PERSPECTIVES ON
Freedom of Speech

Selected Essays from the Journals of the Speech Communication Association

Edited by Thomas L. Tedford, John J. Makay, and David L. Jamison

Southern Illinois University Press

Carbondale and Edwardsville

Copyright © 1987 by the Speech Communication Association

All rights reserved

Printed in the United States of America

Edited by Timothy Burns

Production supervised by Natalia Nadraga

90 89 88 87   4 3 2 1

Library of Congress Cataloging-in-Publication Data

Perspectives on freedom of speech.

Bibliography: p.

1. Freedom of speech—United States.   I. Tedford, Thomas L.   II. Makay, John J.   III. Jamison, David L. IV. Speech Communication Association.

KF4772.A75P47   1987   342.73′0853   86-6706
    ISBN 0-8093-1307-3   347.302853
    ISBN 0-8093-1308-1 (pbk.)

Contents

Preface   vii

Part One: Historical Perspectives

1. From Small Acorns Mighty Oaks Grow: The Legislatures and Free Speech in Colonial Connecticut and Rhode Island   3
   J. Louis Campbell III

2. Freedom of Expression in the Confederate States of America   24
   Stephen A. Smith

3. The Right to Speak: The Free Speech Fights of the Industrial Workers of the World   46
   Terry W. Cole

4. Patriots versus Dissenters: The Rhetoric of Intimidation in Indiana during the First World War   53
   Clark Kimball

Part Two: Philosophical and Theoretical Perspectives

5. Free Speech: The Philosophical Poles   69
   Cal M. Logue

6. Implications of Herbert Marcuse's Theory of Freedom for Freedom of Speech   77
   Joyce Flory

7. The Supreme Court and Communication Theory: Contrasting Models of Speech Efficacy   90
   William Bailey

Part Three: Legal Perspectives

8. Toward a More Realistic View of the Judicial Process in Relation to Freedom of Speech   109
   Ruth McGaffey

9. The United States Supreme Court on Libel   120
   Wayne C. Minnick

10. Protecting Political Speech: *Brandenburg v. Ohio* Updated   136
    Paul Siegel

11. A Rhetoric of Ritual and Desecration   154
    William I. Gorden and Richard Goodman

Part Four: Case Perspectives

12. The Worst Case of Racial Equality He Ever Saw: The Supreme Court, Motion Picture Censorship, and the Color Line   173
    Nickieann Fleener

13. The Birth of a Baby Photo Essay: Was it Obscenity or Censorship?   185
    Michael D. Sherer

14. *Deep Throat* in Deep Trouble on a College Campus: An Academic Freedom Case Study   199
    Churchill L. Roberts

15. Nazis in Skokie: Anatomy of the Heckler's Veto   216
    Franklyn S. Haiman

Part Five: Ethical Perspectives

16. Free Speech, Persuasion, and the Democratic Process   229
    Thomas R. Nilsen

17. An Ethical Basis of Communication   241
    Karl R. Wallace

Notes   255

Annotated Bibliographies

    Essays on Freedom of Speech from the National and Regional Speech Communication Journals   309
    John J. Makay

    Essays on Communication Ethics from the National and Regional Speech Communication Journals   332
    David L. Jamison

Preface

In the early 1960s a group of Communications educators founded the Committee on Freedom of Speech within the organizational framework of the Speech Communication Association (SCA). One of the primary goals of the new committee—the status of which was later elevated to that of an SCA commission—was (and still is) to promote scholarship in the field of the First Amendment in a profession whose viability depends upon the freedom to communicate. Consequently, this committee began issuing a mimeographed yearbook of free speech research. In 1970 the SCA began publishing the *Free Speech Yearbook* in a paperbound volume; it has appeared each year since 1970.

The Commission on Freedom of Speech did more than stimulate submissions to its yearbook; it also stirred interest in national and regional programs that featured free speech themes, thereby feeding the growing interest in research papers, theses, and dissertations. Furthermore, major portions of courses, and sometimes entire courses concerning the First Amendment were initiated in departments of speech communication around the nation. The result has been a steady output of scholarship concerning the "First Freedom" in both national and regional speech communication journals.

This volume, which is sponsored by the Speech Communication Association and its Commission on Freedom of Speech, brings together a representative collection of free speech essays published prior to 1985 in the *Free Speech Yearbook* and in the journals of the SCA. In addition to the essays themselves, which are organized according to five perspectives—historical, philosophical and theoretical, legal, case, and ethical—this anthology concludes with two unique annotated bibliographies derived from national and regional speech communication journals. The Makay bibliography focuses on free speech scholarship, and Jamison focuses on communication ethics—i.e., the responsible use of free speech.

The result, we trust, is a collection of essays and bibliographical materials which will be of use to persons in a variety of fields, ranging from those who have a general interest in the First Amendment to students and teachers in academic disciplines such as speech communication, journalism, mass media studies, political science, library science, English and history. Above all, we hope that our efforts contribute to the ongoing national debate over the meaning of the First

Amendment and the issue of how much freedom of speech our society should permit.

For assisting in the development of this project we are indebted to Professor Daniel Chandler of Herbert H. Lehman College of the City University of New York, who in early 1983, acting in his position as Chair of the Commission on Freedom of Speech, urged SCA to appoint us to an anthology editorial committee; to Professor Kenneth E. Andersen of the University of Illinois, who in his capacity as President of SCA in 1983 made the appointments requested by Chandler; to William Work, Executive Secretary of SCA for his enthusiastic support of this project; and to Kenney Withers, Director of Southern Illinois University Press, for his faith in the proposal. Also, we are grateful to the members of the editorial and production staffs of Southern Illinois University Press for their assistance during the development and publication of this book.

Thomas L. Tedford
John J. Makay
David L. Jamison

Part One

Historical Perspectives

From Small Acorns Mighty Oaks Grow: The
Legislatures and Free Speech in Colonial
Connecticut and Rhode Island
J. Louis Campbell III

Freedom of Expression in the
Confederate States of America
Steven A. Smith

The Right to Speak: The Free Speech Fights of the
Industrial Workers of the World
Terry W. Cole

Patriots versus Dissenters: The Rhetoric of Intimidation
in Indiana During the First World War
Clark Kimball

1

From Small Acorns Mighty Oaks Grow: The Legislatures and Free Speech in Colonial Connecticut and Rhode Island

J. LOUIS CAMPBELL III

J. Louis Campbell III teaches speech communication at the Altoona campus of Pennsylvania State University. Before coming to Altoona he taught freedom of speech at Rutgers University. He holds a law degree from Louisiana State University and is a member of the Louisiana and American Bar Associations. Professor Campbell also participates in the work of the American Civil Liberties Union. This essay first appeared in the Free Speech Yearbook: 1977.

In 1960 Leonard W. Levy, first incumbent Earl Warren Professor of Constitutional History at Brandeis University, declared in his *Legacy of Suppression: Freedom of Speech and Press in Early American History:* "This book represents a revisionist interpretation of the origins and original understanding of the First Amendment's clause on freedom of speech and press. I have been reluctantly forced to conclude . . . that American experience with freedom of political expression was as slight as the theoretical inheritance was narrow. Indeed, the American legislatures, especially during the colonial period, were far more oppressive than the supposedly tyrannous common law courts."[1]

Dr. Levy lays waste to a tradition that many Americans have long held dear, that our Union has from its earliest settlement treasured the ideal of freedom of expression: "The persistent image of colonial America as a society in which freedom of expression was cherished is an hallucination of sentiment that ignores history. . . . The American people simply did not understand that freedom of thought and expression means equal freedom for the other fellow, especially the one with the hated ideas."[2] Tracing "The American Colonial Experience," Levy mentions the role of common-law courts and royal governors in restricting free expression. But he develops his contention that "The most suppressive body by far . . . was that acclaimed bastion of the people's liberties: the popularly elected Assembly."[3]

Though Levy spends his greatest effort on Massachusetts, New York, and Pennsylvania, he indicates by example that regulation of liberty to speak and print occurred throughout the colonies. His spacial sweeps are at times broad, and his coverage thin.[4] Notable omissions from his colonial treatment are the colonies of Connecticut and Rhode Island, Delaware, and New Jersey. The present research tests Levy's thesis that Americans inherited a legacy of suppression by examining in detail the records of the colonies of Connecticut and Rhode Island. According to Horatio Rogers, "The colonial charter of Rhode Island . . . was unsurpassed in liberality. That of Connecticut alone approached it, and in these two colonies only, until after independence, were the governors elected by the people. So liberal were the royal charters of these two colonies that they alone survived the Revolution, Connecticut abandoning her charter in 1818, and Rhode Island clinging to hers until 1842."[5]

Further reports of historians are quite favorable in regard to the role of Connecticut in the dawning of American independence. John Fiske argues that "The government of the United States today is in lineal descent more nearly related to that of Connecticut than to any other colonies."[6] Charles Edward Perry lauds Connecticut as bringing forth "the first attempt, in the history of this country, to draft a frame of popular self-government. . . ."[7] Herbert L. Osgood identifies political independence in Connecticut as "even more prominent than was commercial and territorial isolation. . . ."[8] Clinton Lawrence Rossiter, though denying that Connecticut was a democracy, declared that it was an unmistakable step away from the Massachusetts oligarchy and toward a free society.[9] And J. Mark Jacobson considers that Connecticut advanced the development of democratic seeds.[10] The loyalists of the period were not unmindful of Connecticut colonists: "Sedition, said the Tories and British, flowed from their pulpits and through the public prints."[11]

Rhode Island is seen in no-less-stellar light. "Freedom of speech is necessarily affected by the exclusion of aliens for their opinions."[12] And, rather than exclude individualism, Rhode Island encouraged it.[13] This atmosphere led to fiery political discourse, "name calling and calumny," which were thought by many to be "part and parcel of self-government."[14]

The Islanders of Roger Williams codified in their first charter their belief that all men were equal and could aspire to public office; all could meet in public assemblies. They also required that before each law could take effect, it had to be approved by citizens in their public meetings.[15] The first Articles of Agreement were adopted in Providence in 1640. According to Arnold, "The largest liberty of the citizen, civil as well as religious, consistent with the existence of society, was their cherished object.... Latitude of opinion upon fundamental points of civil government still existed. Theories subversive of all legal restraint were broached...."[16] The General Assembly, meeting on May 19, 1647, recorded: "It is agreed by this present Assembly, thus incorporate, and by this present act declared, that the form of government established in Providence Plantations is DEMOCRATICAL, that is to say, a government held by the free and voluntary consent of all, or the greater part of the free inhabitants.... And otherwise than thus, what is herein forbidden, all men may walk as their consciences persuade them, every one in the name of his God."[17] Samuel Greene Arnold finds that the democratic proviso "was no less novel and startling to the statesmen of that day, than was the idea of religious freedom. ..."[18] Rhode Island maintained its vanguard position on May 4, 1776, when it became the first colony to declare its independence.[19] And when the Islanders ratified the Constitution, they were so concerned about the absence of a free-speech clause that they included one in their ratification.[20]

Thus, we have a significant body of circumstantial evidence that shows Connecticut and Rhode Island to be generally more favorable to individual liberty than their sister colonies. If it is found that even in these two most liberal colonies there was a significant degree of suppression of speech, then Levy's thesis must be confirmed. However, if Connecticut and Rhode Island resist Levy's interpretation of evidence obtained elsewhere, we must conclude that Levy has overgeneralized and neglected to note important differences in the colonies.

The present study should be viewed in light of two limitations: First, only freedom of speech, as opposed to freedom of the press, is considered. Second, only *de jure* restrictions are covered—that is, only structural bounds and applications of those bounds originating with the legal system and legislature.

The general assemblies are pinpointed by Levy as being the agents of most-repressive measures vis-a-vis freedom of expression. So let us first answer the question: Were the assemblies of Connecticut and Rhode Island the primary sources of restrictions on speech in those colonies? The evidence leads to an affirmative answer.

There was a minimum of royal authority in Connecticut. Indeed, Connecticut was not a royal colony. It was established without the authority of the King, and his influence was not foremost militarily, diplomatically, or commercially.[21] Connecticut was a corporate colony formed when dissenters separated from Massachusetts and farmers sought richer lands.[22] Connecticut, along with Rhode Island, existed

> largely beyond the limits of English knowledge, for neither the Privy Council, the Board of Trade, the Treasury, nor the Admiralty had much information about them, either how their people lived, how their governments carried on business and acquired revenue, or how their towns managed local affairs. Between the mother country and these colonies there was little communication, as far as administration and finance went, for the King had no power to appoint any of their officials or to concern himself with their legislation, unless clearly contrary to the laws of England.[23]

The assemblies in Connecticut and Rhode Island had the real power.[24]

We now have ground to compare Levy's colonies with two of those he neglected—the two most liberal of all. If we find that Connecticut and Rhode Island were more liberal with respect to free speech, we have discovered new benefactors and the true legacy of liberty.[25] Now, throughout the voluminous colonial records of the two colonies there appear four areas of limitation on absolutely free speech: provision for parliamentary order, protection against criticism of the colonial government, promotion of the established social order, and guidance of religious beliefs.[26] Part I of the essay will discuss these restrictions on speech. Part II will offer a rhetorical explanation for why free speech developed in Connecticut and Rhode Island the way it did.

Part I

Restrictions to Suppress Free Discussion in Representative Bodies of Government

The legislatures made rules regarding *in camera* speaking. In Connecticut, for example, the members had parliamentary privilege: that is, they had general freedom of speech while the Assembly was in session, exclusive of treasonous declarations.[27] The Code of Laws of 1650 stipulated: "It is ordered by this Court that whosoever doth disorderly speak privately during the sitting of the Court, with his neighbor, or two or three together, shall presently pay twelve pence, if the Court so think meet."[28] To further promote decorum among its members the Assembly fined anyone who spoke without first being recognized the sum of one shilling.[29]

Rhode Island also felt the need to maintain order in its deliberative bodies. For example, on May 16, 1648, for "the Good Order of the Assembly" the legislators voted that "every man shall have liberty to speak freely to any matter propounded yet but once, unless it be by lease from ye moderator . . . he that stand vp first vncovered shall speake first to the cause."[30] That cool deliberation was not always preserved is evident from a restriction of June 30, 1655. The Assembly declared that, "'in case any man shall strike another person in ye Court, he shall either be fined ten pounds, or be whipt, accordinge as ye Court shall see meete.'"[31]

Both colonies enacted measures to deal with indecorous speech in town meetings. On May 8, 1729, the Connecticut Assembly promulgated legislation entitled "An Act to prevent Tumults and Disorders in Town Meetings, Society Meetings, and Proprietors Meetings." Fines were prescribed for persons vilifying the moderator or speaking out of order.[32] If one suspects that there was much agitation in the deliberative meetings of Rhode Island, one is correct to the letter of the law. For on May 19, 1647, the Rhode Island Assembly ordered "that all cases presented, concerning General Matters for the colony, shall be first stated in the Townes . . . that is, when a case is propounded, the Towne where it is propounded shall agitate and full discuss the matter in theire Town Meetings. . . ."[33] And discussion was plentiful as well as fierce debate.[34] The Island Assembly enacted at least one law giving moderators power to keep the peace in town meetings—a broad delegation of power under which probably came restrictions on speech.[35]

The Rhode Island Assembly allowed for dissent in its deliberations. Within Assembly sessions dissents or protests by members to Assembly action could become pointedly hostile. Referring to various acts, Benjamin Ellery and Peter Bours used the words "very injurious to the colonies,"[36] William Ellery and others used the phrase "highly unjust,"[37] Samuel Wickham and friends warned of "most pernicious consequence,"[38] Peter Bours and Edward Scott issued claims of manifest absurdity, unreasonableness, and injustice,[39] and Samuel Ward charged a "violation of the Act of Parliament, and a breach of the faith of this government."[40] Colony administrators did not always mince words regarding England, either. Governor Samuel Ward of Rhode Island was the only colonial governor to refuse to take an oath to sustain the Stamp Act.[41] The Assembly ordered an anonymous speech attacking England to be printed in the records on November 30, 1784.[42] For all the blunt language no retribution was exacted from those who dissented and criticized.[43] Rhode Island did, however, ask a small compensation for printing the dissents, i.e., two shillings.[44] The privilege of dissent in that colony obtained for mid-echelon officials as well: "'if any magistrate on ye bench dissent from ye rest of ye magistrates,'" he could have it recorded for eighteen pence.[45] It has been speculated that these charges may have reduced the number of dissents recorded,[46] though not necessarily voiced.

Secrecy was a salient concern of Connecticut leaders. In the debate over the Fundamental Orders "strict secrecy" was imposed, and no records were made of the issues raised therein.[47] The Assembly formalized its precept of silence in October, 1639[48] and again in the Code of Laws, 1650, when it declared "that whatsoever member of the General Court shall reveal any secret, or shall make known to any person what any one member of the Court speaks concerning any person or businesses that may come into litigation in the Court, shall forfeit for every such fault ten pounds, and shall be dealt otherwise withall at the discretion of the Court."[49]

Thus, we have seen that the legislatures under study made provisions for parliamentary order which affected free speech. But the classes of provisions discovered are not unconscionable. They do not impact on free speech in an evil manner. Further, Connecticut and Rhode Island seem more liberal, judging by Levy's work, than the other colonies. Levy declares that "None of the available evidence suggests that freedom of speech or press existed before the revolutionary controversy."[50] As partial proof he cites two examples where government officials were punished for dissenting speech during official functions.[51] Connecticut and particularly Rhode Island, where dissents were officially publishable, were clearly more liberal and suggestive of freedom of speech. We are now ready to move on to a second motive the legislatures had to bind speech: they wanted to protect the colonial governments from unbridled public criticism.

Restrictions to Protect the Government Against Criticism

In 1642 Connecticut enacted a law forbidding advocacy of the forcible overthrow of the government. The penalty was death.[52] In 1675 the penalty was downgraded to other punishment.[53] No case was discovered which was brought specifically under this statute. In numerous cases adjudicated by the Connecticut legislature it had taken offense at a colonist's speech. The case of Richard Gyldersly is typical. On June 11, 1640, Gyldersly was found guilty of "casting out pernicious speeches tending to the detriment and dishonor of this commonwealth." He was fined forty shillings and required to post a bond of twenty pounds to guarantee his appearance at the next session of Court.[54] Sundry reports raise the issues of scandalous allegations, distempered speeches, loud language, defamation of the Assembly. A few accounts are illustrative.

On May 17, 1715, in a public session of the General Assembly and Court of Election, Captain Joseph Wadsworth challenged the validity of the Assembly's acts vis-a-vis the Charter of Connecticut. He was subsequently brought before the bar of the Assembly "and behaving himself with due submission" was forced to publicly declare: "I do sincerely profess . . . I had no design to reflect or expose the proceedings of the . . . Assembly. . . . If what I said had any tendency thereunto, it was more than I intended or perceived; and I am heartily sorry that what I said was of such tendency as to give offense to this Assembly, for which, as for the Charter, I had a great regard and honor."[55]

The Assembly was sensitive to the words of one William Leet. He declared that he could either bully them verbally or intimidate them by sword; he charged one member, "You are a lying, scounderling, ill-bred fellow." The Assembly ordered Leet arrested.[56]

Preacher Benjamin Pomroy certainly gave the Assembly cause to spring into action. It did so. On May 10, 1744, he was convicted for having said, among other things, that "the state law of this colony, made concerning ecclesiastical affairs, was a great foundation to encourage persecution . . . that the great men had fallen in and joined with those that are on the devil's side and enemies to the kingdom of Christ . . . there is no colony so privileged as Connecticut was, and now there is no colony so bad as Connecticut for persecuting laws, I never heard nor read of such persecuting laws as in Connecticut, nay there is no such thing among the heathen. . . ."[57] In the face of such inciting utterances one would expect Pomroy's fate to have commenced with drawing and quartering. But the Assembly was content to slap the wrist of this man of the cloth. It required him to post a bond of fifty pounds, to be returned to him at the end of the session if he maintained equable conduct.[58]

Public apology to the Court was frequently required. "To resist in any way the authority of the people's representatives was a serious matter. The man who submitted humbly was more common than the one who did not; and the one who did not do so at first was likely to be very humble indeed before the incident was over."[59]

Though Rhode Island had structural protection for some dissent, the legislature's record in tolerating dissent is not spotless. By 1672 Islanders had been tumultuous in their opposition to series of new taxes. The Assembly bristled at this resistance and expressed its outrage in the first Sedition Act in the colony:

... if any person or persons in any town or place within this jurisdiction, shall at any time more especially in any town meeting or other publique assembly of people, appear by word or act, in opposition to such rates and impositions, made from time to time by the General Assembly of this Colony, or shall appear in opposition against any of the Acts and Orders of such Assembly made accordingly to the Charter, by speaking against such Acts or Orders openly, in any concourse of people together, or that shall move to the rejecting such Acts and Orders when published in any such meeting in any town or place, or that shall endeavour by word or deed to send back or otherwise to slight such Acts and Orders; all and every such persons shall be questioned and proceeded against as for high contempt and sedition. . . .[60]

The punishment for violation was a fine of up to twenty pounds, whipping up to thirty stripes, or imprisonment of up to twelve months.

It has been suggested that the Assembly did not act out of an evil purpose. Land disputes with Connecticut, Indian wars, and internal dissension were justifications for the reactionary measures of the Assembly.[61] Notwithstanding circumstances the people of Rhode Island were emphatic in their resentment of the strong-arm tactics of the Assembly, and applied the ultimate political remedy: Shortly after the Sedition Act of April 2, 1672, elections were held, and the Assembly members were replaced.[62] On May 14, 1672, the new Assembly voted to repeal the Sedition Act, "forasmuch as severall acts and orders were made in the Generall Assembly in the Aprill last, some whereof seeminge to the infringeinge of the libertyes of the people of this Collony, and setting up an arbitrary power, which is contrary to . . . the fundamentall lawes of this Collony from the very first setling therof. . . ."[63] Thus, declared contrary to the essence of Rhode Island, the act had a life of little more than one month.

In 1699, during border disputes with Connecticut, the Assembly enacted a second Sedition Act.[64] Unpopular again, the act was repealed on March 24, 1701/1702.[65] Though not officially labeled sedition, a law passed on March 30, 1761, called for a fine of five pounds or imprisonment for thirty days for anyone convicted of dissuading a colonist from joining the Rhode Island army. Persons convicted of persuading an Islander to join the army of a neighboring colony were to be fined twenty pounds and jailed until the next court session of that county.[66]

The Island Assembly also passed laws under the rubric "An Act for Punishing Criminal Offenses" which demanded that respect (including speech) be shown by nonofficers to officers of the colony[67] and by inferiors to superiors.[68] But even before these laws the Assembly began exercising some overseership as early as 1640. Samuel Gorton was sentenced to be whipped and banished from the Island after he challenged the Court's right to exist without royal authorization, called the magistrates "asses" and the deputy governor "an abettor of riot" and "unfit to make a warrant," charged the judges with being corrupt and "wresting witnesses," called a freeman a "jack-an-apes," and made ungentlemanly aspersions about one of the female witnesses.[69] In one case the Assembly wrote to the entire town of Warwick, "protesting against such expressions as tending to discredit the authority of the Assembly, thereby weakening the government. . . ."[70] That the Assembly did not always take a dim view of criticism is illustrated by an incident of May 16, 1671. The Court of Justices, sitting under the authority of the Assembly, was interrupted by a group of people challenging the authority of Rhode Island and favoring that of Connecticut. The justices were willing "to pass it by as an act proceeding only from some vnruly passions."[71] The Assembly did not review the case.

Clearly Connecticut and Rhode Island legislatures were sensitive to criticism, as are Congress and the state legislatures today. But, compared with the colonies studied by Levy, they tended to be more liberal. For example, Levy cites Massachusetts' suppression of advocacy of the election of rulers.[72] In Connecticut and Rhode Island popular choice of officials was mandated. Levy declares that the legislature was the "unexceptioned superior" in clashes with free debaters;[73] but in Rhode Island almost an entire Assembly was replaced when the colonists resented strong-arm measures regarding free speech. Even that Island law, as it stood, was more tolerant than sedition laws in some other colonies. It called for limited fines, imprisonment, or whipping, while a Virginia proclamation cited by Levy in his proof threatened loss of life or limb for seditious speeches. Thus, contrary to Levy's thesis that "Freedom . . . did not include a right to criticize the legislature . . ."[74] we have found that *some* freedom, even if imperfectly measured, indeed existed in Connecticut and Rhode Island. Let us now move on to the third area of restrictions on free speech: those promoting the social order.

Restrictions to Promote the Established Social Order

When Connecticut was first established, laws were promulgated to meet the most immediate needs. Relations with native Americans were a pressing concern at that point. Hence, the General Court, acting at Hartford, March 8, 1637, ordered that "no commissioners or other persons shall bind, imprison, or restrain, correct, or whip any

Indian or other, nor give them any threatening or menacing speeches . . . ." unless provoked by an Indian assault on person or property.⁷⁵

As the colony became better organized, the governing body enacted a code of laws specifying the crimes for which a person would forfeit his life. On December 1, 1642, the General Court adopted the "Capitall Lawes," of which three dealt with the spoken word. Law eleven dealt with bearing false witness; Law twelve, with advocacy of the overthrow of the commonwealth (the English monarchy was not mentioned); and Law three, with blasphemy: "If any prson shall blaspheme the name of God the Father, Son or Holy Ghoste, with direct, expres, prsumptuous, or highhanded blasphemy, or shall curse God in the like manner, he shall be put to death."⁷⁶ Biblical verses were cited in support of each stricture in the capital code.

In 1650 the Ludlow Code was enacted, adding several articles to the "Capitall Lawes." Among them was Law thirteen: "If any childe or children above sixteen yeares old and of sufficient vnderstanding, shall curse or smite theire natural father or mother hee or they shall be put to death. . . ."⁷⁷ The only justification a child could plead under the law was that his parent or parents had been "very unchristianly negligent" in providing education for said child or had exercised such "cruell correction" that the child was in danger of death or maiming.⁷⁸ The year 1675 saw a moderation of penalties prescribed in "Capitall Lawes." A blasphemer, under the 1675 revision, was to be reprimanded by "having his tongue bored through with a red hot iron . . ." as opposed to the presumably harsher 1642 penalty of death.⁷⁹

By 1713, as Connecticut continued to grow and as transients and nonestablishment persons became more numerous, the General Assembly apparently felt the need to reiterate its role in providing for the welfare of its people in the area of oral expressions. To wit, in a law entitled "An Act for the Correcting and Restraining of Rogues and Vagabonds, and other Persons of Evil Name and Fame, for Rude and Prophane Discourse, etc.," the Assembly moved against "wanderers and others, who have by their vile and prophane discourses and actions proved a snare to youth especially, and tend to the great detriment of religion, being of pernicious consequence. . . ."⁸⁰ In applying such laws the Connecticut Assembly acted as a kind of colonial vice squad, sanitizing the colony's moral fiber by punishing liars, cursers, swearers, and others whose speech posed a danger of "infection to others." For example, on August 22, 1665, Robert Pinion was convicted of lascivious and corrupt speeches in that "he spake many things of making maids loving of him and kissing him in the stocks, and that he said to [Joshua Bradley's] sister that had he but half hour's speech with her he could make her come to him [if he were in the stocks] and kiss him, to which she said, do you go and sit in the stocks and see if I will come to you. . . ."[81] Pinion was sentenced to a whipping to serve as a "future warning and terror to himself and others." Samuel Ford made the mistake of asking a young pregnant wife to sleep with him for only half an hour. The Court sentenced him on October 1, 1667, to a whipping and required him to pay the *husband* of the girl ten shillings for the *husband's* trouble.[82]

Edward Vickers, a runaway slave, was charged with "cursing and swearing, and . . . giving threatening speeches against the Clark of the ironworks."[83] Vickers confessed that he had cursed and pleaded for mercy. He argued that he had fallen in with the wrong crowd. The Court was unmoved, however, and ruled: "The Court upon the evidence present . . . do find him rightly guilty of common and frequent cursing and swearing in a most prophane and blasphemous manner, horrible to be heard or uttered, and the like not formerly known among us, to the great dishonor of God and the danger of infection to others. . . ."[84]

Typical of the defamation suits in which colonists were litigants before the Assembly was the case of Josiah Wilkinson v. George Tong and wife. Wilkinson charged the Tong couple with slander after the couple accused him of operating a whorehouse and being a rogue and liar. He won a fifty-pound judgment.[85] Apparently Mr. Tong disapproved of the decision, for "shortly thereafter the Court fined Tong another ten shillings for cursing. Plaintiffs and defendants minced no words even before the bench."[86]

Rhode Island's Assembly provided for social order in similar fashion. For example, slander was a major topic of legislative concern and vividly scorned. "Forasmuch as a good man is better than precious ointment, and slaunderers are worser than dead flies to corrupt and alter the savour thereof, it is agreed . . . to prohibitt the raysing and spreading of false rports. . . ."[87] Examples of what constituted slander were given: "to Say A man is a Traytor a fellon a thief a cutpurse . . . a Bankrupt . . . a young man Unmarried a whoremaster and to say a man keeps a house of Baudery. . . ."[88]

Another legislative concern was cursing. Cursing, "notorious and customary," was against the law.[89] Additional statutes that regulated speech dealt with perjury,[90] children's and servants' respect for their parents and masters respectively,[91] vexatious lawsuits,[92] conspiracy,[93] and what today might be considered the "symbolic speech" of Indian dances.[94] Incidents in which colonists were involved in defamation suits were also similar to those found in Connecticut.[95]

A comparison with the results of Levy's study is impossible because Levy concerns himself only with political expressions. Nevertheless, one might conclude that the morality-type restrictions were less sinister than the political-type and thus not subsumed under the forboding "legacy of suppression." We must also consider the taut Puritan culture that frowned on one who "spake many things of making maids loving of him" and resist judging by the criteria of our more-permissive age. While neither lying (except perjury) nor cussing nor lewd and lascivious language are now proscribed, defamation of character is still very much a cause for legal redress. Reasonably enough, one citizen cannot destroy the reputation and good name of another without penalty.

The final motive for restricting free speech was to support religious beliefs. Because variety of worship was tolerated in Rhode Island, this motive was found to exist only in Connecticut.

Restrictions to Support Religious Beliefs

Connecticut was emphatically Protestant. And Protestants had a good measure of liberty in speech on religious matters. For example, in 1744, Elisha Williams, speaker of the Connecticut Assembly and former president of Yale, "brilliantly pleaded for the right of private judgment without any control from civil authority, not only as to affairs of conscience but on all issues."[96] He declared for "the Right that every one has to speak his Sentiments openly concerning such matters as affect the good of the whole."[97] Non-Protestants, however, were less favored in Williams's universe.[98]

The tolerance of the Assembly in regard to Protestants' religious jousts can be seen in the case of the Reverend Mr. Stow, fired by the Assembly on March 4, 1660, from his ministry in Middletown.[99] During the decade between 1650 and 1660 a good deal of turmoil existed in the churches of Windsor, Wethersfield, Hartford, and Middletown. This contention "gave opportunities for a good deal of free speaking."[100] During the bouts Stow was charged with having said that "'those that were not in visible covenant were dogs and among dogs and in the Kingdom of Sathan and at Sathan's command.'"[101] Though the Court deprived Stow of his official pulpit, it went on to declare that he "is not infringed of his liberty to preach in Middletown to such as will attend him, until there be a settled minister there."[102]

The only case of capital punishment discovered in this research was the case of an unnamed woman hanged in 1663 for calling Christ a bastard.[103] Other penalties were far milder. Any Christian who acted "contemptuously . . . toward the word preached or the messages thereof . . . by interrupting [the preacher] or by charging him falsely with an error . . ." was to be censured upon the first offense; a second offense called for a fine or standing "two hours openly upon a block or stool four foot high, upon a Lecture day, with a paper fixed on his breast written with capital letters, 'AN OPEN AND OBSTINATE CONTEMNER OF GOD'S HOLY ORDINANCES,' that others may fear and be ashamed of breaking out into like wickedness."[104] This issue of punishment for speech provides a good basis for comparing perspectives on free speech in England, Levy's colonies, and Connecticut and Rhode Island, with the assumption that the degree of punishment is some indication of the considered degree of seriousness of the offense.

Comparative Punishment. From earliest times free speech had some restriction in England. Slander was a civil offense, pitting person versus person, while slander of the King and other government officials might be punishable as treason.[105] In 1275 Edward I decreed that "from henceforth none be so hardy to cite or publish any false news or tales whereby discord or occasion of discord or slander may grow between the king and his people or the great men of the realm. . . ."[106] Statutory control of speech continued throughout English history.[107]

Punishments cited as exemplary are stunning. Quaker James Nayler was granted mercy in 1656 on a charge of blasphemy. His punishments were: two hours in the pillory at Westminster, from whence he was to be whipped by the hangman into the town Cheapside, there to be pilloried two hours "for the sport of another mob," after which he was to have his tongue burned through with a hot iron and his forehead branded with the letter *B*.[108] Fines were at times extravagant: for example, ten thousand pounds down to five hundred pounds.[109] Some sentences combined fines and corporeal punishment: Samuel Johnson was fined five hundred marks, pilloried three times, and whipped from Newgate to Tyburn.[110] If one persisted in caustic or impudent address, one might suffer unusual detriment. In 1637 John Lilburne began a sixteen-year ordeal, during which the Star Chamber fined him five hundred pounds, raised "two hundred bloody welts" on his back. The House of Lords fined him four thousand pounds and sentenced him to seven years in prison. Parliament fined him three thousand pounds and exiled him for life; Cromwell tried him for treason in 1653.[111] Though Lilburne was acquitted, he had suffered greatly for his remarks. Historians record that next to the stark nature of British intolerance was the frequency with which it was expressed. Between April 30 and November 28, 1684, there were sixteen trials involving seditious expressions.[112]

In the colonies surveyed by Levy punishments were also stiff. Levy cites a fine of one hundred pounds levied on one Buckner[113] plus a fine of fifty pounds coupled with a bond of one thousand pounds.[114] Shades of English brutality were discernible. Branding, boring through the tongue, and death are cited by Levy as having in fact been administered to punish speech.[115] Levy concludes that the evidence "suggests that open political debate had been scotched. . . ."[116]

By comparison Connecticut and Rhode Island were more liberal. Penalties for the various offenses were at times harsh in the letter of the law. But capital punishment occurred only once—when a person described Christ as a bastard. Boring a hole through the tongue with a red-hot iron was prescribed by law as punishment, but no case applied such torture as a remedy. Fines seem to have been the commonest form of retribution. A fine of ten or twenty pounds for many offenders was difficult to bear. However, "the gradations of wealth among Connecticuts population . . . were moderate and the majority of farmers within it was overwhelming."[117] Examples of salaries of non-farmers paid by the legislature may shed light upon the severity of some of the fines assessed by the same body. The salary for the keeper of the House of Correction in 1650 was ten pounds a year.[118] In 1655 Daniell Porter was retained as the colony's surgeon at six pounds a year plus a few shillings per case.[119] In a letter to the General Assembly dated October 10, 1745, Timothy Green requested full payment of his annual salary of fifty pounds a year for printing government publications.[120] And Jeffrey Amherst wrote a letter to Thomas Fitch (dated February 21, 1762) offering five pounds as an inducement for men to join the army.[121] Thus, it appears that some fines levied by the Assembly were equal to annual salaries paid by the same bodies. It is at least conceivable that the coincidence was not accidental. Fines may have been assigned with an eye to the legislative budget. The absence or diminution of punitive designs in writing statutes and handing down sentences would conform with the thesis of this article that Connecticut and Rhode Island departed from the examples of suppression in the mother country and sister colonies.

Other penalties were imposed as well. Sitting in stocks and public whippings were not infrequent sentences among the cases cited herein. "Public humiliation proved to be an effective deterrent to future crimes in many cases."[122] Some jail sentences were imposed.

In Rhode Island fines were the most frequent form of punishment.[123] Imprisonment, whippings, recantation, and an occasional deprivation of franchise[124] may also be found in the records.

Thus, Connecticut and Rhode Island were clearly milder in treating violations of their restrictions on communication than were England and Levy's colonies: the incidence of punishment was less; fines were approximately 1/10 as great; corporal punishment was less frequent and drastic; there was a wider gap between the maximum statutory punishments and those actually applied; and there were more reductions in statutory sentences. All of these actions suggest that decriminalization of speech was under way in Connecticut and Rhode Island.

Summary

"This case and the others which have been reviewed indicate that liberty of expression in principle or practice barely existed, if at all, in the American colonies during the seventeenth century. By 1763, the situation was substantially unchanged. . . ."[125] Levy's conclusion may be true for the colonies he surveyed; but, regarding speech, Connecticut and Rhode Island were different. The founders of these two colonies were, in large measure, dissidents who left Massachusetts Bay in opposition to the severe limitations placed on personal freedoms therein. They established popular systems of government, under which expression was freer. Part II of this essay will offer a theory as to how the soil in Connecticut and Rhode Island nourished free speech.

Part II

I have argued that in practice Connecticut and Rhode Island were more liberal in allowing freedom of speech than the other colonies and that, therefore, Leonard Levy was careless in locating the source of our legacy as well as in characterizing that bequest. It now remains to explain, in rhetorical terms, why these two colonies proved best able to give impetus to the development of free speech as we know it.[126] The theory of rhetorical vision was advanced by Ernest Bormann in "Fantasy and Rhetorical Vision: The Rhetorical Criticism of Social Reality."[127]

According to Bormann a rhetorical vision is a symbolic reality, which serves large groups of people "to sustain the members' sense of community, to impel them strongly to action (which raises the question of motivation), and to provide them with a social reality filled with heroes, villains, emotions, and attitudes."[128] This symbolic reality is the result of a set of fantasy themes that have caught on in a group of "people with similar individual psychodynamics" who have met "to discuss a common preoccupation or problem. A member dramatizes a theme that catches the group and causes it to chain out because it hits a common psychodynamic chord or a hidden agenda item or their common difficulties vis-a-vis the natural environment, the socio-political systems, or the economic structures."[129] A form of the vision thus produced is promulgated in consideration of a different and larger audience. As the vision emerges as a unified construct, *dramatis personae* are identified as reference persons who can be expected to generate the original emotional feeling. The dramatic situation can touch people to the extent that individuals will be transported to an idealized world, responding as they would to a work of art. Stirred, these people act: "The rhetorical vision of a group of people contains their drives to action. People who generate, legitimize and participate in a public fantasy are . . . 'powerfully impelled to action by that process.'"[130] With this in mind a critic can predict the behavior of participants. That behavior will fulfill the value aspirations of the vision. What has this to do with free speech? Can we use Bormann's theory in studying a legal system of free speech? The answer is yes.

According to Thomas Emerson, Lines Professor of Law at Yale University, "a perfect set of legal rules and an ideal array of judicial institutions could not by themselves assure an effective system of free expression. Many other factors are critical. There must be a substantial consensus on the values and goals of the society—some minimum area of agreement or acquiescence."[131] In other words, there must be a vision, a symbolic reality, to sustain a sense of community. Among other prerequisites, according to Emerson, are an economic system that provides a broad base of sharing of the wealth and political institutions with some basis in tradition, some degree of acceptance by the people, and the capability of adjustment and change.[132] Emerson affirms the importance of communication (or dramatization) as reinforcement when he says: ". . . the theory of freedom of expression is a sophisticated and even complex one. It does not come naturally to the ordinary citizen, but needs to be learned. It must be restated and reiterated not only for each generation but for each new situation. . . ."[133] Thus, a vision analysis is appropriate to this study. Let us now proceed to isolate two *fundamentally* different colonial visions: the royal vision and the democratic vision.

Rossiter has identified two types of colonies: those established by royal authority and those established without it. In the royal colony the body politic was one in which "the crown was immediately supreme and sovereign. In theory, all officials and institutions existed at the pleasure of the King."[134] Eleven of thirteen colonies were thus influenced by the crown. The two remaining colonies—Connecticut and Rhode Island—were founded without royal authority.[135] They governed independently of the crown. One Boston Tory wrote—and "not too far from the truth"—that "'The people in those Colonies chuse their Governors, Judges, Assemblymen, Counsellors, and all the rest of their officers; and the King and Parliament have as much influence there as in the Wilds of Tartary.'"[136] Where the King and Parliament did have a significant role the royal vision obtained. The themes susceptible to dramatization were a kingship with a tincture of divinity; an established church; a hereditary peerage and the House of Lords; a Parliament supreme over other branches of government; and the suppression of freedom of speech, press, and religion.[137]

It is important to know the foundation of the English policy of restricting expression. That foundation was the divine fantasy that surrounded the King and his government. Because the Monarch and his government were transcendental in nature (this was reinforced by the King's role as head of the Church as well as the government), they were superior to ordinary persons and immune to criticism.[138] This divine fantasy obtained among the institutions in the colonies except Connecticut and Rhode Island. The difference is the essence of the writer's argument.

Connecticut was founded as "one farther step removed from English oversight, a colony in which the fermenting process of self-government could take place with the least possible interference from the home country."[139] It was "symbolically, . . . the first overt indication of the popular urges [fantasies] beneath" autocratic Puritanism and royal government.[140] Part of this symbolic reality or vision, founded by people with similar psychodynamics, was the American "Spirit of political liberalism."[141] The vision was promulgated to others by documentary means as well as the spoken word. The independent constitution of Connecticut, called the Fundamental Orders of Connecticut,[142] failed to pledge allegiance to the King (whether "dread sovereign" or "gracious king"), Lord Protector, Colony of Massachusetts Bay, or any other outside force.[143] Thus, symbolically, *rhetorically*, the colonists separated themselves from the divine fantasy, which in England and the other colonies was the center piece of the government's claim to immunity from criticism.

Rhode Island also broke with the royal vision. As a result of rhetoric of which history deprives us, a document was promulgated in 1640, setting the fantasies of a small group of people into a symbolic whole: "It is ordered and unanimously agreed upon that the Government which this Bodie Politick doth attend unto in this Island . . . is a Democracie, or Popular Government."[144] A 1644 patent from England ordered that the Island's laws conform to those of England only insofar as the nature and constitution of the place would allow.[145] In 1647 Rhode Island a constitution was promulgated: "one of the few constitutions in history to proceed directly from the people."[146] "Lenient," "free play," and a "general spirit of democracy and independence" are descriptions applicable to the Rhode Island version of the democratic vision.[147] "The colonial records testify that Rhode Island was the closest thing to democracy in seventeenth-century America."[148] Thus, we have the royal vision, emphasizing duty to King, and the democratic vision, establishing the people as their own rulers. Fantasy themes or dramatizations regarding free speech and lending support to their respective visions might be stated as follows:

> If the ruler is regarded as the superior of the subject, as being by the nature of his position presumably wise and good, the rightful ruler and guide of the whole population, it must necessarily follow that it is wrong to censure him openly, that even if he is mistaken his mistakes should be pointed out with the utmost respect, and that whether mistaken or not no censure should be cast upon him likely or designed to diminish his authority.
>
> If on the other hand the ruler is regarded as the agent and servant, and the subject as the wise and good master who is obliged to delegate his power to the so-called ruler because being a multitude he cannot use it himself, it is obvious that this sentiment must be reversed. Every member of the public who censures the ruler for the time being exercises in his own person the right which belongs to the whole of which he forms a part. He is finding fault with his servant. If others think differently they can take the others side of the dispute, and the utmost that can happen is that the servant will be dismissed and another put in his place, or perhaps that the arrangements of the household will be modified. To those who hold this view fully and carry it out to all its consequences there can be no such offense as sedition. There may indeed be breaches of the peace which may destroy or endanger life, limb, or property, and there may be incitements to such offences, but no imaginable censure of the government, short of a censure which has an immediate tendency to produce such a breach of the peace, ought to be regarded as criminal.[149]

The participants in the royal vision installed the King as the *dramatis persona*. They fantasized themselves in the role of subjects to their King or servants to their master. Thus, they stressed harsh treatment of insubordination. The democratic vision omitted the King as a leading character. Participants dramatized making the servants into masters and assuming responsibility for the household. The crucial difference is royal authority and the consequent fantasy theme regarding free speech under that authority.[150] Now, Levy makes the point that the legislatures of the colonies, especially the popularly elected Assemblies, were most suppressive of speech. How did the royal vision affect these bodies?

In the colonies were "conciliar" organizations of men who exercised executive, legislative, and judicial functions. These councils acted in the legislatures as upper houses, the assemblies being the lower houses. The councils were "often as powerful an agent of royal authority as the governor. The normal method of appointment of councilors was by the Crown, on recommendation of the governor."[151] Thus, sitting as part of the colonial American legislatures were advocates of the royal vision. Proponents of deference to the King and the master-over-servant theme regarding free speech were among those legislating and adjudicating restrictions on expression. And, indeed, though Levy claims that the popularly elected assembly was most suppressive, his evidence is replete with cases from the Governor's (King's) Council and the Governor himself. The assemblies, under the influence of a royal vision and royal agents present to reinforce that vision, may have redrawn the fantasy whereby subjects did not criticize their rulers to one where citizens did not criticize their representatives.

Not so with Connecticut and Rhode Island. I have already established the comparative independence of these two colonies from their beginnings. Now, their legislatures also had councils. But they were free of significant royal influence. In neither colony did the King or Parliament have authority to verify appointments or oversee elections.[152] Members of the councils and assemblies were free of royal interference and elected by the townspeople.[153] In Connecticut loyalists were not even supported by the presence of a royal army to which they could turn, from which they could take strength.[154] Thus, organized under a democratic vision, by which servants became masters in the conduct of government and free of the elsewhere-ever-present influence of agents from the competing rhetorical vision, legislators in these colonies were not constrained to suppress free speech to the same significant degree. Well, in the absence of a royal *dramatis persona* and his agents, who were the *personae* of the democratic vision? Other *dramatis personae* appeared, and their presence was just as important as the presence of the King in the royal vision.

One such *persona* in Connecticut was Thomas Hooker, the founder of that colony. He was highly revered by his fellow colonists: "He was the sage, 'the grand old man,' the philosopher, the accommodator of differences, the typical colonial father."[155] His counsel was sought and advice followed. "He faced toward freedom."[156] Hooker propelled Connecticut to the documentation of its democratic vision when he declared, in a sermon of May 31, 1638, that "the choice of public magistrates belongs unto the people by God's own allowance" and that "the foundation is laid, firstly, in the *free consent* of the people"[157] (emphasis mine). Hooker's central importance is enhanced by the fact that he spearheaded the first attempt at unifying the colonies: the New England Confederation of 1643. The Confederation was the spark of the Albany Congress of 1754 and the first and second Continental Congresses of 1774 and 1775.[158]

One *dramatic persona* of Rhode Island was its founder: Roger Williams. Williams was a "friend of toleration."[159] He was the rod and staff of the "most popular system of government in the colonial period."[160] Williams was of the persuasion that the ultimate source of a civil government's power was God; the earthly "Root of Power" was the people.[161] Thus, in Connecticut and Rhode Island agents of the rhetorical vision stressing uncritical subservience were absent, while *personae* of the vision emphasizing the direct role of the people in the affairs of the state and the servants-over-masters fantasy theme regarding free expression were present.

The question now arises: What sort of responses, if any, did the democratic vision produce among the people? Did it become a work of art, prompting idealistic acts? Yes. In both Connecticut and Rhode Island colonists were motivated to respond in support of their vision. For example, in 1687, James II attempted to seize Connecticut's charter. "While Sir Edmund was bandying threats . . . in the course of their evening the candles were suddenly blown out, and when after some scraping of tinder they were lighted again the document was nowhere to be found, for Captain Wadsworth had carried it away and hidden it in the hollow trunk of a mighty oak tree."[162] "Charter Oak" is today a cherished historical site in the State of Connecticut. In Rhode Island, when the colony was threatened with economic boycott if it did not proscribe the activities and expressions of the Quakers, colonists remained loyal to their vision and wrote to Cromwell, announcing their intention to remain firm.[163] Rhode Island was the only colony not to enact laws against the Quakers, and Connecticut enacted the mildest of laws.[164]

I submit that the evidence gathered on free speech in Connecticut and Rhode Island is further indication that these colonies were acting out their fantasies, if imperfectly, with regard to the relationship between the governed and the governing. It seems unlikely that in this boisterous period there were only thirty instances in Connecticut where the legislature could act against speech and only twenty-four in Rhode Island, if indeed these legislatures were comparable to those studied by Levy.

Further evidence of the strength of the vision in these two colonies is available. The royal vision eroded as the psychodynamic bond between the colonies and the English deteriorated. The fantasy proscribing criticism of a ruler by a subject faded. In 1735 John Peter Zenger provided material for new fantasies, which spread through the colonies—fantasies that ultimately raised citizens up from their knees and subservient roles. But they were fantasies that had already begun to be celebrated in Connecticut and Rhode Island. When the coexistence between the royal vision and the democratic vision finally ended, only the democratic vision remained. Only Connecticut and Rhode Island continued their governments essentially unchanged for years after the Revolution ended, Connecticut abandoning her charter in 1818, and Rhode Island clinging to hers until 1842. And the states that were forming a new American Republic formed constitutional governments with Connecticut and Rhode Island as exemplars.

It is one of the greatest ironies of all that early charters granted to Connecticut and Rhode Island by Charles II were made extremely liberal for the purpose of quelling the growing power of Massachusetts.[165] To protect the royal vision Charles II unwittingly confirmed the democratic vision that had developed in Connecticut and Rhode Island—a rhetorical vision destined to prevail.

The resolution of this research is at hand: Connecticut and Rhode Island were established when persons with psychodynamic bonds left the royal compound of Massachusetts in order to promulgate a symbolic reality that would give greater play to their fantasies concerning citizen government. Led by friends of tolerance, they documented the vision that made servants into masters, silence into sound. When all about them were searching for new scripts after the Revolutionary clamor, Connecticut and Rhode Island alone remained true to their existing rhetorical visions. These two colonies were more liberal with regard to free speech than those colonies studied by Levy because their rhetorical visions, fundamentally different from the competing royal vision, demanded that they be so. In view of the fact that our present government rests so heavily on that same democratic vision, we should recognize that our legacy is one of liberality, not suppression, and that our benefactors are those free spirits who gathered in Connecticut and Rhode Island, that from small acorns mighty oaks would grow.

2

Freedom of Expression in the Confederate States of America

STEVEN A. SMITH

Stephen A. Smith is Associate Professor of Communication at the University of Arkansas where he teaches a course entitled "Freedom of Speech: Issues and Cases." For a number of years he has been a member of the Commission on Freedom of Speech of the SCA; he is also a member of the Freedom and Responsibilities of Speech Division of the Southern Speech Communication Association, serving as chair of this division for the academic years 1976–77 and 1984–85.

Professor Smith edited the Communication Law Review *from 1983 to 1985 and is serving as editor of the* Free Speech Yearbook *for 1985–88. His publications in the area of free speech include "Scientific Creationism in Arkansas: A Study in Public Opinion, Public Persuasion, and Public Policy,"* Communication Law Review *2 (1984): 13–17; and "The Uncivil Servants: Public Employees and Political Expression,"* Free Speech Yearbook: 1983, *pp. 51–61. For the following essay, which was published in the* Free Speech Yearbook: 1978, *Smith was awarded the H. A. Wichelns Memorial Award for the most significant article published in the 1978 yearbook.*

During the formative years of the Republic the South provided some of the abler advocates of freedom of speech and press. Virginia became the first state to include protection for freedom of the press in its constitution in 1776. Thomas Jefferson wrote the Virginia Statute of Religious Freedom in 1785. Charles C. Pinckney, of South Carolina, tried to insert a clause protecting freedom of speech in the original draft of the Constitution in 1787. North Carolina demanded a Bill of Rights protecting the freedom of speech and press during its ratification debates on the Constitution in 1788. James Madison authored the First Amendment in 1789. Ten years later he and Jefferson took the lead with the Virginia and Kentucky resolutions against the federal sedition act.

This early libertarian heritage, however, faded with the growth of abolition sentiment during the first decades of the nineteenth century. Clement Eaton, one of the leading authorities on the antebellum South, dates the major turning point at 1830, when state legislatures first responded to "incendiary" tracts advocating slave rebellions. The fear of servile insurrection had always been present among the slaveholding class, and these publications from the North led to "a drastic regulation of freedom of speech and of the press."[1] This legislation and subsequent acts aimed at related issues are believed to have been responsible for "the loss of freedom of thought and speech after 1835."[2]

Leonard W. Levy has examined the legal and philosophical development of the concept of freedom of expression during the colonial and early national period.[3] Clement Eaton has written of the southern experience leading up to the Civil War.[4] Harry Kalven, Jr., has discussed important developments during the "Second Reconstruction" of the 1950s and 1960s.[5] Other scholars have concentrated on the constitutional controversies that have developed in the period since 1917.[6] Only scant attention, however, seems to have been given to the concept of freedom of expression during the Civil War. This article focuses upon the concept and practice of freedom of speech and press in the Confederate States of America, 1861–1865. While filling an important void in the scholarly studies tracing the development of First Amendment theory, such an examination should also provide comparative insights to the only other government of English heritage to exist within the present boundaries of the United States.

Constitutions and Courts of the Confederacy

While presidential and congressional Reconstruction plans differed as to whether or not the eleven southern states had actually withdrawn from the Union, the elected representatives of those states certainly presumed the right and action of secession. On February 4, 1861, delegates from South Carolina, Georgia, Florida, Alabama, Mississippi, and Louisiana, soon to be joined by delegates from Texas, met in Montgomery, Alabama, to form a new national government. The product of their deliberations, the "Confederate States of America, claiming and exercising empire from the Atlantic to the Colorado and from the Gulf to the Ohio, was a federal republic, organized in all branches of government."[7]

The first procedural actions of the Montgomery convention did not encourage those who might have expected or hoped for an open government. In a letter to his wife on February 5 one delegate wrote:

". . . we cleared the galleries this morning and went into secret session. The outsiders were very much outraged at the movement. . . ."[8] He further explained that the delegates, like the framers of the United States Constitution, were "doing the most important work in 'secret session' and a member is expelled for divulging the matter in any manner."[9] The press, upset, voiced its displeasure by charging the convention with conspiracy and deceit. But one member responded that to assure calm, unbiased deliberations "it was of the highest importance that our actions not be anticipated and misrepresented through the appliances of news mongers and sensational telegrams."[10]

On February 5, 1861, the second day of the convention, Memminger of South Carolina proposed "that a committee be appointed to report a plan of the provisional government . . . upon the basis of the Constitution of the United States."[11] Such an action might seem somewhat inconsistent for recently seceded states; but, as another delegate later explained, they had withdrawn "not from the Constitution, but from the wicked and injurious perversions of the Compact."[12] The committee presented a draft on the afternoon of February 7. It was debated in secret session and adopted on the evening of February 8.[13]

Article I, Section 7.9 of the Constitution for the Provisional Government of the Confederate States of America stated: "Congress shall make no law respecting a establishment of religion or prohibiting the free exercise thereof; or abridging the freedom of speech, or of the press; or of the right of the people peaceably to assemble and to petition the Government for a redress of such grievances as the delegated powers of this Government may warrant it to consider and redress."[14]

This paragraph differs from the First Amendment to the Constitution of the United States only with respect to its qualification concerning the types of grievances mentioned. Rather than an authorization to limit freedom of assembly this change reflected two significant currents in southern thought of the period: (1) a states'-rights view of limited national government and (2) a response to abolition petitions that had been received by the United States Congress in previous decades.

The permanent Constitution of the Confederate States of America, which was presented on February 28, adopted on March 11, and ratified on March 29, 1861, did not include the additional language. Article I, Section 9.12, in phrasing identical to the First Amendment to the United States Constitution, declared: "Congress shall make no law respecting an establishment of religion, or prohibiting the free exercise thereof; or abridging the freedom of speech, or of the press; or of the right of the people peaceably to assemble and to petition the Government for a redress of grievances."[15]

The debates on this paragraph reveal that on March 6 two attempts were made to modify its scope, but neither would have changed the protection of speech and press. Delegate Cobb tried to insert a clause prohibiting Congress from requiring any citizen to perform secular labor on Sunday,[16] and Delegate Wither moved to again add the restriction "such as the delegated powers herein contained may authorize Congress to redress."[17] Both motions were defeated.

In view of the prevailing states'-rights philosophy and the growing regional resentment against decisions of the United States Supreme Court during the years preceding secession it is also necessary to examine the Confederate judicial system. Article III of the Provisional Constitution provided for a system of district courts, each state constituting a judicial district, and a Supreme Court consisting of a majority of the district judges sitting together.[18] In the permanent Constitution, after realizing the difficulty of assembling judges from distant districts, the delegates authorized Congress to establish an independent Supreme Court to hear appeals. Although legislation was offered in every session of Congress, no Supreme Court was ever established. Some members opposed a Supreme Court's having appellate jurisdiction over state courts. Some feared centralizing of national power should President Jefferson Davis appoint former United States Supreme Court Justice John Archibald Campbell of Alabama.[20] Some were afraid that Davis would appoint former U.S. Senator Judah P. Benjamin, his most influential secretary. Others were more concerned about such matters as the conduct of the war. One member said: "We had no time for Courts. We had no use for Beat Courts, nor for County Courts, nor for the State Courts, nor for Confederate Courts."[21]

The Confederate district judges were appointed by Davis and confirmed by Congress in May, 1861. Most of the former U.S. district judges resigned their positions, took an oath to support the Confederate Constitution, and were reappointed as Confederate district judges.[22] The transition from one federal judiciary was so smooth that some of the clerks "merely turned a page in the United States record books and went on with the business of the day."[23] The judges of the state supreme courts made even more effortless adaptations to the new order than did the federal judges. They merely took an oath to uphold the new Constitution and remained in office to rule upon the continuing dockets and state laws.

Both federal and state courts continued to cite the decisions of the U.S. Supreme Court almost as if the states had not seceded. One state court cited *The Federalist* in support of the Confederate government's power of military conscription.[24] Another relied on Mr. Justice Marshall's decision in *McCulloch* to grant the Confederate government power in a conflict of jurisdiction with a state.²⁵ In the words of one scholar, "So far as the character of the decisions was concerned, it would be difficult as a rule for a reader of the Southern judicial literature to discover that there had been a withdrawal from the Union."²⁶

With regard to district-court decisions, however, that literature is rather limited. Sidney D. Brummer, an early Confederate legal historian, was unable to locate any Confederate district-court opinions in either manuscript or print.²⁷ Another writer seemed to infer from this that the district courts had an insignificant role.²⁸

Although they may have been overshadowed in importance by the state supreme courts,²⁹ there were other reasons for the lack of published reports. The reports of only one federal district court had been published in the antebellum South,³⁰ and the war period was not the most opportune time to begin such a practice. The excitement and confusion of war did little to encourage the keeping of better records, for as early as August, 1862, thirteen of the forty-three regular district-court seats had been abandoned because of hostile military activity.³¹ Some reports did survive in the form of newspaper accounts and pamphlets. These give some idea of the character of judicial opinions.

Neither the extant federal decisions nor the numerous reported state-court opinions, however, reveal very much regarding the meaning of freedom of speech and press. In only about half the states did constitutional issues arise. These dealt with the national government's power of military conscription, which the state courts upheld, and the power to suspend the privilege of the writ of *habeas corpus*, on which no state supreme court ruled.³² Restrictions on freedom of speech and press were not challenged on the basis of Article I, Section 9.12, just as the First Amendment was not invoked in the United States during that time. One must turn elsewhere, then, for a better understanding of the concept and practice of freedom of expression. It would seem profitable to examine the legislative enactments, executive decisions, military activities, and extralegal restraints.

Legislative Acts and Attitudes

Congressman Cocock, Speaker of the Confederate House of Representatives, once quipped that the *Richmond Examiner* should be destroyed and its editor hanged.³³ Congressman Leach also made the same hyperbolic suggestion with regard to the treatment of editors in general.³⁴ Congressman Conrad also resented the press and said that he saw no need to exempt editors from the conscription law, that newspapers in the Confederacy had done more harm than good, and that the South could probably do just as well without newspapers for six months.[35] Despite these comments indicating congressional disdain, when proposals were presented to curb the press or establish penalties for publishing military information, Congress refused to take such action.[36]

On two occasions, however, the members were angered enough to suggest action against those who attacked their deliberations. An article written by George C. Stedman in the *Richmond Enquirer* on February 24, 1863, drew the ire of the Senate. Stedman had accused Senator Albert Gallatin Brown of Mississippi, an opponent of exempting newspaper editors from conscription, of having done some rhetorical grand-standing in a bid for popularity. The Senate viewed the remarks as "an attack upon the personal and political character of a Senator, couched in indecent and offensive language."[37] On February 25 the Senate passed Senator Wigfall's resolution establishing a committee "to inquire into the rights and duties of reporters admitted to seats upon the floor of the Senate, and also to inquire as to whether there had been any breach of those duties in certain comments made by a reporter in the columns of a newspaper published in this city . . . ."[38] The committee report, issued on March 11, concluded that admission to the floor of the Senate was a privilege that could be withdrawn for either inaccurate or insulting reporting without violating the rights of the press.[39] Following the report the Senate adopted a resolution withdrawing privileges from Stedman, but it rejected two other proposals that would have withdrawn the privilege of the floor from the *Richmond Enquirer* and given the presiding officer the power to withdraw the privilege from any reporter or newspaper at his discretion.[40]

The Senate's action in this incident suggests that the Confederate senators had progressed beyond the concept of seditious libel but had not yet reached the conclusions of the present generation regarding the right to cover and report governmental proceedings under the First Amendment and freedom-of-information legislation. Two years later, though, the House went even further than the Senate. On January 14, 1865, the *Richmond Sentinel* ran an article charging the Congress with treasonable activity for attempting to secure a negotiated peace. Two days later Congressman Lester moved to suspend the rules and allow his introduction of a resolution denouncing the newspaper. He was supported by several members who took exception to the insulting language in the article. Congressman Smith of Alabama even threatened to resign in protest. But the House, by a vote of 32–36, refused to allow Lester to even introduce the measure.[41]

The Congress did pass several pieces of legislation which affected the rights of citizens to engage in communication: an act against enticing desertion from the military forces[42] and another to prevent improper communication with the enemy.[43] Under the second of these any person "corresponding with the enemy in any manner with intent to injure the Confederate States of America" could suffer death or up to twenty years in prison. Later, following futile attempts to secure convictions for treason, Congress enacted another bill "to define and punish conspiracy against the Confederate States," which made punishable by five years' imprisonment any conspiracy "to hold any secret Communication with the enemy" or to "promote disobedience of military orders, or desertion."[44]

On the other hand, newspaper operations were aided by special postage rates for newspapers, magazines, books, circulars, and other printed materials, and by free postage on newspapers mailed between publishers. Congress even enacted, over Davis's veto, legislation extending the frank to newspapers mailed to soldiers.[45] Further protection was given the press by exemption from conscription of "one editor of each newspaper now being published, and such employees as the editor or proprietor may certify, upon oath, to be indispensable for conducting the publication."[46]

Another important medium of communication—the telegraph—was placed under the control of the President as early as May 11, 1861. The Postmaster General was designated to take charge of the lines and supervise communications passing through "to the end that no communications shall be conveyed of the military operations of the government to endanger the success of such operations, nor any communication calculated to injure the cause of the Confederate States. . . ."[47] Such language, considered overbroad by today's standards, reflected the war-time atmosphere. The statute went even further by limiting the transmission of communication "calculated to affect the public welfare" and allowing the military censor to strike "whatever he thought improper."[48]

As in the foregoing examples congressional attitudes toward freedom of expression were usually developed against the background of some military activity. In September, 1863, Senator Haynes of Tennessee offered a resolution that has received differing assessments by historians, some viewing it as an attempt to protect freedom of speech and others describing it as a sedition bill aimed at curtailing it.[49] The legislative history of the resolution and the subsequent bill suggests that the latter view is the more correct. The Haynes resolution asked the Judiciary Committee to "inquire into the expediency of providing by law, under proper sanctions, that no military commander . . . shall suspend or abridge the freedom of speech or of the press, and fixing suitable penalties for the abuse of such freedom when exercised to disturb the public peace, or incite to domestic violence or rebellion against the Confederate States."[50] The Senate amended the resolution to delete any reference to the abuse of freedom of speech before passing it,[51] and prevented the enactment of a companion bill aimed at punishing insurrection and rebellion when Senator Wigfall read a section of the Sedition Act of 1789 for "odious comparison."[52]

The pressures of war and military necessity did, however, combine to force Congress to pass three acts that had a profound effect upon the exercise of individual rights—acts that would never have been passed in peace time. Twice in 1862 and once in 1864 Congress enacted legislation authorizing the President to suspend the writ of *habeas corpus* for a combined period of sixteen months.[53]

The first act declared that during the invasion of the Confederate States, "the President shall have the power to suspend the privilege of the writ of *habeas corpus* in such cities, towns, and military districts as shall, in his judgement, be in such danger of attack by the enemy to require the declaration of martial law for their defense."[54] During the first two weeks of suspension Richmond Provost Martial John Winder's troops made more than thirty arbitrary arrests, leading one resident to describe the period as a "reign of terror."[55] One citizen arrested by military authorities charged that the legislation had been enacted "for the purpose of putting a padlock upon every man's mouth, and thus annihilating all freedom of speech. . . ."[56] This vigorous exercise of power led Congress to amend the law within two months, setting a date for the termination of the authority and limiting its application to "arrests made by authority of the Confederate government or offenses against the same."[57] When the law was renewed for a second time, Congress retained the above restrictions, eliminated the reference to martial law, and required the President to order the investigation of the cases of all persons arrested under the act.[58]

In February, 1864, President Davis again asked for legislation allowing suspension of the writ, citing acts of treason and plots to incite slave rebellions as reasons necessitating the power.[59] The law was enacted a third time, but both public and congressional opposition was growing. The legislatures of Georgia, North Carolina, and Mississippi passed resolutions declaring the law to be unconstitutional,[60] and the North Carolina Assembly went so far as to impose a fine and imprisonment for anyone failing to honor a writ of *habeas corpus*.[61] In general "prevailing opinion in the South held the suspension law unconstitutional and the practice dangerous."[62] Congress considered repeal of the legislation, but the threat of a veto prevented that action.[63] In May and again in November, Davis requested that the authorization be renewed; however, both times Congress refused to grant the request.[64]

The controversy surrounding the executive suspension of the privilege the writ of *habeas corpus* and the accompanying military actions under martial law were among the more-emotional issues considered by the Confederate Congress. Under the suspension of the writ some of the most-oppressive actions concerning freedom of expression were taken. These led to grave congressional concern. An examination of the attitudes and activities of the executive branch, especially those of the War Department, is necessary for a full understanding of the reasons for and the reactions to these restrictions on freedom of speech and press.

Executive Department Actions

Although President Davis had requested authority to suspend the writ of *habeas corpus* during periods of military crisis, he was otherwise tolerant of citizens exercising their freedom of speech and press. A survey of southern newspaper editorials of the war era revealed that Davis was "far from popular among members of the fourth estate."[65] One contemporary writer observed in May, 1863, "I find that it is a great mistake to suppose that the Press is gagged in the South, as I constantly see the most violent attacks upon the President—upon the different generals and their measures."[66] Yet President Davis was said to have remarked that he "would not live in a country that did not tolerate freedom of the press"[67] and, in response to a question as to why he did not suppress the hostile *Richmond Examiner*, replied that nothing would be gained if the South were "to win independence by losing liberties."[68] The only suggestion that Davis was inclined to retaliate occurred when he vetoed a bill allowing free postage for newspapers mailed to military personnel. Some critics charged that it was to spite editors who had been critical of his administration.[69]

In July, 1861, Thomas A. R. Nelson made a speech in Carter County, Tennessee, urging the audience to resist the actions of the seceded state government and pledging his support for the Lincoln administration. While on his way to Washington he was arrested by a company of home guards in Lee County, Virginia, transferred to a jail in Richmond, and held on charges of treason. Davis ordered his release, stating that it was the Confederate government's policy "not to enter into questions of differences of opinion hereafter existing."[70]

While advocating freedom of expression at home Davis was often critical of measures employed by the United States government in response to political opposition, citing the suppression of newspapers and the jailing of editors in Ohio and Pennsylvania as well as the arrest of public officials in Maryland.[71] In his inaugural address at Richmond on February 22, 1862, after almost a year of military hostilities, he compared the experience in the South with that of the North, saying:

> For proof of the sincerity of our purpose to maintain our ancient institutions, we may point to the Constitution of the Confederacy and to the laws enacted under it, as well as to the fact that through all the necessities of an unequal struggle there has been no act on our part to impair personal liberty or the freedom of speech, or thought, or of the press. The courts have been open, the judicial functions fully executed, and every right of the peaceful citizen maintained as securely as if a war of invasion had not disturbed the land.[72]

One historian, acknowledging the government's toleration of hostile criticism, suggested that there might have been too much freedom of expression in the South, blaming the lack of censorship of military news and soldiers' mail for the destruction of public and military morale.[73] Even some editors thought that the press had little to fear from the Davis administration but cautioned that it could be endangered by "the reckless abuse and excessive license practiced by some of its [freedom of the press] advocates and expounders."[74] Another historian agreed that in addition "to the malignancy of the anti-Davis newspapers was an overzealous feeling for freedom of the press—the right to publish anything the editor chose—and a lack of understanding of what might give aid and comfort to the enemy."[75] That assessment differed little from that of T. C. DeLeon, who, in 1890, wrote:

> Nowhere on the globe was the freedom of the press more thoroughly vindicated than in the Southern States of America. And during the whole course of the war, criticisms of men and measures were constant and outspoken. So much so, indeed, that in many instances the operators of the Government were embarrassed, or the actions of a department commander seriously hampered by criticisms in a paper. In naval operations, and the workings of the Conscript law, especially was this freedom felt to be injurious; and though it sprang from the perfectly pure motive of doing the best for the cause . . . still it might have been better at times had gag law been applied.[76]

Unfortunately gag law was applied at times. Under the suspension of the writ of *habeas corpus* the military commanders and provost marshals, unable to distinguish between military necessity and political persecution, often infringed upon constitutionally guaranteed freedoms of expression. One of the first conflicts between the army and the press concerned the reporting of military activities. On July 1, 1861, "while professing his belief in an unshackled press and his continued willingness to permit any of the representatives of the press to visit the camps in Virginia,"[77] Secretary of War Walker urged reporters to refrain from mentioning troop strength and movements.[78] Furthermore, the Provisional Congress had authorized governmental control of telegraphic transmissions relating to military activity, so between the requested voluntary censorship and the imposed wire censorship, reporting of military activity was sometimes restricted.[79]

Press response to Secretary Walker's request, however, was not all that he had hoped. The *Charleston Mercury* said that the press would cause greater harm to the nation by concealing vital information from the people than by anything they might print about military activity.[80] One reporter, after having his dispatch severely edited by the telegraph censors, complained that "to be consistent the Government should establish a censorship over the mailbags, over the railway trains, and over the minds and tongues of men. . . ."[81] Another reporter, frustrated over the difficulty of locating the proper officers to approve his dispatches and over the variances in what different officers would allow, suggested that the system of censorship be replaced with legislation "making reporters and editors responsible for censoring their own dispatches and subjecting them to fines and imprisonment for violations of security regulations."[82] Such a system, felt to be an improvement at the time, would have only brought the wartime concept of freedom of expression from a condition of prior restraint up to the definition advanced by Blackstone—actually a step backward under peacetime conditions.

Despite Walker's well-intended suggestions his permission to allow reporters to go into army camps was often of little consequence. Some generals issued orders prohibiting their officers from discussing military affairs with press correspondents.[83] Others totally excluded reporters from their command. One general even prohibited members of the press from remaining within twenty-five miles of his camp.[84]

Several reporters were arrested by military authorities during the war, but none was ever convicted. William W. Screws, of the *Montgomery Daily Advertiser*, was arrested by General Braxton Bragg for reporting troop movements; but he was released after being held for ten days.[85] Samuel Reid, of the *Mobile Register*, once had to flee Bragg's camp to avoid arrest. John Linebaugh, of the *Memphis Appeal*, was arrested on Bragg's orders.[86] Linebaugh was held on charges of treason for having reported troop movements and making unfavorable comments about Bragg, but after about two weeks he was released on a writ of *habeas corpus* by Judge O. A. Bull of Atlanta. Leonidas Spratt, a reporter for the *Charleston Mercury* and a former member of the South Carolina legislature, was arrested on spy charges but was released after convincing the authorities of his loyalty.[87] Another correspondent—Frank Smyth of the *Petersburg Express*—was also arrested by the local militia and jailed in Winchester, Virginia, until the Secretary of War ordered his release.[88] The only case that ever came to trial was that of L. H. Matthews, of the *Pensacola Observer*. He was acquitted of spy charges after having been arrested for publishing information concerning military affairs.[89]

When General Robert E. Lee complained that Richmond papers published reports of troop strength and movements, Secretary of War Randolph had copies of the letter sent to all the newspapers in the city, expressing his hope that no official steps would be necessary to stop such publications. "A more rigid censorship should be established by the papers themselves," he said, "or they will do much mischief. It is the ardent wish of the Department that this revolution may be successfully closed without the suppression of one single newspaper in the Confederate States. . . ."[90]

Others, however, were less ardent in their concern. General Herbert declared martial law throughout the entire state of Texas on May 30, 1862. Among the orders issued were the requirements that every white male over sixteen years of age was to register "and to furnish such information as may be required of him."[91]

Five weeks later, General Earl Van Dorn declared martial law in the military department of south Mississippi and east Louisiana, proclaiming that "the seeds of dissension and dissatisfaction shall not be sown among the troops."[92] The order made it illegal to do or say or write anything undermining Confederate currency, and prohibited the publication of any article in the newspapers regarding troop movements. Furthermore, no article or editorial could be printed which might impair confidence in the commanding officers. Any violations could result in fines, imprisonment, and suspension of publication.

Earlier that same week, in the district to the north of Van Dorn's command, Asa Hodges was arrested on suspicion of disloyalty by order of Brigadier-General Adams and held without being charged. Adams reported that, in a conversation with a neighbor, Hodges "had given utterance to language of a very suspicious and disloyal character."[93] On July 2 General Bragg allowed the release of Hodges but suggested that he be admonished against future despondent talk concerning the Confederate States: "Such language may do as much hurt with the ignorant, weak and hesitant as downright disloyalty. In times like these Mr. Hodges does not play the part of a good citizen but actually of an incendiary when he sets to work to discredit the capacity, conduct and policy of the public authorities, the military especially, and it will not be permitted."[94]

Shortly after these actions Senator T. J. Semmes introduced and passed a resolution calling for a congressional study of means of limiting such military abuses of power. His position was supported in the House by Garnett of Virginia and Jones and Foote of Tennessee.[95] President Davis responded by issuing an order revoking the proclamations of martial law. He later replaced Herbert and Van Dorn.[96]

There were additional infringements by military forces. A civilian named Wigden was held in North Carolina as a prisoner of war for using "treasonable language."[97] Andrew McKee was tried by court-martial, found guilty of treason, and sentenced to be shot before he was released by a judge who ruled that private citizens were beyond the military court's jurisdiction.[98] It was suggested by some that Robert Toombs had been arrested by General Pierre Beauregard for a near-treasonous speech he had given in Savannah.[99] The office of W. W. Holden's anti-administration *Raleigh Standard* was destroyed by troops in September, 1863.[100] However, the incidents mentioned above were not part of any general or sustained pattern such as was found in other areas—like Richmond and East Tennessee.

Richmond, the seat of government, was also the base of an over-zealous provost marshal: John H. Winder. Almost immediately after the writ of *habeas corpus* was suspended, a citizen named John Botts was arrested at his home before daybreak on March 2, 1862. His private papers were seized and examined by military authorities. He was held in a Richmond jail almost two months before being released on a parole of honor. Botts was required to take an oath that he would move to the interior of the state, not go more than five miles from his home, "nor express any opinion tending to impair the confidence of the people in the capacity of the Confederate States to achieve their independence."[101]

In another case Alden Bosserman, a Unitarian minister, was arrested and jailed for "expressing his contempt for the Confederacy in foolishly praying that 'this unholy rebellion should be crushed out.'"[102] Citizens were often arrested on such vague charges as disloyalty or using treasonable language. Winder also made arrests for slogans written on buildings.[103] The provost marshal once went so far as to threaten to suppress publication of the *Richmond Whig* if it did not "abandon its vicious habit of uttering unpalatable truths."[104]

One of the most-striking examples of the wartime restrictions on expression is seen in "General Orders, No. 31," issued by the Adjutant and Inspector General's office in Richmond on March 10, 1864. The writ of *habeas corpus* was suspended for thirteen offenses, nine of which were verbal crimes: (1) treason or treasonable efforts to subvert the government, (2) conspiracies to overthrow the government or conspiracies to resist lawful authority, (3) communicating intelligence to the enemy, (4) conspiracies to incite servile insurrection, (5) encouraging desertions from the armed forces, (6) holding correspondence with the enemy without necessity or permission from the Confederate States, (7) conspiracies to liberate prisoners, (8) conspiracies to aid the enemy, and (9) advising or inciting others to abandon the Confederate cause.[105]

In eastern Tennessee, where citizens of the mountainous counties had voted 2-1 against secession, the military commanders had an especially difficult time maintaining loyalty to the cause. Brigadier-General Carroll, on November 29, 1861, stated that "the Government of the Confederate States has not nor will it interfere with individuals on account of their political opinions," but he would, however, arrest all "who in any manner may aid or abet its enemies or incite rebellion in order that they may be tried by military law."[106]

It appears that either those opinions mentioned above would be tolerated only as long as they were not expressed or that the term "in any manner" was broadly construed. In the case of *Confederate States of America v. W. A. G. Reed* the defendant was charged with treason for circulating a book "calculated to excite discontent and insurrection and rebellion, and with an intent to subvert and overthrow the government of the Confederate States."[107] Reed was released by the court after taking an oath of allegiance to the government—a widespread practice in such cases.

Colonel Wood, who was under Carroll's command, arrested Judge David T. Patterson, son-in-law of Andrew Johnson; Colonel Samuel Pickens, the state senator from Sevier County; several members of the Tennessee House of Representatives; and others of influence and distinction in east Tennessee in connection with armed resistance and the destruction of important railroad bridges. These men, he said, encouraged the rebellion, "but have so managed as not to be found in arms. Nevertheless all their actions and words have been unfriendly to the Government of the Confederate States."[108] Wood said that they "really deserve the gallows . . . [but] it is a mere farce to arrest them and turn them over to the courts."[109]

No jury impaneled in that area of the state would convict the prisoners. The Confederate States district judge was more lenient than

Judge Halyburton in Richmond,[110] who dismissed charges or released on oath 109 of 109 such cases before him.[111] In view of these facts the important prisoners were sent to a detention camp for political prisoners in Tuscaloosa, Alabama.[112] Others who were arrested for related resistance activities were released after being required to take an oath that they would "not directly or indirectly by talking, writing or otherwise seditiously or rebelliously attempt to excite prejudice in the mind of any person or persons against the existence, perpetuity or prosperity of said Confederate States."[113]

The most famous case of political repression in Tennessee was that involving William G. "Parson" Brownlow, editor of the *Knoxville Whig* and a future governor of the state. A vocal and vociferous Union man, with an editorial style that seemed to have been influenced by his pulpit style, Brownlow soon became a target of Confederate States Attorney J. C. Ramsey. Ramsey already had a reputation for arresting citizens and hauling them into court without warrants, merely for being Union men. It was even said that "an old man named Duggan, a Methodist preacher, was arrested . . . and all they had against him was that in February last (before secession) he prayed for the Union."[114] Reports of these activities had prompted President Davis to instruct Secretary of War Benjamin to take action to "prevent as far as we may such proceedings. . . ."[115]

Ramsey once said that Brownlow's paper was "the greatest cause of rebellion in this section and most who have been arrested have been deluded by his gross distortion of the facts and incited to take up arms by his inflammatory appeals to their passions and infamous libels upon the Confederate States."[116] On December 6, 1861, a warrant for Brownlow's arrest was issued by Confederate States Commissioner Reynolds. The warrant, upon Ramsey's affidavit, charged that Brownlow "did willfully, knowingly and with malice aforethought and feloniously commit the crime of treason against the Confederate States by . . . publishing a weekly and tri-weekly paper known as Brownlow's *Knoxville Whig;* and said paper . . . contained weekly divers of editorials written by said Brownlow which said editorials were treasonable against the Confederate States of America, and did then and there commit treason and prompt others to commit treason; by speech as well as publication as aforesaid commit treason and did give aid and comfort to the United States. . . ."[117]

In a letter written to President Davis from his prison cell Brownlow stated that "the publication of a newspaper, however objectionable its matter might be, cannot amount to treason."[118] One of the editorials for which he was arrested gives an indication that he had been harassed previously and was expecting to be arrested. It further illuminates his views on freedom of the press in the Confederate States of America. In the issue of October 26, 1861, he wrote:

> The real object of my arrest and contemplated imprisonment is to dry up, break down, silence and destroy the last and only Union paper left in the eleven seceded States and thereby to keep from the people of East Tennessee the facts which are daily transpiring in the country. After the Hon. Jeff Davis had stated in Richmond in a conversation relative to my paper that he would not live in a government that would not tolerate freedom of the press—after the judges, attorneys, jurors and all others filling positions of honor and trust under the "permanent Constitution" which guarantees freedom of the press—and after the entire press of the South had come down in thunder tones upon the Federal Government for suppressing the *Louisville Courier* and the *New York Day-Book* and other secession journals—I did expect the utmost liberty to be allowed to one small sheet whose errors could be combated by the entire Southern press. It is not enough that my paper has been denied a circulation through the ordinary channels of conveyance in the country but it must be discouraged all together or its editor must write and select such articles as meet the approval of the scoundrels in Knoxville when their superiors in all the qualities that adorn human nature are in the penitentiary of our State. And this is the boasted liberty of the press in the Southern Confederacy.[119]

Brownlow was never tried on the charges, because the President ordered that he be released and allowed to go beyond Confederate lines. Ramsey entered a *nolle prosequi* in late December. After a brief detention by military authorities Brownlow went to the North, where he continued to speak out against the Confederate government.[120] After U. S. forces reoccupied Tennessee in 1863, Brownlow returned to edit the *Knoxville Whig and Rebel Ventilator* and later became governor when the state was readmitted to the Union.

The events in Tennessee and the actions of the military authorities throughout the South represent unique conditions, which must be understood in any analysis of the concept of freedom of expression in the Confederate States of America. These practices were beyond the Constitution in that the privilege of the writ of *habeas corpus* was suspended and martial law sometimes imposed, yet they were within the Constitution in that the Congress had constitutionally authorized the suspension. Their true significance can only be evaluated and understood in relation to other aspects of the problem.

The Pressure of Public Opinion

Even before the formation of the confederacy the states of the South had endured a generation of growing restrictions on the freedom of expression for the white population and several generations of no freedom of expression for the black population. The influence of these trends could scarcely have been expected to disappear with secession, regardless of the new government's policies.

Evidence of a continuing repressive psychology can be seen in several unofficial acts at the local level. In Georgia one grand jury admonished "disloyal citizens who were speaking disparagingly of the government at Richmond, cautioning them to 'stop their impudent and imprudent mouths.'"[121] Another recommended legislation forbidding subscription to the *New York Tribune*.[122] George Fitzhugh, an antebellum defender of the exploitation of both slaves and free labor, held that "newspapers should not be privately run, but that each state and the Confederacy should have their official press and that no other newspaper should be allowed to exist."[123]

Several newspapers, though not destroyed by overt action, were the victims of public pressure. The *New Orleans True Delta* and the *Richmond Whig* were both forced to change their editorial policy to survive.[124] Those papers which did not change their position, such as the *Union Banner* in Athens, Alabama, the *Wilmington Daily Herald* in North Carolina, the *Charlottesville Review* in Virginia, and *The Christian Banner* of Fredricksburg, Virginia, were forced to suspend publication soon after the war began. This was because of a drop in number of subscribers and the withdrawal of official patronage of legal notices.[125]

In some sections vigilance committees took it upon themselves to arrest, try, convict, and punish strangers and local residents whom they considered to be disloyal.[126] One citizen so tried was Robert S. Tharin, a former law partner of William L. Yancey, of Wetumpka, Alabama. He was tried by a local beat court, convicted, and banished from his community "for expressing and endeavoring to propagate sentiments that were *dangerous to the peace of society.* He had conversed with several non-slaveholders . . . [and] said that he was going to establish a newspaper (at Montgomery), to be called the *Non-Slaveholder.*"[127] Among others who were forced to flee their home states were John H. Aughey, a Presbyterian minister in Mississippi; and State Senator Isaac Murphy, of Arkansas.[128]

Mayor William D. Branch, of Lynchburg, Virginia, ordered the arrest of George Gross in May, 1861, and held him without formal charges. Explaining his actions to the governor, Branch said, "He claims now to be a Republican. Having expressed such sentiments I thought he ought not to be allowed to travel through the country and committed him to jail."[129] Although some probably thought republicanism to be "more of a conspiracy against the South than a political party,"[130] Gross was released by Governor Letcher after taking an oath of fidelity to the Confederacy.[131]

On the other hand, the Civil War period was also a time of progress toward a less-restrictive society. In 1862 the Georgia legislature, in contrast with antebellum statutes forbidding teaching slaves to read or write, moved to repeal earlier laws against issuing preaching licenses to Negroes or slaves.[132] While the practice of state regulation of religious expression and the licensing of speakers is foreign to the concept of free expression today, the action was a significant step forward.

There had been an increasing solidarity among southern political leaders in Congress since the debates on the Missouri Compromise, but following secession that trend was either reversed or exposed as a thin facade. Governors Zebulon B. Vance of North Carolina and Joseph E. Brown of Georgia were often critical of the Davis administration and led their states in legal battles against conscription and suspension of the writ of *habeas corpus*. Former Governor Sam Houston of Texas and former Senator Robert Toombs of Georgia were openly contemptuous toward the government. Congressman Henry S. Foote defected to the North before the war was over. Davis was even forced to contend with the often-hostile criticism of his Vice-President: Alexander H. Stephens.

The previously discussed armed resistance of the civilian population in east Tennessee was the most obvious but not the only indication of popular opposition to the Richmond government. In Mississippi one county declared its independence from the Confederacy. The mountain regions of Arkansas, Alabama, Georgia, North Carolina, and Virginia all had strong and active peace societies throughout the war.[133] It was a time of increasingly open criticism of the government as well as a time of continued suppression. To better understand the broader conception of freedom of expression one must interpret these paradoxical events from a comparative point of view.

Summary and Interpretation

The concept and practice of freedom of expression in the Confederate States of America will be evaluated from three perspectives: (1) a comparison with the practices prevailing in the remaining United States during the same period: 1861–1865; (2) an investigation of the concept relative to its understanding and practice in the United States during other periods of war; and (3) an analysis of the concept on a continuum from the Blackstonian definition to the present development of First Amendment theory.

Secretary of War Randolph, in voicing support for freedom of the press, expressed his wish that the Confederate experience would "be able to challenge comparison with our enemy."[134] That seems to have been the same standard of measurement used by President Davis. It has also been applied by later historians. "Taken as a whole . . . the government's answer to disloyal conditions was within constitutional limitations," wrote Robinson. "Its restricted use of martial law and its limited suspension of the writ of *habeas corpus*, only when authorized by Congress, stand in marked contrast to Lincoln's unrestrained use of extra-constitutional measures."[135]

The case of John Merryman provides an example of the contrast of which Robinson wrote. Merryman was arrested by Union troops and held in Fort McHenry without the privilege of the writ of *habeas corpus*, which had been issued by Judge Taney. Both the military authorities and President Lincoln ignored the writ and a subsequent decision declaring Lincoln's exercise of power to be unconstitutional. Merryman was later indicted for treason.[136] President Davis, however, only suspended the privilege upon statutory authority from Congress. This authority was granted only for a period of sixteen months during the four years of war.

Another point for comparison is Lincoln's proclamation of September 24, 1862, ordering that persons suspected of disloyal activities should be subject to trial by courts-martial and military commissions.[137] This practice was never authorized by Congress. The issue was conveniently avoided by the United States Supreme Court until after the war.[138] The Confederate States Congress, on the other hand, passed a resolution denying military authority over civilians or civil courts. The courts ruled to the same effect.[139]

Postal authorities in the South had censored mail, especially newspapers, from the North during the antebellum period. This policy continued during the war, although mail from within the South escaped censorship.[140] Mail censorship, though, was not a practice limited to Confederate authorities. After the capture of New Orleans, United States officers regularly opened and read the personal correspondence of southern citizens.[141]

Likewise, the military authorities of the Confederate government did not always support the press; but one historian proclaimed that "no newspaper was ever suppressed by state or Confederate authority throughout the war. . . ."[142] While that statement could be questioned in regard to the *Knoxville Whig* and the *Raleigh Standard,* the advance of United States forces did not present any remarkable advances for freedom of speech and press. Sherman's troops systematically destroyed the telegraph lines to disrupt transmission of military communications. This also prevented transmission of newspaper reports.[143] Although this effect was secondary, other actions of the general were not. In May, 1863, his troops destroyed the printing plant of the *Jackson Mississippian.* Two years later, in North Carolina, "the destruction of newspaper offices was a primary objective of his army. In Fayetteville, Sherman's soldiers completely destroyed the offices of the *Telegraph* and the *Observer* and were alleged to have offered a reward of $10,000 for the body of E. J. Hale, the senior editor of the *Observer.*"[144]

One author, noting the tendency of myths to control southern history, suggested that "the notion of Southern freedom of the press during the Civil War is another myth that must be discarded in the interest of a proper understanding of the Southern past."[145] A contemporary northern observer in the South, however, suggested that "liberty of the press is carried to its fullest extent."[146] A true assessment probably lies between these two contentions. Freedom of expression, when measured by prevailing practices in the United States during the same period, was no more repressed in the Confederacy than in the United States.

The primary factor that made the *concept* in both countries indistinguishable was the common legal heritage. The primary factor that made the *practice* by both countries indistinguishable was the common military conflict. The government of the Confederate States of America was at war during forty-eight of its fifty-month existence. All wars seem to have devastating effects upon civil liberties, especially freedom of expression.

The activities of the Confederate military commanders have been shown to be no more repressive than those of their contemporary Union counterparts. The same might be said of the civilian governments. As Arthur M. Schlesinger has stated and as Leonard W. Levy has agreed, during the American Revolution "liberty of speech belonged solely to those who spoke the speech of liberty."[147] The experience of the United States during World War I offers numerous examples of judicial repression, from both judges and juries, in regard to political expression.[148] Mr. Justice Holmes suggested, "When a nation is at war many things that might be said in time of peace are such a hindrance to its effort that their utterance will not be endured so long as men fight and that no Court could regard them as protected by any constitutional right."[149]

The Confederate judicial experience was, in some respects, more favorable. When the privilege of the writ of *habeas corpus* was not suspended, the courts proved to be quite lenient. Confederate District Judges James D. Halyburton (Virginia) and West H. Humphreys (Tennessee) both had widespread reputations for issuing writs to release prisoners charged with treason, desertion and discouraging enlistment.[150] In North Carolina, Chief Justice Pearson became notorious for similar practices. In Tennessee juries were sure to acquit almost all such defendants.[151] Few persons were ever indicted for verbal crimes; but when they were, the defendants were usually acquitted or the cases were merely continued from session to session without trial.[152]

The arrest and detention of reporters as well as civilians under suspension of the writ certainly had a chilling effect on political expression during the Civil War; but the abuses by government and military personnel were no more severe than during other periods of war, and the attitudes of judges and juries may have been somewhat less so. In such a comparison it does not appear that the statutory or constitutional provisions of the Confederacy made any significant difference in the way freedom of expression was viewed.

Finally, it should be determined just what the framers of the Constitution and those members of Congress whom they restrained understood freedom of expression to mean. While the convention debates are uninstructive, a review and explanation of the prevailing practices will provide some idea of what was meant by the protection given in Article I, Section 9.12 of the Constitution.

When reporter Samuel C. Reid, Jr. urged his editors at the *Montgomery Daily Advertiser* to lobby for legislation repealing the system of military censorship and making the press responsible for the consequences of their actions, it seemed that he would have been satisfied if the government of the Confederate States of America would only accept the Blackstonian doctrine of "no previous restraints upon publications . . . [with liability] for criminal matter when published."[153] Such a conclusion may be valid with reference to wartime measures, since the authorization for telegraphic censorship was a war statute and generally limited to information concerning military operations; but the practice of free expression was much broader in other areas.

The Confederate House refused even to allow introduction of a resolution censuring a newspaper for attacking the integrity of the Congress, and the Senate gave further evidence that the concept of seditious libel was dead when it amended a resolution by striking language concerning abuses of freedom of speech and press, including speech that might disturb the peace or be considered an incitement.[154] When legislation was presented to curb political expression, its passage was prevented by comparing it with the Sedition Act of 1798.[155] President Davis, too, remained firm in his support of a free press even in the face of hostile personal and political attacks.

The action of the Senate in expelling a reporter for an attack on one of its members serves to illustrate the precise development of the concept of freedom of the press. The committee report on the incident revealed that the solons did not conceive protection to include the right to gather news. That right, with respect to reporting Senate debates, was a privilege to be extended by the Senate—an understanding consistent with the assumed right of the Senate to hold secret sessions but inconsistent with present theory embodied in freedom-of-information legislation. For violation of the privilege the Senate responded by withdrawing it from that particular reporter rather than by enacting punitive measures. Furthermore, the senators rejected a resolution to exclude other reporters from the same newspaper even after the editors had taken responsibility for the publication and voiced their support of the reporter's interpretation.[156]

The concept and practice of freedom of expression in the Confederate States of America, 1861–1865, differed little from that in the United States at the same time, and its response to military conditions was remarkably similar to the response of American governments during other wars. The concept went beyond the Blackstonian definition of no prior restraint to allow unbridled criticism of public men and measures, but it did not include the latitude that has developed in United States constitutional law since the time of the Holmes-Brandeis dissents of the 1920s. While the previous climate of repression with regard to abolition sentiments, the contemporary atmosphere of repression concerning Union sentiments, and the measures connected with the conduct of war all prevented expansion of the rights of speech and press under the government of the Confederate States of America, neither the general concept nor the practice of freedom of expression was diminished as a result of actions by the Confederate government.

3

The Right to Speak: The Free Speech Fights of the Industrial Workers of the World

TERRY W. COLE

Terry W. Cole is Professor of Communication Arts at Appalachian State University where he teaches courses entitled "Ethics and Freedom of Speech" and "Law and Ethics of Communication Media." He is a member of the American Civil Liberties Union and has served on the Board of Directors of the North Carolina Civil Liberties Union. He also has served as chair of the Freedom and Responsibilities of Speech Division of the Southern Speech Communication Association. In addition to a number of papers pertaining to First Amendment topics which he has presented at professional meetings, Professor Cole is the author of "Legal Issues in Library Censorship Cases," published in 1985 in the School Library Media Quarterly. *This essay appeared in the* Free Speech Yearbook: 1978.

> 5,000 men and women, who believe in freedom of Speech, Press, and Public Assemblage, to be in Spokane, Wash., on March 1st and show contempt for home-made laws that are enacted for the purpose of keeping the workers in ignorance.
> ....
> Come and show your contempt for those who tramped the Constitution of the United States into the Earth, and thus break the laws themselves.[1]

With this call to action the Industrial Workers of the World (IWW, sometimes called "Wobblies") summoned its membership to participate in a free-speech fight. In the decade between 1906 and 1918 the IWW conducted more than twenty-six such fights in communities as divergent as Missoula, Montana; San Diego, California; and Paterson, New Jersey.

These colorful episodes were not merely libertarian defenses of abstract First Amendment doctrine but, rather, pragmatic tactics designed to remedy specific denials of free speech while at the same time rhetorically advancing the ideology of the movement. These free-speech fights were unique rhetorical tactics as well as significant episodes in the history of freedom of speech.

History of the Battles for Free Speech

When the IWW was founded in 1905, its leadership had little notion that the organization would become an early defender of the First Amendment; yet within a year the ideology of the IWW and its rhetorical tactics came into direct confrontation with a repressive society. In response to the exigencies of the confrontation the IWW developed its unique rhetorical strategy—the free-speech fight.[2]

It is not surprising that the IWW and its radical ideology met with suppression from reactionary defenders of capitalism.[3] The ideology of the IWW was a product of the dissatisfaction of small groups of socialists, anarchists, industrial unionists, and dissident trade unionists. Advancing a radical, Marxian concept of revolutionary industrial unionism, the IWW sought to organize the working class along industrial lines and to abolish the capitalist system. It also sought to organize society's outcasts—immigrants, the Negroes, and migratory workers.[4]

Suppression occurred in conservative communities of the Pacific Northwest and California, where the IWW had begun active agitation among itinerant lumber workers and migratory farm workers. The campaign relied heavily upon colorful soapboxers to attract large crowds of idle workers wintering in the skid rows of western communities.[5] It was essential that these agitators have free use of the streets if they were to reach workers who might be most receptive to the Wobbly message. Totally hostile to the ideology of the IWW, employers pressured municipal governments to pass speaker-ban ordinances or, in some instances, to use co-operative police-censor squads.[6]

IWW agitators faced several constraints in responding to these legal and extralegal limitations on his freedom of speech. In the first place, the IWW did not have access to the councils of government and consequently could not respond to suppression in normal, institutional ways. Moreover, the IWW's intransigent ideology, rejecting political and judicial avenues of redress as contrary to the class struggle, further limited its available responses.[7] Finally, even if the IWW had chosen to challenge the constitutionality of gag laws, it is doubtful that such appeals would have worked. The Fourteenth Amendment door to First Amendment challenges of municipal or state laws was not to be opened until 1925 with the ruling in *Gitlow vs. New York* (268 US 652). So, faced with suppressive gag laws and with limited avenues of response, the IWW met the situation with direct action.

The pattern of the free-speech fight developed in an almost-classic form of civil disobediance. Once the Wobbly leaders decided to fight an ordinance against street speaking, the call went out through the IWW press and "general office bulletins" for all footloose members of the IWW to come to a particular community and join the fight.[8] Arriving at the scene, Wobblies would line up at a designated corner to speak or read from documents like the Constitution or the Declaration of Independence. As expected, the police would move in and arrest an offending speaker and cart him off to jail. No sooner would one speaker be arrested than another would take his place. In this fashion the protest continued until the jails were filled with Wobblies, each demanding a separate trial. Ultimately the protest made it financially and physically prohibitive to enforce the ordinance, and in most instances it was abolished or significantly altered.

The 1909 Spokane free-speech struggle illustrates the scope and effectiveness of the Wobbly tactic. During the five months of the fight more than six hundred Wobblies were jailed, and more than twelve hundred arrests were made. The jails were filled beyond capacity. Still, fresh Wobblies arrived from points as far away as Pennsylvania, Maine, Canada, and Mexico, willing to stand up, speak out, and go to jail. Five months after the fight began, the city capitulated and granted the IWW most of its demands.

Clearly the free-speech fight was a rhetorical tactic in the civil-disobedience tradition we have come to know in the civil-rights and antiwar movements of the 1960s and 1970s. It was an instrumental act, pragmatic and purposive, a specific means toward a specific end. Clearly it was an available means of persuasion.

Likewise, the free-speech struggle was symbolic. The physical presence of free-speech fighters became symbolic. The IWW's tactic was directed to both the membership of the IWW and the communities in which the fights occurred. By inviting arrest, jailing, and persecution the free-speech fighters were dramatizing and illuminating specific conditions needing change. Citizens observing the agitation were forced to address themselves to the condition. Many felt compelled to take the side of the IWW and further advance the call for change.

While the primary task of the free-speech fight was to win the right to use the streets, the method of gaining that right augmented other strategies in the rhetorical program of the IWW—a fact not overlooked by IWW rhetors. For example, the free-speech struggle strengthened working-class solidarity.[10] To the IWW solidarity was the power of a united working class, and the free-speech fight became an operational definition of the term. W. E. Trautmann, an IWW leader, confirmed this thinking: "We appeal to a candid world of workers to aid us in this struggle so that the corporations of the West and their city officials of Spokane can be given the lesson that more powerful than the agencies of oppression and brutal force is the power of the combined workers of this country."[11] Likewise, the IWW newspaper *Solidarity* observed: "By use of its weakest weapon—passive resistence—labor forced civic authorities to recognize a power equal to the state."[12]

Equally basic to the ideology of the IWW was the doctrine of the class struggle. This doctrine too was rhetorically advanced through the polarizing effect of the free-speech struggle. Whereas the class-struggle rhetoric argued the existence of a breach between the working class and the employing class, the free-speech fights illustrated and exacerbated that breach.

Insight into this rhetorical tactic may be gained by applying a strategy identified by James F. Klumpp in his analysis of the rhetoric of the 1968 revolt at Columbia University: "polar-rejective identification."[13] According to Klumpp "the strategy's success rests on the rejection of established leadership in a polarized environment." In such a setting an audience (or community) is forced to choose between the establishment and the agents of agitation. "With such a choice forced on the community," Klumpp observed, "the radicals could succeed without the necessity of *pulling* the community toward their position but by creating a situation in which the [establishment] *drove* the community toward the radical alternative."[14] Bowers and Ochs similarly observed that polarization occurs "by forcing such a strong negative reaction to the emotionally charged flag issue [the denial of free speech and police brutality] that condemnation of flag individuals and groups [municipal officials] would follow." "A choice would be forced," they concluded; "neutrality would be most difficult."[15] The polarization is completed when the "radicals" accurately predict the establishment's reactions and the establishment is rejected.

Although Wobbly victories in the free-speech fights did not necessarily spring from a complete rejection of municipal establishments, most factors of the polar-rejective identification strategy were present. During the free-speech struggles IWW rhetors advanced the polarization strategy with an invective campaign labeling as lawbreakers those who would deny free speech to the working class.

The following statement is typical of such arguments: "There is one good thing about this gag-law business; it is causing all thinking working people to see that the 'liberties' of the United States constitution do not exist, and that a working man or woman has no rights that his employer need respect, *unless the workers have the power* to enforce respect.... The employer agents are the ones who have passed the Spokane gag law, and it is, of course, the employing class generally who are responsible for this."[16]

The rhetoric took advantage of every act of brutality on the part of the law-enforcement officers and vigilantes, thus further intensifying the polarization. Many articles and photographs appearing in the IWW press vividly recounted the brutality visited upon free-speech advocates by forces of law and order.

Weapons used against the free-speech fighters were usually as brutal as the victims claimed. Spokane authorities incarcerated freespeech advocates in drafty, unheated buildings in the middle of winter. Prisoners were tortured in eight-by-six sweat boxes and returned to icy cells. Fresno prisoners were fed on bread and water and punished with bruising showers from 150-pound-pressure fire hoses.[17] San Diego prisoners were forced to strip, run a gauntlet of whip-and-blackjack-wielding men and, finally, to kiss the flag and sing the national anthem.[18]

The rhetorical value of polarization was demonstrated in every free-speech fight. The message was clear: The IWW had used nonviolence to gain First Amendment rights. The establishment had violated basic constitutional rights with brutality and inhumane treatment.

Faced with a polarization difficult to deal with, many persons hostile to the IWW were forced by conscience into a position of sympathy for the free-speech fighters. "Free speech became an instrument for possible martyrdom for the cause of economic justice and emancipation of the workers."[19] Liberal voices rose in defense of the IWW in the face of increasingly ugly police tactics. In Spokane civic leaders, respected clergymen, and many leading socialists gave sympathy and support to the cause. In Missoula, Senator Robert M. LaFollette, in town for a visit, spoke in support of the free-speech fighters.[20]

Perhaps the most vivid evidence of the impact of the IWW's strategy came in a report filed by Harrison Weinstock, special commissioner to the Governor of California and an avowed antagonist of the IWW. In part he admitted: "Your commissioner is frank to confess that when he became satisfied of the truth of the stories ... it was hard for him to believe that he still was not sojourning in Russia, conducting his investigation there, instead of in this alleged 'land of the free and home of the brave.' Surely these American men who, as the overwhelming evidence shows, in large numbers assaulted with weapons in a most cowardly and brutal manner their helpless and defenseless fellows, were certainly far from 'brave' and their victims far from 'free.'"[21] Weinstock concluded with a statement that could well have come from the mouth of an IWW rhetor: "The question naturally arises, therefore, who are the greater criminals; who are the real anarchists; who are the real violators of the constitution; who are the real undesirables—these so-called unfortunate members of 'the scum of the earth,' or these presumably respectable members of society?"[22] No IWW soapboxer could have more effectively underscored the polarization of the class struggle.

The Wobbly Philosophy

While some historians attribute a purely pragmatic motive to the IWW and deny that it had any larger philosophical or libertarian motivation in defending free speech,[23] the free-speech fights it conducted did advance the cause of freedom of speech. In the first place, the free-speech struggles drew considerable public attention not only to the IWW and its ideology but also to basic First Amendment principles. As historian Philip Foner observed, the IWW was "dedicated to preserve a basic principle of American democracy—freedom of speech—when no other national organization existed to uphold this principle."[24] Indeed, the free-speech fights were initiated some ten years before the founding of the American Civil Liberties Union. Likewise, those who rallied to support the free-speech fighters—newspapers, socialist groups, townspeople, and even the illustrious Robert M. LaFollette—were defending not merely a radical labor organization but also a principle that was being systematically violated. While many found the association of IWW ideology with free speech a difficult concept to grasp (not unlike the 1978 Skokie, Illinois, experience with the American Nazi Party), the principle of free speech was nevertheless so basic a part of the doctrines and traditions of our government that the struggles could not be ignored.[25] Thus, by defending free speech for its own pragmatic purposes the IWW highlighted First Amendment principles for all to see and learn from.

Finally, the rhetoric itself advanced a clearly defined concept of freedom of speech. Following the arrest of Elizabeth Gurley Flynn for speaking in Paterson, New Jersey, the IWW protested in a telegram to President Woodrow Wilson: ". . . New Jersey denied the civic rights, the inalienable rights guaranteed to citizens. . . . New Jersey has violated the constitution under which the State was chartered. The

Industrial Workers of the World proposes to fight this issue to reestablish the right of free speech and the right of free assembly."[26]

Such a motive was not only followed by the leadership but was proclaimed by the rank-and-file as well. Note, for instance, the position taken by a group of Minneapolis Wobblies: "Freedom of speech is a natural right and no man or set of men, no government . . . has the moral or constitutional right to prevent the exercise of the same."[27] Other Wobbly opinions foreshadowed the Holmes concept that truth can only come from a "free trade in ideas," only in the "competition of the marketplace."[28] For example, a Portland, Oregon, Wobbly wrote: ". . . the raggedest imbecile, if you please, has the right to give his fellow men the thoughts his Creator put in his brain. You do not know but that in the glacial movement of the ages his thoughts may turn out to be truth and yours the lie."[29] Likewise, Wobbly writer Mark Stone penned: "Belief in free speech is the conviction that bad ideas (if there is any such thing) need only complete freedom of expression of opposite ideas to render the bad ones futile, harmless, and ridiculous."[30]

One of the functions of the newspapers and other pieces of literature published by the IWW was to educate workers into whose hands they fell. The fact that newspaper writers for the IWW chose to present detailed, analytical articles on free speech evidences the movement's desire to communicate a clear freedom-of-speech doctrine. While it is impossible to ascertain the number of people within and without the IWW who read and learned from this literature, the fact remains that in the literature related to the free-speech fights was contained a consistent and philosophically sound doctrine of free speech.

Freedom of speech is as frequently taught by episodes of suppression as by textbooks used in civics classes. Such were the free-speech fights of the Industrial Workers of the World. Responding to the exigencies of legal suppression of the right to speak, the IWW developed its unique tactic of the free-speech fight. It was a successful rhetorical strategy and it was an object lesson in First Amendment principles. Labor historian Joseph Conlin accurately summed up the contributions of the free-speech fights: "The Wobblies have neither the benefit of historical remoteness, to romanticize their radical dissent, nor the appearance of respectability. Nevertheless, in a series of 'free speech fights' . . . during the decade following 1906, the I.W.W. stood boldly and steadfastly for the right to speak unhindered when most other Americans were either indifferent to the right or downright hostile to it. To this facet of Wobbly history, Americans owe a real debt, and historians some attention."[31]

4

Patriots versus Dissenters: The Rhetoric of Intimidation in Indiana During the First World War

CLARK KIMBALL

Clark Kimball taught speech communication at James Madison University and the University of Virginia before entering private law practice in 1977. Since 1980 he has been associated with the editorial department of Matthew Bender & Company, one of the nation's largest publishers of legal materials for the professional and academic markets. The following essay appeared in the Free Speech Yearbook: 1972.

> Loyalty to the flag means whole-hearted and
> absolute allegience to the United States.
> No patience can be shown to the man who does
> not accept this definition of patriotism.
> *Richmond Palladium*[1]

During the First World War, when legal duress proved unjustified or impractical as a means of forcing a suspected disloyalist to refrain from offensive behavior, Indiana patriots willingly turned to devices of intimidation to suppress dissent. Refusing to recognize a middle ground between treason and patriotism, war supporters at the least wanted to convince recalcitrants and slackers that public expression of unpatriotic sentiments would be unwise. In many instances patriots tried to compel dissenters to accept a measure of patriotic responsibility or to make a public gesture of loyalty. The case of Isaac Baum, an Indianapolis tailor, illustrated a basic patriotic approach to subduing unpopular actions. On the morning of July 6, 1917, as Baum opened his shop on North Pennsylvania Street, he noticed a small crowd gathered in front of the store. He soon learned why these people had looks of astonishment on their faces as they gazed through the shop window. Two Justice Department agents called on Baum, demanding to know why he was displaying a picture of Kaiser Wilhelm. Warning Baum to avoid such displays in the future, the government operatives departed, taking with them a book which had been opened to the revolting picture of Wilhelm.[2] Revealing the readiness of some patriots to resort to more ominous, direct threats to coerce dissenters, a letter signed by "Black Halk [sic], Fort Wayne Division" informed John Genth that unless he bought war bonds he could look for his "nice big barns to go up in flames" or his house to "get a stick of powder."[3] Both cases reflected a reliance of patriots on the ability of pressure from other persons to affect the behavior of an alleged disloyalist.

Belief in the power of public opinion to achieve uniformity of behavior among some Americans sustained organized tactics of intimidation. A strongly worded letter of reproach would warn the recipient that fellow citizens suspected his disloyal tendencies. A visit from defense or law enforcement officials carried the threat of further action. Persons listed as slackers by defense agencies were threatened with public exposure and the consequent social or economic ostracism. Asserting that no individual or organization could withstand hostile public opinion, the editor of the *Logansport Tribune* cautioned that in wartime all citizens must obey orders regardless of task, regardless of legality.[4]

Avid patriots attempted to suppress dissent by making public examples of selected disloyalists. Charles Dhe, Chairman of the Benton County Council of Defense, called for Secret Service men to investigate pro-German residents in Parish Grove Township. Dhe felt that it was time "to make an example," since "we must shut the mouths of those people before they do more dirt."[5] Circuit Court Judge John Bretz of Jasper told Will Hays, Chairman of the State Defense Council, that "the atmosphere" in the Jasper area would be "clarified . . . very extensively" if "some of our talkative disloyalists were brought up in federal court and dealt with as they appear to deserve."[6] On another occasion, in April, 1918, John Shirk of the Franklin County War Savings Committee expressed his belief that taking up the case of one pro-German in that county "would have a very wholesome effect . . . among those who are not showing their loyalty to the United States that they should."[7]

A Hoosier citizen suspected of disloyalty faced an amazing array of organizations and devices dedicated to his destruction. The official responsibility for investigating alleged disloyalty belonged to the state and county defense councils. The administrative duty fell to protection committees established within the defense council structure. The State Defense Council appointed George Harney, editor of the *Crawfordsville Review*, to the post of state director of protection activities. Under his direction the county defense councils established local protection committees.⁸ In Ripley County twenty-nine men maintained a vigil over the fourteen municipalities in the area.⁹

The State Council instructed Harney's division to discover quietly any evidence of disloyalty "which warrants preemptory action or the reporting to the state for such attention as may be deemed necessary."¹⁰ Although county protection chairmen were known to the general public, officials desired to conceal the identity of other members of the committees. Behind their self-imposed cloak of secrecy and with the excuse of authority, some defense councils extended the scope of the assignment to their groups. Tippecanoe County defense leaders ordered their protection committee to root out and suppress disloyalty.¹¹ In Wells County Sheriff J. A. Johnson appointed deputies in every precinct with power to arrest any person guilty of disloyal talk or action against the government.¹²

Protection committees depended upon citizen informants to report the names of those persons displaying improper sentiments.¹³ Conditioned to expect a pro-German agent behind every suspicious activity, loyal Americans daily reported as many as 1500 cases of disloyalty across the nation.¹⁴ Neither the Justice Department nor the state defense agencies possessed the machinery to investigate each case. To aid in this work, a group of private citizens organized the American Protective League which grew to involve 200,000 members in over 1000 communities.¹⁵

By mid-spring, 1918, the APL had established branches in many Indiana communities, including Batesville, Noblesville, Fort Wayne, Terre Haute, Seymour, Marion, South Bend, Logansport, Kokomo, Muncie, Crawfordsville, and Indianapolis.¹⁶ Each branch consisted of a chief and an assistant chief, known to the public, who had under their supervision a large number of secret operatives known only by assigned number.¹⁷ APL organization proceeded slowly in Indiana where selection of a state director proved to be a troublesome problem.¹⁸ Once organized, the APL actively assisted the State Defense Council in the investigation of cases of alleged disloyalty. By mid-May the League had handled at least 150 inquiries in Indiana.¹⁹ The APL found favor with George Murdock, Indianapolis agent of the Bureau of Investigation. In a report to his Justice Department superiors in Washington Murdock could offer no suggestion for the betterment of the APL in Indiana since he had "absolutely no criticism to make" of their activities.²⁰ By assisting with the organizational work of the APL, the State Council of Defense endorsed the enterprise which closely paralleled the workings of the protection committees.²¹

APL operatives filed reports that summarized information uncovered while investigating disloyalty cases. In Indianapolis a Liberty bond salesman, Patrick Moran, approached citizen J. D. Riggs regarding Riggs' refusal to buy bonds. Riggs expressed a lack of concern for the boys in the trenches. Moran reported the incident to bond drive leaders who in turn assigned it to the APL for study. Operative #411, unidentified on even the official report, obtained affidavits from Moran, Riggs' next door neighbors, Riggs' cousin, and Riggs' employers at the Link Belt company. From the latter he learned that Riggs had access to Link Belt's plans for government work. The other sources indicated that Riggs was pro-German. The APL submitted this report without interpretation to the State Defense Council for whatever action it might undertake.[22]

In some sections of the state groups of patriots formed unofficial protection committees to supplement the work of the defense councils, the APL, and federal agents. The Gary Patriotic Committee was composed of leading professional people who were determined to rid Gary of German influences. They once went out as a Vigilance Committee and compelled a man to tear to pieces a picture of the Kaiser which was hanging in the suspect's home.[23] The Loyal Citizens Vigilance Committee of Miami County emerged as the most conspicuous and most controversial such group. Founded in the spring of 1918, the committee quickly grew to a membership in excess of 2,000 persons including prominent professionals and businessmen, farmers, educators, and ministers.[24] The committee was directed by the assistant chief of the local APL branch.[25] Its stated purpose was to act as a patriotic influence, supporting the war, preserving loyalty, and protecting law and order.[26] In May thirty members of the committee took a rural Miami County man from his home, covered his body with yellow paint, and warned him of more serious punishment to come should he still refuse to display proper sympathy for the United States.[27]

The propensity to violence shown by the Miami County group led to complaints being lodged with Indiana Adjutant-General Lester Smith. In a late August, 1918, meeting of the State Defense Council Smith asked the defense leaders to review the lawlessness in the Peru area.[28] Smith recounted the case of Thomas McGloin, a farmer who was being harassed by the Loyal Citizens. McGloin had complained that the committee was demanding a greater contribution to the War Chest than he was willing to make. Not inclined to follow Smith's suggestion that he make the contribution, McGloin soon reported that a crowd of 2000 persons had surrounded his house one evening and threatened him while he attempted without success to contact law enforcement officers. The Adjutant-General expressed concern that patriots in Miami County were apparently resorting to violence with no objections from defense bodies or law agencies.[29]

The Council seemed inclined to defend the Vigilance Committee. Suggesting that state officials "would do well to keep hands off and let Miami County take care of itself," Frank Wampler called attention to the Miami group's blue-blood composition.[30] Michael Foley, who had replaced Will Hays as State Council Chairman, had found during the course of a recent visit to one of the committee's meetings that the members were a "thoroughly patriotic and representative set of people."[31] In fact in early August Foley had commended the committee for its "courage to publicly denounce any man, or class of men, who are not willing to do their duty."[32] Council member E. M. Wilson disclosed that he and Captain Harney of the Protection Division had met with McGloin in Indianapolis. They were convinced that McGloin's allegations "did not convict the Vigilance Committee in any sense."[33] The State Council finally decided to remand the case to the Miami County Council of Defense. County chairman W. A. Hammond sent back an indictment of McGloin's account of the incident and defended the Vigilance Committee members as "good, law abiding citizens" who had "positive instructions not to violate the law in any way."[34] Regardless of the facts in each such incident the Loyal Citizens Vigilance Committee acquired a public image as an intolerant opponent of any form of dissent. Its reputation encouraged citizens to avoid a confrontation.

Persons reluctant to "do their bit" faced the threat of public exposure by defense bodies. Labeling persons not aiding the Red Cross as "sinners," the *Pulaski County Democrat* announced that it held a list of names of the non-contributors. Before publishing the names, the *Democrat* offered the transgressors a chance to repent.[35] Similar threats were made by the Fulton County Council of Defense, the Fourth Liberty Loan organization in Spencer County, and the Delaware County Defense Council.[36]

Defense leaders displayed great ingenuity in designing means of compiling the lists of slackers. Some war drives depended upon door to door soliciting for contributions. Campaign committees frequently determined prior to the canvas a quota for each person or family in its jurisdiction. If a person refused to subscribe that amount, the canvasser filled out a "yellow card" with details of the individual's economic situation. Loan officials used these cards to determine which persons should receive additional solicitations.[37] On some occasions officials set out to compile patriotic indexes. Women's registration, a national campaign scheduled for ten days in April, 1918, was the most comprehensive such effort. Census takers tried to interview every woman in America to discover what contributions each had made to the war effort and what special contributions each might be willing to make in the future.[38] Wabash County officials compiled a war census card index, recording the patriotic activities of each family in the county. From this census the Council could determine who should be officially encouraged to lend assistance to the war. Those refusing would "be put into the class" in which they belonged.[39] In the Bluffton area the Harrison Township Liberty Association printed pledges of loyalty. A person refusing to sign the card would be subject to a loyalty investigation.[40]

Some reflective citizens objected to the coercive implications of the efforts to compile patriotic lists. Referring to women's registration, Colonel Russell Harrison, Secretary of the Marion County Defense Council, explained that the registration "is entirely a volunteer matter. There is no law requiring women and girls in this city to fill in and sign war service registration cards."[41] Although discounting any attempts to force women to sign up for war work, the government requested that each woman register with the census taker.[42] Enraged by Harrison's open-minded disposition, Anna Essinger of the Sullivan County Defense Council wrote Michael Foley that if "Mr. Harrison is correct, we believe we may as well discontinue the work of registration."[43] Ignoring the issue raised by Harrison, Foley responded that the article by Harrison had been "unauthorized" and emphasized a statement of Governor James Goodrich "decrying any further delay in the women's registration."[44]

The State Council of Defense tolerated the coercive use of lists. During its March 27, 1918, meeting some council members raised minor reservations but overall seemed to support the practice.[45] On another occasion a Crawfordsville editor inquired about the prudency of publishing a list of persons not contributing to the local War Chest. Foley answered that he was not "inclined to protect the feelings of anyone who is against any of the war activities."[46] Foley suggested that the matter was one for local decision but offered his "Amen" should the decision be to publish the list.[47] The Council understood that the matter of contributions to war drives was entirely voluntary; so "practically the only thing that can be done is to bring lack of patriotism to public attention."[48]

Although frequently threatening to do so, officials did not make a habit of distributing lists of slackers to the public. On one occasion each, newspapers in Scott and White Counties published lists of contributors to the Red Cross.[49] Persons whose names did not appear were assumed to be slackers. On another occasion readers of the *Indiana Bulletin* learned that by looking at a map of the Washington Township area of Jackson County they could see "one tip of the Kaiser's mustache curled up from Dudley town and the tip at Sauer's Church, while the Crown Prince and the Empress look out through the eyes of every wooden-shoed lad and pig-tailed lady-chen that you meet on their way to the parochial school."[50] A poor response to women's enrollment in the area inspired this cartographic invective.[51]

Defense groups used lists mainly as threats against dissidents. Indianapolis patriots purchased a full-page advertisement in the *Indianapolis News* in which they spelled out the fate of those "indexed." They threatened to preserve the index "so that coming generations may read it."[52] Fayette County officials discussed plans to erect a large black tablet on the court house lawn, a "Roll of Dishonor" listing in red letters the name of any proven anti-American within the county.[53]

Lists of disloyalists prompted defense organizations to send intimidating letters to those listed. During the Fourth Liberty Loan drive in Miami County in the fall of 1918 the state loan director advised county officials not to be "afraid to tell the truth . . . concerning the slackers, as well as other more influential men who might be indifferent toward the loan."[54] Ninety-eight persons refused to buy bonds. Bond salesmen filled out a card listing occupation, annual income, total worth, record of prior war support, and reason for refusal for each recalcitrant.[55] Freeman Morse wanted to keep his money so he could spend it as he desired.[56] George Allman and Edward Condon each claimed too great a debt to allow bond purchases.[57] Fern Hoffman, a Peru schoolteacher, had subscribed to the first three bond issues and felt unable to buy this time.[58] Dismissing all of these excuses as inadequate, the secretary of the county loan organization noted on each of the cards that the individual must buy bonds.

The loan committee dispatched telegrams and letters to those deemed capable of larger purchases. J. J. Dunn received a curt telegram: "You are reported as not having subscribed adequately to Fourth Liberty Loan. You should buy one thousand dollars. Time is short. If without funds your banker will lend so you can make adequate subscriptions. See your banker before noon tomorrow."[59] Twenty-two area residents received letters reminding them that their failure to buy bonds was having a demoralizing effect on the community. The letter explained that those less able to subscribe could not understand why they should when the better-off citizens did not. The letter urged "shirkers" to reconsider their decisions. If they did not, they faced being stamped forever as having failed the government in its hour of need. The letter ended with an ominous threat: "Please consider the matter deeply; then write us your decision, which we hope will not embarrass you or compel us to take further steps."[60]

Mistakes occurred. G. R. Chamberlain of the Peru First National Bank was assailed for having bought only $300 worth of bonds when $1000 had been the assigned quota.[61] He responded that he had subscribed for not $300 but $3300 worth of the issue and had previously bought $3000 worth of the first three bond issues. Fearing public embarrassment, this victim of intimidation felt compelled to sign up for another $1000 of the Fourth Loan even "if it takes the hide off to pay for them."[62] The bank confirmed his additional purchase.[63]

Checking her family's daily mail, Mrs. Susan Baker of Garrett spotted a letter to her son Parker from J. V. W. McClellan, Chairman of the DeKalb County Defense Council. Opening it, she found a message accusing the youth of not doing his duty as an American citizen. McClellan advised that "there is no room for such yellow dogs in this country. . . . Uncle Sam will not stand for slacking."[64] Incensed by the belligerent note, Mrs. Baker sent it to the State Defense Council, warning: "I expect to carry this to Washington." Referring to the low character of the note's author, the distressed mother asserted that Parker "has been sickly for many years and is physically unfit to do many things that he would like to do."[65]

Should veiled threats to smear an accused disloyalist's public reputation fail to stimulate better behavior, patriots could be more direct in their attacks on one's security. One reprehensible practice was to threaten a person with loss of a draft exemption should he do or say anything which suggested misplaced war sympathies. District Exemption Board No. 2 asked an Elkhart board for the names of farmers who failed to buy Liberty bonds and who did not support the Red Cross. Newspapers reported that "a decision may be made to reopen some army draft cases in which farmers are concerned."[66] When Earl G. Klenck of Evansville reportedly cursed an American soldier, a local committee took him before Albert Funkhouser, the Federal conscription agent, where he agreed to pledge his loyalty, fly the flag, and purchase a bond.[67] Witnesses appearing before the Third Indiana District Army Appeal Board on behalf of registrants seeking exemption were asked if they had bought a liberty bond.[68]

Some individuals were threatened with loss of jobs or economic self-sufficiency. Huntington County defense leaders sent local merchants a list of eight persons certified as not supporting the government. The merchants were directed "to see that the persons named . . . shall not have an equal privilege with loyal Americans."[69] Adams County sources reported that a well-known farmer who refused to buy bonds could not find a customer for a wagon load of fine apples.[70] Near Huntington, Clear Creek Township officials asked merchants not to trade with a certain man. Unable to sell his cream, unable to buy coal, the farmer reportedly mended his ways and bought the limit of Thrift stamps and gave liberally to other war activities.[71]

In other instances patriots threatened the job security of those not willing to fully support the war. Clay County coal miners passed resolutions holding non-bond holders ineligible to work in the mines.[72] Gary Mayor R. J. Johnson fired city engineering inspector Benj Szinyi for not being in sympathy with America.[73] The Secretary of the Marion County Defense Council obtained the discharge of a "disloyal employee" of the Premier Motor Car Company.[74] This individual transferred to the National Motor Car Company, and again he was dismissed at the insistence of the ever vigilant defense official.[75] At a mass meeting in Evansville employees of the Bernstein Overall Company called for the dismissal of Mrs. Alma Kisstinger and Mrs. Mamie Armstrong for not supporting the Red Cross and for making irreverent remarks about President Wilson.[76] Refusing to work with a "hungabbler," fellow employees at the Columbia Harness Company in Indianapolis forced the release of Charles Best.[77] After conferring with state officials, Robert Proctor of the Elkhart County War Savings Stamp Committee asked the county auditor to fire his deputy, A. S. Stuttenrotz, for the latter's failure to purchase stamps.[78] The Indianapolis Board of Public Safety dismissed patrolman Charles Baumann for alleged utterances disloyal to the United States.[79]

Officials interfered with public meetings of dissident groups. By prohibiting gatherings or by infiltrating those that were held, authorities stifled open discussion. Once, when planning a peace meeting to protest the "cossack methods" of local police, Gary socialists encountered seventy-five patrolmen surrounding their meeting hall.[80] Earlier in the day Federal Agent George Bragdon had arrested a Chicago socialist scheduled to address the Gary group and had grilled several local socialist leaders.[81] Mayor Roswell O. Johnson pledged the use of the entire police force, if necessary, to prevent the meeting.[82] In Boone County the Defense Council publicly commended Sheriff D. N. Lewis for his prompt action in suppressing a socialist meeting.[83] The state's Lieutenant Governor, temporarily at the helm of Indiana during Governor Goodrich's serious illness in the fall of 1917, assured Marion County patriots that he would "prevent the holding of a disgraceful peace meeting."[84]

Often government representatives would attend meetings of dissident groups. In Indianapolis a number of citizens called a meeting to form an anti-conscription organization. The *Indianapolis Star* reported that during the meeting so thick was the gloom cast by the presence of Captain Thomas Hall of the Secret Service, United States Marshal Mark Storen, and Deputy Marshals Frank Barnhart and Frank Ream that the expected organization was not perfected.[85] As soon as participants recognized the officers, "oratorical ardor subsided."[86] Marshal Storen delivered a brief speech, pointing out "the risks they ran in attempting to hold such a meeting . . . when the entire secret service was on the alert to discover and root out just such propaganda."[87] The *Star* warned that every person at the meeting would be an object of interest to Federal authorities.[88]

Frustrated by the ineffective efforts of courts to cope with all varieties of disloyalty and determined to invest their actions with authority, some defense bodies constituted themselves into extra-legal courts of justice. Their purpose was ostensibly to decide on the merits of evidence presented against alleged disloyalists to ascertain whether further action might be justified.[89] Without authority, they assumed the right to subpoena and examine suspects and witnesses and to mete out punishment to violators of whatever policy was at issue.

Although stressing the need for reasonable procedures, the State Council of Defense nevertheless approved these extra-legal activities. Shelbyville lawyer and county defense leader Ed Adams questioned state officials as to his power to compel persons to appear before the council.[90] George Harney responded that "no power was given . . . to summon witnesses and take testimony."[91] Disregarding his own admission, Harney continued: "In Indiana we have been proceeding as though we had this power and have been obtaining very satisfactory results."[92] He then outlined the means by which a local defense council could assume these court-like powers: "You can summon them by letter, directing them to appear before the Council (registered letter the best method). For the protection of the offender and all concerned he should be sworn and his statements taken by a reporter and such final disposition made as the case seems to warrant." He pointed to the use of this system in Vigo, Huntington, Randolph, Miami, and LaPorte counties.[93]

In practice the assumption of unwarranted powers by defense groups led to abuses of the rights of private citizens. Although devoid of statutory authority, summonses were treated by patriots as though they were law. The Elkhart County Council of Defence dispatched the Goshen police chief to escort Reverend Henry Weldy to a meeting of the Council.[94] A more blatant violation of standard legal procedure occurred in Randolph County when an extra-legal committee placed a suspect in jail after deciding on his disloyalty. Committee members agreed that they would be willing to take the blame in case of any further legal action.[95]

Sitting as court, the Miami County Loyal Citizens Vigilance Committee terrified the Peru area. In late September, 1918, the committee sent a delegation to Macy to usher J. E. Ewer to the group's meeting place in the old Peru postoffice. Ewer declined to accompany the group, asserting that they had no authority to compel him to leave his home.⁹⁶ A week later the committee instructed another delegation of ten men to produce Ewer before the meeting.⁹⁷ Forcing their way into the Ewer home, they seized the alleged slacker and carried him to a waiting car, pointed revolvers to ward off curious neighbors, and sped with their captive to the waiting Loyal Citizens.⁹⁸ After a fiery session Ewer agreed to buy War Savings Stamps since it was the only way to assure the safety of his family. His pragmatism offended the members of the Vigilance Committee. They refused Ewer's offer and sent him on his way.⁹⁹ Commenting on the action, the *Peru Journal* proclaimed that "the time has passed when refusals upon the part of men charged with disloyal remarks and acts against the government will be allowed to take the form of refusing to come before the Committee for examination."¹⁰⁰

Ewer refused to drop the matter. Believing that the Committee had flagrantly misused an illegally assumed authority, he carried his case to L. Ert Slack, United States District Attorney in Indianapolis. Ewer convinced Slack that there should not only be a Federal investigation of the case, but that state officials as well should become involved.¹⁰¹ However, the war ended before any action could be initiated. By refusing to investigate the activities of the Miami County group earlier, officials put a tacit stamp of approval on terrorism, kidnapping, and kangaroo courts as long as they were designed to subdue disloyalists.

In August, 1918, the Putnam County Defense Council sat as a court to hear the case of Jennie Wolf who stood accused of publicly upholding the Kaiser while criticizing President Wilson.¹⁰² Benjamin Crowin served as the prosecuting attorney; Jackson Boyd represented the defendant. The first witness, Dela Pickett, testified that Mrs. Wolf became enraged at co-workers at the Reed-Murdock tomato processing plant who were uttering hateful remarks about the Kaiser. Seven other witnesses corroborated Mrs. Pickett's account of the affair. Taking the stand on her own behalf, Mrs. Wolf admitted criticing the President but proclaimed her patriotism. Although the hearing unearthed no substantive evidence of an illegal act, officials nevertheless berated Mrs. Wolf. At the request of C. C. Hurst of the Putnam County Council Michael Foley wrote the woman a letter outlining the sins of the Kaiser, adding: "Hereafter I shall expect you . . . to refrain from any comment in public or in private that is intended to defend the German Kaiser or a single act of his bloody career."¹⁰⁴ After the "trial" Mrs. Wolf left her job at the packing plant.¹⁰⁵

Although possessing no authority to compel behavior, the threats posed by extra-legal courts were often sufficient to frighten people into the desired action. After formally investigating five men in Spencer County for disloyalty a Defense Council committee demanded and received loyalty pledges in the form of monthly contributions to the Red Cross, promises to display the flag, and assistance in stopping disloyal talk in the community.[106] Called before Elkhart County's defense body, farmer Jacob Bechtel agreed to purchase "not less than $2,500 worth of the next Liberty Loan issue."[107] John Wilson of the State Council of Defense reported to national defense officials that "in very few instances did this procedure [calling persons before the local councils] fail to secure a larger subscription from the individual."[108] Officials depended on the force of public pressure to legitimatize extra-legal courts. After holding two hearings involving disloyalty, Vigo County officials noted that giving publicity to the hearings "lets the man's neighbors and the people he works with know what kind of man he is."[109] The result would be that the "people will point the finger of scorn at them—best punishment there is."[110]

Occasionally a lonely voice protesting intimidation arose above the patriotic clamor that so marked the state. When merchants threatened a boycott, Huntington area farmers composed a defense of their allegedly disloyal actions. Rebuffed in efforts to publish this defense in Huntington papers, they forwarded it to the State Defense Council. Claiming loyalty to the President, they asserted that each had contributed his share to "nearly every fund that came along."[111] Threatened during a recent fund drive with fines up to $10,000 and imprisonment for fifteen years, they strongly disapproved of "these misrepresentations to the good people of our county, and neither will we submit to coercion and fraud." Poignantly they queried: "Where is your law and your court for such judgments?"[112] The farmers carried their protest to federal officials. Lawyer John C. Cline wrote the Treasury Department a letter protesting the tactics of coercion used against his clients.[113] Treasury officials agreed with Cline, condemning the use of any methods even resembling compulsion in connection with war fund drives. They foresaw the danger that over-zealous patriots could create citizen resentment rather than unity and support for the war.[114] But the merchants maintained their boycott until the farmers threatened to seek restraining orders and to file major damage suits against them.[115]

A few Hoosiers so resented efforts of patriots to intimidate them that they assaulted their harassers. James Himelick of Peru struck bond worker Bill Hood with a post digger.[116] In Indianapolis Elbert Martz used a sledge hammer on another bond salesman, Rolland Garrison, after Garrison called Martz a slacker for saying he could not afford a bond due to his daughter's serious illness.[117] In another incident a Liberty bond solicitor was assaulted near Spencer by an alleged pro-German wielding a hatchet.[118]

Regardless of occasional public criticism most Indiana defense officials encouraged the intimidation of slackers. The *Indianapolis News* argued that threats were not methods of sound sense. Sensing that persons forced to make a show of patriotism act hypocritically, the *News* allowed that threats and coercion may bring forth a small amount of money, but felt the moral effect would be better if slackers would be left to their consciences.[119] However, as late as October 1918, after the situations in Miami and Huntington counties had been in the public spotlight, Michael Foley was commending the Liberty Loan organization for pressuring two Cloverdale men who had not bought bonds.[120] Foley felt that Will Wade, director of bond sales in Indiana, had handled the matter in fine style: "While the amounts are not large, the purchases by these gentlemen will have the desired effect in this neighborhood."[121]

The willingness of Hoosier patriots to resort to coercive or illegal practices to enforce patriotism stemmed in part from the fervor of their own patriotism and in part from their conception of the Indiana situation. Believing that pro-German sympathizers endangered effective war work in the state, patriots felt a need to arouse people to a full awareness of the seriousness of the war and the need for total loyalty at home. By challenging those who might be inclined to express contrary opinions, leaders sought to achieve the unity they considered important. To be effective, challenges had to be strong. Courts of law had proved unequal to the task. Although achieving great support for the war, public persuasion failed to silence those who disagreed with official policy. Persons resistant to ordinary methods of persuasion might not be so resistant to threats to their personal security. By obtaining statewide publicity for the scattered battles against disloyalists, state officials hoped to bring the cases ultimately to the Court of Public Opinion which they believed capable of influencing a recalcitrant to change, if not his attitudes, at least his public behavior.

Part Two

Philosophical and Theoretical Perspectives

Free Speech: The Philosophical Poles
Cal M. Logue

Implications of Herbert Marcuse's Theory of Freedom for Freedom of Speech
Joyce Flory

The Supreme Court and Communication Theory: Contrasting Models of Speech Efficacy
William Bailey

5

Free Speech:
The Philosophical Poles

CAL M. LOGUE

Cal M. Logue is Professor and Chair of the Department of Speech Communication at the University of Georgia. He is one of the founders of the Freedom and Responsibilities of Speech Division of the Southern Speech Communication Association, and in 1976–77 served as president of that association. Professor Logue is the author of numerous articles in the field of rhetoric and public address, and is the author, co-author or editor of several books in that field, including Oratory of Southern Demagogues, *edited with Howard Dorgan (Baton Rouge: Louisiana State University Press, 1981); and* No Place to Hide: The South and Human Rights, *2 vols. (Macon: Mercer University Press, 1984). The following essay was published in the* Free Speech Yearbook: 1972.

We hear much talk about "free speech" today. Persons of every persuasion voice their opinions on the limits of free expression. Such discussions have implications which are legal, moral, rhetorical, political, and philosophical. In this essay the writer will consider the essentials of the philosophy of liberty, i.e., some of the choices one confronts concerning the nature of man's involvement with society and himself.

To limit this discussion, the essay will consider only "modern" political philosophy. Modern political philosophy begins with "the rights of the individual, and conceives the State as existing to secure the conditions of his development." Classical political philosophy, on the other hand, starts with "law" and the "right of the State."[1]

Although modern political thought is premised on the rights of the individual, there has been considerable debate over the meaning and role of liberty in society. One still confronts many critical choices: What is "liberty" and "free speech"? Who shall have it? When? How much? Who shall grant it? Or is it a "natural" right? Under what conditions, if any, shall it be denied?

If one plots the extreme philosophical positions (within modern thought) along a continuum of how much individual-right man should have, one will find Thomas Hobbes' (1588–1679) absolute "Sovereign" at one end and John Stuart Mill's (1806–1873) absolute libertarianism on the other. Between these two extremes will fall the beliefs of our founding fathers, John Milton and, more recently, Alexander Meiklejohn. A comparison of the views of Hobbes and Mill on free expression provides considerable insight into the potential benefit, as well as the possible perils, of liberty. Often a person will advocate one view or another, whether liberal or conservative, with less than adequate consideration of its means or its implication for man and society. Here the writer will define and compare the polar philosophies of free speech advocated by Hobbes and Mill. This comparison reveals the matrix of philosophical choice one must consider when studying human liberty.

Thomas Hobbes

Thomas Hobbes "valued security far more than liberty."[2] Hobbes believed that man's primary need was to survive. He felt that people, before they establish some kind of government, are equal; but most important is their equal ability to kill each other.[3] In this pre-political predicament there is no security because, according to Hobbes, "each man" has the "Liberty . . . of doing any thing, which is his own Judgment, and Reason, he shall conceive to be the aptest means thereunto."[4] Hobbes considered such a condition to be dangerous. He argued that man must organize politically to find self-protection. Blair Campbell explained what Hobbes had in mind:

> The self must be harnessed, disciplined, and indeed coerced, if man is to live without fear; his behavior must be circumscribed by rules. Moreover, he requires sanctions if his vanity is to be kept within peaceful bounds; and since he is in a state of constant psychic flux, he cannot rely on his own self-admonitions. Therefore, these sanctions must be given external force, they must be politicized.[5]

Hobbes assumed that men are not naturally social and political; man has to create an artificial framework to find order and protection. Hobbes' ideal government is an absolute sovereign (individual or assembly, monarch or democracy) which rules authoritatively after it has been contracted by the people. Through this "social contract" individuals swap their freedom for personal safety. In his *Leviathan*, Hobbes explained the nature of this agreement:

The only way to erect such a Common Power . . . is to conferre all their power and strength upon one Man, or upon one Assembly of men, that may reduce all their Wills, by plurality of voices, unto one Will: which is as much as to say, to appoint one Man, or Assembly of men, to beare their Person; and every one to owne, and acknowledge himselfe to be Author of whatsoever he that so beareth their Person, shall Act, or cause to be Acted, in those things which concerns the Common Peace and Safetie; and therein to submit their Wills, every one to his Will, and their Judgements, to his Judgement.[6]

Hobbes' condition of consent remained the same regardless of the machinery of government. He wrote, "Whether a Common-wealth be Monarchicall, or Popular, the Freedome is still the same."[7] The stability of this sovereign was to be preserved at all cost, because upon that condition depended man's security. Harvey C. Mansfield, Jr. believed that Hobbes "wished to suppress private judgments of good and bad in politics because such judgments endanger civil peace."[8]

Hobbes, then, argued that because man in his "state of nature" (before government) is unsafe, he should seek safety under the shelter of a sovereign. Individuals should do nothing to disrupt this situation. J. B. Stewart interpreted Hobbes to mean that people should "seek concord within the commonwealth in every expedient way; be not enthralled by other goods, for they are inferior; endeavor always—quieting, appeasing, adjusting, compromising in all things—to prevent the death of the commonwealth."[9]

Hobbes believed it was necessary to restrict man's freedom. Under Hobbes' sovereign state one gives up freedom of expression for security and, as some interpret Hobbes, for "human happiness."[10] Hobbes recognizes, however, that when man contracts with the sovereign, he retains certain liberties. Men continue to have the right to move bodily about, to do "what their own reasons shall suggest" when there are no laws preventing it, and to disobey "if the Soveraign command a man (though justly condemned,) to kill, wound, or mayme himselfe; or not to resist those that assault him; or to abstain from the use of food, ayre, medicine, or any other thing, without which he cannot live. . . ."[11]

Although Hobbes describes certain minimum rights of man, they are linked more to life-essentials and the will of the state than to any concern for human freedom. What, for example, does Hobbes say about individual free expression? He argued that government should rigidly control not only man's actions but also his opinions. Hobbes considered free discussion to be dangerous because ". . . the Common-peoples minds . . . are like clean paper, fit to receive whatsoever by Publique Authority shall be imprinted in them."[12] Hobbes' remedy for "the poyson of seditious doctrines"[13] is preventative. The sovereign simply does not allow it. Hobbes wrote:

> It is annexed to the Soveraignty, to be Judge of what Opinions and Doctrines are averse, and what conducing to Peace; and consequently, on what occasions, how farre, and what, men are to be trusted withall, in speaking to Multitudes of people; and who shall examine the Doctrines of all bookes before they be published. For the Actions of men proceed from their Opinions; and in the well governing of Opinions, consisteth the well governing of mens Actions, in order to their Peace, and Concord. And though in matter of Doctrine, nothing ought to be regarded but the Truth; yet this is not repugnant to regulating of the same by Peace. For Doctrine repugnant to Peace, can no more be True, than Peace and Concord can be against the Law of Nature.[14]

Hobbes' absolute sovereign could take the form of democracy, though he warns that it will be the most troublesome. Hobbes felt that participation would weaken the power of the sovereign. Laurence Berns explained Hobbes' reservation about a sovereign-democracy:

> For within democracy there is always keen competition between popular orators, or demagogues, and the power of each demagogue is dependent upon his power to control and dispense patronage. . . . From this it is easy to understand the chief defect of democracy, the tendency to breed factions and civil wars. . . . Those who complain of lack of liberty under monarchy do not understand what they really want. . . . It is not liberty but dominion or power and its attendant honor that they want. The true cause of their disaffection is that monarchy deprives them of the opportunity to show off their wisdom, knowledge, and eloquence in deliberating, or seeming to deliberate, about matters of the greatest importance. The love of liberty, according to Hobbes, turns out to be only a mask for the desire for praise, for vanity.[15]

Hobbes, then, believed that for man to have security he had to be governed by authority. This meant giving up much of his personal freedom. While Hobbes permits people to move physically, to do things not prevented by law, and to protect their own lives, they must remember that there can be, not individual will, but the one will of the sovereign—one ruling opinion, voice, decision, and action.

John Stuart Mill

In his *On Liberty*, John Stuart Mill advocated a libertarian philosophy, the right and need ("utility") of man to be free. In this section, the writer will compare the thoughts of Hobbes and Mill.

The first area for comparison is their treatment of personal protection. Both Hobbes and Mill were concerned for man's safety. Hobbes, however, stressed the sacrifice of individual freedom for security. "The end of Obedience is Protection."[16] Mill, on the other hand, maintains "that the only purpose for which power can be rightfully exercised over any member of a civilised community, against his will, is to prevent harm to others."[17] Mill's attitude about personal protection, then, resulted more from a concern for the freedom of the other man. In no other sense was a government or a person to interfere with man's freedom, even for that man's own protection. Mill argued that a person's "own good, either physical or moral, is not a sufficient warrant. He cannot rightfully be compelled to do or forbear because it will be better for him to do so, because it will make him happier, because, in the opinions of others, to do so would be wise, or even right."[18]

The second subject of interest to both Hobbes and Mill is the nature and role of sovereignty. Because Hobbes believed that guarantee of safety was justification enough for rule by authority, he spends little time defending this arrangement. When he does he clothes this condition in a spirit that seems somewhat foreign to it. He speaks of "a Common Power" and a "Common Peace," and concludes that "nothing the Sovereign Representative can doe to a Subject, on what pretence soever, can properly be called Injustice, or Injury; because every Subject is Author of every act the Sovereign doth. . . ."[19] Hobbes denies individual free expression, but claims the "Sovereign Representative" to be at-one with the people.

Mill would have none of this. Regardless of its effectiveness or efficiency, any sovereignty, other than that of the individual over himself, is by its very nature bad. Richard Lichtman declared that Mill "questions not merely the wisdom of the decrees that society imposes on its constituents, but the very right of society to impose decrees, wise or ignorant."[20] Even in a relatively open society Mill warned of pressures which pull the human spirit to conformity. He was greatly concerned that modern society tends to intimidate man. "Our merely social intolerance kills no one," he wrote, "roots out no opinions, but induces men to disguise them, or to abstain from any active effort for their diffusion."[21] According to Henry Magid, Mill meant that "the individual is sovereign over himself" and "the thoughts of the individual are part of himself, and therefore the principle requires that society exert no control over them."[22]

The third topic of concern for both Hobbes and Mill is that of individual participation in affairs of society. When Hobbes discusses "democracy" he means a sovereign-democracy. Even within this context, however, he considers democracy to be weakness. Hobbes believed democracy not only led naturally to "factions and civil wars,"[23] but, says Mansfield, "to the extent that democracy does increase participation, it is bad, for it ceases to do the work of sovereignty."[24] Hobbes' conviction was founded on a faith in a form of government—absolute rule.

Though Mill felt a need for government, his emphasis seemed to be upon a condition of society, rather than any particular plan of polity. Government was necessary to "prevent harm to others"; however, government was not to infringe upon man's freedom. Herein is where Hobbes and Mill are poles apart. Although Hobbes recognized that man would retain the right to save his own life, he gives the sovereign absolute rule over man's opinions and actions. Mill emphasizes the importance of individual freedom. Neither government nor society is to restrict man's freedom as long as he does not harm others. Mill wrote:

> Let us suppose, therefore, that the government is entirely at one with the people, and never thinks of exerting any power of coercion unless in agreement with what it conceives to be their voice. But I deny the right of the people to exercise such coercion, either by themselves or by their government. The power itself is illegitimate. The best government has no more title to it than the worst.[25]

Mill placed liberty above any total loyalty to government. And his "theory of liberty," according to Henry Magid, "is practically relevant only when society becomes more important than the state."[26]

Some critics of Mill think that his degree of devotion to liberty will lead to a breakdown in societal order. They ask what will be the nature of man's existence in Mill's free society. While Mill reserves for government the responsibility of human safety, his faith in freedom, unlike Hobbes, not only allows but encourages a liberal license for personal advocacy of opinion. We find here another basic difference between Hobbes and Mill. Hobbes believed free opinion to be poisonous to his sovereign form of government. Willmoore Kendall, in his attack on Mill's "open society," predicts that "such a society" would "descend ineluctably into ever-deepening *differences of opinion,* into progressive breakdown of those common premises upon which alone a society can conduct its affairs by discussion, and so into the abandonment of the discussion process and the arbitrament of public questions by violence and civil war."[27]

Even Mill placed some restrictions on his free society. He warned of the "tendency of the most idealistic and high-minded reform movements to harden into dogmatic systems which forced conformity and thereby inhibited future progress."[28] Mill warned that for his free society to work man had to be reasonable. As John Ward found, "it is his faith in reason that buttresses Mill's plea for the freedom and primacy of the individual."[29] Mill added:

> It is, perhaps, hardly necessary to say that this doctrine is meant to apply to human beings in the maturity of their faculties. We are not speaking of children, of young persons below the age which the law may fix as that of manhood or womanhood. . . . For the same reason, we may leave out of consideration those backward states of society in which the race itself may be considered as in its nonage.[30]

While Mill pauses to point out a few conditions he considers important for the success of his kind of society, his main emphasis is upon the potential of free man for individual and societal progress. Mill has faith in free man. Freedom produces, not poison, but a transfusion of new life in individuals and in society. For Mill liberty is a condition necessary for progress. Life must have liberty.

Mill argues so vigorously for freedom that liberty becomes not only a condition for progress, but possibly its cause. He warned, however, that "the dictum that truth always triumphs over persecution is one of those pleasant falsehoods which men repeat after one another till they pass into commonplaces, but which all experience refutes."[31] The freedom to do something, then, is sterile without the doing. The very practice of public involvement is generative of good. Profit is inherent to the pursuit. Mill wrote:

> The human faculties of perception, judgment, discriminative feeling, mental activity, and even moral preference, are exercised only in making a choice. He who does anything because it is the custom makes no choice. He gains no practice either in discerning or in desireing what is best. The mental and moral, like the muscular powers, are improved only by being used.[32]

Mill believed that free involvement can produce personal development. But what does freedom do for society in general? When opinion is "fully, frequently, and fearlessly discussed," he wrote, it can become "a living truth" and not just "a dead dogma."[33] Specifically, Mill developed three reasons why a majority opinion in society is never justified in suppressing a minority opinion:

1. If the opinion is right, people are deprived of the opportunity of exchanging error for truth.
2. If the opinion is wrong, people lose, what is almost as great a benefit, the clearer perception and livelier impression of existing truth, produced by its collision with error.[34]
3. When the conflicting doctrines, instead of being one true and the other false, share the truth between them; and the nonconforming opinion is needed to supply the remainder of the truth, of which the received doctrine embodies only a part.[35]

Conclusion

When considering the philosophy of free expression, one confronts many choices. Within the context of modern political philosophy, there is a range of opinion from Hobbes' sovereign ruler to Mill's free man. Hobbes requires the individual to position himself to be at-one with the will of the sovereign. Mill argues that freedom is essential for individual and societal good, if not a cause of it. Hobbes had men exchange liberty for security. Mill wanted government to preserve protection, but the very thought of power to control man's freedom, regardless of how fair or efficient, was unacceptable to him. Man must be free both to discover and to discern the desirable for himself. "A person whose desires and impulses are his own," he wrote, "are the expression of his own nature, as it has been developed and modified by his own culture—is said to have a character."[36]

6

Implications of Herbert Marcuse's Theory of Freedom for Freedom of Speech

JOYCE FLORY

Joyce Flory is Director of Communications of the American College of Hospital Administrators, Chicago, Illinois. Her essay on Marcuse was published in the Free Speech Yearbook: 1977.

Herbert Marcuse, apostle of the student left of the 1960's, provides the theorist of freedom of speech with profound criticisms of its practice, particularly as it functions in current society. Drawing his philosophy from the dialectical tradition of Hegel and Marx, the existentialism of Heidegger, and the psychoanalytic theory of Freud, Marcuse argues that tolerance as currently understood and practiced forms a repressive tendency within society. Marcuse makes clear his position in his *Essay on Liberation:*

> The author is fully aware that, at present, no power, no authority, no government exists that would translate liberating tolerance into practice, but he believes that it is the task and duty of the intellectual to recall and preserve historical possibilities which seem to have become utopian possibilities.[1]

Marcuse's View of Freedom: An Overview

Marcuse vacillates between two apparently contradictory ideas of freedom.[2] Marcuse partly upholds the liberal view of freedom, defining freedom as doing what one chooses to do and as the absence of restraint. Advocated in various forms by Hobbes, Locke, and Thoreau, this view supports a minimal role for government.[3] It permits government to exercise control only to the extent that it prevents persons from harming one another.

Marcuse, however, fails to restrict himself to this liberal view. Like Plato and Hegel, he views freedom as the capacity to implement the "ought" and to perfect the self.[4] Both Plato and Hegel view the self as a field of conflicting forces. While government must function to prevent harm to its members, so does one aspect of the self function to govern and restrain the whole self. If a conflict exists within a person between reason and passion, that person is only free if his passions are under the control of reason. However, if his passions reign supreme, he will not have freedom despite the absence of governmental control.

Marcuse thus alternates between liberal theory and the theory of perfectibility. He believes that society must restrain individuals and limit their freedom of choice. He rejects the notion that the opportunity to exacerbate violence and repression constitutes part of freedom. Nor does he believe in the free market place of ideas. Instead he views the dialogue and exchange of ideas as weighted heavily on the side of violence and suppression.

With violence and suppression already in control society hardly practices neutrality in allowing all persons to speak freely; rather, it confers an advantage to those who espouse violence and suppression. Despite his pessimism concerning the practice of free speech in current society Marcuse justifies its existence and outlines recommendations for its restoration through the revolutionary process.

A Definition of Tolerance

Marcuse views tolerance as government without violence or "surplus repression." This definition distinguishes Marcuse, since modern democratic society views tolerance as open acceptance of various points of view. He lends a new perspective to tolerance by connecting tolerance to the elimination of violence and excessive suppression. His use of the term "excess" is critical, since he believes that all societies require a measure of suppression in order to function. While acknowledging that every society requires suppression, he also holds that every society reaches a point at which it exercises more suppression than is necessary to function. At this point suppression becomes "excess" or "surplus."[5]

After defining tolerance Marcuse attempts to define the practice of tolerance in current society. He finds it unfortunate that our society bestows tolerance even upon those actions which result in misery and suffering. If society tolerates such negative acts, it actually works against the principle of tolerance. In such cases tolerance functions directly to advance those acts which it seeks to prevent. Thus tolerance functions not to advance liberty and eradicate violence but to harbor and protect acts of violence and suppression of freedom.[6]

The Controlling Force of Affluence

To comprehend Marcuse's view of a society devoid of true tolerance one must understand the controlling force of affluence. In *One-Dimensional Man*, Marcuse labels freedom from want as the "concrete substance of all freedoms."[7] Because contemporary society possesses the capability of fulfilling man's material needs, it has the concurrent capability of buying off its members from seeking further liberation. In Marcuse's view affluence enables society to co-opt or buy off dissent. He believes that free speech operates freely only because society realizes that free speech is devoid of any real power of change; yet he acknowledges that society withdraws freedom of speech when it deems necessary. Moreover, society distributes free speech unequally with certain interests benefiting.

The Pleasure Principle

While Marcuse views technology, in *One-Dimensional Man*, as possessing inherently evil characteristics, in *Eros and Civilization* he sees technology as a vehicle with which to liberate humanity to engage in erotic activities.[8] Technology thus has the capacity to liberate people for enjoyment rather than postponement of pleasure created by society's imperative to work.

Marcuse perceives the pleasure principle as fundamental in decision making. Human beings act on the basis of their desire for pleasure.[9] However, he acknowledges the limitations of this view, since pleasure alone is unable to sustain a community. To sustain a community its members must defer pleasure to perform functions that will insure their immediate and pressing needs. In cases where these interests conflict, they must act on the basis of the reality principle rather than the pleasure principle.

The Performance Principle

The specific form taken by the controlling reality principle is the performance principle.[10] Marcuse finds that the performance principle is most strongly manifested in a desire to perform work. He writes:

> The restrictions imposed upon the libido appear as more rational: the more universal they become, the more they permeate the whole of society. They operate on the individual as external objective laws and as an internalized force: the societal authority is absorbed into the "conscience" and into the unconscious of the individual and works on his own desire, morality, and fulfillment.[11]

In Marcuse's view an individual thus internalizes the repressiveness of society. This repression operates with dual power: it functions both as an external force on an individual and as part of his internal personality. In *One-Dimensional Man*, Marcuse argues that an individual requires no repression by agencies of the state because society has already shaped his instincts sufficiently to channel and direct needs in an appropriate direction.[12] Marcuse thus refuses to view the absence of restraint as freedom, for he believes that society has already shaped and molded the individual. He writes of this principle:

> A Society governed by the performance principle must impose such distribution (of pleasure into scattered moments of spare time) because the organism must be trained for its alienation at its very roots—the pleasure ego. It must learn to forget the claim for timeless and useless gratification, for the "eternity of pleasure." Moreover, from the working day, alienation and regimentation spread into free time. Such coordination does not have to be, and normally is not, reinforced from without by the agencies of society. The basic control of leisure is achieved by the length of the working day itself, by the tiresome and mechanical routine of alienated labor; these require that leisure be a passive relaxation and a recreation of energy of work.[13]

Possessed with such a work ethic, people abandon their desire for pleasure. They view both their bodies and minds as agents of production, profit, and consumption rather than vehicles for immediate pleasure and gratification. Marcuse thus reinterprets the Freudian evolution of human sexuality. He views this evolution as an artificial restriction by society to localize and limit sexuality to certain zones of the body, liberating the rest of the body for work.[14]

Material Needs

Marcuse's concept of the supremacy of the reality principle is intimately connected to the concept of material needs. He notes that if humans satisfy basic material needs, they possess little desire to modify social institutions. People perceive the society that fulfills as a good society; a society that provides these needs undermines ideals. Marcuse believes that ideals no longer represent unrealized possibilities or a critical attitude. As ideals diminish in power and status, our vision of social change ebbs and diminishes. As society meets the material needs of people, people lose their concern for ideals, and their behavior changes. Marcuse summarizes his position:

> I have just suggested that the concept of alienation seems to become questionable when the individuals identify themselves with my existence which is imposed upon them and have it in their own development and satisfaction. This identification is not illusion, but reality. However, the reality constitutes a more progressive stage of alienation. . . .
>
> Society compensates for our impotence by bestowing upon us the freedom to consume. . . . Freedom has become not the determining of one's life, but the passive consumption of goods and objects produced by those around us. . . .[15]

Marcuse views traditional civil liberties developing through the bourgeoisie's struggle for power. As long as the bourgeois class required civil liberties in order to assert power over society, those liberties possessed real significance; but now that the bourgeois class has won its battle, the traditional liberties have lost their importance.[16]

Marcuse thus views the failure to protest injustice, not as "moral or intellectual deterioration or corruption," but as "a rational technological attitude." With material wants satisfied people possess no need for freedom:

> A rising standard of living . . . is an almost unavoidable by-product of the politically manipulated industrial society, once a certain level of backwardness has been overcome. The growing productivity of labor creates an increasing surplus-product which, whether privately or centrally appropriate and distributed, allows an increased consumption. As long as the constellation prevails, it reduces the use-value of freedom; there is no reason to insist on self-determination if the administered life is the comfortable and even the "good" life. This is the rational and material ground for the unification of opposites, for one-dimensional political behavior.[17]

The productivity of society tends to subvert the meaning of traditional civil rights. "Freedom from want," Marcuse states, "is not merely a necessary precondition, but is the concrete substance of all freedoms." With established freedoms no longer possessing much importance, Marcuse believes that "a comfortable, smooth, reasonable democratic unfreedom prevails in advanced industrial civilization."[18] He concludes elsewhere that society's "supreme promise is an evermore comfortable life for an ever-growing number of people, who, in a strict sense, cannot imagine a qualitatively different universe of discourse and action, for the capacity to contain and manipulate subversive imagination and effort is an integral part of the given society."[19]

The Function and Justification of Freedom of Speech

Despite his cynicism Marcuse sets forth both positive and negative functions for freedom of speech within the society: "The exercise of political rights . . . in a society of total administration serves to strengthen this administration by testifying to the existence of democratic liberties which, in reality, have changed their content and lost their effectiveness."[20] In Marcuse's view, the facade or mask of opposition obscures the absence of any real opposing force.

Marcuse views American society as possessing only the deceptive appearance of freedom. University professors, politicians, and the media appear free, for society grants them permission to say anything within certain bounds. Since physical violence does not serve as a weapon of totalitarianism, no military forces work to threaten their right. However, the freedom that results is not genuine. While people may think and speak freely, they are restrained in their effort to change the basic structure of institutions. As individuals we practice a diluted version of freedom of thought and speech, but we must accept the class and institutional hierarchies and structures initiated and perpetuated by others.

While Marcuse criticizes freedom of speech, he still supports its maintenance: "The existence and practice of these liberties remain a precondition for the restoration of their original oppositional function, provided that the effort to transcend their original (often self-imposed) limitations is intensified."[21] Despite the fact that these political rights mislead the populace, he argues, they cannot be abandoned. Marcuse recognizes two options for those interested in liberation: (1) They can repress the corrupt elements in the society, though at present there exists no force capable of selective repression, or (2) they can await the end of the revolutionary process when the government deserving repression falls from power. He believes that the power to repress does not exist when it is actually needed—that is, when those who hold power repress liberation.

Since Marcuse believes that we need liberties to carry out a revolution, he finds the espousal of repression imprudent. The call for repression merely places a tool in the hands of those who wield power. When corrupt forces are defeated through a revolutionary process, repression is superfluous. Marcuse thus recognizes that power cannot be withdrawn from certain groups, for those groups with the power to repress tolerance would not repress those from whom Marcuse wants to withdraw tolerance. Neither would they bestow tolerance on those whom Marcuse perceives to be for forces of liberation.

The Nature of Tolerance

Marcuse uses his analysis of the futility of repression to discuss the nature of tolerance of established policies. He holds that tolerance is extended largely to established attitudes; but he also believes that there exists an abstract tolerance of every position. The sciences are dominated by procedures, but on the periphery of each field rest certain practitioners or mavericks who initiate new actions and whom society pleasantly tolerates. Marcuse explains the nature of this tolerance:

> [Tolerance] is of two kinds: (1) the passive toleration of entrenched and established attitudes and ideas—even if their damaging effect on man and nature is evident; (2) the active official tolerance granted to the Right as well as to the Left, to movements of aggression as well as to movements of peace, to the party of hate as well as to that of humanity. I call this non-partisan tolerance "abstract" or "pure" inasmuch as it refrains from taking sides—but in doing so it actually protects the already established machinery of discrimination.[22]

Marcuse acknowledges that tolerance has never been defended in a way devoid of all value. When the principle of tolerance was formulated, liberals craved tolerance in order to acquire freedom from church and government. Liberal theory has already placed an important condition upon tolerance: it is to apply to human beings in the maturity of their faculties.[23]

Marcuse believes that if authentic tolerance were to be achieved, it would demand intolerance for what presently exists and tolerance for what is currently suppressed or labeled illegal. Tolerance, as currently practiced and defended, is actually repressive in its effects.[24]

Marcuse asserts that the system of constitutionally guaranteed civil rights and liberties rests on the underlying principle that "the established society is free and that any improvement, even a change in the social structure and social values, would come about in the normal course of events, prepared, defined, and tested in free and equal discussion, on the open marketplace of ideas and goods."[25] This belief assumes a system by which "different pressures, interests, and authorities balance each other out and result in a truly general and national interest."[26] In practice, however, power remains unequally distributed. With both economic and political power concentrated in the hands of a few and with technology used as an "instrument of domination" effective dissent is thwarted.[27]

Our affluent democracy presents only a facade of tolerance. Our society permits the hearing of all points of view and treats with equal respect the intelligent and misinformed opinion, propaganda and education, truth and falsehood. However, the ability of the populace to distinguish right from wrong and good from bad and the capacity to deliberate and reach a decision, depends on its access to "authentic information" and that it can evaluate it on the basis of "autonomous thought." In Marcuse's view, the standard democratic defense for abstract tolerance "tends to be invalidated by the invalidation of the democratic process itself."[28]

Tolerance, as currently practiced, thus serves to nurture and reinforce repression. In Marcuse's view this perversion, gradual dehumanization, and development of "false consciousness" in individual members of society can be counteracted only through the blocking of "words and images which feed this consciousness." He thus sanctions censorship or precensorship of "regressive movements before they become active" on the grounds that this "withdrawal of tolerance" works to combat the more covert forms of censorship which permeate the "monopolistic media—themselves mere instruments of economic and political power."[29] Paradoxically Marcuse believes that these "antidemocratic" acts of censorship will ultimately function to create "the conditions where tolerance can again become a liberating and humanizing force."[30]

The Relationship Between Truth and Freedom of Speech

Marcuse poses a crucial question, which seeks to establish the relationship between truth and freedom of speech:

> Mill's often quoted words have a less familiar implication on which their meaning depends: the internal connection between liberty and truth. There is a sense in which truth is the end of liberty and liberty must be defined and confirmed by truth. In what sense can liberty be for the sake of truth? Liberty is self-determination, autonomy—this is almost a tautology, but a tautology which results

from a whole series of synthetic judgements. It stipulates the ability to determine one's life: to be able to determine what to do and what not to do, what to suffer and what not.[31]

Marcuse is emphatic in asserting the certainty of knowledge and the ability of a reasonable human being to know the truth:

> Tolerance of free speech is the way of improvement, of progress in liberation, not because there is no objective truth, and improvement must necessarily be a compromise between a variety of opinions, but because there is an objective truth which can be discovered, ascertained only in learning and comprehending that which is and that which can be and ought to be done for the sake of improving the lot of mankind.[32]

This truth, however, must be discovered, not through intuition and insight, but through a delicate process of interpretation, evaluation, and synthesis. "It has to be uncovered by 'cutting through,' 'splitting,' 'breaking asunder' (dis-cutio) the given material—separating right and wrong, good and bad, correct and incorrect." Criticizing the "sacred liberalistic principle of equality for the 'other side,'" Marcuse asserts that there exist issues for which there is no "other side, for which the other side is 'regressive,' aggressive, or destructive in character and impedes possible improvement of the human condition."[34]

Marcuse appears to define freedom as freedom of choice. Yet he complicates his position by speaking about the distinction between real and apparent will: "But the subject of this autonomy is never the contingent private individual as that which actually is or happens to be. It is rather the individual as human being who is capable of being free with others."[35] He thus unites the dual notions of self-determination and self-perfection:

> The problem of making possible such harmony between every individual liberty and the other is not that of finding a compromise between competitiveness and between freedom and law, between general and individual interest, common and private welfare in an established society, but of creating the society in which man is no longer enslaved by institutions which vitiate self-determination from the beginning. In other words, freedom is still to be created even for the freest of the existing societies. And the direction in which it must be sought and the institutionalized and cultural changes which help to attain the goal are at least in developed civilizations comprehensible—that is to say, they can be identified and projected on the basis of experience by human reason.[36]

Marcuse argues that we can recognize the possibilities of our own fulfillment. He argues that self-determination and self-perfection are interdependent and that self-determination necessitates self-perfection. Having asserted the connection between self-perfection and self-determination, he discusses the implications of this relationship. First he implies the necessity for choices and alternatives. He believes that for self-determination to exist genuine options must also exist. However, there are limitations to this position. Society cannot permit any one individual to make a free choice among alternatives. One individual choice may preclude another from retaining the option to choose. This limitation is further reinforced by the fact that every society both controls the availability of some alternatives and deliberately advances other alternatives.[37]

Marcuse asserts that for a person to choose well he requires, not merely alternatives, but an awareness and consciousness of alternatives. Marcuse recognizes that just as all things cannot be real, an individual cannot know all things. An individual's awareness must possess some ordering. Yet Marcuse recognizes that even such an ordering is difficult, for society itself chooses to cultivate an awareness of certain alternatives while at the same time obscuring an awareness of other alternatives through its programs of education, through the media, and through the total socialization process. Society cultivates specific skills and motivations within the individual. In such an environment Marcuse believes that freedom achieves self-determination only when it incorporates the concept of self-perfection. Freedom thus involves both the ordering of alternatives and the power to actualize those alternatives.

The Limits of Tolerance

Having established a background on the dimensions of the concept of freedom and its functions, Marcuse advances his case for freedom of thought. Though failing to distinguish between thought and action, he argues that freedom of thought, although not unlimited, is necessary for a society to function.

> Tolerance cannot be indiscriminate and equal with respect to the contents of expression, neither in word nor in deed; it cannot protect false words and wrong deeds which demonstrate that they contradict the possibilities of liberation. Such indiscriminate tolerance is justified in harmless debates, in conversation, in academic discussion: it is indispensable in the scientific enterprise, in private religion. But society cannot be indiscriminate where the

pacification of existence, where freedom and happiness themselves are at stake. Here certain policies cannot be proposed. Certain behavior cannot be permitted without making tolerance an instrument for the continuation of servitude.[38]

Throughout Marcuse develops a series of standards for the practice of tolerance. Often he contradicts himself. While labeling tolerance as "indispensable" in scientific enterprises he nevertheless states that the restoration of freedom would in many cases demand an intolerance "toward scientific research in the interest of deadly 'deterrents' of abnormal human endurance under inhuman conditions."[39] He does, however, discuss the necessity of strict regulations governing the curriculum of educational institutions. At the same time he acknowledges that withdrawal of tolerance toward regressive, repressive opinions could result only from extensive pressure and a reversal of current trends.

Marcuse appears less optimistic when he discusses the likelihood of withdrawal of tolerance for the repressive practices of businesses and publicity. Such practices "pertain to the basis on which the repressive affluent society rests and reproduces itself and its vital defenses."[40]

Marcuse urges a reconsideration of the extension of tolerance to certain acts of violence. He asserts the "natural right" for oppressed minorities to use extralegal means.[41] In most cases his principle of liberating tolerance implies intolerance of rightist movements and tolerance of the left. He labels the entire post-Fascist, post-Nazi period as one of "clear and present danger." He urges existing society to shun the precedent of Nazi Germany, where propaganda quickly evolved into action. Instead society must achieve pacification and liberation through the withdrawal of tolerance before the deed when communication is still in the realm of word, print, and picture. Maintaining that this is an "emergency situation" and a "society of extreme danger," Marcuse dismisses the standard liberal defense of free speech: "Different opinions and philosophies can no longer compete peacefully for adherence and persuasion on rational grounds; the 'marketplace of ideas' is organized and delimited by those who determine the national and individual interest."[42] Only by "breaking the tyranny of public opinion and its makers in the closed society" will there develop individuals with mature faculties, capable of rational and independent thought, desirous of participation in dialogue and discussion, capable of making decisions about tolerance.[43]

Despite the specific conditions Marcuse constructs for the limitation of tolerance he insists that "there is an objective truth" that can be revealed by "'cutting through,' 'splitting,' 'breaking asunder,' the given material." He acknowledges the existence of "incorrect arguments" but suggests that there is a specific process of separating right from wrong arguments. However, in his concluding remarks, he acknowledges the difficulties of this process and thus comes out on the side of unlimited tolerance. At the same time he recognizes that true freedom does not really exist.

To develop his concept of the absence of true freedom Marcuse asserts that a complete sifting of right from wrong arguments can rarely occur, for even objectivity is prejudiced. He offers an example of such prejudiced objectivity:

> When a magazine prints side by side a negative and a positive report on the FBI, it fulfills honestly the requirements of objectivity. However, the chances are that the positive wins because the image of the institution is deeply engraved in the mind of the people.[44]

In Marcuse's view, even when the media realize their neutrality, they rarely maintain that neutrality in their impact on the public mind. To Marcuse such neutrality tends to benefit the existing system. It aids the system by divesting the moral dimension of its power. Though adherence to the principle of neutrality presumes that there exist valid points worthy of presentation on both sides of the issues, nothing in fact is actually presented. The harm in the absence of a two-sided presentation is exacerbated by the non-neutrality of the persons being addressed. Controlled and manipulated by the society, the auditors have relinquished their neutrality. Marcuse makes this point in a concluding passage:

> The people exposed to this impartiality are no *tabulae rasae;* they are indoctrinated by the conditions under which they live and think and which they try to transcend. To enable them to become autonomous to find by themselves what is true and what is false for man in the existing society, they would have to be freed from the prevailing indoctrination (which is no longer recognized as indoctrination). But this means the trend would have to be reversed: They would have to get information slanted in the opposite direction. For the facts are never given immediately and never accessible immediately; they are established; "mediated" by those who make them; the truth "the whole truth" surpasses these facts and requires rupture with their appearance.[45]

Marcuse thus suggests that for freedom to exist there must also be a rupture between facts and reality. While such a rupture is impossible within the existing society as Marcuse views it, he views unlimited tolerance as serving to enhance the probability of the all-encompassing liberation to which he refers.

Marcuse explores the process by which freedom biased in favor of particular groups is to be converted to freedom available to all citizens. Using Freud as a foundation, he suggests that the social structure is introjected into the individual. He suggests that a biological foundation for revolution will evolve. New needs will evolve to become an inherent part of an individual's personality so that failure to satisfy them will disconcert the individual. These new needs will require satisfaction as strongly as those needs currently viewed as simply biological. Thus, a revolution, in Marcuse's view, would change not only those who control social institutions, but also those who carry out the revolution. Since the culture is introjected into us and pervades the organism, we must engender and make the revolution not only against the society but, more importantly, against ourselves:[46]

We would have to conclude that liberation would mean subversion against the will and against the prevailing interests of the great majority of people. In this deep-rooted, "organic" adaptation of the people to a terrible, but profitably functioning society, lie the limits of democratic persuasion and evolution. On the overcoming of these limits lies the establishment of democracy.[47]

7

The Supreme Court and Communication Theory: Contrasting Models of Speech Efficacy

WILLIAM BAILEY

William Bailey is a lecturer of communication at the University of Arizona. This essay, originally published in the Free Speech Yearbook: 1980, *received the H. A. Wichelns Memorial Award for the most significant contribution to the* Yearbook *for 1980.*

Chafee wrote some years ago that the "real issue in every free speech controversy is . . . whether the state can punish all words which have some tendency, however remote, to bring about acts in violation of law, or only words which directly incite to acts in violations of law."[1] Thus the question of incitement readily reduces to a question of causal relationships between the speech and the violation of law. Chafee marked off the free speech boundary by postulating a series of statements that ranged from disapproval of war to direct advocacy of resisting induction, and a series of audiences that ranged from women in an old women's home to inductees starting for a training camp: "Somewhere in such a range of circumstances is the point where direct causation begins and the speech becomes punishable as incitement under the ordinary standards of statutory construction and the ordinary policy of free speech. . . ."[2]

In this view, what must be determined is the real or probable efficacy of the speech in a given set of circumstances and with a given audience. But we may note now for later reference that the concern with the audience is with its direct involvement in the issues, and not with its attitudes or predisposition toward the issues. And another assumption of this view needs explicit statement: the law against incitement is not arbitrary; advocacy of acts in violation of law is a positive harm in that it brings about, causes, the unlawful acts, and it is this harm that justifies the abridgment of free speech. If the laws were arbitrary, if speech caused no harm, presumably incitement laws would be unconstitutional.

A central problem for this view of incitement is that causation is not observable but is an inference of relationships between or among phenomena. In an ordinary mechanical sequence of effects—say, one man pulling the trigger of a loaded gun pointed at another man—the sequence follows patterns of physical law. The chain of effects is empirically demonstrable, repeatable, and is of unquestionable harm to the man shot. But suppose bullets were no more harmful than water from a water pistol unless the person shot, for some reason, wanted them to be lethal. The law would take a much different position on the harm of shooting a man because the volition of the man shot would be the critical factor. This situation, while not wholly parallel with the speech situation, illustrates something of the problem of free speech prosecution: a speech is not "shot" at a man with the kind of predictable effects which characterize a gunshot, and to a considerable degree because the efficacy of the speech is extremely dependent upon the volition of the audience. Traditionally, the situation that follows a speech is taken as the measure of the effect of the speech, but in part this is an instance of the *post hoc* fallacy in classic form; the response made to a speech by an audience may be a more accurate measure of the predisposition of the audience than the power of the speaker to persuade. The speech act to a considerable degree serves as an occasion for the audience to manifest their convictions; most often the audience probably hears a speaker with which it is already in agreement, but some members of the audience may be there to heckle and disagree. In sum, the efficacy of a speech or speaker is very difficult to demonstrate.

Aspects of speech efficacy assuredly tend to follow certain patterns of probability, but the variables are so plentiful and so complex that it is doubtful the cause-effect relationships of the speech act can ever be shown to approach the regularity of mechanical cause-effect relationships.

This essay will argue that the Supreme Court has, like Chafee, assumed a very mechanistic model of speech efficacy: it will (1) attempt to illustrate the origin and nature of the model expressed in selected Court decisions; (2) attempt to present a typical, empirical model of speech efficacy; (3) attempt to relate the significance of the empirical model to free speech prosecution. In brief, the contention to be supported is that the Court has both overdetermined and over-estimated the efficacy of the speech act because of an inadequate model of the communication process. This essay will concern itself with Court decisions that are primarily applications or derivations of the "clear and present danger" test,[3] but the study is relevant to any test that assumes speech efficacy. The intention is to illustrate factors relevant to the Court's model, or concept, of speech efficacy, and not to account for either the development or abandonment of the clear and present danger test. Whatever contentions may be subsequently made concern only the pragmatics of the Court's view, and surely will not be mistaken for arguments of constitutional law. When the Court considers questions of probability or clear and present danger, it enters the realm of pragmatics, and it seems reasonable to suggest that when the Court's pragmatic assumptions fail to accord with contemporary knowledge, they should be revised or abandoned.

The Nature of the Court's Model

It is significant that the spirit of the Espionage Act of 1917 was in part influenced, according to Chafee, by the "fear of German propaganda and the knowledge of legislation and administrative regulations guarding against it in Great Britain and Canada."[4] The motivational strength of this fear is suggested by Attorney General Gregory's argument for expansion of the Espionage Act as reported by Chafee:

> He stated that although it had proved an effective instrumentality against deliberate or organized disloyal propaganda, it did not reach the individual casual or impulsive disloyal utterances.[5]

The Espionage Act, *per se*, was less a threat to free speech than was the emotional tenor of the country:

> No one reading the simple language of the Espionage Act of 1917 could have anticipated that it would be rapidly turned into a law under which opinions hostile to the war had practically no protection. Such a result was made possible only by the District Court test and by the tremendous wave of popular feeling against pacifists and pro-Germans during the war. This feeling was largely due to the hysterical fear of spies and other German propaganda.[6]

In his study of propaganda Terence Qualter dates the concern of the general public with propaganda as beginning with World War I.[7] He notes that the linkage of propaganda with falsehood was widespread after 1918.[8] As the Espionage Act was intended to be a weapon against propaganda, the linkage of propaganda and falsehood goes far to explain the false statement clause of the Espionage Act and the convictions under the clause.⁹ Qualter goes on to comment with obvious surprise:

> Even so eminent a scholar as James Bryce could, in 1921, accept uncritically the then popular attack on the war propagandists, and he defined propaganda as "that dissemination by the printed word of untruths and fallacies and incitements to violence."¹⁰

J. A. C. Brown states that it was with World War I that people began to have the "ambivalent feeling that propaganda is something sly, unpleasant, and frequently silly, yet also a weapon of devastating power for 'getting at' people without their consent."¹¹ Roger Brown comments that even today:

> In both popular and academic social psychology the "masses" are thought to be unable to resist certain kinds of persuasion. An unscrupulous propagandist can persuade the masses to act in a way that is not consonant with their own best interests.¹²

Americans, Roger Brown argues, believe they have in the past acted as masses and are afraid of a recurrence;¹³ in parody of the American attitude towards propaganda he cites William Empson:

> They believe in machinery more passionately than we do and modern propaganda is a scientific machine, so it seems to them obvious that a mere reasoning man can't stand up against it. All this produces a curiously girlish attitude toward anyone who might be doing propaganda. Don't let that man come near. Don't let him tempt me, because if he does, I'm sure to fall.¹⁴

The response that society has made to this view of the weak, virtuous-because-untempted general public is manifested in incitement statutes and incitement clauses of statutes. It is most significant that the history of the Supreme Court's treatment of free speech and the general public's fear of propaganda began together with World War I.

That in the aftermath of World War I the Court worked with a concept of propaganda is unquestionable. Justice Clarke seems to have been particularly responsive. In the *Abrams* majority opinion he wrote that excerpts from the publication in question showed "the plain purpose of their propaganda was to excite . . . sedition, riots, and, as they hoped, revolution. . . ."¹⁵ He again designated as propaganda the material before the Court in *Milwaukee Social Democratic Publishing Company*, saying that while it was "written more adroitly than the usual pro-German propaganda of that time," it still clearly proved its publishers intended to interfere with the war effort.¹⁶ Material designated as propaganda by the lower courts was also coming before the Court. In the *Gitlow* majority opinion Justice Sanford noted that the Appellate Division had held the convicted men ". . . planned for militantly disseminating a propaganda."[17] In *Dennis* the Court argued that "propaganda will answer propaganda."[18] Justice Jackson concurred with the majority, but apparently had less than full faith in the statement on propaganda; he rejected the clear and present danger test on the grounds that it involved imponderables, among which was the prediction of "the effectiveness of Communist propaganda."[19] No effort has been made to cite all instances in which the Court or its members classified material as propaganda or spoke of propagandists, but it seems clear that the Court had an early and enduring concern with propaganda. It can also be shown that the Court viewed some speech as "compelling speech," speech that was inherently effective.

The landmark case of the clear and present danger test was, of course, *Schenck*, in which Justice Holmes wrote for the Court:

> The question in every case is whether the words used are used in such circumstances and are of such a nature as to create a clear and present danger that they will bring about the substantive evils that Congress has a right to prevent.[20]

The passage provides obvious parallels to the citations from Chafee with which this essay began: by examining the language and the circumstances the question of causation is readily resolved. Note the assumption that words may have a certain "nature," may inherently be such as to create the danger. The Holmes-Brandeis dissent in *Gitlow* makes more apparent the quality of this inherency.

Justice Sanford wrote for the majority in *Gitlow* that a "single revolutionary spark may kindle a fire that, smoldering for a time, may burst into a sweeping and destructive conflagration," and the State "to protect the public peace and safety . . . seeks to extinguish the spark without waiting until it has enkindled the flame or blazed into the conflagration."[21] Holmes shifted this fire imagery from the broad social plane to the specific speech situation. He argues that the principle difference between expression of opinion and incitement "in the narrower sense is the speaker's enthusiasm for the result. Eloquence may set fire to reason," but in his view, "the redundant discourse before us . . . had no chance of starting a present conflagration."[22] The emphasis upon fire tempts speculation,[23] but it is at least safe to say the kind of persuasion the masses are unable to resist in the Holmes view, and agreed to by Brandeis, was that in which eloquence and enthusiasm—emotionality—overwhelmed reason.

The Holmes-Brandeis dissent in *Gitlow* rejected the broad view of the majority that tended to make doctrine punishable. In such a view, the dissenters argued, every idea must be considered an incitement.[24] The majority had turned away from examination of the specific speech situation for dangerous potentials and instead examined ideas. Cushman has argued that Gitlow was punished because he published "not dangerous words but forbidden words."[25] Such a contrast is rather difficult to maintain; presumably the words are forbidden because they are dangerous, inherently dangerous. Indeed, this view is precisely Sanford's argument. While disclaiming the possibility, and therefore the need, of the Court precisely to measure and foresee the impact of an utterance, Sanford wrote that the utterances of the Gitlow variety "by their very nature, involve danger to the public peace and to the security of the State. They threaten breaches of the peace and ultimate revolution."[26] In other words, Sanford, along with Holmes, felt that certain speech had inherent efficacy, but that efficacy was not, as for Holmes, limited to a particular time and place. The danger was no less clear because not immediately present. The effect of this approach was to discard the obligation to show cause-effect relationships in the speech act; the Court needed to show only tendency since the time-place frame of reference was unlimited.

Brandeis wrote a concurring opinion for *Whitney* that, functionally, was another attack on the *Gitlow* decision: he pointed out that every advocacy or opinion contrary to law increased to some degree the probability of the *future* transgression of the law and insisted the Court confine itself to determining *present* danger, and danger of a serious nature.[27] The essence of the Holmes-Brandeis attack on the *Gitlow* opinion is the effort to lead the Court back to confront directly the question of speech efficacy.

The consequence of the Court's freeing itself of the burden of demonstrating speech efficacy becomes apparent in the logical problems confronting Justice Vinson in *Dennis*. He could not conceive that the clear and present danger test meant the government must "wait until the putsch is about to be executed," or must assume the putsch would not be attempted until "success or probability of success is the criterion."[28] Yet Justice Vinson accepted Judge Hand's formula that "the gravity of the 'evil' discounted by its improbability must be held to justify invasion of free speech to avoid the danger."[29] Assumedly, the evil is the speaker's goal, is success, and how that evil may be discounted by its improbability without invoking the criterion of probability seems less than clear.

In *Yates* efficacy is less a question than whether the speaker advocated an action or a belief.[30] This view suggests that the Court at this time held a rather arbitrary view of incitement; certain utterances had already been held to be inherently dangerous, and these were advocacies of certain actions. There was no need to consider the efficacy of the particular utterance in a particular time and place but only whether it fell into the advocacy of action category. The same sort of categorical approach is manifested in *Scales:* Justice Harlan stated "It was settled in *Dennis* that the advocacy with which we are here concerned is not constitutionally protected speech."[31] The advocacy of the Communist Party was inherently dangerous, and Scales could therefore not claim individual First Amendment protection. Here is a consequence of shifting away from consideration of individual speech efficacy in a given time and place toward a doctrinal approach; the defendent comes before the law not as an individual, but as a part of a whole already damned. The Court would have perhaps served its ends better if it had confronted more directly the problems germane to its assumptions concerning speech that had inherent efficacy, and therefore was inherently dangerous.

The Court's decision in *Kingsley International Picture Corp. v. Regents of University of New York* represents a shift back to the Holmes-Brandeis conception of clear and present danger, i.e., a danger that is both *imminent and likely*.[32] The shift was affirmed in *Brandenburg v. Ohio*, where the court distinguished between mere advocacy and incitement to imminent, likely, lawless action.[33] In his concurrence with that decision, Douglas discusses the Court's prior abandonment of the Holmes-Brandeis conception of clear and present danger, and argues cogently the lack of necessity to punish speech.[34] The "imminent and likely" criteria was again the controlling factor in the court's decision in *Communist Party of Indiana v. Whitcomb*.[35]

At this point two cases will be considered that fit neither the foregoing class of national security cases nor the subsequent class of public order cases, but are still relevant to the concerns of this essay and may be dealt with briefly in relevant aspects. In *Musser v. Utah* there is found a germinal differentiation between persuasive and coercive speech drawn apparently on the basis of pressure applied by a group upon individuals to practice polygamy.[36] This differentiation constitutes the clearest expression of a notion of "compelling speech," but it is of course complicated by religion and other factors that are peripheral to speech. The second case is *Beauharnais* wherein Justice Jackson dissented and argued the validity of the clear and present danger test in libel cases. Jackson said of the test: "It is the most just and workable standard yet evolved for determining criminality of words whose injurious or inciting tendencies are not demonstrated by the event but are ascribed to them on the basis of probabilities."[37] The principal reason for citing Jackson's statement is that it makes explicit the certainty that in speech events where harm occurs, harm may be ascribed without question to the words involved. And it is also explicit that in the absence of such an occurrence of harm, but where there is suspected "clear and present danger" of harm, again the only place to seek for efficacy in producing the harm is the speech.

Court decisions pertaining to violation of public order have also manifested the concept of efficacy inherent to some forms of speech. In *Kunz* the question was primarily one of prior restraint, but Justice Jackson's dissent reveals the same suspicion of emotionalism in speech as was expressed by Justice Holmes:

> Written words are less apt to incite or provoke to mass action than spoken words, speech being the primitive and direct communication with emotions. Few are the riots caused by publications alone, few are the mobs that have not had their immediate origin in harangue.[38]

This passage follows Jackson's statement that the purpose of First Amendment protection of speech "is to foster peaceful interchange" of information, thoughts, and ideas: "Its policy is rooted in faith in the force of reason,"[39] and, it might be added, "in suspicion of the forces of emotion." In this psychology of dichotomized reason and emotion, assuredly outdated, the danger arises from the emotional, irrational side of man. It is worth noting, too, that the communication is considered to be a direct instrument, to be directly in touch with the primitive emotions and can therefore "get at" people without their consent. The final proposition can be reversed: it can be logically argued that mobs encourage harangues.

In *Cantwell* Justice Roberts stated for the Court that the power of the state to punish or prevent clear and present danger of riot, disorder, or other threats to the public well-being was obvious.[40] Also stated was the speaker's responsibility for the reasonably expected consequences of his speech, whether or not the consequences were intended.[41] These statements are relevant to the subsequent discussion of *Feiner*. In *Chaplinsky*, Justice Murphy designated a "class" of utterances that enjoyed no protection; this class included lewd, obscene, profane, libelous, and insulting or "fighting" words, all of which were held by the Court to be of "no essential part of any exposition of ideas," and that "by their very utterance inflict injury or tend to incite an immediate breach of the peace."[42] The phrase "by their very utterance" parallels Justice Sanford's statement in *Gitlow* that the utterances "by their very nature" endangered the peace and security of the state. Inherent efficacy of some words is again manifested, and it is reasonably clear that the words are of the expressive or emotional variety and are held in contrast with reason, or the exposition of ideas.

Justice Douglas insisted in *Terminiello* that there be demonstrated "a clear and present danger of a serious substantive evil that arises far above public inconvenience, annoyance or unrest."[43] Terminiello's speech taken in conjunction with the Court's decision suggests that the "classes of speech" concept of *Chaplinsky* may be specious. The Court did not feel it had to rule on the "fighting words" question in *Terminiello*.[44] Justice Jackson certainly had a strong and logical point in his dissent; the epithets for which Chaplinsky was prosecuted *were* mild in comparison with those Terminiello employed.[45] Yet, it must be conceded that Terminiello was indeed engaged in the exposition of ideas. The question as to whether some classes of speech are nonessential to the exposition of ideas would seem to turn on the adequacy of the speaker's vocabulary. Educationally and culturally deprived citizens or citizens of limited intelligence cannot be expected to express their attitudes with the turn of a phrase requiring the literary skills exhibited by some Court justices. But the question of First Amendment disenfranchisement of the illiterate and poorly educated is a constitutional question beyond the scope of this essay. More relevant is the Court's suspicion of expressive or emotional language and its concept of inherent efficacy. Even for Justice Douglas there was no question that Terminiello was the cause of "inconvenience, annoyance or unrest."

The Court's concept of unidirectional influence—that the speaker does something to the audience as the sole causative agent—is apparent in *Feiner*, where Justice Vinson ruled for the Court that Feiner was "neither arrested nor convicted for the making or the content of his speech. Rather, it was the reaction it actually engendered."[46] Vinson went on to point out that it was not necessary to conclude from the general prohibition of using police to suppress free speech that the police were powerless "when as here the speaker passes the bounds of argument of persuasion and undertakes incitement to riot. . . ."[47] It may be recalled that Feiner had more to fear from a riot than did the state; the audience was hostile.

Although Feiner was presumably seeking support for his ideas from the audience, the court did not have to weigh his intentions heavily against the effect it presumed his speech caused. That was settled in *Cantwell*. In holding the speaker responsible for the consequences of the speech situation regardless of the effects the speech was intended to have, the Court thus makes clear the completeness of its commitment to the view of the speaker as the sole cause of whatever effects accrue. It may be argued that if Feiner had not made the speech, or if he had made a different speech, the disorder would not have occurred.

It is equally obvious that if the audience had not been present, or if a different audience had been present, the disorder would not have occurred.

In the rash of cases involving public disorder during the late sixties and early seventies, the Court had occasion to apply and refine the "fighting words" doctrine, and did so with considerably more sophistication as to speech efficacy than had been evidenced before.[48] The principal case of the group to be considered is *Cohen v. California*.[49] At issue was Cohen's jacket which bore the motto, "Fuck the Draft." Justice Harlan, writing for the Court, reaffirms the right of the States, under *Chaplinski*, to ban "fighting words," defined by Harlan as "those personally abusive epithets which, when addressed to the ordinary citizen, are, as a matter of common knowledge, inherently likely to provoke violent reactions."[50] However, such was not the case with Cohen's jacket since the motto was addressed to no one in particular and unlikely to be taken as a personal insult by anyone.[51] Furthermore, a particular epithet cannot be excluded from public discourse on the grounds that its use is "inherently likely" to cause violence in the absence of evidence that a substantial proportion of the citizenry will react violently when the execration is uttered.[52] In brief, the simple use or display of a word cannot be banned.[53] The Court notes that linguistic expression serves both cognitive and emotive functions, and that the emotive function may be the most important in some messages,[54] and thus takes a position quite different from earlier Court decisions in which the emotions were suspect.

In *Gooding v. Wilson*,[55] a situation in which murderous threats and abusive language were directed to policemen, the Court dismissed the case because of the overbreadth of the law as indicated by Georgia appellate decisions. In *Rosenfield v. New Jersey*,[56] which involved a prosecution for indecent language at a public school board meeting, the Court remanded the case to New Jersey Courts that had decided Rosenfield without benefit of *Cohen* and *Gooding*. *Lewis v. City of New Orleans*,[57] in which a woman had been convicted of reviling police officers, and *Brown v. Oklahoma*,[58] in which the conviction was for obscene language in a public place, were also remanded to the respective state courts.[59] *Plummer v. City of Columbus*,[60] involved a taxicab driver's conviction for verbally abusing a customer. Like *Gooding*, the words may have been "fighting words," but the ordinance was overly broad. In *Hess v. Indiana*,[61] the conviction was for uttering in the context of an anti-war demonstration, "We'll take the fucking street later [or again]." In a *per curium* opinion it was held that while the words might be offensive to some individuals, the words were not addressed to anyone in particular and therefore could not be "fighting words."[62]

It would appear that Justice Murphy's conception in *Chaplinsky* of "fighting words" that "by their very utterance inflict injury or tend to incite an immediate breach of the peace" has been eviscerated by the more recent Court's reluctance to decide cases simply on the basis of words uttered.[63] As Haiman notes, the "fighting words" category is restricted to personal epithets in a face to face situation and "limited also to circumstances where it can be demonstrated to a degree that is more than just speculative, that physical conflict was likely to ensue."[64] Even so, we are still at some remove from a position that recognizes the capacity of the "ordinary citizen" to walk away from "fighting words," to resist incitements to breaches of the peace or other illegal acts. If there is to be any kind of meaningful presupposition of innocence for a speaker prosecuted for incitement, recognition of the audience as a causal factor in speech situations must be made. It may be properly argued that if the audience is admitted as a causal factor in the speech situation, nothing the speaker says or does may be taken as proof of incitement. That is precisely the point of the following section of the essay.

Before moving to the next section, a summary here may be helpful. The early free speech cases occurred during a period of time when society was frightened virtually to hysteria by the threat of propaganda. It was, and still is, feared that the persuader could "get at" an audience without its consent. Especially suspect were the emotional appeals that could cause men to act irrationally. In this view, speech is a direct instrumentality that compels behavior, and the flow of influence is unidirectional, from the speaker to the audience. This view of speech is inherent to the rationale behind prosecution of incitement and has manifested itself in the opinions of the Court.

The Empirical Model of Speech Efficacy

This section will be devoted to the presentation of a reasonably typical empirical model of speech efficacy. Rather than attempt to integrate individual experiments or theories, the presentation will draw upon summary opinions of scholars and researchers making comment upon such broad areas of study as propaganda and public opinion. There is no intent to present a thorough, scholarly survey, but only to present as clearly as possible in the least amount of space the contemporary view of speech efficacy based upon empirical research.

At the outset it seems advantageous to contrast the model discussed in the prior section with the model to be presented in this section.

Professor Bauer accomplishes the contrast with considerable efficiency:

> The *social model* of communication is a model of one-way influence in which the communicator presumably has power and "does something to the audience," with or without its consent. This model of communication emphasizes the exploitation of man by man. . . . In fact, however, the history of communication research seems to offer more support for a different model.
>
> The *scientific model* of communication more accurately reflects what is known from communication research. It views communication as a two-way transaction between communicator and audience in which each party is engaged in problem solving, and in which each party both gives and gets something.[65]

The transactional aspect of the model is important. As Professor Bauer points out, in the latter model we are led to look not only for the influence of the speaker upon the audience, but as well "for the audience's effect upon the communicator."[66] Bauer feels that "Perhaps the most important implication of the transaction is that when we try to change others we get changed ourselves."[67] The social model has been wholly abandoned and the emphasis is upon constructing a model adequate to the transactional elements of the communication process.[68] There is no question that the speech situation is effective in changing attitudes or behavior; however, the efficacy depends to a significant degree upon the audience.[69] Both the hidden and overt persuader are far less powerful than previously thought. The study of propaganda has brought forth considerable information on this point.

A common and significant insistance of propaganda studies is that decided differences in both kind and efficacy of propaganda exist between democratic and totalitarian societies. Qualter points out that the greater power of the totalitarian propaganda does not derive from superior techniques but from a monopoly control over the means of propaganda and the use of force to exclude rival propaganda; this fact leads him to conclude that in a genuine democracy there will be the greatest possible free competition among the propagandists for a variety of causes:

> This competition is desirable, not only to prevent the emergence of a totalitarian monopoly . . . but also because the fillip of new, controversial ideas is in itself a stimulating educating force. . . . Rival propaganda campaigns are one of the most important forces for provoking individual thinking on any issue. Now, although a democratic government may give a lead to public opinion . . . it is

not part of its function to determine the religious, philosophic, economic, social, or purely eccentric beliefs of its people. The government is not the guardian of the public conscience and has no authority to object to the faith of any of its citizens or to their desire to convert others to that faith.[70]

Qualter goes on to point out that the average propagandist in a democracy may have ambitions of "moulding a public mind to his own design," but the competition forces his propaganda to take on an educational function, about which the audience makes up its own mind: "The propaganda makes the people aware of the issues to be considered, but it seems to have less effect than once imagined in determining how people will react to these issues."[71] Similarly, Klapper points out that "The condition believed to render persuasion most effective is a monopoly propaganda position. In the United States, such a position can be achieved only by persuasion for attitudes which already enjoy almost universal sanction."[72]

George A. Miller finds that the "power of the propaganda campaign is not as alarming as it might seem on first consideration. People seek out and believe what they want to believe, and they let themselves be pushed in the way they want to go."[73] Roger Brown concludes that the power of propaganda has been "oversold,"[74] and that fear in this country of Russian propaganda that appears to hold the Russians in its grip fails to recognize the difference between the monopoly situation in Russia and the competitive situation in the United States.[75] Roger Brown makes a very significant point on speech efficacy when he states, "Speech is not directly instrumental, it does not compel action. The consent of the audience is won by convincing them that the recommended action is in their own best interests."[76]

J. A. C. Brown concludes:

> ... it would appear that the main lesson to be drawn from our present study of propaganda is how very resistant people are to messages that fail to fit into their own picture of the world and their own objective circumstances, how they deliberately (if unconsciously) seek out only those views which agree with their own.[77]

J. A. C. Brown makes a quite ironic point: he argues that in their study of Gallup polls and motivation research to find out what the people really think, the "would-be brainwashers of Western democracies are being brainwashed"; only in the Communist "people's democracies" are the brainwashers "performing their proper function."[78]

Berelson writing on public opinion and communication provides from that point of view a close parallel with the opinions already expressed:

> The point is that the nature of one's audience places certain limits upon what one can say to it—and still have an audience. . . .
>
> It is important to take account of this direction in the flow of influence between communication and public opinion in order to appreciate the reciprocal nature of that influence, i.e., to recognize that it is not all a one way process. It is also important to note that the total effect of this reciprocal process is probably to stabilize and "conservatize" opinion since ideologies are constantly in process of reinforcement thereby. The over-all picture then, is that of like begetting like begetting like.[79]

It is clear that the efficacy of the persuader had been in the past overestimated and that a considerably greater danger may attach to limiting speech significantly than to giving it free rein. One of the most relevant statements with regard to policy concerning free speech was made by Daniel Katz, commenting on the study of attitudes. Katz defines two streams of thought that have been traditionally held and that assume contrasting models.[80] On the one hand is the tradition that assumes an irrational model and holds that men are very limited in powers of reason, reflection, discrimination, self insight and memory, and that "Whatever mental capacities people do possess are easily overwhelmed by emotional forces and appeals to self-interest and vanity."[81] In the second tradition, a rational model is invoked. This model assumes that man "seeks understanding . . . , consistently attempts to make sense of the world about him, that he possesses discriminating and reasoning powers . . . and that he is capable of self-criticism and self-insight. It relies heavily upon getting adequate information to people."[82] Both of these viewpoints have been supported by research, and Katz concludes:

> Now either school of thought can point to evidence which supports its assumptions, and can make fairly damaging criticism of its opponent. . . .
>
> The conflict between the rationality and irrationality models was saved from becoming a worthless debate because of the experimentation and research suggested by these models. . . . In general, the irrational approach was at its best where the situation imposed heavy restrictions upon research behavior and response alternatives. . . . On the other hand, where the individual can have more adequate commerce with the relevant environmental setting, where he has time to obtain more feedback from his

reality testing, and where he has a number of realistic choices, his behavior will reflect the use of his rational faculties.[83]

The import of this position is clear: if irrationality is the desired end for man, restrict his access to communication, effect a persuasive monopoly; if rationality is the desired end, give him free access to all possible views and advocacies, make a persuasive monopoly impossible. But the primary force of the arguments of this section should be directed against the concept of incitement. It should be evident that the Court has assumed wrongly that the speaker is *the* causative agent in the speech situation, and it is this unwarranted assumption that modern communication research most strongly rejects.

Conclusion

This section will conclude the essay with an attempt to sharpen the relationship and significance of the empirical model to free speech prosecution. To that end a very contemporary complaint about the lack of empirical analysis on the part of the Court is relevant. In his free speech arguments relating to black power advocacy Paul Harris contends, "The clear and present danger test sidesteps the question whether or not there was a real causal connection [between advocacy and violence] by requiring only that reasonable men agree that the advocacy could have caused the violence."[84] Harris continues:

> The Court has never made a full empirical analysis of the advocate's relationship to the expected danger. It may be that the judicial process is not adequate to make these kinds of determinations. But if the Court is committed to a formula which requires determinations as to when there is an actual danger and as to the likelihood speech causing action, then its refusal to attempt empirical answers to these issues results in vague notions of danger and causality determining the scope of free speech.[85]

The arguments of this essay support the contentions of Harris but point in a direction other than empirical determination by the Court of individual speech efficacy. As Harris intimates, the judicial process does not seem adequate to make such determinations. Nor does it need to. The empirical model is a generalization of empirical findings with regard to speech efficacy. If the Court were guided by such a model in its deliberations, it could not affirm incitement convictions but would hold that too many variables enter to allow the conviction and that no audience can be compelled by words to commit acts they do not want to commit.

The major function of the empirical model of communication in free speech prosecution would be the correction it would make of the older model's over-estimation and over-determination of the efficacy of a speaker or a speech. Correction would be accomplished primarily through the model's inclusion of the audience as a definite and possibly determinant factor in speech efficacy, and this inclusion renders the causal factors traditionally assigned to the speaker possibilities rather than certainties. The empirical model, if incitement prosecution could be contemplated under its auspices, could as easily lead to prosecution of an audience for incitement of a speaker as the reverse. But in fact, the model destroys the concept of incitement.

The significance of the empirical model is that it wholly denies the notion of inherent efficacy which was the enabling assumption of the Espionage Act convictions. Guided by such a model the Court could not assume that words "by their very nature" or "by their very utterance" have any efficacy, because the efficacy of the words is dependent upon the audience hearing them. In brief, guided by the empirical model the Court would hold the position that the speech act is at least as much determined in its efficacy by the mind of the listener as by anything the speaker may do.

It is plain then, that should the Court adopt an empirical view of speech efficacy, the abridgment of free speech by incitement prosecution would end. "Reasonable men" could not agree that an advocacy could cause violence in the absence of a predisposition toward violence on the part of the audience. And assuming such a predisposition could be demonstrated, "reasonable men" would not agree that the speaker's contribution could be separated from the audience's contribution.

At this point some objections may be considered. One objection might be to the general tenor of an argument against incitement prosecution: why should advocacy in violation of law receive First Amendment protection? This question reflects an increasingly popular attitude, and since the Court's decisions have affirmed incitement convictions, the burden of proof seems to rest on the libertarian. But the easy assertion that freedoms are not absolute is not a rationale for limiting those freedoms in the absence of a clearly defined harm. The arguments of this essay have raised substantive questions concerning the pragmatics of the Court's assumptions relating to incitement. If incitement convictions cannot be upheld by the Court upon an empirical, factual basis, surely everyone would agree the very notion of incitement is one that the judicial process is better off without. It is not necessary for one to approve of the radical's method or message to see the injustice of prosecution or conviction based upon erroneous premises. The fore-going arguments attack the basis of incitement prosecutions: the assumption that incitement has inherent efficacy and therefore causes violation of the law. If it cannot be maintained that speech is the direct instrument of violation of law, the argued need for abridgment of First Amendment protections by incitement statutes is without substance.

It may be objected that "incitement" is used in this essay in a far stronger sense than it has in legal usage, where it means only to "urge," "stimulate," or "advocate," and not at all "to compel by speech." Citations from the Court opinions given above manifest assumptions of inherent efficacy that argue to the contrary. Besides, if "urging," "stimulating," or "advocating" were not deemed highly effective in causing the proscribed act, if "incitement" does not in meaning approach "compelling speech," then why should it be prosecuted?

The assumption of a rational audience may be considered excessively idealistic, but that has already been answered in part, above, by Katz. The counter-assumption, that man is irrational, carries its own condemnation: how does he who asserts man's irrationality exempt himself and his statement? Most probably he does not mean *all* men, and when pressed will reveal the elitist assumption of irrational masses. But the questions of whether or not the masses are rational must assume the masses have free access to opinion and information.

Finally, whether or not men are rational, or have free will, the law obviously assumes they do, and it makes each man responsible for his individual acts. Even the most hardy opponent of the arguments offered here against incitement prosecution must surely concede that it is inconsistent for the law to assume individual responsibility, but yet punish a speaker for what an audience did, or might have done, as if the speaker were some warlock or wizard who could deprive the individual of his reason and autonomy. Future generations may well look back upon the speech prosecutions of this age with the same feelings we experience when we contemplate the earlier period of our history when men burned witches.

Part Three

Legal Perspectives

Toward a More Realistic View of the Judicial Process in
Relation to Freedom of Speech
Ruth McGaffey

The United States Supreme Court on Libel
Wayne C. Minnick

Protecting Political Speech:
Brandenburg v. Ohio Updated
Paul Siegel

A Rhetoric of Ritual and Desecration
William I. Gorden and Richard Goodman

8

Toward a More Realistic View of the Judicial Process in Relation to Freedom of Speech

RUTH MCGAFFEY

Ruth McGaffey is Professor of Communication and Director of Graduate Studies in the Department of Communication at the University of Wisconsin-Milwaukee, where she teaches the course "Contemporary Problems in Freedom of Speech." She is a member of the Commission on Freedom of Speech of the Speech Communication Association and is a former editor of Free Speech, *the Commission's newsletter. McGaffey's activities in the American Civil Liberties Union include serving on the board of directors of the Milwaukee chapter of the Wisconsin Civil Liberties Union. Professor McGaffey is the author of a number of essays concerning the First Amendment, including "Group Label Revisited,"* Quarterly Journal of Speech *65 (April 1979): 157–70; and "The Hecklers' Veto,"* Marquette Law Review *57 (1973): 39–65. The following essay was published in the* Free Speech Yearbook: 1972.

Thurmond Arnold, former Professor of Law at Yale, once wrote, "Human institutions, in an environment which worships reason, fail in influence and prestige unless they appear to be firmly grounded on reason and fundamental principle."[1] He then described "The Law," "The Sanctity of the Constitution," and "The Impartiality and Rationality of the Judicial Process," as myths which most Americans find necessary to accept. He said:

> In spite of all the irrefutable logic of the realists, men insist upon believing that there are fundamental principles of law which exist apart from any particular case, or any particular human activity. . . . The truth of such a philosophy cannot be demonstrated or proved. It exists only because we seem unable to find comfort without it.[2]

Arnold argued that Americans are made insecure by the idea that the law is made by men and that it thus changes from day to day. Even more disturbing, perhaps, is the concept that the constitution is what the prevailing power group says it is.

Thurman Arnold was talking about lawyers, legal scholars, law students and the general public. He contended that those law professors who attempt to inject a note of reality into their lectures must deal with "the temper of students who expect to find law to be something which they can take down in notebooks, and who do not wish to be confronted with the confused picture of what is actually going on."[3]

Departments of speech communication are often confronted with the same type of students. Recently many of these departments have added courses relating to the operation of the judicial process. This essay concerns one of these courses, Freedom of Speech. Students and faculty often approach such a course as "true believers" in two ideas. The first is that "Freedom of Speech" is guaranteed in our society. The second is that "The Law" is a logical entity formulated by wise men immune to their own prejudices or outside influence. These ideas are myths. In order for students to intelligently consider the problem of free speech in contemporary society, they must realize this. One need only to recall the Alien & Sedition Acts, the Espionage Act of 1917, the Smith Act and the McCarran Act to refute the first belief. The second requires more attention. This essay will attempt to show that constitutional interpretation and related judicial decision-making are chancey, subjective processes. The first way to observe this subjectivity is to examine the very factor which is thought to insure orderly, logical legal development, *stare decisis*.

Stare Decisis in First Amendment Law

Stare Decisis is a legal term which means, "let the decision stand."[4] It is an important element of the common law whereby a decision applies in similar cases and is binding on the lower courts. It relies on the application of reasoning by analogy in which the conclusion drawn from one set of facts is applied to a similar set of facts. It is capable of manipulation, however. There is often no really analogous situation from which a precedent can be drawn. This has been particularly apparent in the development of the legal concept of "symbolic speech." As each new activity has been considered for First Amendment protection on the grounds of its non-verbal expression, it has not been found so obviously analogous to one model that others were automatically excluded. Draft card burning is not clearly analogous to any other activity. The flag salute is not the same as the display of a red flag. Wearing arm bands in a public school is not the same as carrying placards on a public street. Even demonstrating in front of a courthouse is not the same as marching through a legislative chamber. Therefore, as each new behavior has been brought into the judicial arena, judges have had an opportunity to select from among several models. A judge could choose to use a situation in which another activity had either been accorded or denied First Amendment protection. This can be seen in the treatment of "demonstrations." Those judges who were in favor of restriction selected labor picketing as the relevant model. Justice Hugo Black exemplified this method of reasoning. Those who would give more protection to demonstrators suggested public forum and leaflet analogies. Justice William O. Douglas has taken this position.

A second factor allowing for individual decision-making is the existence of several contradictory decisions. This situation is common prior to a Supreme Court ruling on an issue. Before the Supreme Court decision in *Davis v. Massachusetts*,[5] there were cases available to support either the argument that city officials could have discretionary authority over streets and parks or that they could not. Thus a judge had some freedom to select those opinions which supported his beliefs. The same situation arose in relation to picketing, draft card burning and school regulations. During the formative period of a legal concept, law is very fluid. Different jurisdictions arrive at different conclusions, and these results can be used by still other courts.

Other factors allow for individual interpretation of the law. A judge can distinguish away a relevant case if the result does not support his position and can avoid an unfavorable precedent by showing that the situation has changed since the Court made the earlier pronouncement. This latter technique was especially apparent in the *Hague v. CIO* conflict where the District and Circuit Courts argued that, while their decisions might be contrary to an old Supreme Court holding, they were consistent with recent rulings of the Court.[6] Reference was made to the change in constitutional interpretation resulting in the application of the First Amendment to state action. Mention was also made of recent decisions of the Court which, while not strictly analogous, supported a more libertarian position than the earlier *Davis* case.

A lower court judge can also avoid using a Supreme Court decision as precedent if he can point out something about the decision itself which destroys its weight. This was particularly obvious in judicial reaction to the *Hague v. CIO* decision. That decision had not expressly overruled the earlier *Davis* ruling, and there was not a majority opinion. Both of these facts were pointed out in *State v. Fowler*, where the judge of the Rhode Island Supreme Court upheld the validity of a discretionary permit ordinance in seeming opposition to the intent of the *Hague* decision.[7]

The Justices of the Supreme Court have even fewer limits on their ability to make subjective decisions. Very important, of course, is the power of that Court to decide which cases it wants to hear. A case is considered if four of the Justices want to hear it. Thus the Court can refuse to hear cases that would force decisions of hard questions in ways either consistent with or departing from precedent. Even when the Court has decided to hear a case it may use precedent subjectively. By the time a case reaches the Supreme Court, the issue has usually been considered a number of times at lower levels. The Supreme Court Justice can select from among lower court cases those with which he agrees and use them to support his arguments. If a similar case has not been brought before the Supreme Court, a Justice can simply articulate a new doctrine. This was done in the red flag case of *Stromberg v. California*.[8] In articulating such a doctrine, the Court is free to use whatever models it chooses. At first there were few freedom of speech cases from which to choose. As the law developed, however, the Court could choose from public forum cases, leaflet cases, picketing cases or several other types.

The only precedents that the Supreme Court must consider are its own earlier rulings. Ways can be found to avoid following these rulings. For example, Justices can simply admit that they were wrong, or that an earlier Court was wrong. This has not happened very often, but it did happen in the flag salute controversy, and it is an available technique.[9] A Justice who did not participate in a prior decision can formulate a new doctrine which makes the old case obsolete. The Court can decide the instant case on its facts without overruling the earlier case. This was done in *Hague v. CIO*. The Supreme Court can also make distinctions on the facts. Such distinctions were made in several of the sit-in and demonstration cases. *Adderley v. Florida*[10] relied on the difference between a jailhouse and a legislative chamber to distinguish it from *Edwards v. South Carolina*.[11] The same distinction was employed in *Cox v. Louisiana*.[12]

Thus even the most conservative element in the judicial process, the application of precedent, cannot be depended upon to provide consistent legal interpretation of the constitution. This conclusion can be verified by a brief look at traditional literature in jurisprudence and at more recent social science writings in the field.

Legal and Social Science Viewpoints

Traditional Literature in Jurisprudence

Students of public address are familiar with the "great man" approach to history. In the field of jurisprudence, much of the "classical theory" has been the work of such men. While they may not have completely described what the law is and how it works, their views helped to determine what, in fact, it became. Those views give little support to the idea of judicial decision-making independent of human variables.

In 1881 Oliver Wendell Holmes wrote:

> The life of the law has not been logic; it has been experience. The felt necessities of the time, the prevalent moral and political theories, intuitions of public policy, avowed or unconscious, even the prejudices which judges share with their fellowmen, have a great deal more to do than the syllogism in determining the rules by which men should be governed. The law embodies the story of a nation's development through many centuries, and it cannot be dealt with as if it contained only the axioms and corrollaries of a book of mathematics.[13]

Perhaps in all the writing since 1881, there has been no better description of the law.

A second classic work in jurisprudence, *The Nature of the Judicial Process* by Benjamin Cardozo, was published in 1921.[14] Cardozo's introductory remarks help to explain why no one has been able to describe exactly how the judicial process works. He wrote:

> The work of deciding cases goes on every day in hundreds of courts throughout the land. Any judge, one might suppose, would find it easy to describe the process which he had followed a thousand times or more. Nothing could be farther from the truth. Let some intelligent layman ask him to explain; he will not go very far before taking refuge in the excuse that the language of craftsmen is unintelligible to those untutored in the craft.[15]

Cardozo discussed four methods of arriving at a decision. Each began with the finding of applicable precedents and the determination of what to do with them. He noted, "*Stare decisis* is at least the everyday working rule of our law."[16] He suggested, however, that exceptions should be made when precedent conflicted with the best interests of society. Cardozo realized that judges will disagree as to what constitutes this "best interest." He admitted that personal opinions, values and prejudices would be factors in that decision. He was optimistic, however, about the results of such interpretation. Cardozo wrote, "The eccentricities of judges balance one another . . .[;] out of the attrition of diverse minds there is beaten something which has a constancy and uniformity and average value greater than its component elements."[17]

Roscoe Pound was Dean of the Harvard Law School for many years. He agreed that a judge has the opportunity to make decisions according to his view of what the law should be. He suggested that a judge is fooling himself as well as society if he claims to be judging by any other method. He concluded, "The element of most enduring effect in legal development is professional and judicial ideals of the social and legal order."[18]

Whether William O. Douglas will be considered a "great man" is for history to decide. He is a former law professor as well as a Justice of the Supreme Court. Thus his philosophy of law is relevant. Douglas does not entirely discount the doctrine of *stare decisis*. In a 1949 *Columbia Law Review* article he wrote, "*Stare Decisis* provides some moorings so that men may trade and arrange their affairs with confidence. . . . It is a strong tie which the future has to the past."[19] Douglas also stated, however, that in deciding which precedents to follow, the judge may make room for his own philosophy. He made an even stronger point in relation to constitutional issues. To rely on precedent as a binding factor in such situations would be to "let men long dead and unaware of the problems of the age in which he lives do his thinking for him."[20]

Another "great man," Thomas Reed Powell, contended that a strict application of precedent would be possible only if the law were a completely logical system. Professor Powell, who taught at Harvard and Columbia law schools, argued that the law is not simply a matter of logic. This is because minor premises are often the result of qualitative judgments rather than "such a simple assurance that Socrates is a man." The resulting illogic of the law makes it a confusing process to those within the system as well as those without. Powell concluded, "The force of precedents and the decisions of the future lie within the determination of perhaps one Justice or also of two, who may very well have been unable to tell themselves just what turned them one way or the other."[21]

Some scholars have reacted against what they regard as ad hoc decision making without due regard to either logic or principle. One of these was Herbert Wechsler who wrote, ". . . judgment must distill a principle that determines the case at hand and that is viable in respect of those other situations, now forseeable, to which the logic of the principle demands that it apply."[22] He contended that if the decision were not supportable in such general and neutral terms, it did not satisfy the minimal conception of "equal justice under law." Thurmond Arnold would argue that belief in the existence of such neutral principles is an illustration of our need for myths.

Most scholars have agreed that precedents are to be followed unless there is a good reason not to follow them. The reasons for exception depend on the specific judge. As was noted in the *Yale Law Journal*, "In the suppressed moral premises of judicial opinions, in the choices between words of different value tones, in the selection, classification and interpretation of facts and precedents, and in the tracing of lines of causation, we find prime indicators of the value patterns of a judge, a judiciary, or a society."[23]

Social Science Literature

In the early 1940's C. Herman Pritchett began to publish voting records of Supreme Court Justices arranged according to values supported.[24] In 1955 Felix Cohen suggested that there was a need for "increased use of statistical methods in the scientific description and prediction of judicial behavior. . . ."[25] By 1961 Joseph Tanenhaus could point out several areas where social science techniques had been used to analyze the judicial process.[26] This research also supports the position that legal decision-making is a subjective process. It examines factors which may influence the ways decisions are made.

Backgrounds and Decision-Making. There has been increasing recognition that judges' backgrounds might be a factor in the way they make decisions. In a 1966 article in the *Harvard Law Review*, Joel Grossman summarized some important studies in this area.[27] He described three categories of research. The first attempted to collect background data about judges. According to Grossman, the most influential of these was John Schmidhauser's "Collective Portrait of the Justices of the Supreme Court."[28] This study showed that most Supreme Court Justices have been recruited from the upper middle class.

A second category of research has attempted to correlate backgrounds with voting records. Grossman listed several such studies. Nagel tried to correlate party affiliation with voting performance.[29] He concluded that Democratic judges were more likely than Republican judges to support the designated liberal position. It is doubtful that this was much of a surprise. Schmidhauser concluded that among justices who took extreme positions, party and sectional background seemed to strengthen attitudes toward regionally divisive issues.

Among moderate and neutral judges, party frequently proved stronger than regional background. He also found that justices with experience on lower courts had a greater propensity to abandon precedent than did those without such experience. He noted that justices who dissented most often were those with the lowest propensities to overrule. Schmidhauser concluded, therefore, that the typical dissenter was not an innovator, but an advocate of "traditional doctrines which were being abandoned."[30]

In the third category of research on judicial backgrounds—to determine to what extent these findings can account for the variance in judicial behavior—little of significance was reported. Bowen noted that none of the variables most significantly associated with judicial decisions explained more than a fraction of the total variance among judges. Grossman concluded that these findings cast doubt on the explanatory power of background variables taken by themselves.[31]

Values and Attitudes. Closely related to background studies have been studies of attitudes and values held by judges. These have attempted to find out whether identification of particular attitudes and values would permit predictions of voting behavior. In 1961 Glendon Schubert analyzed all of the cases on which the Supreme Court divided on the merits during the 1961 term. On the basis of voting behavior, he designated three types of political attitudes; the liberal attitude, the idiosyncratic attitude, and the conservative attitude. Applying these attitudes to cases that were to be considered in the 1962 term, he found that he was able to predict voting behavior.[32]

The study of values as variables in decision-making began with the studies of C. Herman Pritchett in the 1940's. A later study by David Danielski attempted to support the hypothesis that disagreements in the court were the results of differences in values.[33] He suggested that justices had been committed to certain values long before they arrived on the Court. His particular study compared the values of Justice Butler and Brandeis as determined from an analysis of a speech given by each. Values did indeed appear to be ranked in different order of importance, and could have explained differences on particular decisions. These studies seem to support the statement by Murphy that "since the constitution is written in broad terms . . . saying what this is allows, perhaps even requires, the Justices to apply their own value preferences."[34]

Small Group Theory. Some studies have attempted to apply small group theory to the process of decision-making. Two early studies by C. Herman Pritchett and Eloise Snyder indicated that the Supreme

Court could be divided into subgroups or voting blocs.[35] Later Walter Murphy argued in *Elements of Judicial Strategy*[36] that a Justice of the Supreme Court could maximize his influence through a process of bargaining. He contended that a Justice has a valuable object with which he can bargain. That object is his vote or his concurrence in an opinion. His sanctions are his ability to change his vote or to write a dissent. Murphy indicated several hypothetical and some real instances where this process of bargaining may be a realistic one.

Another study which employed small group analysis was done by Richard Richardson and Kenneth Vines.[37] They explored interpersonal relationships on three United States Courts of Appeal and concluded, "Since in all circuits, the reversal of cases by the appeals courts is largely directed toward turning non-libertarian decisions into libertarian ones, we suggest that dissent in the lower appellate courts is usually an expression of non-libertarianism."[38]

Inter-Court Interaction. Jack Peltason was the first "new breed" political scientist to study the impact of the Supreme Court's decisions on lower courts.[39] In 1955, Peltason noted that the Supreme Court does not always have the final decision in a conflict. He said that lower courts represent a variety of interests, and these interests are frequently different from those represented by the Supreme Court.[40] He compared the relationship between the lower courts and the Supreme Court to that between the Supreme Court and the Constitution. He argued that, ". . . just as it is said that the Constitution is what the judges say it is, so it can be said that a Supreme Court decision is what the subordinate judges who apply it say it is."[41]

Murphy pointed out that state judges are more apt to disagree with the Supreme Court than are lower federal court judges.[42] This is logical since state judges are not only closer to the situation, but owe their appointments to local political groups and can be removed, if at all, only by state action. Murphy agreed that, ". . . the Supreme Court usually does not render either the initial or the final decision in a case."[43]

Other Elements

Other factors affecting judicial development have received comment. Some scholars have speculated about the influence of law journals. Peltason compared these to reviews by drama critics. Their effect may not be that great, but they appear to have some influence. Many law review articles are cited in legal opinions. In 1959 Chester Newland published a study of "Law Reviews and the Supreme Court," in which he summarized the citations of legal periodicals by the Supreme Court from 1924 through 1956.[44] His findings indicated that those judges who cited law review articles the most were the ones in favor of change. A law professor commented that the Supreme Court follows not the election returns, but the law reviews. On the other hand one author thought that the judge made up his mind first, and then consulted law reviews to support his decisions.

Perhaps the most influential factor in the development of law is outside of the legal system. That factor is the historical situation in which a court or litigant finds itself. This situation determines to a large degree what laws legislatures will pass, what will thus become indictable offenses and, consequently, what issues will face the courts. The First World War, for example, eventually resulted in the Espionage Act with its subsequent trial in the courts. The Red Scare of the early twenties resulted in laws prosecuting those who displayed a red flag. This in turn led to the decision of the Supreme Court that such display was a form of speech. The Second World War brought compulsory flag salute laws and a further expansion of the term "speech." The post World War II Communist scare resulted in the McCarran Act which again changed the law. The developing labor movement in the 1930's and the civil rights movement twenty years later also clearly influenced the way in which the First Amendment Law developed.

Even outside the broad context which determines which laws are passed, however, there are many other contextual factors which influence the development of legal concepts. The mechanics of the judicial process allow for arbitrary decisions and for the influence of pure luck. The law enforcement officials in any area have vast discretion as to how stringently they will enforce the law, and whom they will indict for its violation. Once a person has been indicted, financial resources, publicity, availability of group backing and volunteer legal services may affect the quality of legal aid given to the defendant. All of these things may in turn be influenced by the timing of the offense in relation to the development of current issues. During the time when flag desecration was an important issue to the ACLU, a Milwaukee girl was indicted for violation of the Wisconsin desecration statute. Her picture appeared in *The Milwaukee Journal*, and immediate offers of legal assistance were forthcoming. Perhaps five years earlier she would not have been so fortunate.

Legal help is an important variable. This is true not only because the skill of a lawyer may determine success or failure, but because the lawyer decides which arguments are used in a legal contest. This in turn affects the possibility of appeal to a higher court, and may eventually determine which issues are decided by the Supreme Court. Benjamin Twiss compared the arguments of counsel to a cafeteria. The judges are not apt to use all of the arguments in their decisions, but their selection is often limited to those arguments in the lawyers' briefs.[45] Melvin Wulf wrote, "Though a lawyer cannot confidently predict that he will win any given case, he controls to a large extent the grounds upon which the court will decide his claims if they are decided favorably."[46] Such decisions of strategy may entail more than the lawyer's guess as to which arguments will be more effective. They may also be based on that lawyer's ideas of the proper function of courts and judges. There is some thought, for example, that the rationale used for decision in the case of the Pentagon Papers might have been different if Alexander Bickel had not represented the *New York Times*. Bickel is the leading academic advocate of judicial restraint, and it may be that his brief reflected that point of view.

Conclusion

Neither our historical experience in the development of First Amendment law, nor the literature in the field of jurisprudence gives much support to the thought that constitutional interpretation is a logical and rational procedure immune from societal or personal pressure. Many freedom of speech teachers and students have little faith in the good judgment of legislators or of citizens. Most writers would prefer that the judiciary have the last word in determining what speech should be constitutionally protected. Such a conclusion should be reached only after looking at reality and realizing that in the judicial process also, we are resting our faith in fallible men who often make subjective judgments.

History supports the position that the men on the courts and their personal, political and social biases determine legal development. One may look with fear or with joy at the Nixon appointees to the Court, but it is already clear that their effect will be noticeable. We must realize that when we speak of "the law," we are describing a way of writing about human institutions in terms of ideals. The Law "meets a deep-seated popular demand that government institutions symbolize a beautiful dream within the confines of which principles operate, independently of individuals."[47] It is perhaps desirable to have such an ideal; it is not desirable to act and to teach our students to act as if a myth were in fact real.

9

The United States Supreme Court on Libel

WAYNE C. MINNICK

Wayne C. Minnick is Professor of Communication at Florida State University. His numerous publications in the field of rhetoric and public address include The Art of Persuasion, *2nd ed. (New York: Houghton Mifflin, 1968); chapter 11 of this work concerns "the ethics of persuasion" in a free society. The following essay was published in the* Quarterly Journal of Speech *in November, 1982.*

In recent years many Americans have shown their displeasure with the United States Supreme Court by attacking decisions on such sensitive topics as busing, abortion and school prayer. These dissatisfied Americans accuse the Court of usurping law-making powers not granted to it by the United States Constitution and, thus, mandating social changes that ought to be the sole province of state legislatures or the Congress. The Court, on the other hand, takes the position that the Constitution guarantees citizens certain rights and the Court has a duty to clarify the meaning and implementation of those rights, stating when and under what conditions legislation, or the lack of it, infringes them.

In deference to the Court's position, it must be said that the provisions of the American Constitution need clarification. What, for example, is the meaning of "freedom of speech and of the press" when applied to specific passages of speech or writing alleged to be an exercise of that right? What is "due process of law" in a case where a particular person claims he has been wrongfully deprived of life, liberty or property? In such instances, Justices have had little choice; being forced to decide they have done so pretty much according to their own social philosophies.

Many Court decisions are responses to legislation or to the action of public officials and require that these be measured against constitutional standards. In some instances, however, the Court's decisions seem to fill a void created by inaction on the part of popularly elected legislatures which are paralyzed by the political interests of their members, by the demands of antagonistic pressure groups, or by simple neglect of felt needs. A good example is the problem of reapportionment of state legislatures. In 1946 in *Colegrove v. Green*,[1] the Court held that state and federal electoral districting was a political question and not for the courts to decide. For eighteen years the Court maintained that position, presumably awaiting a political disposition of the problem. None came. In 1964, in *Reynolds v. Sims*,[2] the Court acted, declaring that "the Equal Protection Clause requires that the seats in both houses of a bicameral state legislature must be apportioned on a population basis."[3]

In addition to clarifying the promulgated rights and privileges of the constitution, the Court has made decisions expanding the explicitly stated powers of that instrument to include an array of powers whose existence is only implied by the need to implement guaranteed rights. In this sense, the Court's decisions have provided a substitute for constitutional revision. The founding fathers made the amendment process cumbersome, so hedged with difficulties that reform via that route is exceedingly time consuming and difficult. The 19th Amendment, which gave women the right to vote, was the product of long agitation extending, in organized form, from 1848 to 1920. Yet the Supreme Court has promoted social changes just as profound as woman suffrage by handing down decisions having the force of constitutional amendments. The Court has upheld, for example, actions of the Presidents of the United States that suspended constitutional guarantees of free speech and due process during wartime. Beginning with Abraham Lincoln's executive orders relating to Clement Valandingham and including Roosevelt's internment of Japanese-American citizens in World War II the Court has upheld Presidential exercises of power nowhere expressed or implied in the Constitution itself. Justices have ". . . accepted the proposition that during crisis periods the basic law is subject to suspension and acquiesced in the exercise of whatever power the government deemed necessary to meet the crises successfully."[4]

This tendency of the Court to modify the meaning of vague Constitutional terms and/or to invest the instrument with new, if implied, powers for the purpose of serving an end the Justices think desirable shows up clearly in the Court's policy toward libel as it has grown over the years. This paper will attempt to trace the historical evolution of the Court's libel policy while examining the underlying reasons given in support of it, and will offer some critical judgments about the wisdom of that policy.

Growth of the Court's Policy on Libel

In English law libel was any published utterance that damaged a man's good name and the law applied uniformly either to a private person or a magistrate (or public person). Initially even true statements were considered libelous, but in America by 1735, in the case of John Peter Zenger, a colonial publisher, the right to present evidence concerning the truth of printed statements was established as a defense against a libel charge. It should be noted that libel laws in the United States are not uniform because they are enacted by the separate state legislatures; however since the Zenger case truth has remained a sufficient answer to the charge of libel although some early state laws asserted that, in order not to be libelous, truth had to be published with good motives and for justifiable ends.[5]

Until about 1845, the United States Supreme Court considered the rulings of state courts in libel cases, especially criminal libel, final and not subject to review. States went unmolested and, although they often paid little regard to constitutional guarantees of freedom of speech and press, the Supreme Court did not use that fact as a reason to take jurisdiction. The Court did, however, retain jurisdiction in some civil libel cases that transcended state boundaries. In *White v. Nichols* (1845), a case involving an allegedly libelous letter written by a group of Georgetown residents to the President of the United States protesting the political activities of the Georgetown collector of customs, the Court heard the defense claim that the letter was not libelous because it was about the conduct of a public official, and, therefore, privileged. The Court agreed, saying that publications involving public officials were exceptions to the general laws of libel in that the mere publication of a writing which would be considered libelous in the case of a private person, was not *prime facie* to be considered a libel on a public official. A public official, complaining that he has been libeled, must accept a burden of proof to show "the existence of malice as the true motive" of the defendant's conduct.[6] This case was important for two reasons. First, it singled out malice as a punishable, though not clearly defined motive, and, second, it placed the burden of proof on public officials to prove the existence of malice whereas with private persons malice was implied from the mere publication of odious material. It might be said that in this case the test that was later to be known as the "actual malice rule" was really born.

In 1912, in *Gandia v. Pettingill*, the Supreme Court extended its position requiring proof of malice to newspaper discussion of a public official, as opposed to the letter writing involved in *White v. Nichols*.

The official involved in this instance was a United States district attorney in the territory of Puerto Rico.[7]

Though the above cases established important principles concerning libel law, they applied only to instances in which the alleged libel transcended state lines or occurred in a territory. It was not until 1925 that the Court, in *Gitlow v. New York*, ruled it had the power to review state court decisions on the ground that freedom of speech and press "are among the fundamental rights and liberties protected by the due process clause of the Fourteenth Amendment from impairment in the states;" and, shortly thereafter, in *Near v. Minnesota ex rel Olson*, it reaffirmed this judgment and struck down a Minnesota law imposing prior restraints on the publication of potentially libelous material about public officials.[8] In subsequent years numerous cases arose in which (1) the term public official was variously defined, if only on an *ad hoc* basis, and ultimately expanded to include public figures, (2) an "actual malice" rule was elaborated and clarified, and (3) a rationale was offered for distinguishing between and according different treatment of ordinary citizens and public officials/figures.

Definition and Expansion of the Term, Public Official. In the 1845 *White v. Nichols* case, the Court said public officials were persons elected to office or candidates for office. In 1966, in *Rosenblatt v. Baer*, the Court held that the term public official was not limited to elected officials, but included government employees believed by the public to have substantial responsibility for governmental affairs.[9] This ruling seemed to make every elected or appointed governmental employee at the federal, state and local level, potentially at least, a public official. In clarification one opinion offered the following guideline, "The employee's position must be one which would invite public scrutiny and discussion of the person holding it, entirely apart from the scrutiny and discussion occasioned by the particular charges in controversy."[10] Later the Court failed to reinforce this position in *Hutchinson v. Proxmire*. The district court had held that Hutchinson was a public official because he was Director of Research at the Kalamazoo State Mental Hospital. The Supreme Court disagreed, holding that since the Court of Appeals had not considered this aspect of Hutchinson's case, the issue was not before it. It did state, however, in a footnote, that the term public official "Cannot be thought to include all public employees, however."[11] From inspection of these cases, one has difficulty, after passing from elected officials and certain highly visible appointed officers, in determining who is and who is not to be classified as a public official.

In addition to efforts at defining public official, the Court attempted to specify those aspects of a public official's conduct that could be commented upon under the protection of "privileged communication." In its earliest consideration of this matter, *Gandia v. Pettingill* (1912), the Court said that any comment on an official's private life that pertained to his qualifications for office was a legitimate subject of statement and comment. Later in *New York Times Co. v. Sullivan* the Court held that comments on a public official's "official conduct" were privileged,[12] and in *Garrison v. Louisiana* it went even farther to say that "anything which might touch on an official's fitness for office" was protected.[13] That conduct bearing on fitness-for-office could be very far ranging was made clear in *Monitor Patriot Co. v. Roy* when the Court held that a candidate's conviction for bootlegging twenty-six years prior to his standing for office was relevant and comment about it was to be considered privileged.[14]

As the Court dealt with the reasons for applying different standards of proof to public officials as opposed to private citizens, it was drawn inevitably, perhaps, to recognize that another class of citizens played an important role in public policy determination. These it labeled "public figures," defined as persons who participated prominently in the discussion of public issues, even issues that were not governmental ones. The delineation of "public figures" as a legal entity came about in the Court's decisions with respect to the prominent libel actions in 1967, *Curtis Publishing Co. v. Butts* and *Associated Press v. Walker*.

Butts was Athletic Director at the University of Georgia; however, he was employed by the Georgia Athletic Association, not the State of Georgia, a fact which made it difficult to classify him as a public official. He sued Curtis Publishing because of an article printed in the *Saturday Evening Post* which alleged that he gave away, in an overheard telephone conversation, Georgia football team plays and defensive patterns to the coach of the Alabama team, prior to those schools meeting on the football field. The significant thing about the Court's ruling was that it declared Butts a public figure on the basis of the prominence of his position and required him to meet the same "actual malice" standard that applied to public officials.[15]

Walker's case was somewhat different. Walker had become involved in public resistance to court-mandated admission of the first black student to the University of Mississippi. He appeared on radio and television programs urging defiance of the order and, on the night of the campus demonstration, he was present and highly visible. An AP reporter alleged, in a story about the campus disturbances, that Walker had led the demonstration. Walker disputed this assertion and sued for libel. In the lower courts he won a verdict, but the Supreme Court overturned the award on the ground that Walker had made himself a public figure by "injecting his personality into the vortex of an important public controversy." Hence, he would have to meet the same standard for providing libel as applied to public officials.[16]

So now, to the public official category, the Court had added a group called "public figures," i.e., persons whose positions made them prominent in the discussion of public issues, or persons having the anonymity of private parties but who, on their own initiative, interjected themselves into public controversies.

Elaboration and Clarification of the Actual Malice Standard. The actual malice rule was best stated in *New York Times v. Sullivan* in the following language: "The constitutional guarantees require, we think, a federal rule that prohibits a public official from recovering damages for a defamatory falsehood relating to his official conduct unless he proves that the statement was made with 'actual malice'—that is, with knowledge that it was false or with reckless disregard of whether it was false or not."[17] Later the Court declared "only those false statements made with a high degree of awareness of their probable falsity . . . may be the subject of either civil or criminal sanctions."[18] Lack of ordinary care or negligence in checking facts was not evidence of a high degree of probable falsity, nor was the establishment of "bad or corrupt motives" or "personal spite, ill will or a desire to injure plaintiff."[19] Even "subjective awareness of probable falsity" was insufficient.[20] Instead, convincing proof was required that the source of the alleged libel knew the statement was false and recklessly, but not carelessly or imprudently, disregarded its falsity.

Rationale for Holding Public Officials/Figures to a Standard Different from that Required of Ordinary Citizens. In creating two different classes of citizens and imposing upon one class extremely difficult standards of proof not required of the other, the Court was obliged, in its opinions, to provide reasons justifying the dichotomy. The basic justification was well expressed in *New York Times v. Sullivan*. Here, the Court argued that the First Amendment was "an attempt to secure the widest possible dissemination of information from diverse sources," and recognized "a profound national commitment to the principle that debate on public issues should be uninhibited, robust, and wide-open, and that it may well include vehement, caustic, and sometimes unpleasantly sharp attacks on government and public officials."[21] The Court disagreed with Sullivan's argument that the Constitution did not protect libel by citing a previous decision in which the Court had exercised authority to "nullify action which encroaches on freedom of utterance under the guise of punishing libel."[22] In *Garrison v. Louisiana*, the Court amplified its position, saying, "honest utterance, even if inaccurate, may further the fruitful exercise of the right of free speech,"[23] and, finally, in another case, it maintained that false statements of fact were "inevitable in free debate."[24]

With respect to public figures, the Court said that the public opinion generated by the discussion in which they were involved might be the "only instrument by which society can attempt to influence their conduct;"[25] therefore, the necessity for robust debate on those issues overrode the right of public figures to an easy standard for the protection of their good names.

In summary, it is clear that, in balancing a citizen's right to protect his good name against the need of society for uninhibited debate of public issues, the Court has been willing to sacrifice the former for what it views as a greater good–robust debate. In implementing this preference, the Court's decisions have not been without problems, nor has the Court's assumption of the social value of robust, uninhibited debate been fully demonstrated.

Criticism of the Court's Position on Libel

When the Court said that, because a democracy required robustness of debate, the Constitution afforded less protection against libel to public officials than to private citizens, it assumed a cause and effect proposition that contained serious implications. If holding *public* officials to stringent standards of proof was necessary to insure robust debate, why not hold all public employees, not merely elected ones or ones who were candidates for office, to such a standard? By its own reasoning the Court was impelled toward including all public employees in the actual malice rule, but it still tried to avoid this outcome by saying that the term *public official*, while not clearly defined, did not include all public employees. What the Court did, therefore, was to define public official on a case by case basis, making first a judge and then a jury the determiner of that status. Yet, this was a crucial distinction for both the person uttering the alleged libel and the person seeking redress. Two quite different constitutional standards were at stake and the question: Has libel been committed? was shifted from substantive argument, in large part, to one of classification.

Also, if robustness was desirable in debate of political issues by public officials, should it not be desirable as well in the discussion of all issues affecting public policy by all persons? If it answered affirmatively then, to be consistent, the Court would have to rule that all persons, whether public or private, who engaged in debate of public issues should have their right to recovery for defamation constrained by the actual malice rule.

The Court avoided this when it created "public figures," defined as persons who have "voluntarily exposed themselves to increased risk of injury from defamatory falsehoods . . . by assuming a role of prominence in society or in a particular controversy."[26] This classification still left unanswered questions. If in order to insure robust debate it is necessary to hold some persons who are not public officials to an actual malice rule is it not also necessary, to achieve the same end, to hold all persons discussing important public issues to the same rule? Robust debate, it would seem, is important for public enlightenment because of the nature of the issue, *per se*, rather than because of the position of the participants.

In a plurality decision in *Rosenbloom v. Metromedia*, written by Justice William Brennan, Jr., the force of the above argument was admitted. Brennan wrote: "It is clear that there has emerged from our cases decided since the *New York Times* the concept that the First Amendment's impact upon state libel laws derives not so much from whether the plaintiff is a 'public official,' 'public figure,' or 'private individual' as it derives from the question whether the alleged defamatory publication concerns a matter of public or general interest,"[27] in which case First Amendment restraints would apply. But the reasoning of the plurality in *Metromedia* was shortly repudiated in *Gertz v. Welch* when the Court reaffirmed the dichotomy between the public official/figure and the private citizen. Gertz, who sued Robert Welch as publisher of *American Opinion* magazine, for allegedly libelous statements made in an article Welch had printed, was declared not to be a public official nor a public figure because there was "no clear evidence of general fame or notoriety in the community, and pervasive involvement in the affairs of society."[28] Justices declared that Gertz, because he was a private person, did not have to prove knowing and reckless falsehood, but they did say that in order to collect damages he had to show "competent evidence" of injury to reputation. No presumed damages or punitive damages could be assessed without the plaintiff proving a knowing and reckless disregard of truth.[29] On this basis Gertz's case was sent back for retrial.

Although renouncing the reasoning it had developed in cases leading to and including *Metromedia*, the Court still threw the protection of the First Amendment over publishers sued by private citizens by erecting more stringent requirements for the ascertainment of injury. The private individual didn't have to prove actual malice as did a public official/public figure, but he had to present "competent evidence" of injury which reduced the likelihood of a substantial award and practically eliminated punitive damages unless he assumed a different and heavier burden of proof.[30]

Criticism of the Court's approach to libel would not be complete without examination of the validity of the basic premise used to justify its decisions. The issue can be sharply drawn with this question. Has the Court in its concern to insure debate that is free, robust and untrammeled by anxious concern about possible libel action, improved the public's ability to make responsible decisions on public issues? The Court has assumed that its decisions have done just that. There seems, however, to be some confusion in the Justices' minds about the propriety of widespread tolerance for error of *opinion* and *ideas* versus error of *fact*. When the Court assumes that the widest latitude for diversity of opinion and idea is essential to quality in public discussion, it appears to be on sound ground. In *Gertz v. Welch*, the Court said: "There is no such thing as a false idea" nor could there be anything libelous in error of opinion. However pernicious an opinion may seem, we depend for its correction, not on the conscience of judges or juries, but on the competition of other ideas." But it went on to say that although opinions and fact were different, false statements of fact were "inevitable in free debate" and, therefore, the media could not, under the First Amendment, "be required to accept liability for proving the truth of all injurious factual statements."[31]

The standards of journalism encouraged by the Courts' dictum that false statements of facts are "inevitable in free debate" are certainly not high standards and may even be said to encourage the press to use unreliable sources and utter poorly investigated charges. A few opinions regarding press responsibility gleaned from various cases will illustrate the Courts' willingness to protect careless journalism. In *New York Times v. Sullivan* the Court acknowledged that the evidence would support a finding of "negligence in failing to discover the misstatements" of the open letter which was the cause of the action but held that this was "insufficient to show the recklessness that is required for a finding of actual malice."[32] In *Beckley Newspapers Corporation v. Hanks* the Court said failure of a publisher to make a prior investigation of alleged facts which the publisher supposed to be true but which were actually false was not sufficient to establish actual malice.[33] In *St. Amant v. Thompson*, it was held that actual malice could not be measured by "what a reasonably prudent man would have published or would have investigated before publishing,"[34] and this conclusion was reiterated and reinforced in *Metromedia*. In *Garrison v. Louisiana* the Court held that misstatements that arose out of hatred, anger, or ill will were protected by the Constitution. In the same ruling it held that a lack of reasonable belief in a statement's truth was not sufficient proof of actual malice, but only of lack of ordinary care. The Court then said: "The test we laid down in *New York Times* is not keyed to ordinary care; defeasance of the privilege is conditioned, not on mere negligence, but on reckless disregard of truth."[35] In *Gertz v. Welch* "Subjective awareness of probable falsity"[36] was declared protected, one presumes, by a showing of hatred, anger, or ill will.

In the Butts case, with respect to public figures, four Justices tried to establish a rule requiring a publisher to show reasonable care before publishing a potentially libelous assertion of fact. They would have denied First Amendment protection for publishers "on a showing of highly unreasonable conduct constituting an extreme departure from standards of investigation and reporting adhered to by responsible publishers."[37] But the majority, while admitting the *Post* showed a serious lack of good journalistic practice, rejected the suggested rule, and based the decisions on "reckless disregard" because the *Post* had substantial evidence, before publishing, that the charge was false. They thus avoided condemning the *Post* for shoddy journalism.

In all of this exegesis of the actual malice doctrine, the Court seems to have distinguished two kinds of false factual statements. There is one kind, called honest utterance, that springs from exuberance in debate, carelessness, political bias, or possibly from spite, and of whose falsity the communicator is unaware, or at worst probably only subjectively aware. Another kind is the lie, "knowingly and deliberately published." The former, the honest utterance, says the Court, "even if inaccurate, may further the fruitful exercise of the right of free speech" while the latter does not.[38]

One could raise the question, how is it that false facts are fruitful when uttered honestly i.e. without awareness of their falsity, but pernicious if uttered knowingly? One would think that false facts in public debate are undesirable regardless of the purveyor's state of mind concerning them. One can logically go with such a distinction if "fruitful" means, as it certainly does, "abundant," and abundance in debate is all one cares about. But if "fruitful" also means that public debate should be based upon good evidence, a qualitative dimension must be reckoned with. Does abundant debate, regardless of quality of evidence, produce responsible public policy? If debate consisted merely of ideas and opinions one might say, yes, because an abundance of ideas and opinions is the means by which poorly thought-out ideas and reckless opinions are exposed. But what is the corrective for false statement of fact about the conduct and qualifications of persons? The law of libel is the *prima facie* corrective, but in placing rigorous standards for proof of libel upon public officials and public figures the Court has, to a large extent, denied such persons that recourse. We are supposed to tolerate this condition on the assumption that abundance of debate on public issues overrides the right of public officials/figures to use the same corrective for false and injurious statements open to private citizens.

It might also be argued that the situation is tolerable because public officials and public figures have some way of correcting libelous statements not available to private citizens. Such a corrective might be ready access to the media for purposes of rebutting a libel, and, in some cases, the Court seemed to be offering that kind of reasoning. It held in *Farmer's Cooperative v. WDAY, Inc.* that libel laws do not apply to statements made when the electronic media are complying with equal time requirements.[39] But for obvious reasons, this could not be extended to the press which had no legal responsibility to allow rebuttal in its pages to allegedly defamed public officials. In another case, *Gertz v. Welch*, the Court said that the states have a greater interest in protecting common people from libel because they did not have access to the media to combat defamatory falsehoods as do public people. But it never made this reason into a justification equivalent to the "robust debate" formulation which remained the crux of its position.

In several instances where the Court has refused or reversed libel judgments, evidence can be found suggesting that the constitutionally protected but careless publication of false facts may have had an adverse effect upon the decisions the public was obliged to make. In 1971 the *Ocala Star-Banner v. Damron* case was decided against Damron. The facts were these: Leonard Damron was mayor of Crystal City, Florida which was served by the *Ocala Star-Banner*, and he was also candidate for tax assessor. He was accused by the paper of having been indicted in federal court for perjury. His brother James was in fact the person who had been indicted, and as originally written the story named James as that person. However, a new area editor who had handled several stories about Leonard, but had never heard of James, assumed that the reporter had made a mistake and changed the name to Leonard. Leonard sued and the lower courts awarded him a libel judgment, but the Supreme Court overturned the judgment saying that Leonard failed to show that the newspaper acted with knowledge of falsity or reckless disregard of falsity.[40] It seems difficult, in this instance, to argue that the public's decision in choosing a tax assessor was enhanced by debate that, while fruitful, gave the electors false information upon which to act.

Ill informed charges printed in a newspaper editorial were protected in another Supreme Court case, *Beckley Newspaper Corporation v. Hanks* in 1967. *The Beckley Post Herald* printed an editorial charging Hanks, who was standing for reelection to public office, with threatening a newspaperman and a woman official. When, at the trial, it was shown that these charges were baseless, the newspaper publisher testified that no investigation of the charges had been made, but "it was our opinion that that was as near the facts and truth as we could get."[41] The Court reversed the libel judgment of the lower court and said the papers' failure to make prior investigation was not proof of reckless disregard of truth. Although Hanks' reelection campaign has been seriously tarnished, and the people of his community misled about his qualifications for office, the Court continued to justify its position on the robust and fruitful debate principle.

One must look carefully at the kind of message the Supreme Court had been sending to the media concerning debate on public issues. It seems to be this: Broadcasters and publishers should have the utmost freedom to present all matters of fact and opinion relating to a public issue. No idea or opinion can ever be considered libelous. False facts, however, while possibly libelous *per se*, are inevitable in public debate and the media should not be intimidated by too strict a standard of accountability. Only deliberate, knowing lies are to be punished. Carelessness, lack of investigation, lack of reasonable prudence, existence of malice and ill will, even "subjective" knowledge of falsity—none of these is grounds for a libel judgment if the plaintiff is a public official or a public figure. This message may be interpreted as an opportunity to defame public persons with impunity. The existence of false facts in public debate may indeed be inevitable, as the Court asserts, but should the media be given a license tending to make the publication of falsehood endemic?

The Court needs to reexamine its notion of what constitutes good debate in democratic society. Prolixity, abundance, quantity are not the only indices of robust debate. If one takes robust to mean "healthy," then quality as well as quantity has to be considered. Have the Court's decisions neglected quality in devotion to quantity? The foregoing discussion seems to suggest strongly that they have. The unfortunate thing about it all is that, not only has the quality of public debate been neglected, but a whole class of American citizens called public officials and public figures has been deprived, on a dubious premise, of the equal protection of the laws guaranteed them by the Fourteenth Amendment.

Is it possible to change the Court's handling of libel cases so that some of the problems of present practice are avoided? Any new policy would need to meet certain tests. For instance, it should not inhibit debate on public issues by encouraging frivolous and intimidating libel actions, but, likewise, it should not suggest that some classes of citizens are fair game for defamation because standards of proof to establish libel are, for them, almost impossibly high. Further, it should recognize that while public debate may be vehement, caustic and sharp, even vitriolic in opinion, publishers and broadcasters cannot use that fact as an excuse to sacrifice reasonable standards of investigation and ordinary prudence in the handling of potentially defamatory charges.

Within this framework the Court might substitute for the "actual malice" rule, a standard that false assertions are libelous whenever there is clear failure to adhere to ordinary standards of investigation and reporting expected of responsible publishers. This rule would erase the double standard that now separates public persons and private persons and extricate the Court from its present illogic which holds that, in the debate of public issues, a private person can be defamed by a statement published in a given set of circumstances while a public person, made the object of the same statement in exactly the same circumstances, cannot. In addition, the Court could limit general libel awards, for all persons, to actual damages and require competent evidence of damage to reputation. Finally, punitive damages would be awarded only on demonstration of "actual malice" in decisions to publish or "gross" negligence in investigation, and would be limited in amount to some figure justified by the extent of actual damages.

The elements of this proposal have already been supported by various justices, at one time or another, in dissenting opinions. As was previously indicated, four justices, in connection with the Butts case would have denied First Amendment protection for publishers "on a showing of highly unreasonable conduct constituting an extreme departure from standards of investigation and reporting adhered to by responsible publishers."[42] In *Rosenbloom v. Metromedia*, three justices expressed the view that lack of reasonable care, which was the basis of the jury's decision in the lower court, was a proper rule for deciding whether to invoke constitutional privilege in cases involving private persons.[43] Indeed, Justice Harlan wrote, "To begin with, it does no violence, in my judgment, to the value of freedom of speech and press to impose a duty of reasonable care upon those who would exercise these freedoms. I do not think it can be gainsaid that the States have a substantial interest in encouraging speakers to carefully seek the truth before they communicate, as well as in compensating persons actually harmed by false descriptions of their personal behavior."[44]

Thus, some justices saw the importance of discouraging careless reporting and recognized the possibility that another standard than actual malice would be appropriate in instances involving private persons. An extension of this view to include public persons/public figures would be warranted if the distinction between public and private persons were found to be unsound.

Referring again to opinions in the Rosenbloom case, a plurality of justices declared that an artificial barrier had been built up between public and private persons. One justice wrote: "If a matter is a subject of public or general interest, it cannot suddenly become less so merely because a private individual is involved, or because in some sense the individual did not choose to become 'voluntarily' involved. The public's primary interest is in the event; the public focus is on the conduct of the participant, and the content, effect and significance of the conduct, not the participant's prior anonymity or notoriety."[45] If the public/private distinction is a legal fiction how can one justify a double standard for the two categories?

Other justices have recognized that a factor seriously chilling democratic debate is less an actual conviction for libel than the magnitude of damages often awarded. A jury, for instance, awarded Butts $60,000 in actual damages and $3 million in punitive damages. In another case, Rosenbloom, whose award was overturned by the Court, had received $25,000 in general damages and $750,000 in punitive damages. Although it is common for judges to reduce these awards (Butts' award was subsequently reduced to $460,000 total) the intimidating effect of such figures is substantial. Of outsized awards Justice Marshall wrote, "The unlimited discretion exercised by juries in awarding punitive and presumed damages compounds the problem of self-censorship that necessarily results from the awarding of huge judgments. This discretion allows juries to penalize heavily the unorthodox and the unpopular and exact little from others. Such free wheeling discretion presents obvious and basic threats to society's interest in freedom of the press."[46] Marshall and Stewart, in this same case, would have allowed no punitive damages and would have limited all damages to actual injuries.[47] Harlan would have sanctioned punitive damages if private individuals proved actual malice, but even then punitive damages would have to show "a reasonable and purposeful relationship to the actual harm done."[48] In a later case, *Gertz v. Welch*, the Court criticized the awarding to Gertz of $50,000 in compensatory damages because he had shown no evidence that he had been actually injured,[49] and used that complaint as a reason, in part, to return the case to a lower court.

The application of a reasonable care standard would be no more intimidating, in fact probably less intimidating than application of the actual malice standard. The actual malice standard requires plaintiffs to focus on the mental set or state of mind of the defendant which sometimes can be inferred from his actions but frequently cannot. This induced the Court in *Hebert v. Lando*[50] to acknowledge the right to inquire into a defendant's state of mind, a decision which evoked widespread expressions of fear from media representatives. A reasonable care standard would require no such intimidating right. While probably not definable *a priori*, reasonable care can be ascertained by the use of already noted guidelines such as fabricated stories, unverified phone calls, dependence without investigation upon sources whose truthfulness is questionable, use of allegations so improbable that a reasonable person would investigate before publishing, etc. All of these have at one time or another been cited in Supreme Court opinions. Further guidelines would be established case by case.

Not every publication of false fact would be grounds for an award. In *New York Times v. Sullivan*, for example, the Court held that the *Times* had followed normal procedures in checking the advertisement that was the cause of Sullivan's action. It was checked routinely by the *Times'* Advertising Accountability Department and found to contain no personal attacks, and the *Times* relied on the good reputation of the sponsors.[51] Only serious departures from reasonable standard of investigation would be actionable, and, while a "serious departure" is open to debate it can be settled by objective criteria rather than by state of mind inferences. Moreover, the policy would apply uniformly to public as well as to private persons and force argument into substantive reasons rather than into ones of classification.

Finally, damage awards, in cases of infraction, would not likely be of a magnitude that could threaten the financial stability of a publishing house or broadcasting station, or, conceivably, cause their failure. But they would not be so insubstantial as to lack deterrence. Damages would be keyed to financial injury and/or injury to reputation. Such things as "impairment of reputation and standing in the community, personal humiliation, and mental anguish and suffering"[52] would be considered, as they always have been, but some evidence other than plaintiff's mere assertion would be necessary. Such evidence, it can be expected, would be unlikely to produce million dollar awards either in actual or in punitive damages; but substantial awards, upon demonstrated injury, would still be forthcoming.

The effect of such a policy on public debate ought to be beneficial. The policy erects safeguards to prevent frivolous and intimidating libel suits. These are such that the robustness of public debate should be unaffected, because publishers and broadcasters, while being put on notice that they can more readily be held accountable for defaming public officials, will know that accountability requires no more than adherence to reasonable and prudent journalistic practices. Moreover, they will know that damages, in cases of infractions, will not likely be of magnitude that could threaten the financial stability of their company or its possible destruction.

Though quantity of public debate should be undiminished, its quality should improve. Greater reliance should be placed upon reliable sources at the expense of doubtful ones, potentially libelous assertions of fact should be more thoroughly investigated before a publication decision is made, and a greater reluctance should exist to disseminate uninvestigated rumour.[53] All of this, of course, depends upon the willingness of Justices to revise their notion of what constitutes "good" public debate. If "good" is no more than uninhibited, they will probably stick with present practice, but if "good" means not only uninhibited but includes a preference for prudent standards of investigation and verification of evidence, then a new and better policy may emerge.

10

Protecting Political Speech: Brandenburg v. Ohio *Updated*

PAUL SIEGEL

Paul Siegel teaches in the Department of Communication at Illinois State University where his classroom responsibilities include a course dealing with freedom of speech. He is the former executive director of the Kansas and Western Missouri affiliate of the American Civil Liberties Union. His publications include "Privacy: Control over Stimulus Input, Stimulus Output, and Self-Regarding Conduct," Buffalo Law Review *33 (1985): 35 ff. The following essay, which was first published in the* Quarterly Journal of Speech *in February 1981, has been revised and updated for this anthology.*

The current test used by the Supreme Court in determining whether or not a particular act of advocacy should enjoy first amendment protection was set forth in *Brandenburg v. Ohio*.[1] In a per curiam opinion, a unanimous Court overturned Brandenburg's conviction for having advocated anti-black violence to a gathering of his KKK cohorts. In so doing, the Court ruled that the states may not prohibit or proscribe political speech unless such speech "is directed to inciting or producing imminent lawless action, and is likely to produce such action."[2]

Implicitly, any advocacy which falls short of a call for illegal action is wholly protected (assuming it does not fall into other categories of unprotected speech, such as libel or obscenity). More crucially, speech which does call for illegal action can still be protected if either of these two conditions obtains: (a) the illegal action is not being sought *immediately*, or (b) there is reason to believe that the listeners will not actually commit the illegal action.

As Hans Linde notes, the Court phrased its decision in *Brandenburg* so as to suggest that it was really saying nothing new.[3] Thus, in pointing out that the earlier decision in *Whitney v. California*[4] had been "thoroughly discredited"[5] in later verdicts, the Court suggested that those later decisions themselves (especially *U.S. v. Dennis*[6]) had already "fashioned a principle"[7] to be set forth explicitly in *Brandenburg*.

Staughton Lynd correctly points out, however, that it is the very *combination* of the requirements of "incitement to illegal action" and that the unlawfulness sought be "imminent" which is itself the unique feature of *Brandenburg*.[8] Thus, in *Schenck v. U.S.*,[9] the Court seemed to permit states a great amount of latitude in the regulation of political advocacy: "The question in every case is whether the words are used in such circumstances and are of such a nature as to create a clear and present danger they will bring about the substantial evils that Congress has a right to prevent."[10] Note that there is no reference to purposeful "incitement" here; rather, it is the nature of the "circumstances" that will produce the feared danger.

Almost forty years later, in *Yates v. U.S.*,[11] the Court seemed to suggest quite a different standard. For advocacy to be punishable under the *Yates* doctrine, those to whom it is addressed "must be urged to do something, now or in the future, rather than merely to believe in something."[12] Here the "imminence" requirement implicit in the "clear and *present* danger" test is discarded completely, as the Court makes clear that the illegal action sought may very well be future action. The *Yates* Court, however, does require that the speaker must explicitly *seek* such action on the listener's part, a protection rejected in the earlier "nature of the circumstances" doctrine from *Schenck*.

In *Brandenburg*, of course, we have both references to "imminence" *and* to the speaker's explicit seeking of illegality ("directed to inciting"). Thus the *Brandenburg* Court combines the two earlier protections.

The purpose of this essay is to describe the manner in which the courts have interpreted and applied *Brandenburg* since it was handed down in 1969. Every U.S. Supreme Court and federal appellate ruling in which the landmark decision has been cited constituted the primary research materials.[13] Answers to the following four queries were sought:

1) How imminent need "imminent" be? Do speakers forfeit first amendment protection only when they demand that their listeners engage in illegality immediately?
2) Has the speaker's intention been construed as part of the *Brandenburg* test, or can speakers be held accountable for consequences that a reasonable person should have realized would result from an act of advocacy?
3) Do advocacy of violent lawless actions (such as those for which

Brandenburg himself was initially convicted) and advocacy of nonviolent crimes (e.g., tax evasion) or even victimless crimes (e.g., fornication or sodomy) receive different treatment by the courts?
4) Are some settings more protected than others (e.g., the military, the prisons, and the campuses)?

The Eminence of Imminence

The *Brandenburg* test dictates that political speech can be curtailed only if the speaker appears to be advocating imminent lawless action. Moreover, the "likely to produce *such* action" language suggests that, not only must the illegality be sought immediately, but it must also be immediately forthcoming. How seriously have the courts heeded these requirements?

Of all cases reviewed, the one in which the *Brandenburg* test was applied in its purest form was *Hess v. Indiana*,[14] involving an anti-Vietnam War demonstration on the Indiana University campus in Bloomington. In overturning Hess' conviction, the Supreme Court took very careful note of the precise words uttered by the appellant. Hess was overheard to yell at the demonstrators, in response to the police having barricaded the street, that "we'll take the fucking street later." (Some witnesses heard "again" for "later."[15]) The Supreme Court overruled, offering this interpretation of Hess' utterance: "At best, the statement could be taken as counsel for present moderation. At worst, it amounted to nothing more than advocacy of illegal action *at some indefinite future time.*"[16]

Another case in which the "imminence" requirement received special attention is *Eisenstadt v. Baird*.[17] The case involved a lecture given by population planning advocate Bill Baird, during which he handed a tube of contraceptive foam to one of the women in his audience. Inasmuch as fornication was a crime in Massachusetts, the local sheriff arrested Baird for inciting the woman to commit such a crime. The Supreme Court, in affirming the Court of Appeals' earlier reversal of Baird's original conviction, relied upon a two-pronged argument.

The Court's first contention was that, since the official charge against Baird was providing contraceptives to an unmarried woman, the issue of whether or not that law was an effective deterrent against fornication had to be addressed. The Court found the law an ineffective one, in that married persons could use the contraceptives they purchased legally to engage in illegal, extramarital relationships.

The second line of reasoning asserted that, even if Baird's action was an instance of disobeying an *effective* statute, that action was still protected, in that one could not conclude with certainty that imminent lawless action was in the offing. Indeed, had the sheriff not so swiftly arrested Baird, the woman might simply have examined the tube of contraceptive foam and handed it back to Baird.[18]

The alleged advocacy of sexual practices frowned upon by society was also very much at issue in a 1985 case that many observers thought would produce the first ruling by the Supreme Court in the area of gay rights in almost 20 years. *National Gay Task Force v. Board of Education*[19] found the gay rights group seeking a declaratory judgment that a statute affecting the first amendment rights of teachers in Oklahoma was unconstitutional. The statute provided for, among other things, the termination of public school teachers whose statements "advocated," "promoted," or "encouraged" public or private homosexual activity if such statements were likely to come to the attention of students or coworkers.[20]

The Tenth Circuit Court of Appeals invalidated this portion of the statute, and the Supreme Court affirmed that judgment (by a 4-4 vote, thus not providing a nationwide precedent and not giving us a hint as to which Justices voted which way and why). Concerning *Brandenburg*'s imminence requirement, the appellate court indicated that "the first amendment does not permit someone to be punished for advocating illegal conduct at some indefinite future time."[21] The court was clearly troubled by the tremendous breadth of proscribed first amendment activities covered by this statute:

> A teacher who went before the Oklahoma legislature or appeared on television to repeal the Oklahoma anti-sodomy statute would be "advocating," "promoting" and "encouraging" homosexual sodomy and creating a substantial risk that his or her speech would come to the attention of school children.... Such statements, which are aimed at legal and social change, are at the core of first amendment protections.[22]

There is a series of decisions involving the attempts of "fringe" political groups to use a public facility for a planned meeting, and in which explicit reference is made to *Brandenburg*'s imminence requirement. Representative of such cases is *Collin v. Chicago Park District*,[23] in which a local Nazi group won the right to rally in Chicago's Marquette Park. The city's brief had argued that at least one of Collin's previous demonstrations had produced a good deal of violence, and that a permit could be denied on those grounds. The Seventh Circuit Court of Appeals rejected this reasoning, however: "The fact that plaintiff and/or his followers apparently had taken relish in breaking up downtown peace rallies is not indicative of how they would act at a rally in a neighborhood more sympathetic to them in which the bulk of their supporters reside."[24]

In the Nazi case, then, past violence could not be used to predict "imminent" *future* violence. This doctrine was not adhered to in *Krause v. Rhodes*,[25] in which the parents of the four Kent State victims sued the governor of Ohio. The parents' most relevant argument for present purposes is that their children's first amendment rights had been violated when the students were prohibited from demonstrating on the day of the shootings. The Circuit Court's reaction:

> In /the parents'/ view, prior restraint is never justified, and the authorities must always indulge the presumption that the next assembly will be peaceful, no matter how violent the preceeding ones have been. That is not the law, particularly in a school or college setting.[26]

The apparent contradiction in "imminence" criteria between *Collin* and *Krause* lies in this reference to the peculiarities of the school or college setting. We will return to this issue in a later section.

Whether instances of past violence could be used under *Brandenburg* to predict future violence was also very much at issue in *Alliance to End Repression v. City of Chicago*,[27] in which the activist group sought to have the federal courts invalidate then-Attorney General Smith's proposed new guidelines governing when the FBI would be justified in initiating an investigation against a political group. The Alliance's argument was that the proposed guidelines violated the spirit, if not the letter, of a previous consent decree imposed upon the FBI when it had been caught spying on such groups as the ACLU and the NAACP. That earlier judgment had provided that "the FBI shall not conduct an investigation solely on the basis of activities protected by the First Amendment."[28]

The Smith guidelines, after paraphrasing the restrictions imposed upon the agency by the earlier decision, added the following qualifying statement: "When, however, statements advocate criminal activity or indicate an apparent attempt to engage in crimes of violence, an investigation may be warranted unless it is apparent, from the circumstances or the context in which the statements are made, that there is no prospect of harm."[29]

The Seventh Circuit Court of Appeals sided with the Administration, and in so doing seemed to cast the imminence requirement from *Brandenburg* aside completely:

> /The FBI/ may investigate any group that advocates the commission, *even if not immediately*, of terrorist acts in violation of

federal law. It need not wait till the bombs begin to go off or even till the bomb factory is found. . . . The FBI cannot hope to nip terrorist conspiracies in the bud if it may not investigate proto-terrorist organizations.[30]

The court did, however, recognize that this would appear to be a departure from established doctrine concerning the level of first amendment protection granted political advocacy. *Brandenburg*, the court rejoinded, was never meant to apply to situations other than those in which activists would suffer "punitive measures" for the advocacy. Being the subject of an FBI investigation is not a punitive measure.[31]

Perhaps the key to understanding this dilution of the *Brandenburg* test can be found in the court's reference to "terrorist" activities and to "bombs." Such words call to mind the most heinous kinds of violence imaginable. As we shall see in a later section, the court quite consciously intended to draw a line between advocacy of violent and nonviolent illegality.

The final case demanding our attention in our attempt to assess judicial handling of the "imminence" requirement under *Brandenburg* provides a change of pace from the terrorists and the Nazis and the bombs. In *Cinevision Corporation v. City of Burbank*,[32] the contracted-for use of a municipal amphitheatre was denied because the City Council of Burbank determined that such "hard rock" artists as Jackson Browne, Patti Smith and Todd Rundgren would attract antinuclear fanatics, drug users, and "homosexual crowds."[33] The Ninth Circuit Court of Appeals felt justified under *Brandenburg*'s imminence requirement to conclude that "a *general* fear" that laws might be broken or that the wrong kinds of persons would tend to congregate "cannot justify a content-based restriction on expression."[34]

Judicial Attention to Speaker's Intention

Under the *Brandenburg* test, a speaker's first amendment rights may be curtailed if his or her utterance "is directed" towards incitement. The test is phrased in the passive voice, and this may be significant. When someone *incites* us, or *directs* us, to do something, we feel justified in attributing intentionality to the speaker. Indeed, common parlance probably does not even recognize the possibility of accidental incitement.

We are less certain about intention when confronting the passive voice. If the speech in question "*is directed*" to inciting or producing illegality, is someone doing the directing, or is the incitement to be found somehow in the words themselves? This section examines cases which have cited *Brandenburg* and in which some concern is expressed by the courts regarding the speaker's intention.

Perhaps the most illuminating case is *U.S. v. Kelner*.[35] Russell Kelner was a leader of the Jewish Defense League charged with threatening the life of PLO leader Yasser Arafat. In November of 1974, Arafat was to arrive in New York for a United Nations assembly. A reporter for New York's Channel 11, WPIX (which has a three-state viewing area), covered a news conference given by Kelner, who was dressed in military fatigues and had a .38 caliber "police special" visibly nearby. The television account of Kelner's words included the following:

> We have people who have been trained and who are out now and who intend to make sure that Arafat and his lieutenants do not leave this country alive. I am talking about justice . . . equal rights under the law. . . . We are planning to assassinate Mr. Arafat. . . . Everything is planned in detail. . . . It's going to come off.[36]

Kelner was convicted under a federal statute prohibiting the transmission "in interstate commerce" of any communication that threatened the kidnapping or injury of another person.[37]

Two of the arguments set forth by Kelner in his unsuccessful appeal dealt with the intention issue. First, he maintained that he himself had no control over his statement's being transmitted across state lines, only WPIX could do that. Secondly, he asserted that there was no threat intended by his words, which should more accurately be seen as mere political hyperbole.

The court swiftly dismissed the first argument, concluding in effect that any reasonable person should have known that when you hold a press conference in a major media outlet, interstate transmissions of communication will likely result.[38] Kelner's "political hyperbole" defense received far more attention, although it too was eventually rejected. The court admitted at the outset that there can be such a thing as a speech that sounds like a threat but is not one. To be a "true threat," the court held, an utterance must be "so unequivocal, unconditional, immediate, and specific as to the person threatened as to convey a gravity of purpose and imminent prospect of execution."[39] The court further held that the *words themselves* were capable of expressing an "intention of being carried out."[40]

In *Kelner*, then, the court claims to adhere to the *Brandenburg* test, interpreting that test so as to require a finding of intention on the part of the speaker. Whereas this court handily avoids the difficult issue of assessing Kelner's sincerity by finding the intention in his words themselves, a 1984 judicial opinion goes so far as to conclude that the *Brandenburg* test does not apply at all to "threatening" utterances. In *U.S. vs. Howell*,[41] an inpatient at a state hospital in Texas had been convicted of threatening the life of the President, an action explicitly covered by federal statute. "It's too bad that John Hinckley did not get him," Mr. Howell confided in an FBI investigator.[42] In upholding Howell's conviction, the federal appeals court said:

> Far from attempting to influence others, Howell was merely stating his own unambiguous and apparently quite serious intention to take the life of the President.... While Howell's statements may have been unlikely to incite or produce imminent lawless action, the *Brandenburg* test applies by its terms to advocacy, *not to threats* such as those made by Howell.[43]

In 1976, a difference of opinion surrounding the attribution of intention in a classic first amendment battle between freedom of speech and freedom of the press prompted an almost comic exchange between two judges in the Fifth Circuit Court of Appeals. In *MGA v. Goudelock*[44], the Mississippi Gay Alliance sought to place an ad in the campus newspaper (the *Reflector*) at Mississippi State University. Student-editor Bill Goudelock refused to accept the ad, which would have advised the *Reflector's* readers that MGA offered "counseling, legal aid, and a library of homosexual literature." Judge Coleman, writing for the majority and upholding Goudelock's editorial prerogative, pointed out that "... the advertisement tendered by the Gay Alliance offered *legal* aid. Such an offer is open to various interpretations, one of which is that criminal activity is contemplated, necessitating the aid of counsel."[45] Judge Goldberg, in his dissent, replied: "The suggestion ... that the criminal taint in the ad is demonstrated by the offer of "legal aid" implies a presumption of illegality whenever lawyers are involved—surely the level of respect for the profession has not yet reached this nadir."[46]

Although the bulk of the court's time in *MGA* was spent determining that Goudelock functioned independently enough of the university administration so as to remove "state's action" from his editorial judgment, it is interesting to note the judges' perceived need to say something about the "speaker's" intentions, under *Brandenburg*.

One set of cases in which the speaker's intention was wholly ignored also involved gay groups. Representative of this set is *Gay Lib vs.*

University of Missouri,⁴⁷ in which the plaintiffs sought official recognition as an organization. The university argued, and called in expert witnesses to testify, that taking such a step would lead to an increase in the number of sodomy violations. The closest thing to an "utterance" examined by the court was the gay group's Statement of Purposes. Predictably, "incitement to commit illegal acts" was not a formally stated purpose of the group.

Although the Circuit Court of Appeals overturned the lower court, thus compelling the university to recognize the gay group, it did so on the grounds that defendants had failed to establish a plausible nexus between such recognition and sodomy statute violations.⁴⁸ The implication, of course, is that had such a nexus been more convincingly established, the ruling may have been a different one, the gay group's intentions notwithstanding.

Advocacy of Non-Violent Illegality

We proposed at the outset to compare the courts' handling of true criminal syndicalism (typically involving advocacy of rioting or other violent illegality) with their handling of non-violent, often victimless, advocacy. The comparison will be strained, however, because so few *Brandenburg* citations involve actual prosecutions for the advocating of truly violent illegality.

Moreover, those cases that do involve the kinds of violent illegality for which Brandenburg himself was convicted tend to have been decided on technicalities, or skirted altogether. Thus, in *Krause v. Rhodes*, the Kent State case, the Sixth Circuit Court of Appeals based its final decision upon charges of jury tampering. In *U.S. v. Dellinger*,⁴⁹ the Chicago Seven conspiracy trial, the convictions were overturned on the grounds that the original judge had failed to adequately screen jurors in the voir dire process. In the two remaining criminal syndicalism cases citing *Brandenburg*, the federal courts refused to intervene in what they saw as ongoing state investigations.⁵⁰

Still, some clues can be gleaned from the language in decisions involving non-violent advocacy. One clear statement is found in *U.S. v. Buttorff*,⁵¹ a case involving a defendant charged with travelling the country, lecturing on methods of cheating on income tax reporting. Upholding Buttorff's conviction, the Eighth Circuit Court of Appeals opined:

> Although the speeches here do not incite the type of imminent lawless activity referred to in criminal syndicalism cases, the de-

fendants did go beyond mere advocacy of tax reform. They explained how to avoid withholding and their speeches and explanations incited several individuals to activity that violated the law.[52]

In *Buttorff*, then, the court is attempting to say that advocacy of violent and non-violent illegality will be treated the same. The court's analogy is a bit flawed, however, given the reference to "mere advocacy of tax *reform*." Under *Brandenburg*, of course, even the advocacy of inarguably illegal tax return preparation might be protected—as long as the "imminence" and "likely to produce" illegal action standards are not met.

More recent cases have attempted to fine tune the *Buttorff* doctrine. In *U.S. v. Dahlstrom*,[53] for example, the conviction on advocacy of tax evasion charges was overturned, in that the legality of the specific "tax shelters" at issue was not clearly settled as a matter of law. Less fortunate was the criminal defendant in *U.S. v. Holecek*,[54] who was found not only to have advocated tax evasion, but also to have practiced it. The Eighth Circuit Court of Appeals had no difficulty concluding that such conduct simply removed the case entirely "from the ambit of both *Brandenburg* and the First Amendment."[55]

As was previously mentioned, the Supreme Court's handling of *NGTF v. Board of Education*[56] left the appellate court's ruling intact but without the force of a majority opinion from the high court. The arguments raised by the advocates in that case before the Supreme Court are highly relevant to our current discussion of violent vs. non-violent illegality.

The Oklahoma statute, it will be recalled, would have permitted the firing of any teacher who "advocated" or "encouraged" the commission of sodomy. Harvard's Professor Laurence Tribe, who argued the case for the gay rights group, felt that the first amendment relevance of such a statute could be seen most clearly when contrasted with the more violent kinds of illegality originally covered by the *Brandenburg* test:

> This Court has long since held that the first amendment forbids the proscription of mere abstract advocacy of, or mere expression of belief in, even the criminal overthrow of the government by force and violence. . . . If such protection is accorded even speech advocating criminal terrorism and sabotage against our government, clearly no less can be accorded speech abstractly advocating, encouraging, or promoting intimate and consensual homosexual activity which, although deemed a crime in Oklahoma, has been decriminalized by over half the states.[57]

In *NAACP v. Claiborne Hardware Company*,[58] the most relevant question posed was whether those who led a long-term boycott of white merchants could be held accountable for the occasional violent incidents associated with the boycott. In other words, can advocacy of non-violent conduct be actionable when it results in violent conduct? Despite the fact that organizer Charles Evers' speechmaking was seen by some as in fact a call for violent illegality, the Court viewed it otherwise: "Strong and effective extemporaneous rhetoric cannot be nicely channeled in purely dulcet phrases," the Court reminded us.[59]

We have already seen how in *Alliance to End Repression v. City of Chicago*,[60] the Seventh Circuit Court of Appeals ruled that the FBI may commence investigations against political groups that advocate illegality. One impetus for the litigation, it will be recalled, was an earlier consent decree entered into by the FBI when it was found to have engaged in surveillance against the ACLU and other political groups. The Court of Appeals makes a fascinating reference to that earlier case when it tries to comfort the unsuccessful litigants that the FBI is not being unleashed to again embark upon illegal campaigns of surveillance: "The organizations that the decree sought to protect, organizations such as the ACLU and the NAACP, do not go around making threats to commit *violent* acts, and are not the acorns from which grow such trees as the FALN, the Posse Comitatus, . . . and the White Knights of the Ku Klux Klan. . . ."[61]

From the court's point of view, the opinion continued, the FBI was not being empowered to begin investigations based solely upon the advocacy of non-violent illegality. So should a future set of facts arise, in which an unfriendly FBI official concludes (rightly or wrongly) that the ACLU is "advocating draft resistance" and opens an investigatory file on that basis, the ACLU would be able to bring suit just as it had in the earlier case.[62] In this case, advocacy of violent and of non-violent illegality does appear to be handled differently.

The general rule, however, appears to be more in keeping with the *Buttorff* doctrine of treating the two kinds of advocacy identically under the *Brandenburg* test. Further evidence for this position can be inferred from noting what the courts sometimes choose *not* to say. In the cases involving recognition of groups of gay college students, for example, nowhere is there the slightest hint that sodomy is not so serious a crime as homicide.[63] The issue is rather restricted to whether or not the sanctioning of a gay organization on campus will lead to increased acts of sodomy. In *Eisenstadt v. Baird*,[64] similarly, the seriousness of the crime of fornication was respected. At issue was the effectiveness of a specific statute in deterring fornicators.

Special Settings: The Military, The Prisons, The Campuses

One thing that becomes clear in reviewing those cases which have cited *Brandenburg* since 1969 is that the first amendment protection granted in that decision is not consistent across all life situations. Indeed, the courts have explicitly stated that, at least in three special settings—the campuses, the military, and the prisons—the *Brandenburg* test either does not apply, or applies only in a loosened form.

In *Kiiskila v. Nichols*,[65] Carolyn Kiiskila was dismissed from her civilian employment on a military base for passing out anti-war literature near, but not on, a local navy base. The Seventh Circuit Court of Appeals ruled in her favor, but hastily added that it did not mean to imply that "off-the-base conduct can never be considered in determining the validity of /such dismissals/."[67]

Also emerging from the Vietnam era were the facts leading up to the Supreme Court's disposition of *Greer v. Spock*,[67] invalidating a lower court injunction that had compelled the military personnel at Fort Dix to allow presidential candidate Spock and his followers to speak on the base. In its ruling, the Court tersely noted that the primary function of army bases is "to train soldiers, not to provide a public forum."[68]

Two years earlier, the Court, in *Parker v. Levy*,[69] had upheld the findings of a court-martial of an army physician. Levy had been accused of disobeying orders by advising Black enlistees to refuse to serve in VietNam. The Court took the opportunity to set forth explicitly that speech within and without the military are entirely different matters:

> Disrespectful and contemptuous speech, even advocacy of violent change, is tolerable in the civilian community, for it does not directly affect the capacity of the government to discharge its responsibilities. . . .
>
> In military life, however, other consierations must be weighed. The armed forces depend on a command structure that at times must commit men to combat, not only hazarding their lives but ultimately involving the security of the nation itself. Speech that is protected in the civil population may nonetheless undermine the effectiveness of response of command. If it does, it is constitutionally unprotected.[70]

Clearly *Brandenburg* carries little if any weight in a military setting. As we shall next see, the same can be said of prisons. There are actually two separate prison contexts addressed in the citations, one involving current prisoners and one involving former prisoners (i.e., parolees). In *Blue v. Hogan*,[71] a Georgia inmate charged prison officials with infringing upon his first amendment rights by having censored his reading material. The trial court applied the *Brandenburg* test and granted Blue an injunction. The appellate court overruled, however, flatly stating that *Brandenburg* is inoperative within a prison.

In *Pickens v. Texas*,[72] parolee Pickens witnessed the shooting of a close friend on a downtown street. He and a group of cohorts followed the ambulance to the hospital, where they congregated in the lobby of the emergency room. Pickens was visibly upset, concerned that his friend might not be getting the best of care. He was overheard to say to his cohorts, referring to the emergency room staff: "There ain't many of them in there. If we rushed them, we could get in." The hospital staff complained that their functioning was hindered, and their complaints eventually led to the rescinding of Pickens' parole. The Fifth Circuit Court of Appeals upheld that action. Judge Rives' dissent is reminiscent of the Supreme Court's handling of *Hess vs. Indiana*,[73] as he carefully assessed Pickens' precise wording: "Pickens nowhere made the outright suggestion that the persons gathered join together and storm the door; he simply stated what appeared to be a fact; i.e., *if* they all stormed the door, they could get in."[74] Explicit in *Blue v. Hogan*, and implicit in *Pickens v. Texas*, is the caveat that neither prisoners nor parolees should expect the full first amendment protection available to others under *Brandenburg*.

The other setting in which *Brandenburg* does not seem to apply with full force is the campus. We have already dealt with the efforts of gay groups to achieve full campus recognition. The major precedent in this area involved not a homophile group but a left-wing political group. In *Healy v. James*,[75] a local chapter of the Students for a Democratic Society (SDS) was initially denied official status at Central Connecticut State College. Although the Supreme Court ruled in favor of the students, it went out of its way to state that political speech on campuses may be curtailed whenever it is likely to "materially and substantially disrupt the work and discipline of the school."[76] In other words, the imminent lawless action demanded under *Brandenburg* need not be lawless at all; it merely must be "disruptive." Although the vast majority of the student cases citing *Brandenburg* resulted in pro-student decisions, the *Healy* language opens the door wide for intrusions upon students' freedom of association.

In *MGA v. Goudelock*,[77] the courts upheld the right of student editor Bill Goudelock. That case, it will be recalled, involved a delicate balancing of Goudelock's first amendment rights with those of the homophile group. In less complex cases, student editors have fared at least as well. Thus, in *Thonen v. Jenkins*,[78] the Fourth Circuit Court of Appeals demanded the reinstatement of a group of students who had been suspended for writing a letter to the editor, referring to the college president in "obscene terms."[79] And in *Joyner v. Whiting*,[80] the administration of North Carolina Central University chose to punish students by cutting off funds from the school paper, which had published an editorial calling for an end to the influx of white students into what had been a black college. In taking this action, the university president argued that the fourteenth Amendment, together with recent civil rights legislation, prohibited the spending of state funds to encourage segregation. The Fourth Circuit Court of Appeals ruled that since no illegal action had been prompted, the *Brandenburg* test had not been satisfied, and the paper could continue to publish.

In *Norton v. Discipline Committee*,[81] the students' chosen forum was not a newspaper, but the campus grounds of East Tennessee State University itself. A number of students were expelled for distributing leaflets which made multiple charges against the competency of the school's administration. The courts upheld their expulsion. As in other cases we have already examined, the specific wording of these litigants' message was carefully scrutinized, a message that referred with approval to the lawless action that had occurred on other campuses:

> And how has the ETSU student body reacted? Have they participated in revolution like French students? No. Have they brought about an entirely new and liberal administration like Polish students? No. Have they seized buildings and raised havoc until they got what they were entitled to like other American students? No. They have sat upon their rears.[82]

The final case we will discuss also deals with the school as a special setting, but this time the concern is with the first amendment rights of teachers, not students. We will spend a considerable amount of time examining *Acanfora v. Board of Education*,[83] as it is rare to find one case touching upon such a wide range of first amendment issues. When Joe Acanfora's homosexuality was discovered, the Montgomery County, Maryland school board's first action was to transfer him to non-teaching duties. By the time the case reached the federal trial court, Acanfora had been discharged. In a complicated ruling, the court concluded that the initial action on the part of the board—the transfer—was unjustifiably arbitrary, but that its later decision to dismiss Acanfora was wholly justifiable. How could a court have reached such a conclusion?

It seems that, in the interim between the transfer and the dismissal,

Acanfora had taken his case to the public. He granted numerous interviews that appeared in both local and national media, including CBS' "60 Minutes." In expressing disfavor with Acanfora's decision to go public, the trial court allowed that "freedom of speech may best serve the political process, and political discussion within the educational process, when it induces a condition of unrest." The court further allowed that "the promotion of legal rights for homosexuals is a political undertaking."[84]

Nonetheless, the court was extremely sensitive to the special nature of Acanfora's position as a role model for his pupils:

> The instruction of children carries with it special responsibilities whether a teacher be heterosexual or homosexual. The conduct of private life necessarily reflects on the life in public. There exists not only a right of privacy, so strongly urged by the plaintiff, but also a duty of privacy.[85]

Acanfora appealed the ruling. The appellate court affirmed the lower court's decision, but for very different reasons. Disagreeing with the lower court's findings regarding the appellant's media appearances, the court concluded:

> There is no evidence that the interviews disrupted the school, substantially impaired his capacity as a teacher, or gave the school officials reasonable grounds to forecast that those results would flow from what he said. We hold, therefore, that Acanfora's public statements were protected by the first amendment, and that they do not justify . . . the action taken by the school system.[86]

The reason the court was able to affirm Acanfora's dismissal concerned the application form used by the Montgomery County school system. The form required applicants to furnish information about "professional, service, and fraternal organization" memberships and about extracurricular activities engaged in as an undergraduate. Acanfora opted not to volunteer the fact that he had been active in a campus homophile group during his years at Pennsylvania State University. Based upon this omission, the court concluded that he did not have standing to challenge the school board's employment policies:

> Acanfora purposely misled the school officials so he could circumvent, not challenge, what he considers to be their unconstitutional employment practices. He cannot now invoke the process of court to obtain a ruling on an issue that he practiced deception to avoid.[87]

The appellate court's ruling is a puzzling one, in that not even passing reference is made to the Supreme Court's ruling in *Shelton v. Tucker*,[88] which struck down as unconstitutional the Arkansas practice of requiring teaching assistants to disclose all of their recent group associations. That requirement, in the Court's words, would tend to "impair a teacher's right of free association, a right closely allied to freedom of speech."[89]

Conclusions

We can now answer the four questions posed at the outset. As we have seen, the "eminence of imminence" under *Brandenburg* is well established. Whether the feared danger is the storming of a police barricade or a "hard rock" concert attracting "undesirable elements" or even the likelihood of a public school student learning that her or his teacher is pro-gay, the courts have adhered rather well to the imminence requirement. Perhaps the differing result in *Alliance to End Repression v. City of Chicago*[90] can be explained by reminding ourselves that the particular government sanction involved was a hypothetical one. That is, the only question before the court was whether, as a matter of law, it would always be improper for the FBI to commence an investigation of a group known to advocate illegality. Perhaps the court's reluctance to issue such a broad prohibition is best interpreted as a preference to deal with such matters on a case by case basis, as needed.

Whether or not the speaker's intention is part of the *Brandenburg* test is not entirely clear. In *Gay Lib v. University of Missouri*,[91] the potential for increased sodomy violations, not the group's intention, was the key issue. The Supreme Court's concern with Bill Baird's intentions, by contrast, was crucial to his vindication on the charge of inciting the crime of fornication. One could not conclude he was advocating imminent illegality in that one could not even say with certainty that he was advocating illegality at all.

The appellate court's handling of Russell Kelner's claim that he was engaging in mere political hyperbole, rather than uttering genuine threats, seems to rely upon the speaker's intention. But that "intention," it will be recalled, was held to be discoverable in the utterance itself! The federal appeals court in *U.S. v. Howell*[92] also seemed to rely in part upon its finding that Mr. Howell's threat against President Reagan was a real one. But here the court used the speaker's intention not as a way of applying the *Brandenburg* test, but rather of concluding that *Brandenburg* was wholly inapplicable when threats, rather than advocacy directed towards a third party, are involved.

However amusing the exchange between Judge Coleman and Judge Goldberg regarding the Mississippi Gay Alliance's intentions (i.e., that they would offer "legal aid"), it can not help us much in assessing the importance of intention to the *Brandenburg* test. This is because Coleman's assertion was mere dicta, the case having turned on the finding that the first amendment was not at issue, in that student editor Bill Goudelock was not a state's agent.

Concerning courts' handling of violent vs. non-violent advocacy, the *Buttorff*[93] doctrine of treating the two identically is generally followed. We have seen at least one judicial exception, in *Alliance to End Repression v. City of Chicago*,[94] where the court seemed to agree that special deference should be paid the FBI when dealing with groups that espouse *violent* illegality. Justice Powell's illness, which helped to create the 4-4 tie vote in *National Gay Task Force v. Board of Education*,[95] robbed us of the chance to see how the Court would address Professor Tribe's contention that advocacy of non-violent, victimless sexual conduct should receive more protection than violent advocacy.

Regarding the inconsistency of first amendment protection granted by *Brandenburg*, we have seen some explicit language to the effect that the *Brandenburg* test is simply inoperative in some settings. The necessity that the chain of command operate efficiently compelled the Circuit Court of Appeals in Washington, D.C., to rule that *Brandenburg* does not apply to the military. It is unclear whether Carolyn Kiiskila won her case because it pre-dated that ruling, or because she was a civilian employee of the military base.

In *Blue v. Hogan*,[96] we also found very explicit language effectively excluding the prisons from the *Brandenburg* test. Again we saw the judicial inclination to defer to the judgment of government officials whose jobs put them on the front lines in special settings with special needs for discipline and order.

On the campuses, as we have seen, *Brandenburg* applies in a diluted form. Advocacy of conduct that might "materially and substantially disrupt" the school may be prohibited, whether or not such conduct would in fact be illegal. It is interesting to note that Maryland teacher Acanfora's case was not decided on the basis of this standard, presumably because it could not have been met. Indeed, much evidence offered at trial indicated that most of Acanfora's colleagues and students wanted him reinstated.[97]

It is also interesting to note that, despite the restrictive language from *Healy*, only one of the students' rights cases examined here was won by the administration over the students,[98] and that case pre-dated *Healy*. It thus seems as if the net effect of the dilution of the *Brandenburg* test on the campuses is the precise opposite of that which one would expect. That is, students' first amendment rights seem to have found added vigor after *Healy*.

It is a truism of constitutional history that some of our most cherished rights have been won for us by litigants who were themselves not very nice people. This is certainly true of the long-term impact of KKK leader Brandenburg's utterances back in the 1960's. As first amendment issues become more and more complicated by the advent of new technologies that dramatically increase both the potential for speech and the potential for government intrusion upon the speaker, it is sometimes helpful to return to our most basic free speech values for guidance. It is comforting to see that the courts continue to treat the 1969 pronouncement in *Brandenburg v. Ohio* as a reminder that political speech is at the heart of our democratic system of self-government.

11

A Rhetoric of Ritual and Desecration

WILLIAM I. GORDEN AND RICHARD GOODMAN

William Gorden is Professor and Coordinator of Organizational Communication Studies in the School of Speech Communication, Kent State University, where he teaches the course "Speech in a Free Society." He is a member of the Commission on Freedom of Speech of the Speech Communication Association, having served as both secretary and chair of the Commission. In addition, he is active in the work of the American Civil Liberties Union.

Professor Gorden is the author of Nine Men Plus: Supreme Court Opinions on Free Speech and Free Press *(Dubuque, Iowa: William C. Brown, 1971). His essay (with Robert Kelley) "A Look at the Fire Symbol Before and After May 4, 1970" appears in the* Free Speech Yearbook: 1974; *a second essay (with Dominic A. Infante) on "Attitudes Toward Free Speech: Trends, Measurement and Individual Difference Considerations" was published in the* Free Speech Yearbook: 1980.

Richard Goodman is Director of Continuing Education, State University College, Fredonia, New York. The following article was first published in the February 1971 issue of the Quarterly Journal of Speech; *it has been revised and updated for this anthology.*

In September 1634 a rumor reached the Massachusetts Bay Colony that the king would demand obedience to the ceremonies of the Church of England. John Endicott, that puritan of puritans, was disturbed by the news, and upon hearing the fiery eloquence of Roger Williams publicly cut out with his sword the red cross of St. George from the banner of the train band at Salem because he said the cross "savoured of popery."[1] For this act he was prohibited for one year from holding public office. His militiamen, however, refused to serve under the flag that bore the "idolatrous emblem" and the cross was removed.[2]

Desecration of the patriotic symbol has a dramatic and odious heritage that bears witness to serious socio-legal conflict between those who believe desecration is intolerable, treasonous behavior and those who argue that desecration is symbolic speech deserving the protection of the first amendment.

The purpose of this investigation, therefore, is to compare and contrast the rhetoric of flag ritual and flag desecration. The first part of this essay examines the rhetoric of that ritual and the historic emotional character which has endowed the flag with special power. The second section focuses upon the rhetoric of desecration and the disruptive agenda and resurgence of support for establishment values raised by that rhetoric.

Rhetoric of Ritual

The normal situation in which the flag plays a major role is ceremonial. The circumstance is largely a ritual that begets words and actions as a "constituent part of being a certain sort of person," in Sesonske's words, "part of a way of living."[3] Or, as Duncan asserts, "the *structure* of such action is dramatic, but from a sociological point of view the *function* of this drama is the creation and sustainment of social order."[4] Placing one's hand over the heart as Ol' Glory passes is to join with one's fellow in affirmation both as an individual and as a member within a social order. To paraphrase a line from Aristotle's *Rhetoric*, "To praise a *flag* is in one respect akin to urging a course of action."[5] Perhaps more correctly, when it comes to government, to praise is to reinforce a course of action already begun. Thus, publicly, chorally to pledge allegiance to an adopted tangible symbol fuses the verbal with the nonverbal activities of that society. It is in effect a group utterance linked with the other senses of sight (red, white, and blue intermittently lapped by the breeze), touch (the muslin and stitching), with the muscles and viscera (often marching, saluting, and the kinetic events of pageantry).[6]

The usual human response to occasions where pivotal symbols are present Probert likens to "a means of mutual identification in the literal sense of communion: a coming together by means of a symbol. If the thought seems mystical, it may be because we have as yet explored too little the significance of symbols where faith is obviously involved. Exploration reveals that faith symbols are obviously involved everywhere, abundantly in law."[7]

The flag entails, as Whittick suggests in his discussion of the Greek origin of the meaning of the term symbol, "a bringing together . . . of ideas and objects."[8] Likely no other symbol has so ancient an embodiment of collective loyalty and will. Justice Jackson wrote wisely when delivering the opinion of the high court in *West Virginia State Board of Education v. Barnette*, 319 US 624 (1943), with his reference to the flag salute as a "form of utterance" and symbolism which is a "primitive, but effective way of communicating ideas."[9]

Flags can be traced back to tribal totems and military standards. Deep within the collective unconsciousness of modern peoples is this primitive archetypal symbol. It is little wonder that so much ceremony and state institutional life displays the flag. Few other national symbols are so taken-for-granted and expected. As a nation comes into being and matures, its flag is a symbol which as the philosopher Whitehead suggests "gathers emotional significance from its emotional history" and "this is transferred . . . to its meaning in present use."[10] There is a kind of "comfortable as an old shoe" quality about so established a collective symbol, and as Lindmark reasons, therefore the average citizen normally gives little thought to its meaning.[11]

Collective enterprise, particularly the multifaceted complex enterprise we know as the State, naturally uses and needs whatever symbolic help it can muster to bring a sense of order[12] to disorder within and protection from threats without. The flag symbol provides a reigning image that is conceptually understandable. Without such, Gordon argues, collective "conviction or thought or feeling . . . would otherwise be impossible to generate."[13] Langer explains that people need to be anchored into symbols "charged" with historic meaning to which they "seem to respond instinctively."[14]

Colonial settlements formed militias as defense against the Indians, Dutch, French, and later English. These militia and each colony had their own flags. These flags took on a defiant rattlesnake "Don't Tread on Me" character. And a new body of myth grew about the emergent flag design. The Betsy Ross legendary creation of the five-pointed star and Washington's commission given her to sew a flag is part of the emotional history of the flag. The oft repeated and embellished remarks of the First Commander and Chief add a mystical component: "We take the stars from heaven, and the red from our Mother country, separating it by white stripes, thus showing that we have separated from her; and the white stripes shall go down to posterity representing liberty."[15] Most probably these words were imaginary and echoed the European custom of assigning meaning to coats of arms and such symbols, known as heraldry.

Other romantic stories were spun about the first flag, such disputed tales as the making of a battle flag at Fort Schuyler in 1779—the white from a soldier's shirt, the blue field from a captain's cloak and the red stripes from the flannel petticoat of a soldier's wife. Another tells of a colonial quilting party sewing strips cut from their best silk gowns. Another of a young bride donating her wedding dress for the flag which John Paul Jones took into battle, and placed with those buried at sea "who had given their lives to keep it flying."[16] These are the stuff of Fisher's narrative paradigm, "a theory of symbolic actions—words and/or deeds—that have sequence and meaning for those who live, create, or interpret them," and "has relevance to real as well as fictive worlds, to stories living and to stories of the imagination."[17] Note how the flag is made from apparel and from emotional events such as wedding gowns, thus adding special narrative images to its symbolic significance.

The form of flag-waving rhetoric of ritual is narrative; indeed it is a public ceremonial expression of indebtedness to those who made supreme sacrifices. In addition it is an affirmation of loyalty and pledge to carry on under the same banner. The ends of the rhetoric of flag ritual thus are "moral inducement."[18] In a dictatorial state use of such symbols obviously are manipulation of the collective unconscious. In a democratic society, grassroots control of patriotic symbols and dialectic about these symbols can battle against such manipulation.

Varying forms of the flag were flown during the revolutionary period, none of them corresponding to the seven red, six white stripes and 13 five-pointed stars in a circle upon a blue canton popularized by the Ross story. General standards for the flag were set by the Continental Congress June 14, 1779 (that date is now observed as Flag Day) and again in 1794 after Kentucky and Vermont were admitted as states making the flag one of 15 stars and 15 stripes.

Such a flag, flown over Ft. McHenry the night of September 14, 1814, was an audacious 30 by 42 feet, the remains of which are mounted in the Smithsonian. That was the flag Francis Scott Key "watched through the night until through the dawn's early light he could see it yet waved." The emotional history of the flag was growing.

Codification became more explicit in 1818 when Congress limited the number of stripes to 13 and determined that only stars would be added as states were admitted to the Union. Resolutions by Congress have elaborated upon the flag, creating exacting protocols of design and display.[19]

In view of the deliberations which resulted in many state and federal flag laws, there should be no doubt as to the legitimization of this national symbol. Little is left to chance as to what one should know and do in order to honor the country. "To know what one must do" when coupled with the "emotivations" of collective custom and ritual is the essence of acculturation. Herein lies the function of the epideictic of flag myth and ritual.

Literalness in following ritual affirms collective expectations and sense of appropriateness. So it is that elaborate flag codification has evolved with tradition and has been legitimized by law. Collective identity is imprinted on the psyche by ceremony, and coordination of purpose is expressed in homogeneity of public performance. The "communion" of a people is thus experienced and observed, a la Burke's "consubstantiation," by means of the flag's many ongoing dramas.[20]

Yet a dangerous measure of blind obedience may accompany symbols with which one is too comfortable. Chase likens such a subordination of the will to following the Holy Grail, "suffused with ethereal light" and to a naive willingness to die for "a vast figure called the Nation—majestic and wrapped in the flag."[21] Symbols so "charged," if challenged, Langer asserted, arouse "the most fantastic bursts of chauvinism and self righteousness."[22]

On the other hand, the situation in which the flag is desecrated or the ceremony is mocked disrupts the act of communion and negates rather than affirms the social order. The rhetorical impact of flag desecration time and again has accented the struggle over the treasured values of this society. For example, in the fall of 1968 at a House Un-American Activities investigation, Yippie leader Abbie Hoffman, with his dramatic flair for adding insult, defiled the sacred political taboo by wearing a shirt fashioned from an American flag. Hoffman was a radical. His purpose was to mock, not to clown. The context was one of interrogation, if not presumed guilt as in a trial of political heresy, and the "House Un-Americans" were in no mood to be told by the jester Hoffman, "I regret that I have only one shirt to give for my country!"

Being subpoenaed as "Unamerican" brought a certain exigence to the situation,[23] and Hoffman had to speak. His wearing the flag was obviously an act of communication, an act of "symbolic speech," which caused the legislators to react more forcibly to his message. So strong was the reaction that he was convicted of flag desecration, although the conviction was reversed by the Court of Appeals for the District of Columbia.[24]

In the discussion thus far, the flag symbol has been considered equal to if not more important than language as symbolic communication. Few who have an appreciation of the role of tangible symbols in the construing and maintenance of culture would reason otherwise. In a society which constitutionally pledges that no law should abridge its people's use of language, one would assume equal protectiveness of the unabridged use of its significant symbols. Not so.

The U.S. courts, while acknowledging that the use of tangible objects such as the flag may be used symbolically in unconventional ways, have created a less protected category of communication called "speech plus." Failure to stand when others stand to salute the flag would fall into the category of "speech plus," as would more abusive behavior such as raising a foreign flag above Ol' Glory or burning the flag. All are "speech plus," though different in the degree of offensiveness.

In a case involving the destruction by fire of a draft card, Chief Justice Warren passionately explicated the difference between first amendment protections for speech and nonverbal symbolic acts. Delivering the opinion of the High Court he said, "We cannot accept the view that an apparently limitless variety of conduct can be labeled 'speech' whenever a person engaged in conduct intends thereby to express an idea. . . . This Court has held that when 'speech' and 'nonspeech' elements are combined in the same course of conduct, a sufficiently important governmental interest in regulating the nonspeech elements can justify incidental limitations on the first amendment."[25]

Study of the many varied degrees of "speech plus" flag cases leads to the impression that the more passive the noncompliance with the ritual (such as refusal to salute the flag) the more likely first amendment "pure speech" protection. Tedford puts it succinctly, "The more 'plus' to the symbolic expression the less protection the Constitution provides."[26]

The apparent theory underlying a speech-plus doctrine is regulatory; the regulatory function of government in such instances takes precedence over the truth seeking model.[27] The truth seeking model posits that the remedy for falsity or discordant opinions is more rather than less communication, that a free society should be an open marketplace for ideas whatever the form. Particularly in an age when media is king and access to the media is necessary in order to rally support, one might argue that symbolic nonverbal expression is uniquely suited to communication because of its functions within the visual as well as the auditory channel, and as such should deserve first amendment protections.

Rhetoric of Desecration

Let us begin with the inception of this struggle, which had its roots in the American drive to make an easier dollar. Following that, the remainder of the essay will discuss the flag and the red scare, the flag and teaching patriotism, and finally the most destructive of all desecrations—fire and mutilation.

The flag's for hire. At the turn of the twentieth century several legal skirmishes involved the flag and advertisers. Ruhstrat and Company was tried for placing a picture of the flag on their cigar boxes in defiance of an Illinois law.[28] The Court decided this state statute, which could be so interpreted, was unconstitutional because (1) it was incompatible with the federal constitution and (2) it exceeded the police powers of the state. The police powers of the state, the Court reasoned, were not intended to promote or attempt the elevation of public morals, and the legislatures could not determine restraints against the constitutional rights of citizens. This was, the Court also declared, discrimination against the use of the flag in advertising while permitting its use for public or private exhibitions of art; its essence was class legislation.

An almost identical case came before the New York courts in *McPike v. Van De Carr*.[29] The state court here again decided for a cigar manufacturer. Restricting the use of flag reproductions on labels would constitute an infringement on personal liberty. If stationers, book publishers, and jewelers were permitted to use the flag in advertising to sell their products, to forbid tobacco companies to do the same was once again class discrimination if not selective enforcement. The distinguishing mark of *McPike* was the court's ruling that there was no provocation unless the message was actually attached to the flag.

State legislators argued that the *Ruhstrat* and *McPike* decisions had usurped the police powers of the state and their powers as law makers. The advertisers on the other hand had no complaint, for the flag could now help sell merchandise, even tobacco, in Illinois and New York. However, the matter was not settled for the nation. A Nebraska case, decided by the U.S. Supreme Court in 1907, provided for the states' guidelines that exist to this day. Halter and Company had been convicted in both the lower and the Supreme Courts of Nebraska for distributing bottled beer with the United States flag on the label. The Nebraska statute forbade any exhibition of the flag on salable merchandise and provided for a fine not exceeding $100, or imprisonment for not more than thirty days, or both.

This situation once again was rhetorical because the flag had been "put to an ignoble use." The High Court in concurring with the Nebraska courts agreed that the flag was too sacred to appear on a beer bottle. The Nebraska Supreme Court opinion stood:

> Such inhibitions against the irreverent use of sacred things are not mere arbitrary fulminations, but are grounded on sound practical considerations and the conviction that such use of the sacred emblems of religion is inimical to the cause of religion itself. The

legislation under consideration may be justified under the same principle. The flag is the emblem of national authority. To the citizen it is an object of patriotic adoration, emblematic of all for which his country stands—her institutions, her achievements, her long roster of heroic dead, the story of her past, the promise of her future; and it is not fitting that it should become associated in his mind with anything less exalted, nor that it should be put to any mean or ignoble use.[30]

This opinion of the U.S. Supreme Court went on to say: ". . . that the citizen resents any improper use of the flag of his country, and that his resentment is frequently carried to the extent of a breach of the peace, are matters of common knowledge."[31]

The dramatic moment had arrived, and the High Court performed its sacrifice. The evil deed must be punished. The sacred political symbol had not been kept pure. As Duncan puts it, "The high moment in traditional socio-drama is the moment of victimage, the personification of evil powers which threaten community order."[32] And so he who had defiled the flag by using it to sell beer was sentenced.

Current flag statutes pertaining to commercial usage parallel the *Halter* decision. The 1968 Ohio flag law, for example, makes it a crime to "print or place a word, figure, mark, picture, or design upon a flag . . . or have in possession an article of merchandise upon which is placed or attached a representation of such flag."[33] However, the legislators added exceptions for the military, for newspapers, magazines and books, or certificates related to society lodge or emblem, ornamental picture, stationery, or "placed said flag disconnected from an advertisement."[34]

So flag decals are given away at Gulf stations, and the flag is pictured on a Nabisco Shredded Wheat carton for those who might wish to purchase one, but of course not for the purpose of helping sell that breakfast food. Uncle Sam Cereal, packaged in the red, white, and blue, is not quite so subtle but boasts in bold type—"Since 1908 A Natural Laxative." The flag frequently is pictured on newspapers and supermarket ads. The July, 1969 *Reader's Digest* cover pictures stripes of small red firecrackers against the white and a square of blue upon which one sees a family viewing a fireworks display. In the same month a *Look* cover carried a close-up of a flag in which the stitching and warp and woof of the threads seem to almost give it a texture. Another advertisement has the words FREEDOM OF SPEECH in the flag colors, stars and stripes, and just below that caption a tube of Poli-Grip for "dentures that ssslipp or ssslide." But whether one might argue that it is appropriate to place the flag on most merchandise in a materialistic society, it is obvious that present laws concerning the commercial use of the flag are not rigidly enforced and that these laws do permit exceptions. The current wide distribution of the red and white striped and starred top hat behind the bottle of Old Crow whiskey certainly contradicts the spirit if not the letter of the 1907 *Nicholas v. Halter* ruling, but these are post-prohibition times. That is to say, the red, white, and blue may be hired to sell products "respectable" and acceptable to the vast majority of the society. Commercial use of the flag did not diminish through the '70s and into the '80s. Reputable magazines such as the *Saturday Review of Literature* and *Time* carried flag dressed caricatures; AT&T dressed a beautiful woman in a formal red, white and blue gown; and sports companies advertised their wears with variations of flag designs.

Likely there will be no further legal battle for the right to use the flag for commercial purposes. Such costly confrontations would seem unnecessary when the same marketing objectives can be achieved by placing a product in the vicinity of the flag as might be achieved by putting the flag on a label or the product itself.

The flag sees red. Thomas Crawford, the sculptor who created the famous Statue of Freedom that surmounts the great dome of the capitol in Washington, summed up the feelings most of us have been taught to have for our flag: "A country puts its dreams and its ideals into symbols—a flag, a plot of ground, a monument. The people grow to love these symbols, fight for them, die for them. A symbol and what it stands for must stay together. They are indivisible!"[35]

The 1918 Sedition Act made it a crime, during wartime, to say, print, write, or publish anything disloyal, profane, or abusive about the form of government of the United States or the flag or the uniform of the Army or Navy. It is, therefore, understandable that raising a foreign flag on American soil would have been extremely provocative following World War I in the wake of the Russian revolution. Many states enacted "red flag" laws. For example, a segment of Section 403a of the California Penal Code provided the following: "Any person who displays a red flag, banner or badge or any flag, badge, banner or device of any color or form whatever in any public place or in any meeting place or public assembly, or from any house, building or window as a sign, symbol, or emblem of opposition to organized government or as an invitation or stimulus to anarchistic action or as an aid to propaganda that is of a seditious character is guilty of a felony."[36]

In the late twenties Yetta Stromberg, a nineteen-year-old United States citizen and member of the Young Communist League, was convicted in the Superior Court of San Bernadino County, California, for violation of that law. While acting in the capacity of a summer camp counselor, Miss Stromberg led her ten- to fifteen-year-old charges in a daily raising of a reproduction of the Russian flag, which was followed by the pledge of allegiance to the "workers red flag." The Stromberg defense based its case solely on the unconstitutionality of the California statute.

Chief Justice Hughes in the Supreme Court's decision to strike down the California "red flag" law pointed out that under such an act a third party displaying any banners at a convention could be convicted for opposition to organized government. As unpatriotic and unpopular as it may be, since the Stromberg decision, it has been legal to raise a flag of any color, even of an enemy government, in this land. States however, continue to pass such laws. Ohio, for example, as recently as 1968 voted a much broader statute:

> No person shall carry in a parade or display upon any street or building a red or black flag, or any banner, ensign or sign having upon it any inscription opposed to organized government or which is sacrilegious or which may be derogatory to public morals, or display the flag of any anarchistic society upon any public or private building or carry or display such flag in any street procession or parade within the state.
>
> This section does not apply to the pennants of any university or college or recognized institution of learning.[37]

To raise an enemy flag is provocative. To do so is to advocate a change of government for this land. The tolerance for freedom of expression indeed is put to the test when enemy flags are carried down Pennsylvania Avenue and raised around the Washington Monument.[38]

The flag as God.

> Thou shalt not make unto thee any graven image . . .; thou shalt not bow down thyself to them nor serve them.
> —Exodus, Chapter 20

In the late thirties, Lillian and William Gobitis, aged twelve and ten, were expelled from the Minersville, Pennsylvania, public schools for refusing to salute the flag as part of a daily exercise. These children of Jehovah's Witnesses, as part of their religious training, were taught to regard the flag as a "graven image." After the expulsion and a series of unsuccessful appeals, their parents therefore had no choice but to enroll them in a private school at considerable expense. Their case arrived at the Supreme Court in 1940.[39] In delivering the opinion of the court, Justice Frankfurter held the Pennsylvania flag-salute law to be constitutional. "We live by symbols," he declared, and therefore it is the duty of the schools to *train* "children in the patriotic impulse."[40]

The social repercussions for members of this sect were shameful. In some parts of the nation Jehovah's Witnesses were beaten and driven from their homes and several school districts saw in the *Gobitis* decision the opportunity to enforce flag-salute laws vigorously, which meant that a number of Witness children were classified as delinquents and sent to state reform schools. Their disrespect to our patriotic symbol had to be avenged.[41]

Three years after the Gobitis decision, in one of the most striking reversals in the history of the court, the compulsory flag-salute statute of West Virginia was held unconstitutional, and it was a Jehovah's Witness family who won this "right to silence."[42]

The right to silent dissent has more recently been challenged in the halls of academe. Consider, for example, how the sports event seems to demand that the national anthem be played and the flag raised, and that the crowd and players must respond appropriately. Chris Wood, an Adelbert College (Case-Western Reserve University) basketball player, was on the starting team during the first few games of the season. When the national anthem was played and the crowd and players stood, Wood remained standing. And no one was the wiser concerning his true feelings about the flag. Seemingly the constraints of the ritual were working and always would work. The situation was not rhetorical. There was no exigence, no imperfection marked by an urgency. But in midseason young Wood happened not to be selected as a member of the starting five. He was, therefore, seated on the bench that night when the national anthem was played, and all with one accord stood facing the flag—all except Wood.

The rhetorical situation had arrived. At half time, the coach told Wood he was no longer a member of the squad; in subsequent exchanges Wood, the board of trustees, Wood's father, student leaders, vice presidents of the television stations, and newspaper editors all felt constrained to address themselves to the immediacy of one act of insult toward the flag. Wood insisted that he was consistent. He was consistently displeased with the posture of his country. He stated that he would not change his posture upon sight of the flag. If he is standing at a flag ceremony he remains standing; if seated, he remains seated. "The flag," he insisted, "is just another piece of cloth."[43]

The flag on fire and other abuses. The federal flag bill (signed into law July 8, 1968) does not rule out burning as the preferred method for destroying old flags. It does, however, make clear that public burning, tearing, spitting, or otherwise dirtying the flag, or representation thereof, are illegal desecrations subject to up to $1000 fine and as long as a year in jail.[44] The bill did exempt from punishment those who cast contempt "by word," and thus in effect repealed the 1917 act and its 1947 renewal which made that kind of speech a crime in the District of Columbia.[45] Several attempts were made to amend the bill to make the fine $10,000 and the imprisonment five years.[46]

The flag burners themselves may claim to have inflamed the House and got the bill out of committee. They were labeled "rats" and "pinkos" by Representative Bray of Indiana, "unshaven beatniks" by Kuykendall of Tennessee, and "dirty, longhaired Communist-led beatniks" by Baring of Nevada. Early in the debate, Representative Haley of Florida recommended that our government should transport them by boat to "500 miles out in the ocean and handcuff them, with hands behind their backs, chain the anchor around their neck[s] and throw them overboard and tell them to swim to any country that they want to whose flag they can respect."[47] The major incident that provoked this vituperative oratory was the antiwar demonstration, April 15, 1967, in Sheeps Meadow in Central Park in which a flag was burned. The House debate was also an occasion for an epideictic of praise, for urging patriots to rally round the flag by reciting the historic battles at Valley Forge, Fort McHenry, Sumter, Gettysburg, Antietam, Bull Run, Mount Suribachi, and Bloody Ridge.

Other flag desecration incidents were party to the debate: one was a New York case in which a sculptor and gallery owner were fined for stuffed-flag sculptures.[48] In 1966 an artist, Marc Morrell, had constructed 12 soft sculptures shaped from Vietcong, Russian, Nazi and American flags. Morrell and gallery proprietor Stephen Radich were convicted, probably because the American flag in one piece was stuffed in the shape of a person hanging from a noose, in another in the form of a gun caisson and in the third was shaped as an erect penis. The U.S. Supreme Court, without announcing an evenly split opinion, let the conviction of lower courts stand.[49] Later, Radich, before a U.S. District Court, successfully argued that the tie vote was equivocal.[50] But it was the initial "desecratory sculptures" which provided material in congressional deliberations. Another incident, a demonstration at the University of Hawaii, involved the presence of a Viet Cong flag and a large caricature of a United States flag with dollar signs for stars and the stripes dripping blood.[51]

The Hawaiian court ruled that the drawing was "symbolic of the defendant's feeling about certain policies of his country, but that he did not intend by his drawing to dishonor the flag which to him still symbolized everything that he loved and honored about America."[52] Ms. Mink, Representative of Hawaii, stated that she had planned to vote for the flag desecration bill until her state was attacked for not convicting those involved in this demonstration. She was one of the small minority of 16 in the House to vote against the bill.[53] The debate precipitated by a flag desecration bill made possible the weighing of political questions and answers not yet clearly articulated, such as: what is truly a clear and present danger?

The High Court in 1969 spoke to the case of a flag burner and in so doing overturned a New York law that made it a misdemeanor to "publicly mutilate, deface, or defy, trample upon or cast contempt upon [the state or national flag] either by word or act." Sidney Street, a Negro bus driver and World War II winner of the Bronze Star, immediately upon hearing a radio bulletin that James Meredith had been shot from ambush on his 1966 march for civil rights through Mississippi, went to a Brooklyn street corner and burned a 48-star flag, and in outrage declared, "If they let that happen to Meredith, we don't need an American flag."[54]

In a five to four decision the U.S. Supreme Court side-stepped the crucial issue of whether or not flag burning deserves First Amendment protection as "symbolic speech" by limiting its ruling to the *speech* of Sidney Street. The New York statute had overstepped the mark, the Court majority opined, when it made illegal *talk* disparaging of the flag.

Fire with all its kinetic destructive nature carries with it the threat of burning and looting and comes close to the final act of alienation. Czech youth, for example, set afire the Soviet flag as Russian tanks invaded the streets of Prague. This symbolic act preceded by a few short weeks the self-immolation of Jan Hans Polach. However one may assess the soundness of mind of those who have chosen fire death, whether they were Buddhists in Saigon or a Quaker father who held his babe in arms until the moment before he was caught up in flames before the Pentagon, one cannot help but be profoundly moved by these final acts of communication.[55] Desecration by fire is not far from these macabre events of *destruction* by fire, and this may be why desecration by fire to the patriotic symbol poses so potent a threat to the social order. Even the long-time critic of the American government, socialist Norman Thomas, expressed the kind of words that might have been spoken by a member of the Establishment, "I don't like the sight of young people burning the flag of my country, the country that I love. A symbol? If they want an appropriate symbol they should be washing . . . it."[56]

To burn an enemy flag is heroism. To burn the flag of one's own nation is to become the enemy. This simple reasoning outrages those who would prosecute flag burners and sentence the draft card burners to federal penitentiaries.⁵⁷ To ignite bears an historic relationship to that extravagant rhetor William Lloyd Garrison, journalist and abolitionist, who on July 4, 1854, burned the United States Constitution. He branded it a source and parent of atrocities, "a covenant with death and agreement with hell," and as he lit the fire, he proclaimed, "So perish all compromises with tyranny."⁵⁸

Those who wish to demonstrate their displeasure with the direction of this country by flag burning should not expect First Amendment protection; the case of Sidney Street likely will prove an insufficient precedent. Neither will one find support for such behavior in the High Court's admonition in *Smith v. Goguen* against vaguely drawn and ambiguous terminology such as "treats contemptuously." Nor is there support in their ruling in *Spence v. Washington* (to be more fully discussed later) that the flag may be used in defiant symbolic protest sufficient argument for so destructive a symbol as fire. However, in two individual convictions for flag burning, one from Illinois and the other from Iowa, the Supreme Court remanded them in light of *Smith v. Goguen* and *Spence v. Washington*.⁵⁹

The clear reluctance of the High Court to view flag burning as protected symbolic expression can be seen in their denial of review of a more recent case, *Kime v. U.S.* (1982). Teresa Kime and Donald Bonwell, members of the Revolutionary Communist Party, on March 27, 1980, burned a flag they owned in front of the federal courthouse in Greensboro, North Carolina. The demonstration was peaceful. The announced purpose was to publicize a future scheduled political rally of their party.

Only Justice Brennan voted to hear this case and in his statement wrote that he believed if the case were heard that the court would be persuaded that the convictions of Kime and Boswell "violate their First Amendment rights. . . ."⁶⁰

Flag to wear, tear and deface. The *Street* case did not clearly exonerate the flag burning as symbolic expression guaranteed First Amendment protection. Nor did the High Court's dismissal of the case of Alfred Tennyson Cowgill, a Californian arrested in Hermosa Beach for wearing a flag vest on election day in 1968. The refusal to hear *Cowgill* in effect permitted the states to prosecute and convict those who desecrate the flag by wearing or defacing the flag.⁶¹ This ruling, for example, is supportive to a Lynn, Massachusetts, judge who ordered a 19-year-old youth, Donald Ryan, who had sewed pieces of an American flag to his trousers, to write and deliver an essay on the flag to his classmates.⁶² Contrast young Ryan's punishment with the accolades accorded Raquel Welch pictured in a stars and stripes bikini or Mae

West wrapped in a broad striped red, white, and blue gown.[63] Both Ryan and Welch costumes carried the same colors, but their audiences knew that in the motives lay the difference. Ryan was testing the tolerance for protest. The performers, in spite of their bizarre characterizations, were appealing to our love of traditional values in the respected let's pretend of movieland.

One such state case, however, did free a youth in Toledo, Ohio, who had cut a hole in a flag and wore it in a supermarket. The argument in the brief was persuasive: "There is no logical differentiation between wearing the flag and burning in effigy the President. Our flag is really the effigy of a nation. As such it is not immune from symbolic criticism."[64]

Indeed, it seems trifling for a flag-on-the-seat-of-the-pants case to be brought before the Supreme Court. Yet early in 1970 Valarie Goguen was arrested and convicted under the Massachusetts flag desecration statute for wearing a small cloth flag sewed to the rear of his blue jeans. A U.S. District court reversed the conviction reasoning that the state law was vague and overly broad because of such language as "treats contemptuously," and the Supreme Court agreed with that reversal on the vagueness grounds alone.[65] Incidentally no arrests were made in the 1984 Olympics in which many of the athletes wore flag designed costumes. Gold medal winner Mary Lou Retton and her companions on the women's gymnastics team tumbled with their red, white and blue flag designed costumes stretched over their bodies.

Those who are creatively discrete when using the flag to symbolize their dissent may find some support in such a case as *Spence v. Washington*. In May 1970, a Seattle college student attached a peace symbol made with black tape to each side of an American flag which was his. As a sign of his distress over U.S. involvement in the war in Vietnam and the shooting of students by the national guardsmen at Kent State, he then hung that flag upside down from his apartment windows.

The majority of the Supreme Court reversed Spence's conviction under the state of Washington's flag desecration law[66] (Chief Justice Burger and Justices White and Rehnquist dissenting). The Court in a similar case affirmed a federal Circuit Court opinion that the New York law prohibiting placing any design on an American flag was void because of its vagueness and overbreadth. That case also pertained to a 1970 arrest and conviction for showing a peace symbol with a stars and stripes background.[67] The rationale which overturned Spence's conviction for his peace symbol attached to the flag protest was that *that* flag was his on his own property, the act was peaceful and a form of communication.

Desecrators will continue to be arrested and convicted for offense to the flag whether the offense be unintentional or purposive,[68] cities will continue to receive words of praise for being the "flagflyingest city in the world," manufacturers of flags will continue to prosper as the war between the "silent majority" and the desecrators accelerates,[69] and nations will continue to plant their national symbol on new territory on this planet and on other terrestial bodies.[70]

Bill Mauldin caricatured a situation that well illustrates the political impact of the rhetoric of desecration. President Nixon is pictured with the flag wrapped completely around his body and he carries a picket sign which reads "Criticism is Practically Treason." Ex-president Johnson, leaning on a rail fence, drawls, "It didn't work for me either, Dick. Nobody respects the flag any more."[71] We have witnessed a unique phenomenon in American history, a rhetoric of desecration, an epideictic of blame, ridicule, and censure directed toward the patriotic symbol.

The prolonged 1979 incarceration of U.S. citizens by Iran was a cause for displays of more and more flags at places with great historic significance such as Valley Forge. Also the U.S.'s unexpected gold medal victory over the Russian hockey team in the 1980 Lake Placid Olympics was another time when latent chauvinistic patriotism was aroused. It is fortunate a people can find reason to celebrate their unity, whether during times of crisis or in victory. Yet the nagging question persists: How can those who love their country equally well as the establishment flag-wavers, graphically symbolize their dissent if they are prohibited by law from doing so? To paint one of the white stripes of the flag black, for example, might be a graphic way to symbolize corruption in government. Nuclear freeze demonstrators who now carry the flag while costumed in black and skeletal mask, perhaps, have found such a dramatic, yet nondesecratory protest.

Whatever one's feelings about the flag desecrator, one must grudgingly admit that those who have dared to desecrate have caused this nation to pause and attend to a different agenda. The established course of action consequently was reexamined because in part of a dramatic rhetoric of blame.

The toughest kind of patriot may be that one who both loves to fly the flag and can find ways to symbolically desecrate it when the direction of the nation seems wrongheaded. To invert Aristotle's epideictic prescription referred to earlier in this essay: "To blame our flag is in a very real respect akin to urging a different course of action for this nation." As disturbing as that may be, our forefathers were very precise in their pledge to protect that right.

Part Four

Case Perspectives

The Worst Case of Racial Equality He Ever Saw:
The Supreme Court, Motion Picture Censorship,
and the Color Line
Nickieann Fleener

The Birth of a Baby Photo Essay:
Was it Obscenity or Censorship?
Michael D. Sherer

Deep Throat in Deep Trouble on a College Campus:
An Academic Freedom Case Study
Churchill L. Roberts

Nazis in Skokie: Anatomy of the Heckler's Veto
Franklyn S. Haiman

12

The Worst Case of Racial Equality He Ever Saw: The Supreme Court, Motion Picture Censorship, and the Color Line

NICKIEANN FLEENER

Nickieann Fleener is Associate Professor of Communication at the University of Utah. Her publications include D. W. Griffith's "The Birth of a Nation": Controversy, Suppression, and the First Amendment as it Applies to Filmic Expression, 1915–1973 *(New York: Arno Press, 1980). The following essay appeared in the* Free Speech Yearbook: 1979; *it won the 1979 H. A. Wichelns Memorial Award for the most significant essay in the yearbook.*

"The worst case of racial equality he ever saw" was the reason given by Memphis motion picture censor Lloyd Binford when he justified censorship of the film *Imitation of Life* in 1950.[1] Thus, Binford suppressed the film because of his belief that *Imitation of Life* contained black characters that the predominately white Memphis audiences would find offensive or demeaning to their race. Although Binford later approved the film with changes, his interpretation of the word offensive to include the presentation of equality of races is not unique in the history of motion picture censorship.

Virtually from the public introduction of the motion picture medium in the United States, "offensive" thematic content has been censored from films. In the earliest instances "offensive" content tended to be defined in moral and sexual terms.[2] However, censors rather quickly expanded their definitions of offensive to include racial, political, and religious themes.[3] The almost total discretion of the censor to determine what was offensive was finally restricted in 1952 when the United States Supreme Court first brought the motion picture medium within the scope of the First Amendment.[4] More specifically, a unanimous

Court ruled in *Burstyn v. Wilson* that the standard of sacrilegious under which the New York censors had banned the film *The Miracle* was "far from the kind of narrow exception to freedom of expression which a state may carve out to satisfy the adverse demands of other interests of society."[5] Thus, the Court rejected sacrilegious as an acceptable censorship standard as the standard existed in the New York statute but left in question the constitutionality of a number of other film censorship standards including censorship based on the treatment of a racial or ethnic group.

No one aware of today's censorship climate can fail to see that the freedom of speech issue raised by censorship of the treatment of racial or ethnic groups remains a serious question. For example, as recently as January 1979, a censorship controversy raged in Bloomington, Indiana, over a scheduled screening of D. W. Griffith's classic film, *The Birth of a Nation*.[6] The controversy began after the American Guild of Organists announced that it would sponsor a mid-February showing of *The Birth of a Nation* on the Indiana University campus. Several individuals argued that the film should not be shown because the film represented a classic example of the perpetuation of negative racial stereotypes and because the showing was scheduled during Black History Month.[7] After receiving the protests, the Guild cancelled its sponsorship of the film and stated that it did so because the film "presents sensitive material in a prejudicial manner which might not be appreciated by some viewers."[8] The Guild's action prompted other individuals to argue not only for the right of the film to be shown but also for their rights to see the film.[9] The Guild renewed its sponsorship of *The Birth of a Nation* after determining that the "film had historic, artistic, and educational merit."[10] While protesters peacefully marched and distributed literature concerning a concurrent showing of *The Birth* elsewhere on campus sponsored by the Black Student unions "in proper context," *The Birth* was shown in the I.U. Auditorium, March 19, 1979.[11]

A similar controversy surrounds the more contemporary film, *Deer Hunter*. Critically acclaimed and selected by the Motion Picture Academy as best picture of 1978, *Deer Hunter* has also been condemned as "a racist attack on the Vietnamese people" and a misinterpretation of history.[12] Among the complaints against the film are that it negatively stereotypes all Vietnamese as inscrutably evil and that the central metaphor of the film which shows the absurdity of the war is a lie.[13] Specific protests against the film have taken the forms of pamphleteering and demonstrations. Although the film has not been suppressed, at least one writer has expressed the belief that if the Academy Award ballots had been distributed only one week later, the film would have not been selected as 1978's best film.[14]

Perhaps an even more serious indication of the importance of this issue can be found in Congressional attempts to regulate film content dealing with racial or ethnic groups. For example, a resolution that asked the film and broadcast industries to remove voluntarily negative stereotypes of ethnic, racial, and religious groups from all films and programs was introduced into the U.S. Congress in 1971.[15] Co-sponsored by over 69 members of the House of Representatives, the resolution contained a provision for federally enforced censorship if the voluntary effort failed.[16] Hearings were held concerning the resolution, but it was not voted on by the House.[17]

Although the preceding examples illustrate attempts at censorship designed to suppress stereotypes the groups involved considered negative, Binford's censorship of *Imitation of Life* is a reminder that sensitivity as a basis for censorship is an issue with two separate yet related faces. Binford's censorship indicates that statutes written to permit censorship based soley on the thematic treatment of race may also be used to support prevailing social norms such as segregation.

Censorship based on treatment of race is not peculiar to the motion picture medium.[18] However, because the scope of First Amendment coverage determined by the Supreme Court has varied from medium to medium, it is appropriate to discuss the issue as it relates to one medium. The purpose of this research is to study the constitutional issue of whether films can be censored for racial portrayals. More specifically, the research has been guided by this question. Has the U.S. Supreme Court squarely faced the question: Is motion picture censorship soley for treatment of racial themes constitutional?[19] To answer this question, the research specifically considers only those Court cases involving films censored for racial portrayals. However, a general background concerning film censorship for racial reasons precedes the discussion of the cases.

An Overview of Film Censorship for Racial Reasons Prior to Supreme Court Involvement With The Issue.

Although the argument that films should be censored because of content judged racist is not new, the standard was not applied to films on a wide scale until the 1940's.[20] During the 1940's, censors (primarily in the South) began frequently cutting scenes featuring black actors and actresses from films. For example, *Variety* reported in 1944 that "some local censors are attacking scenes indiscriminately leaving the continuity blurred and the entire film choppy and confused."[21] In particular, the Memphis censors led by Lloyd Binford were characterized as considering all films which even hinted at equality between the races "inimical to the public welfare, health, morals, and safety" of that city.[22] For example, the Memphis censors banned the Jack Benny film *Brewster's Millions* because Rochester's antics were deemed "too familiar," eliminated Lena Horne from any movie in which she appeared because "white people don't want to see her," and rejected *Lost Boundries* because it dealt with "social equality between whites and negroes in a way that we do not have in the south."[23] During World War II, newsreel sequences showing black troop actions were cut "in several southern towns."[24] *Variety* summarized the situation:

> The crux of the problem is that although white southern audiences enjoy negro sequences in films for their entertainment value, they will not countenance any scenes showing the negro on a basis of social equality with the whites. Local censors will eliminate such scenes regardless of the effect on the artistic side or the continuity of the film.[25]

This situation came to the attention of Thurgood Marshall, then special counsel to the National Association for the Advancement of Colored People, who called racial censorship "one of the worst evils that can be imagined" and who petitioned the American Civil Liberties Union to combat it.[26] Marshall was disturbed particularly by a Memphis ban of the film *Dixie*. The ACLU responded to Marshall's request for help by saying "certainly we will take up the matter of those southern censorships, although it is going to be a tough job."[27]

The ACLU pursued the matter with little immediate success. In early 1945, Memphis banned *Brewster's Millions*. The ACLU attempted to interest the film's distributor and/or the film's exhibitor into taking legal action against the censors. However, the exhibitor, Harry Kosner of Edward Small Productions, replied that his company would not "dare fight for fear the other southern theatres and circuits will ban the picture."[28] Likewise, the distributor, United Artists, said it "had no definite views one way or another" and would be guided by the exhibitor.[29]

Later in 1945, H.L. Mitchell, president of the Southern Tenant Farmers Union, notified the ACLU that censorship was becoming a major issue in Memphis because "Mr. Benford [sic] has banned a large number of pictures in the past few weeks and both newspapers have carried editorials denouncing the censorship."[30] The ACLU responded that it had tried to bring a test case but that "local exhibitors and distributors . . . are all so afraid of retaliatory action" that none would initiate a lawsuit. Again, the ACLU turned to United Artists and asked that company to initiate a suit:

> As you probably know, the ACLU has been following closely the censorship activities of the Memphis Board of Censors. Earlier in the year when Lloyd T. Binford . . . made the headlines by barring *Brewster's Millions* we attempted to get a test case. Unfortunately, . . . exhibitors are rather loath to defend themselves because of the pressure that can be brought upon them by the municipal authorities. It is therefore gratifying to us to note that United Artists is prepared to combat further censorship. May we offer you our assistance in any case that you might bring? We are prepared to help carry any suit to the United States Supreme Court if necessary.[31]

However, it was two more years before United Artists took the Memphis Board of Censors to Court.

Film Censorship Cases Involving Censorship for Racial Treatment Which Reached the U.S. Supreme Court

During the summer of 1947, United Artists distributed a motion picture comedy, *Curley*, produced by Hal Roach. The film presented a variation upon the structure and theme of the "Our Gang" comedies for which Roach was well known.[32] The film had already been approved in its entirety by censorship boards in New York, Kansas, Ohio, Maryland, Pennsylvania, Virginia, Chicago, and Boston[33] when it was submitted to the Memphis Board of Censors.[34] The Memphis censors rejected the film. In a letter explaining the board's action to United Artists, board chairman Lloyd Binford wrote:

> I am sorry to inform you that it is unable to approve your "Curley" picture with the little Negroes as the south does not permit Negroes in white schools nor recognize social equality between the races even in children.

United Artists (UA) interpreted this to mean that the film had been banned in Memphis and decided to protest. Gradwell Sears, UA president, said, "We are not going to take this lying down. I have instructed our lawyers to test the constitutionality of Binford's censorship."[36]

United Artists and Hal Roach filed a joint petition in the Circuit Court of Shelby County, Tennessee, seeking review of the film without legal authority; that the film censorship ordinance in question was unconstitutional; that the board banned the film solely because negroes appeared in it; and that the board had acted in a "capricious and arbitrary" manner and thus violated the due process guarantees of the Tennessee and U.S. Constitutions.[38] The petition was dismissed by Circuit Court Judge Floyd Henderson, Jr.[39] United Artists and Hal Roach appealed to the Tennessee Supreme Court.[40] The Tennessee Supreme Court heard the case and affirmed Henderson's position. The Tennessee court held that "petitioners were doing business in Tennessee and having failed to comply with statutory provisions for qualification of a foreign corporation to do business in the state could not maintain in the proceeding."[41] In dicta, the court stated that motion picture censorship *might* not be based solely on race or color, but that the constitutionality of the Memphis ordinance could be contested only by someone with standing in the state.[42]

United Artists planned an appeal to the U.S. Supreme Court.[43] The Motion Picture Producers and Distributors Association (MPPDA) supported this action, viewing the case as an excellent opportunity to seek a reversal of the 1915 *Mutual Film Corporation v. Industrial Commission of Ohio*[44] and to have the Court forbid film censorship on racial grounds. MPPDA executive secretary Sidney Schreiber wrote to Memphis attorney Hamilton Little:

> There is no reason to assume that the motion picture should forever remain outside the full protections of the First Amendment. We expect that the Supreme Court will overrule this anachronism when the question is re-presented to it. We expect that the case of *United Artists v. Memphis* will furnish the occasion for the disapproval of the principle enunciated in the *Mutual Film Corp.* case.[45]

Marie Wathen, *Film Daily's* Memphis correspondent, wrote editor Chester Bahn that she was sure "no picture could be banned because of Negro and White children playing together—not in the U.S. Supreme Court."[46] Similarly, the *Louisville Courier-Journal* editorialized that the outcome of the case was "foregone" because "as long as the Constitution guarantees equality of man, it must imply the equality of the pictures of children."[47]

In October 1949, United Artists and Hal Roach filed their petition for a *writ of certiorari* with the U.S. Supreme Court. The petitioners claimed "the basic issue presented is the constitutionality of previous restraint or censorship of talking motion pictures."[48] Major questions in the petition included:

1) Are state laws which provide for previous restraint or censorship of talking pictures in derogation of freedoms secured by the First Amendment and protected against State abridgment by the "due process" and "equal protection" clauses of the Fourteenth Amendment?
2) Even though previous restraint or censorship is not unconstitutional *per se*, may race or color, or the fact that Negro children appear along with white children in school room scenes, constitute a valid ground on which a talking picture may be censored and its exhibition banned?
3) Can state courts evade primary federal constitutional issues by interposing non-federal grounds of decision which, in substance and effect, deny fundamental constitutional rights?[49]

In addition, United Artists asked whether a film's producer and distributor have standing to sue.[50]

On May 8, 1950, the Court denied *certiorari* without dissent.[51] The case seems to have been dismissed because of procedural issues stressed by the Tennessee Supreme Court rather than on constitutional grounds. United Artists and the film industry turned their attentions to another film censored because of a racial theme, *Lost Boundaries*.

In early 1950, *Lost Boundaries* was submitted to Christine Smith, Atlanta, Georgia's film censor, for approval.[52] Smith ruled the film could not be shown in Atlanta because the picture would "adversely affect the peace, morals and good order of said city."[53]

RD-DR Corporation, producer, and Film Classics, distributor of *Lost Boundries*, sued Smith in the U.S. District Court to enjoin enforcement of Atlanta's film censorship ordinance.[54] However, the three-judge federal court upheld the censor's ban and declared the ordinance constitutional.[55] Thus, unlike the Tennessee Supreme Court disposition of the United Artists case on procedural grounds, the Atlanta federal court directly tackled the constitutional issue.

Speaking for the federal court, Chief Judge Neil Andrews said the basic question was "whether motion pictures are entitled to the protection constitutionally accorded the press."[56] Citing the *Mutual* decision, Andrews stated that motion pictures could not be considered part of the press. In spite of Supreme Court Justice William O. Douglas's dicta in *U.S. v. Paramount Pictures*,[57] in which Douglas said "we have no doubt that motion pictures, like newspaper and radio, are included in the press whose freedom is guaranteed by the First Amendment," Andrews said he could not "anticipate that the Court will overrule the *Mutual Film case*."[58] Expressing his personal opinion however, Andrews wrote that he believed the ordinance in question should be interred

> ... in the attic which contains the ghosts of those, who arrayed in the robe of Bigotry, armed with the spear of Intolerance and mounted on the steed of Hatred have through all ages sought to patrol the highways of the mind. In essence that part of the ordinance presently under scrutiny empowers the Censor to determine what is good and what is bad for the community and that without any standard other than the Censor's personal opinion. As here applied it attempts a degree of thought control, but unless motion pictures can be afforded the coverage extended the press, it is clear that the police power of the State has not been exceeded.[59]

RD-DR Corporation appealed to the Fifth U.S. Circuit Court of Appeals. Not only did that court affirm, but also it indicated its conviction that there was no need for a review of the *Mutual* decision.[60]

RD-DR Corporation petitioned the U.S. Supreme Court for a *writ of certiorari*.[61] Though Justice Douglas stated the petition should be granted, the Court refused.[62] So when the U.S. Supreme Court was asked to face squarely the constitutional question of press freedom for motion pictures, it refused.

A few days after the Court denied *certiorari* in the RD-DR Corporation case, the motion picture industry turned its support to another film censored for racial content, *Pinky*. William Gelling had been convicted in the County Court of Harrison County, Texas, for exhibiting *Pinky* without a permit.[63] Gelling had submitted the film to the Marshall, Texas, Board of Censors which denied a film permit. The board held that the film "was of such character as to be prejudicial to the best interests of the people of the city."[64] Gelling exhibited the film without a permit and was arrested.[65]

Gelling appealed his conviction to the Texas Court of Criminal Appeals. He contended the ordinance under which he was arrested was invalid on its face, violating the First and Fourteenth Amendments.[66] The Appeals Court disagreed. In its opinion, the unanimous court drew heavily from Judge Hutchenson's opinion in *RD-DR Corp. v. Smith*.[67] In part, Judge J. Beauchamp, speaking for the court, stated:

> We cannot concede that the motion picture industry has emerged from the business of amusement and become propagators of ideas entitling it to freedom of speech. . . . The desire of a great industry to reap greater fruits from its operations should not be indulged at the expense of Christian character upon which America

must rely for its future existence. Every boy and every girl reaching manhood or womanhood is to an extent the product of that community, and if the communities are divested of all power to surround them with wholesome entertainment and character building education then the product will go forth weak indeed.[68]

The court also said that "the name and character of the picture exhibited are immaterial."[69]

Gelling then appealed to the U.S. Supreme Court. The case was adjudicated just one week after the Court's *Burstyn* ruling. In a one sentence *per curiam* decision the court reversed Gelling's conviction on the authority of *Burstyn* and *Winters v. New York*.[70]

Justices Felix Frankfurter and William Douglas filed concurring opinions in the case. Frankfurter contended that the censorship ordinance "offends the Due Process Clause of the Fourteenth Amendment on the score of indefiniteness."[71] Douglas said the First Amendment had been violated:

> The evil of prior restraint, condemned by *Near v. Minnesota* in the case of newspapers and by *Burstyn* in the case of motion pictures is present here in flagrant form. If a board of censors can tell the American people what it is in their best interests to see or read or to hear, then thought is regimented, authority substituted for liberty, and the great purpose of the First Amendment to keep uncontrolled the freedom of expression defeated.[72]

Thus, two members of the Court seemed to dispatch as unconstitutional the licensing criterion of "prejudicial to the best interests of the people" without considering the specific film involved or the fact that the film had been found potentially prejudicial because of is treatment of a racial theme.

In 1954, the Ohio Supreme Court upheld the censorship of two different films, *M* and *Native Son*.[73] Although three separate cases were actually involved, the court considered the three together because it concluded "the same or similar questions are involved."[74] Nevertheless, the fact situations varied significantly.

The motion picture *M* was banned by the Ohio Department of Education "on account of being harmful."[75] The film's American producer, Superior Films, appealed the ban on the grounds that the film "artistically and dramatically" treated at least five important social problems and was not harmful.[76] Further, Superior Films claimed that the Ohio film censorship statutes violated the First and Fourteenth Amendments of the U.S. Constitution and the First Article of the Ohio Constitution because of indefinite and vague censorship criteria.[77]

The two other cases involved censorship of the film *Native Son*.[78] One was an action in *mandamus* by Classic Picture, Inc., to require the Department of Education to reexamine the film. Prior to this action, the Department of Education denied another review of the film because the film had been considered by the Department on three previous occasions. Despite cuts and deletions, the Department pronounced the film:

> . . . Harmful; because—contributes to racial misunderstanding presenting situations undesirable to the mutual interests of both races; against public interest in undermining conditions at a time when all groups should be united against everything that is subversive.[79]

The other case asked that these censorship orders be set aside and the Ohio film censorship statutes declared unconstitutional.[81] Relying upon the U.S. Supreme Court decisions in *Burstyn and Gelling*, the Court stated:

> From these expressions of the U.S. Supreme Court and otherwise, we conclude that, although a motion picture film may not be rejected because of "sacreligious" expressions or portrayals, there still remains a limited field in which decency and morals may be protected from the impact of an offending motion picture film by prior restraint under proper criteria. There can be no inherent right to publicity which tends to destroy the very social fabric of the community and consequently in such instances there is no right of free speech or free press to be infringed. As we view it, the United States Supreme Court has not ipso facto taken away all community control of moving pictures by censorship, and this court will not do so under the claim of complete unconstitutionality of censorship laws.[82]

Further, the Ohio court ordered the Department of Education to reconsider *Native Son*.[83]

The three cases were joined in an appeal to the U.S. Supreme Court.[84] The Court decided the cases with *Commercial Pictures Corp. v. Regents of the University of the State of New York*.[85] In a one sentence *per curiam* decision, the judgments were reversed on the authority of *Burstyn*.[86] Justice Douglas filed a concurring opinion, with which Justice Black agreed, expressing the broader view that the First Amendment guarantees of freedom of expression prevented a state from establishing censorship over motion pictures. In part Douglas stated ". . . in this nation every writer, actor, or producer no matter what medium of expression he may use should be freed from the censor."[87]

Thus, the Court seems to have considered overbroad the Ohio standard that only films "of a moral, educational, amusing, or harmless character" could be approved and the New York standard forbidding films judged "immoral or tended to corrupt morals."[88] Whether the Court considered the censorship criteria utilized in the *Native Son* cases when deciding the *Superior Film* case is unclear.

Therefore, the U.S. Supreme Court had been asked at least four times to consider cases involving films censored because of racial themes. In at least one of these cases, the Court was asked specifically the question of whether race or color might constitute a valid grounds on which the exhibition of a motion picture might be forbidden. However, in each case, the Court decided the questions involved on broader grounds than the constitutionality of racial sensitivity as a grounds for censorship. Thus, it can be seen that the U.S. Supreme Court has never specifically resolved the constitutionality of treatment of racial themes. It is also interesting to note that in all four cases that reached the Supreme Court, the censorship of the film involved was based on the film's portrayal of black characters judged a threat to existing social norms such as segregation rather than on censorship stemming from the suppression of images blacks argued were demeaning to their race.

Discussion

Some scholars have argued that by reversing lower court decisions in *Gelling* and *Superior Films*, the Court in effect has stated that censorship based solely on the treatment of race is unconstitutional.[89] To support further this position, the validity of the Court's ruling in *Beauharnais v. Illinois* is brought into question.[90] In support of the questionable status of *Beauharnais*, Judge J. Skelly Wright's statement concerning the case in his concurring opinion in *Anti-Defamation League of B'nai B'rith v. FCC* is quoted. Of *Beauharnais* Wright commented in part: "Far from spawning progeny, *Beauharnais* has been left more and more barren by subsequent First Amendment decisions, to the point where it is now doubtful that the decision still represents the views of the Court."[91] On the other hand, it could be argued that because the Court in *Miller v. California* returned to a community rather than a national standard concerning the defining of obscenity, the Court could apply similar reasoning in cases involving censorship for the treatment of race. Thus, the definition of offensive characterizations could be established by community standards. In the extreme, such an interpretation could not only allow one community to ban films like *The Birth of a Nation* and *Deer Hunter*, but also could allow another community to suppress filmic interpretations of the Holocaust because of the allegedly negative images of Germans. Thus, however offensive, allowing suppression of what a racial group considers negative images of itself allows the bigot to suppress films that place racial groups in an equal or positive light.

In addition, many instances of contemporary film censorship based on stereotypes do not reach the courts. For example, as discussed earlier, the February 1979 *The Birth of a Nation* censorship controversy was resolved without court intervention. However, the resolution was not reached without a fight. During the battle several rights to free speech were brought into question including the right of the film to be screened, the right of those who wished to see the film to do so, and the right of those who opposed the film to voice peacefully that opposition by picketing and pamphleteering. Because *The Birth* was eventually shown to an audience wishing to see it, and because the protesters were allowed peacefully to demonstrate their opposition to the film, in this instance all three rights were affirmed. However, the resolution easily could have been otherwise.

Thus, although doubts may exist concerning whether the Court today would recognize censorship based on offensive stereotypes as consistent with the First Amendment, the Court itself has not answered the question. Therefore, the issue remains a viable one and actual or threatened censorship of films for racial themes continues to take place.

13

The Birth of a Baby Photo Essay: Was it Obscenity or Censorship?

MICHAEL SHERER

Michael Sherer teaches in the Department of Journalism at the University of Nebraska at Omaha where he is instructor of the course "Communication Law." He is a member of the National Press Photographers Association and has conducted seminars on freedom of the press and photojournalism for that Association as well as for other groups. He is a member of the editorial board of American Journalism. *Among his publications are "The Problem of Trespass for Photojournalists,"* Journalism Quarterly *62 (Spring 1985): 154 ff.; and "Obtaining the Photojournalist's Work Product Via Warranted Searches and Subpoenas,"* Communications and the Law *6 (August 1984): 3–14. The essay below was published in the* Free Speech Yearbook: 1983.

In photographing what many would say is one of the most beautiful moments anyone can experience, Brian Lanker earned the Pulitzer Prize for feature photography in 1973. His subject was the birth of a baby.[1] This wasn't the first time a baby's birth had been photographed for publication. *Life* magazine did this thirty-five years prior to Lanker's efforts. But rather than meeting with widespread praise and receiving a prestigious prize for photojournalism, *Life* magazine was condemned and confiscated by local police in several cities across the country. Estimates of the number of communities taking action against what was then thought to be an "obscene" publication range from thirty-three[2] to sixty.[3] Whatever the exact number, one fact remains clear, the publication of this photo essay in the April 11, 1938 issue of *Life* led to a widespread attempt at censorship by many local authorities that was at times successful, and at times doomed to failure.

This study is an attempt to piece together the issues involved and to present an overall picture of the assault against this one issue of *Life*. Contemporary news accounts from several cities where this issue came under fire by local authorities will be examined. This examination includes news accounts from newspapers published in New York, Boston, Chicago, St. Louis, New Orleans, and Memphis. In addition to these news accounts, this study will also examine the court opinion written when the publisher of *Life* was charged with publishing an "obscene" publication.

The 1930's

To understand better the attitudes on this issue and the actions taken against *Life*, it might be helpful to recall that life in the 1930's was unique in several ways. It was a period marked by a communications boom. Such things as the first technicolor motion picture were produced at this time. Major photography magazines such as *Life* and *Look* were founded in the late 1930's, and major advances were made in the transmission of news photography by radio and wire. In short, the 1930's was a period when the nation became image conscious.[4]

The 1930's was also a time when movie attendance was at a high level with as many as eighty-five million people going to the cinema each week. What the audience saw at the movies was often a sanitized version of life. For example, in 1934 the Catholic League of Decency started to see that films avoided long kisses, adultery, nude babies, or married couples sleeping in anything but twin beds. And "when Dennis King sang 'to *Hell* with Burgundy,' a thrill ran through the audiences, as though a naked woman had run among them."[5]

One film that became involved in the clash between *Life* and local authorities also had its beginning in the mid-1930's. Produced by the American Committee on Maternal Welfare and sponsored by sixteen medical and social service societies, *The Birth of a Baby* was favorably previewed by a majority of 12,000 doctors and clubwomen. The climax of this seventy-two minute film, which followed a woman's life during pregnancy, was the actual birth of a baby.[6]

> For one breathless minute the camera, with its matchless eye for detail, watches the child's head emerge as the physician moves swiftly to support it, notes an infant arm fling heavenward as it comes into view, shows the physician delivering the child at last from its laboring mother.[7]

A main reason for the film being produced was to help reduce death and sickness among mothers and children through education. The death rate of mothers and babies in birth was high, estimated at a yearly toll of 150,000 lives.[8]

Several stills from this motion picture eventually found their way into *Life* as a part of a special photo essay on the subject of birth. This particular essay was only one of a long series of medically related photo features that *Life* had run early in its career. From 1936 to 1938 several photo features on such topics as epilepsy, syphilis, nursing, socialized medicine, X-rays, tuberculosis, and pneumonia had appeared in *Life*. In the issue dated April 11, 1938, *Life* continued its medical series with a four page spread of thirty-five pictures from the film *The Birth of a Baby*, plus two anatomical diagrams. There was no nudity or unnecessary disclosure in the entire feature.[9]

The publishers of *Life* knew that this particular photo essay could be a cause of concern for some people, so they took the precaution of notifying their 650,000 subscribers in advance of publication by sending them a letter detailing both the content and purpose of the upcoming essay. It was also pointed out in this notice that the photo feature would be printed on the middle pages of the magazine, so that it could be easily removed by family censors. In addition, the magazine's print order for this particular issue was held at the previous week's level of 2,040,000.[10] These actions by *Life* indicated that the magazine knew the potential of the photo essay.[11] By the time the entire episode was over, it was estimated that 17,000,000 people had seen the issue, with sixty-one percent of the public surveyed saying that they approved of this method of teaching the public about childbirth and the care of mothers.[12]

Banned in Boston

Although a majority of Americans may have favored this photo essay, a small but effective minority in many parts of the country was successful in limiting the distribution of this issue despite the fact that the magazine was cleared for mailing by the U.S. Post Office.[13] The first move against *Life* came in Boston and the surrounding area. Boston Police Commissioner Joseph F. Timilty was concerned about the distribution of obscene literature in his territory. In Boston during February and March of 1938, Timilty received agreement among magazine distributors to ban obscene literature. The result was that thirty-five detective, picture, and other magazines with a combined circulation of 1,000,000 copies had been banned from news stands and cigar stores. Although Timilty had no legal power to set himself up as the censor in Boston, or any other area, he could get warrants for the arrest of people distributing obscene literature. Because of this threat news distributors generally cooperated with Timilty by submitting questionable publications to Timility's Board of Censors. This board consisted of Edward W. Fallon, superintendent of police; Capt. Charles F. Eldridge; and Augustine J. Gill, police secretary.[14]

In an effort to extend his censorship powers to other areas outside of Boston, Timilty arranged for a meeting of 107 magazine distributors from six New England states to discuss the issue of obscene literature. After addressing the meeting, which was held in Boston police headquarters, Timilty left the gathering so that the distributors could decide what, if anything, they could do about this issue. When the meeting adjourned the distributors had agreed to a plan whereby a censorship committee of three distributors would be empowered to ban any magazine or periodical from New England on the grounds that it was salacious, obscene or immoral. The distributors agreed to suppress any publication that this board felt was unfit. And in the case of a dispute, the board would submit the issue to Timilty, whose decision would be final.[15]

The first test of this new method of voluntary censorship came when the distributors' censorship committee ruled that the four-page spread in *Life* magazine should be torn out before it was sold on the newsstands. This issue was shown to Timilty who said that the photographs under question were unsuitable for general distribution.[16] If the ruling of the censorship committee was followed, then all newsdealers in New England would not sell this issue of *Life* with the "Birth of a Baby" photo feature still intact. At first it appeared that this plan was working. Boston newsdealers withheld the magazine from the newsstands for a day while some other newsdealers agreed to tear the four page photo feature from the magazine before it was offered for sale. Meanwhile, reports from New Hampshire indicated that all copies of the magazine were taken off the newstands by order of the manager of the affected news agency.[17]

In Pittsfield, Mass., the first city to ban *Life*, Police Chief John L. Sullivan ordered the magazine to be kept from the newsstands. Sullivan called the photographs "muffled propaganda on birth control." He added that "publication of such material hurts what the churches are trying to build up—modesty and virtue."[18] In Boston an employee of a Back Bay newsstand, Morris Baratz, received a summons for selling a copy of *Life* to a police detective.[19] One distributor in Boston was convicted and fined $500 for selling a copy of the magazine.[20] Meanwhile, Timilty moved on to other publications, announcing on April 10, 1938, that he would ban a magazine that contained "photographs of unclad women." This action raised the number of magazines banned in Boston to forty-two in two months. Timilty also used this announcement to restate his determination to "protect the children and decent minded people of Boston from the filth that has been filling some magazines."[21]

In response to the proposed ban of *Life* in Boston and nine other New England cities *Life* publisher Roy E. Larsen said that the purpose of the photo feature was to educate people in an attempt to help reduce the mortality rate among women and their children during childbirth. In response to Larsen's statement, Joseph F. Lamb, State Department of Knights of Columbus, demanded the recall of the issue on "every ground of decency and morality."[22]

One day later, Larsen issued another statement on the banning of *Life* in Boston and other areas. Part of the statement said,

> Local police chiefs and in some instances desk sergeants in several New England cities, with doubtful authority, have set their own opinions of the value of *Life's* "Birth of a Baby" article against the endorsement of national authorities in the fields of education, health, and child welfare. . . . We have no intention whatever of removing the four pages from *Life* containing the "Birth of a Baby" story and are planning to initiate court action in cities when local censorship has banned distribution of the complete issue of *Life*.[23]

Other voices heard in opposition to the ban on *Life* included that of Rev. William G. Stidger, pastor of the Copely Episcopal Church. He said that he was shocked by the ban on the photographs in Boston. Copely added,

> It's a matter of bunk on the part of a group of stupid, narrow minded police commissioners and censors. Birth is the greatest experience in life, and I see nothing indecent in pictures of that experience. *Life's* effort is admirable and the magazine is living up to its name.[24]

Despite the actions taken by New England authorities, *Life* was still available to many readers. Even in Boston the issue was being sold intact by several newsstands. John Tracy of the New England News Company was told by his New York office to offer the magazine to the general public as usual because it was felt that the pictures were educational and could not be considered immoral.[25] And in New Haven, Connecticut City Court Judge Thomas C. Sullivan lifted a police ban on the issue saying, "there is nothing contained in this magazine which could be construed as obscene."[26]

St. Louis Police Seize Life

Censorship of *Life's* photo essay was not confined to the New England area. Another major effort against the magazine occurred in St. Louis. Following a declaration by St. Louis Prosecuting Attorney James P. Finnegan that the photographs were obscene, police were ordered to seize any issue appearing on newsstands in the city. John E. Rogan, manager of the St. Louis News Co., local distributor of *Life*, said that 12,000 copies of the magazine were distributed to 500 local dealers early on April 8. But by the time the police started their confiscation of the issue at 3:30 p.m., only 2,857 copies were left. Rogan was arrested on April 8 at Finnegan's direction and then released on $500 bond. Rogan was charged with selling and offering for sale indecent and immoral matter, a crime that had a maximum penalty of one year in the workhouse and a $1,000 fine. Finnegan said that he took this action after receiving complaints from three church groups and several women who refused to give their names.[27]

Protest about the police action was lodged in an editorial by the *St. Louis Post-Dispatch*. The editorial said in part,

> The protests [against the photo feature] were to have been expected. But if the picture series brings enlightenment that saves the life of only one mother, the controversy will have been paid for.
>
> The action in St. Louis is particularly regrettable. It goes against the city's long-standing tradition of tolerance, and freedom of expression. The authorities are placed in a dubious light by the fact that this honest constructive effort has been suppressed, while dozens of magazines that specialize in suggestiveness or downright filth continue to be sold freely by the newsstands.[28]

In another complaint against the seizure of *Life*, the St. Louis Civil Liberties Committee sent a letter of protest to Finnegan. The committee said, "In our opinion, these pictures do not constitute an offense against public decency or morals. Censorship of any kind is contrary to the tradition of St. Louis. Your action smacks of a self-appointed censorship in defiance of this spirit and tradition."[29] Added to this list of criticisms of Finnegan's actions was the comment from a St. Louis minister, Truman B. Douglass, pastor of the Pilgrim Congregational Church. He said that the seizure of the magazine showed that "puritan prurience now reaches the ultimate by asserting it indecent to be born."[30]

Finnegan responded to this criticism by pointing out that while he had received only three protests of his actions, more than 100 other letters and calls of support for his efforts were sent to him. Finnegan added that he doubted the educational or intellectual value of the photographs. He also said that he would not want his children to see them. Pictures like these, Finnegan said, belong in medical publications.[31] In addition to issuing a defense of his actions, Finnegan ordered that all but fifty copies of *Life* be returned to Rogan. Rogan had agreed that he would not sell the issue in Missouri and that he would seek to withdraw any other issue of *Life* that might still be on an area newsstands.[32]

Memphis Moves Against Birth Photos

Another ruling that the *Life* photographs were obscene led to the magazine's confiscation in Memphis, Tennessee. Using an advisory opinion from the Memphis City Attorney Will Gerber that the pictures violated city and state obscenity laws, Memphis Commissioner of Public Safety Clifford Davis ordered the police to seize all issues of *Life* that were to be offered for sale. But Davis did not stop there. He also contacted the local distributor of *Life*, S. M. Haney of the Memphis News Co., and told Haney of the order before the magazine was even distributed to area news dealers. Davis said that, "Mr. Haney was cooperative, and saved the police a great deal of work." Haney told Davis that no copy of *Life* would be distributed. Haney later said that he had no idea if the photographs would be torn out of the magazine and the remainder of the issue sold at area newsstands. "I have received no instructions from the company," Haney said.[33]

In his opinion on the birth photographs, Memphis City Attorney Gerber said that the photographs were offensive, and "something that delicacy, purity, and decency forbid to be exposed." He added that *Webster's Dictionary* defined obscenity as something "offensive to chastity or modesty, expressing or presenting to the mind something that delicacy, purity, and decency forbid to be exposed." Punishment for a violation of the city's obscenity code carried a maximum of a $50 fine for each offense. Violation of the state code on obscenity carried a maximum punishment of one year in a county jail or workhouse and/or a $1,000 fine. In responding to Gerber's opinion, Commissioner Davis said, "I am glad to see him take this legal position. The relationship of parenthood with respect to childbirth is a most sacred institution and even nature itself has always protected conception and delivery."[34]

Haney said that he accepted the city's ban as a matter of necessity. Haney added that he received many calls on the subject. "A number [of calls] were from people who wanted me to sell them copies secretly," Haney said, "offering as high as $1 a copy and assuring me they wouldn't 'snitch' to the police."[35]

Support for the city's ban came from some members of the Memphis and Shelby County Medical Society. The group issued a statement which said in part,

> Whereas the material presented is scientific, and from our viewpoint not obscene, it is doubtful whether the object that the publishers state they wish to obtain can best be accomplished by this particular kind of publicity. If the publication could be sent through the mail, so that it might be censored by those who take exception to it, and not be open to sale without restriction, it might well accomplish some good.[36]

The April 11 issue of *Life* finally made its way onto newsstands in Memphis, but only in censored form. The four page photo feature on the birth of a baby was torn from the magazines sold on the streets.[37]

Other Areas Ban Life

Just as Memphis moved against *Life*, so too did other cities. In Chicago Lt. Harry M. Costello of the Chicago Police Crime Prevention Bureau ordered the issue to be taken off the newsstands. Costello said the magazine could only be sold if the four page photo feature was removed. He added that newsstands violating his rule would lose their licenses. News store proprietors who refused to comply with Costello's order were told that they would be arrested.[38] The ban was lifted on the following day by Police Commissioner Allman. He said that the restriction was only temporary and that the ban was lifted after police officials determined that the magazine did not violate any city ordinances.[39]

Mayor Maestri of New Orleans also ordered that all copies of *Life* offered for sale at local newsstands and news stores be seized. An 1884 statute was used as justification for this action. It is interesting to note that although a ban was undertaken against *Life* in New Orleans, the *New Orleans Times-Picayune* carried no mention at all of the ban. One reason for this omission can perhaps be seen in a small editorial appearing in the April 9, 1938, issue of the *Times-Picayune*. The newspaper, while not mentioning *Life* by name, said that a national magazine had set out to get the widest possible publicity for what the magazine considered to be a daring article. The *Times-Picayune* said that a publicity buildup was needed because the material itself was actually overplayed in its representation as a daring item. The paper said that other material that is far bolder lies on the shelves collecting dust. For the buildup to be really effective, the editorial continued, "the bait has to be disguised, the rubber frog painted as a leaping devil that will hurdle the morals of the community and corrupt the commoners." This publicity then leads police and other authorities to "impose a censorship, and the financial returns are immense." Few people, the editorial said, think that this material helps anyone while it disgusts many.[40]

Other reports of cities and even a state banning *Life* include rather divergent areas of the country. For example, the magazine was banned in Newport, Virginia, by Police Chief W. E. Mahone. Governor George F. Earle banned the magazine in the entire state of Pennsylvania because of the birth photographs. And the issue was banned in Atlantic City, New Jersey. In Tucson, Arizona, the only far western city to ban the issue, the publisher of the *Arizona Star* sold twenty-five copies of the magazine openly over his own counter in defiance of the police ban.[42] In Miami, Florida, a ban on the sale of the magazine was lifted after the Dade County Medical Association endorsed the photo feature. In contrast, police in Baton Rouge, Louisiana seized all available copies of the magazine, saying that it was objectionable because of the birth photographs. An effort by the police chief in Little Rock, Arkansas, to obtain an issue of *Life* after banning its sale at noon on April 8, 1938 proved futile. By the time he got to the newsstands to buy a copy of *Life* to decide for himself on the status of the pictures, the police chief found that the magazine was sold out. And a ban that was imposed in Syracuse, New York, was lifted on April 8. Other cities banning the magazine included Birmingham, Alabama, and Gulfport, Mississippi.[43]

Banned in the Bronx

Although the list of cities banning *Life* is long, perhaps the most interesting story in *Life's* battle with the censors can be found in the conflict between Bronx City Attorney Samuel J. Foley and Roy E. Larsen, the publisher of *Life*. The confrontation began when Foley declared that the birth photographs were "an outrageous affront to decency." The police, operating with Foley, confiscated 1,000 copies of the magazine in the Bronx in one afternoon. Four newsdealers were also arrested for selling licentious literature. Later in the day, Foley said that he wished to avoid as many arrests as possible, and urged local news dealers to surrender voluntarily copies of the magazine. In a public statement, Foley said,

> I think it [the publication of the birth photographs] is an outrageous affront to decency and an unmistakable violation of the law. It is not in any sense a borderline case. If they like to fight it out in this county as they are reported ready to do, I will be delighted to have the editor, the publisher, and owner come up here and sell me a copy of it, so that I might try it out on them instead of on some newsdealer.[44]

At about this same time, *Life* was also banned in other areas of New York and New Jersey. Essex, Bergen, Hudson, Union, and Mercer counties in New York moved to suppress the issue. Nassau District Attorney Edward J. Neary ordered the county and village police to seize all copies of the magazine that were placed on sale pending a presentation of the issue before a grand jury.[45] The Nassau County grand jury handed down an opinion one week later, saying that "as a matter of public policy, education on the subject presented is highly desirable, but that the printing of such matter should not be permitted in a magazine of general and unrestricted distribution." The grand jury said that the publication of the birth photographs, while not in good taste, was not a violation of the law. Meanwhile, in Mount Holly, New Jersey, Howard Eastwood, Burlington County Prosecutor, ordered police to seize copies of the magazine. Eastwood said that from a verbal description of the photographs, he felt that they were illegal. At about the same time the State Department of the Catholic War Veterans adopted a resolution asking all district attorneys to suppress the magazine, calling it "an insult to decency, morality, and motherhood."[46]

Underlying this movement against *Life* in the New York area was the strong role played by Foley. In sharing his views on the conflict after its conclusion, Foley defended his actions. In a speech before the Holy Name Society of the New York Fire Department in Manhattan, the Bronx, and Richmond, Foley said:

> I try to live as a Catholic and administer my job as a Catholic.
> In these changing times, people are impatient with adherance to standards of decency decreed by Catholic traditions. The people who are impatient with us today are the people who have lost their sense of perspective. Those are the people who swing the pendulum all the way across and bow to the ideology of the day—of sneering at God.[47]

Life *Goes To Trial*

Given the fact that Roy Larsen had seen his magazine being banned in cities across the country, and having been challenged openly by Foley to carry the issue into court, it comes as little surprise that the publisher picked up the gauntlet and agreed to submit himself to arrest for selling an obscene publication.

Prior to announcing his decision to submit himself to arrest, Larsen said that his magazine would defend any news dealer arrested in the Bronx for selling the publication. Harold Medina, an attorney for *Life*, conferred with Foley and said that he (Medina) would press for an early hearing for anyone arrested for selling the magazine. Meanwhile, *Life* officials reported that the sale of the magazine in areas not covered by Foley's ban were moving at a brisk pace.[48] The ban on the magazine in parts of New York reportedly led to a rash of sales in other parts of the city, with supplies of the magazine exhausted, and available copies selling at premium rates. Even the main office of *Life* found itself deficient and had to retrieve several issues sent out to its attorney. No additional copies were published to meet this shortage.[49]

Although Larsen had originally planned to submit himself for arrest on April 9, this move was delayed for two days until April 11 by mutual consent between the attorneys for Larsen and Foley. Larsen's attorney, Morris L. Ernst, expressed confidence before going to trial. He said, "We haven't any doubt we'll win the case. The arrests were silly and stupid. Why if those pictures were obscene, some 800 books in general circulation, many of which can be secured by anyone at any public library, are obscene."[50]

Flanked by three attorneys, Larsen was finally arrested after he had made arrangements with Foley to sell a copy of *Life* to Detective Frank McCarthy. Larsen's reason for submitting himself for arrest was, according to Foley, to test the ban rather than continue to have newsdealers arrested for selling the magazine. Larsen said that the magazine had been sold out and that not more than 10,000 of the 2,000,000 copies printed were confiscated.[51] Following his arrest on April 12, Larsen pleaded not guilty and was released in his lawyer's custody. His case was adjourned until April 19.[52]

Larsen's defense team won an important point early in the trial. The prosecution was overruled on a move to prevent Larsen's attorneys from calling expert witnesses to testify about the photographs. Using twenty-one experts in medicine, education, religion, and social welfare, Larsen's attorney, Morris Ernst, was able to demonstrate that the photographs were valuable, decent, constructive, and dignified. These experts said that the photographs would help allay fears of expectant mothers and help eliminate ignorance on the subject.[53]

On April 26, the three judge court handed down a unanimous decision clearing Larsen of all charges of selling an obscene publication. In the decision of *People v. Larsen*, written by Justice Perlman, the court said,

> ... the picture story, because of the manner in which it was presented, does not fall within the forbidden class. The picture story was directly based on a film produced under the auspices of a responsible medical group. There is no nudity or unnecessary disclosure. The subject has been treated with delicacy.[54]

When learning of the decision, Ernst said, "This means that there will be no more of this nonsense in the country where petty police chiefs set themselves up as censors of the nation's reading."[55]

The Impact of People v. Larsen

Although Ernst felt that the results of *Larsen* would eventually limit the action of other police officials trying to censor publications, the actual legal impact of the case was somewhat limited. Even though the case was never appealed, which would have a tendency to increase the chances of it serving as a guide for future litigation, *Larsen* was cited on six different occasions by courts ruling on a question of obscenity. Five of the six cases citing *Larsen* came from the New England area, while the sixth case was a court decision in the midwest.

The most common use of *Larsen* was to draw upon the definition for obscenity used by Justice Perlman. In *Larsen* obscene material was defined as that which tended "to corrupt morals or to lower the standards of right or wrong concerning sexual behavior."[56] This definition was later used by the City Magistrate's Court in New York in two obscenity cases involving the same defendant.[57] The *Larsen* definition of obscenity was also used in another case decided in a Court of Special Sessions in New York City.[58] The fourth court to rely on the definition of obscenity provided by *Larsen* was also in the same general part of the country. Fifteen years after *Larsen*, the Superior Court of New Jersey called upon the definition of obscenity used in *Larsen*.[59]

The legal impact of *Larsen* was not limited to just a definition of obscenity. Two other concepts concerning ways an item could be judged as being obscene that were put forth in *Larsen* later found their way into two other court decisions. In one instance, the Superior Court of Delaware cited *Larsen's* use of expert testimony to help determine if an item would have a harmful effect on an individual as justification for allowing the use of expert testimony in the case at hand.[60] And in a United States Court of Appeals, Seventh Circuit, decision, *Larsen* was cited as support for the concept that the only real way to determine if the material under question was obscene would be to examine thoroughly the facts of the case.[61]

Even though *Larsen's* legal impact was not overwhelming in its jurisdictions dealing with obscenity cases, it is interesting to note that this trial court decision did manage to find its way into six later obscenity cases. A similar comment can be made about this entire episode's impact on editorial commentary that focused on the question of censorship. For example, *Editor and Publisher* carried an editorial on *Life's* battle with the censors shortly after the event began. The commentary said, in part:

> Its [*Life's*] publication does illustrate, however, how far the frontiers of taboo have been moved since Anthony Comstock successfully prosecuted art and literary productions that might offend today's readers only by the intangibility of their allusions to the forbidden.
>
> Genuine censorship, not by publicity-hungry cops, clergymen or prosecutors, awaits the picture publishers if the dirty-minded segment attempts to exploit *Life's* enterprise by invading fields which the great middle class, buyers of magazines, will not tolerate in the printed page on the library tables.[62]

Other writers have seen *Life's* battle with the censors as a fight for liberty,[63] or a victory "won by the forces of cultural freedom."[64] And one man who played a key role in this episode, Morris Ernst, wrote several years later that the lack of a defense offered by many publishers of books and magazines accused of being obscene can lead and has led to censorship. Ernst wrote:

> Such timidity naturally encourages the censorious. More important, it helps produce unconsidered law on censorship. A street-corner newsstand owner does not make enough profit on the sale of any magazine to warrant the expense of a court defense. It is cheaper to plead guilty. . . .
>
> No wonder vice hunters and police usually level their guns, not at the wealthier publisher who selects the manuscript (and who is really responsible for its publication) but at relatively impecunious retailers who order a few copies, often as samples, and usually on consignment.[65]

In Conclusion

Just as Ernst is able to draw upon his experience in the "Birth of a Baby" episode to conclude that timid defense leads to more censorship, so too can others draw upon this same event to find other thoughts for the future.

The first observation is that when a small, yet highly motivated and vocal minority takes as its cause the suppression of something that violates their standards of morality and decency, they sometimes can have swift and successful results. This is especially true when members of this minority hold positions of local power. Obviously the actions of this moral minority in the 1930's bear some rather striking similarities to a so-called "moral majority" operating in today's society. We are often faced with the same tactics of a small, highly organized and vocal minority who, claiming that the general public holds the same standards of morality as they, move against literature that has been considered informative and educational, not obscene. The issues facing us today on the banning of books and magazines from public and school libraries are fundamentally the same as those issues surrounding the attempt to censor *Life* in 1938.

The second general observation for future consideration that can be drawn from this move against *Life* in the 1930's is that censorship does not work. In the case of *Life's* birth photographs, only a small number of copies of the magazine were actually kept from the general public. If anything, the publicity generated by the attempt to keep the magazine off the newsstands led to an even wider circulation of the magazine. The same is true today. Try to ban a publication or limit its circulation, and you almost certainly make it a best seller.

If only one comment could put into proper perspective the attempt to censor *Life* in 1938, that comment was made by then First Lady Eleanor Roosevelt in her weekly news conference. The First Lady spoke of her friend's five year old son who was shown the four page photo feature depicting the birth of a baby. With a look of complete boredom, he said, "The ostrich in school had a much harder time laying an egg."[66]

14

Deep Throat *in Deep Trouble* on a College Campus: An Academic Freedom Case Study

CHURCHILL L. ROBERTS

Churchill L. Roberts is Professor of Communication Arts at the University of West Florida where he teaches the course "The Constitution and the Press." He is a member of the Freedom and Responsibilities of Speech Division of the Southern Speech Communication Association as well as the Law Division of the Association for Education in Journalism and Mass Communication. His publications include "Attitudes and Media Use of the Moral Majority," Journal of Broadcasting *27 (Fall 1983): 403–10; and "Children's and Parents' Television Viewing and Perceptions of Violence,"* Journalism Quarterly *58 (Winter 1981): 554–62. The essay below was published in the* Free Speech Yearbook: 1981.

Introduction

In 1957 in *Roth v. United States* the U.S. Supreme Court made its first attempt to define obscenity.[1] Justice William Brennan, writing for the majority, said that a work was obscene—and thus devoid of First Amendment protection—if taken as a whole it appealed primarily to prurient interest. The average person and the contemporary community were to be the standards of judgment. In the years that followed, in a plethora of cases, judges, jurors, and justices wrestled with the normative terms used in the definition of obscenity. Who was the average person?[2] And what were the standards of a community? Were they local or national in scope?[3] Brennan himself tried to supply an answer to these questions and others, but by 1973 he concluded that the Court's attempts to formulate a satisfactory definition of obscenity had been futile. "I am forced to conclude that the concept of 'obscenity' cannot be defined with sufficient specificity and clarity to provide fair notice to persons who create and distribute sexually oriented materials, to prevent substantial erosion of protected speech as a by-product of the attempt to suppress unprotected speech, and to avoid very costly institutional harm."[4]

The majority of the Court, however, thought otherwise. Chief Justice Warren Burger fashioned a three-tiered definition of obscenity that included the original Roth test and two other criteria. First, the work had to depict or describe in a patently offensive manner sexual acts proscribed by the relevant state statute, and second, the work had to lack serious literary, artistic, political, or scientific value—the so-called LAPS Test.[5]

Unfortunately, the new test for obscenity provided little clarification for an area Douglas referred to as a "hodge-podge." A year after the *Miller* decision in which Burger announced the revised criteria for obscenity, a jury in Albany, Georgia, applied those criteria and found the film *Carnal Knowledge* obscene. The Supreme Court of Georgia affirmed the lower court's decision. But the U.S. Supreme Court reversed and said that the film, which was widely acclaimed by critics, was simply not its idea of hard-core pornography (obscenity). "Our view of the film satisfies us that 'Carnal Knowledge' could not be found under the *Miller* standards to depict sexual conduct in a patently offensive way."[7] Like Churchill's assessment of the Soviet Union—a riddle wrapped in a mystery inside an enigma—obscenity seemed to represent a jurisprudential quagmire, one that prompted Justice Potter Stewart to exclaim that while he might not be able to define obscenity, he knew it when he saw it.[8]

The Supreme Court's definitions and deliberations regarding obscenity provided the backdrop for a class project in a Regulation of Mass Media course which I taught at the University of West Florida in the Spring of 1977. Students were given a hypothetical situation involving the showing of an allegedly obscene film and were asked to act as jurors and render a legal opinion about whether constitutional protection should be afforded for exhibition of the film. Specifically, they were to assume that a theatre owner had been charged with showing the pornographic film *Deep Throat* in a commercial theatre in Pensacola, Florida (the community in which the university is located). Furthermore, they were to assume that a local jury and the Florida Supreme Court had found the theatre owner guilty of violating the state's obscenity statute (which follows the guidelines enunciated in *Miller v. California*). Thus, students, or groups of students as they were aggregated into groups of three or five, were to act as Supreme Court justices. If the group decision was unanimous, students were to write a single opinion. If there was disagreement, the majority was to formulate a majority opinion while the minority was to fashion a dissenting one.[9]

A videotaped copy of *Deep Throat* was made available for viewing just as it would have been had the case occurred in a real courtroom. Students were forewarned, however, of the content of the film and of the possibility that they could be offended by it. Viewing was therefore voluntary.[10] To insure further that there was no implicit pressure to see the film, viewing took place outside the classroom away from the presence of the instructor. On May 10 and 11, the film was shown in a room near the main office of the Communication Arts department. A secretary scheduled viewing times and turned on the videotape.

Prior to the showing of the film, I had arranged for the local State Attorney, Curtis Golden, to visit the Regulation class to discuss his attempts to control pornography in Northwest Florida. Though no mention was made of the class project, I had no doubt that *Deep Throat* would provoke many questions. It had been shown in Pensacola in 1973 to an estimated twelve thousand people.[11] After the *Miller* decision came down, the State Attorney sought to enjoin exhibition of the film, but it was whisked out of town before law enforcement officials could act.

Arrangements for Mr. Golden's visit were made through his assistant and former campaign manager, Wayne Smith. Later, I learned that Mr. Smith's daughter-in-law was a member of the Regulation class, and through her, the State Attorney's office learned of the screening of the film (See footnote[12]).

On May 11 a student phoned to say he had been asked to appear before the State Attorney. He wondered whether the inquiry might have something to do with his viewing of *Deep Throat*. Within an hour he called again to say that the showing of the film was indeed the subject of the inquiry.[12] The next morning I visited the State Attorney's office to offer an explanation of the class assignment and to point out why I thought my actions were legal. The State Attorney replied, however, that he was obligated to investigate a complaint and would therefore continue to subpoena and question students in the class.[13]

My next step was to inform university officials of what had taken place. During a meeting with the chairman of the department and the dean of the college, I mentioned that the State Attorney would not tell me the name of the person who had lodged a complaint but said that a certain state legislator was very upset about the matter. As it turned out, the legislator was Ed Fortune, Chairman of the House Appropriations Committee and a local resident. His daughter, Felicia Smith, was a member of the Regulation class. She was also the daughter-in-law of the State Attorney's assistant. The meeting with the chairman and dean ended with an assessment of my action: the dean believed I had exercised bad judgment in allowing students to view a pornographic film. Interestingly, the conversation turned out to be my last formal contact with university administrators until a grievance was filed in my behalf by the faculty organization (or union) that is the official bargaining agent for the State University System.

Word of the State Attorney's investigation spread quickly. The local newspaper carried a story on May 13 entitled "UWF Class on Obscenity Sparks Probe."[14] From that moment, the "'Deep Throat' incident" became a cause celebre—"the juiciest controversy to hit Pensacola in months."[15] The publicity prompted a variety of reactions and controversies, each of which revealed important differences in the perceived boundaries of freedom of expression among various segments of the community. First, there was the anticipated town-gown flap—an outcry from fundamentalist ministers and other citizens who were appalled that a college professor would show students a pornographic film and then hide behind the shield of academic freedom and the First Amendment.[16] A second level of controversy took place within the university and the State University System. Concerns about academic freedom were balanced by concerns about legislative retaliation. Finally, the controversy made its way to the courtroom after the State Attorney moved to have the film declared obscene and destroyed. This action, along with the reaction of the public and the legislature, provided a formidable test of academic freedom and academic leadership.

Public Reaction

In addition to carrying stories about the showing of *Deep Throat* and the ensuing investigation, the news media also offered editorial comments. The local newspaper, for example, thought the showing of the film was understandable and that the State Attorney's investigation should be terminated if he were to learn that only the students in the Regulation class were allowed to view it.[17]

> Since the regulation of films deals mainly with obscenity, . . . he asked those students who wanted to do so to view the film, outside classroom hours, in small groups so they would have before them an example of the type of films with which the law deals—"Deep Throat" film being a celebrated case.

He said it was voluntary and that he warned students in advance of the contents of the film. Frankly, we don't see a great deal of harm in this. . . . If only the students are involved, and they tell Golden their interests were academic and not prurient, then the matter ought to end right there.[18]

The only local radio station which editorializes was also tolerant of the film's use in the classroom. "Like it or not, consideration of the movie in a strictly academic atmosphere, with proper restrictions, is, in our opinion, suitable educational material for young adults who are studying the impact of the media on the public."[19]

The area's commercial television station, however, took a different view of the matter. In remarks directed to the students in the Regulation class, the station manager stated:

Just exactly what was it that you hoped to learn from the likes of "Deep Throat"? Admittedly, there have been plagues visited upon Northwest Florida in recent years, but pornographic movies hasn't really been one of them, and we wonder whether the University of West Florida, normally a boon to our area, really wants to count among its credentials and accomplishments the fact that it pioneered hard core pornography in this area. . . . We assume that most of you students are kept at the University as a result of your parents' benevolence and plain hard work. We wonder what they would say if they knew of your activities. Why not write a letter home to dear old Mom and let her know of your new found interest in Linda Lovelace.[20]

A week after the station manager's editorial was aired, another editorial was broadcast—this one by a member of the Regulation class.[21] The student-generated editorial sought to characterize the one delivered by the station manager as emotional and misleading:

You characterize us, that is, the class as "people whose activities were unexpectedly exposed." The clear implication of this is that we were doing something illegal or immoral or otherwise wrong. A survey of class members shows that *not one* of the students felt that he or she had done something wrong. . . . You asked what we hoped to learn from "Deep Throat." The answer is: the law. Whether or not a student saw the entire film clip, walked out on it, or declined to see it at all, the class project enabled us to learn a great deal about obscenity laws and the Constitution, and the difficult job that the Supreme Court and the States have in determining legal questions about obscenity. . . . Secondly, we hardly consider that the *optional*, private showing of the film to the 35 students of the class constitutes "pioneering pornography in this area." . . .

You state that "most of the students are kept at the university as a result of your parents' benevolence and plain hard work." The facts are that *27* of the *30* people in the class available for the survey are either putting themselves through school entirely on their own or at least hold jobs to help with the expense.[22]

While the rebuttal editorial was hailed by most class members as vindication, the station manager had the last word. On May 27 he delivered another editorial on the *Deep Throat* incident. In this one he reaffirmed his belief that the showing of the film was wrong and possibly illegal.

Forty-five minutes of "Deep Throat" as an official act of the University of West Florida is wrong. We said it was wrong last Thursday, and we repeat it tonight—and no matter what benefits on the understanding of law are claimed, we would hope that better ways of communicating the content of pornography can be found in the future. Academic freedom can be absolute no more than free speech can. You can't shout "fire" in a crowded theatre and you can't justify forty-five minutes of pornography by making it part of a college course.[23]

Community reaction to the use of *Deep Throat* in the classroom surfaced in other ways in the media—particularly in newspapers. The "Letters to the Editor" or "Voice of the People" sections of newspapers in the area were overwhelmingly critical of the showing of the film. A letter written by a minister of a nearby community stated: "Showing this material, the professor cheapens the students of the class, cheapens the university as an institution, cheapens the taxpayer and citizens and cheapens his own heritage as a member of the human family."[24] Another, written by a group of ministers in an adjacent county, proclaimed: "We, the Santa Rosa Ministerial Fellowship, hereby express our indignation at the use of pornographic material in the form of the film 'Deep Throat' for teaching purposes in public, tax supported institutions."[25] One letter, expressing the concern that academic freedom might "override the necessity for uniform rules and regulations," suggested a course of action. "I guess what it all boils down to is that it appears that there is a big weeding job laying here for the trustees of our alleged university to tackle."[26]

The Pensacola newspaper carried a public opinion article entitled "If You Ask Me." Photographs of individuals who were interviewed were displayed above their responses to the question, "Do you think the movie 'Deep Throat' should have been shown to university students as a class project?" Surprisingly, perhaps, eight of the ten people who were interviewed found nothing wrong with the class project.[27] A similar survey was conducted by the local public television station. Of the seven persons whose opinions were featured during one of the station's evening newscasts, four indicated that use of the film was proper.[28]

A position quite different from that reflected in the opinion polls was taken by a Christian organization comprised mainly of fundamentalist businessmen. The sponsored a newspaper advertisement labeled "We Protest." The ad stated:

> Anyone that would try to hide behind academic freedom to show the movie "Deep Throat" should be given their walking papers. We are sick of all the filth that has come from many of our institutions of higher learning during the past twenty years under the label of "academic freedom."[29]

The advertisement urged the president of the university to take action, and if he did not, the ad suggested that the Board of Regents take action against the president.[30]

There were few phone calls to me criticizing use of the film—but numerous letters, almost all of which were chock-full of Biblical quotations. One letter declared:

> So the truth is out? But did you not earlier consider the ancient wisdom? "Be sure your sin will find you out." . . . A greater teacher than you or I is recorded to have said, "There is nothing covered that shall not be revealed; neither hid that shall not be known."[31]

An anonymous letter which contained a quotation from the book of Matthew warned, "Hell will be full of your students and you, their stumbling block will be among them."[32] A more conciliatory letter came from a woman in Lodi, California. Aware that the film had been shown in a class, she admonished:

> I would like to remind you that this is a stench in the nostrils of God and you are contributing to the downfall of young people as well as sending your own soul to hell. God loves you and wants for you his richest blessing and life so full and so blessed with God's peace, love and comfort. God can and will forgive no matter what we do and it is this love and forgiveness that I pray you will seek.[33]

Similar letters were received by the president of the university. One told of a family's "concern about the dreadful situation" and of its alertness to subtle and blatant attempts to "polute" the community with "filth related to sex, violence, pornography, and homosexuality."[34] The latter issue seemed to be of equal interest, for the letter asked, "And what is the status of the homosexual on your staff or have I been misinformed?" The note to the president ended with a lengthy complimentary closing: "Yours for decency and IN LOVE FOR GOD AND COUNTRY. Sincerely, A friend-in-Christ, May God bless you as only He can."[35]

The University and Board of Regents Response

The divergent and often polarized views of the public caused a great deal of consternation within the university and the State University System. For the most part, students and faculty were supportive of what had taken place. In fact, as soon as Student Government members learned of the State Attorney's investigation, they issued a call for a special meeting to pass a resolution supporting "Dr. Churchill Roberts in his quest to further academic and intellectual freedom in the university environment."[36]

The university's Faculty Council also took action. In response to an article in the paper in which the president of the university allegedly assured Representative Fortune that no film such as *Deep Throat* would ever be shown again, the Council called a meeting to query the president about his remarks.[37] The president told the Council he did not recall the precise words he used in his conversation with the state legislator, nor did he know at the time the circumstances surrounding the showing of the film. The president declined any further comment, noting that:

> Under Board of Regents policy, and the agreement between the board and the United Faculty of Florida, the contents of official personnel evaluations are confidential. . . .
>
> Therefore, the university will have nothing to say publicly about the faculty member concerned in this incident.[38]

In the week following the president's meeting with the Faculty Council, the chairman of the Florida Board of Regents, Marshall Criser, sent a letter to me criticizing the use of *Deep Throat*. "Despite what might have been considered reasonable safeguards by you I cannot but conclude that you exercised inexcusable bad judgment in involving students of a state university, whether or not on a mandatory basis, in such an offensive presentation."[39] Copies of the letter were sent to other regents and to the president of the university who was asked to include the letter in my personnel file.

The regent who lived in Pensacola concurred with Chairman Criser:

> According to all press reports, it appears you feel you took every reasonable and proper caution prior to showing the movie. However, as a Regent, I have a responsibility to carry out and I strongly urge you to consider making an apology to the University for this incident.
> While your actions did not have criminal intent, I believe you could have exercised restraint and avoided placing the University and the Board of Regents in the position of having to defend or criticize your actions.[40]

Besides sending his own letter, the regent delivered a copy of the chairman's letter to the newspaper which ran it under the heading, "'Deep Throat' Showing Bad Judgment."[41] The letter's appearance in the paper promoted the faculty union to issue a statement to the press. The statement supported my use of the film and condemned the chairman of the Board of Regents for allowing his letter to be published. "For either an administrator or a member of the Board to make an evaluation of a professor which will be a part of his official record and to make it public is a violation of the agreement between the union and the Board of Regents, as Mr. Criser should know."[42]

The majority of students in the Regulation class were also perturbed by Mr. Criser's remarks. Despite an intensive amount of publicity, they had continued to work on the class project and on May 19 presented their results. Five of the eight groups decided the film was worthy of the First Amendment protection, though only one group did so on the basis of its artistic merits. The other four groups took either an absolutist First Amendment position or agreed with Justice Brennan that a definition of sufficient clarity could not be formulated without eroding individual rights guaranteed by the First Amendment. Three groups, however, thought that obscene materials should be controlled and that *Deep Throat* met the test for obscenity. Regardless of their judicial decision, most of them believed the project had been beneficial and that they had learned a great deal about obscenity law. They saw Mr. Criser's assessment as a political reaction, one that cast the project (and the professor) in a false light. A letter addressed to the Board chairman and signed by twenty-eight of the thirty-five students declared:

> It is our contention that the many hours we have spent reviewing the decisions of the United States Supreme Court . . . concerning this confused area of jurisprudence . . . will satisfy the most ex-

acting professional assessment of the educational merit of this assignment.

We feel, further, that it is an injustice to attempt to appease the general public's misunderstanding of the educational validity of our study with the sacrifice of Dr. Roberts' career. Thus, we denounce the ignoble means employed by Dr. Roberts' private, public, and administrative accusers in their attempt to malign his character and impugn his integrity as a professional educator.

We believe that the truth of this issue will live long after the cries of the defamers have ceased. And that truth is: the overwhelming majority of the students in the class are unreserved in their support of the educational discretion exercised by Dr. Roberts in his determination of content for this course; that the project and course have been an invaluable educational experience; and that the noble pursuit of truth in our educational community has been justifiably served.[43]

The actions of the Board chairman and the local regent seemed to be an attempt to placate the chairman of the House Appropriations Committee (Representative Fortune), who controlled the purse strings of the universities. In the days that followed the State Attorney's investigation, Fortune told the press that showing *Deep Throat* was morally wrong and that his daughter had sat through one scene and left. He further stated: "I'm not going to forget this. I want to be continually assured and the community deserves to be assured, that it will not happen again."[44]

Whatever assurances Fortune sought, including the one from the president of the university who supposedly told Fortune that a movie like *Deep Throat* would never be shown again, they were apparently not satisfactory; for the representative introduced a bill to the legislature to establish curriculum review boards at each university and community college in the state. The boards, which were to be comprised of faculty appointed by the president, were to screen all films and other curricula for material which might be pornographic. The final Senate version of the bill, the one which was eventually passed, read as follows:

Curriculum Screening Committee

The Board of Regents of the State University System and the Board of Trustees of each community college are hereby directed to establish rules to require the creation of a curriculum screening committee in each university and community college to review films and course curricula to determine the compliance with community standards on pornography.[45]

Several legislators questioned the Fortune proposal. Representative Bill Sadowski thought the bill would be unconstitutional. Another representative, Alan Becker, stated that "imposing prior restraint on movies and literature for whatever reason now would later lead to restraints on expressing political opinion."[46] When the Senate initially attempted to water down the bill by making the screening committees optional, Fortune read House members a letter from one of his constituents describing a "simulated sex act" which took place in a theatre course at the University of West Florida.

> During the final exam for a drama class at the end of the fall quarter this year, Dr. Thomas Long allowed a male student to strip naked and simulate the acts of intercourse with a female student, almost naked, on stage in front of the entire class.
>
> The student was portraying a deranged individual who had had sex relations with a horse and decided to try a girl, after which he decided he liked horses better.[47]

Fortune said the letter supported his contention that screening committees were necessary.

Though the charges in the letter were denied by students who had performed a scene from the play *Equus*,[48] revelation of the incident prompted the local newspaper, which had opposed Fortune's bill, to call for tighter university controls.

> ... if our university classes are being run, with no front-office direction, by professors who will deliberately choose or allow to be chosen the most offensive and controversial materials around to be presented to students, then the universities themselves are putting the ammunition in the hands of those politicians who want more direct control over the university.
>
> Surely, something other than the degrading and disgusting play "Equus" could have been found with which to teach students the fundamentals of acting; this professor did not even have the excuse that it was necessary to teach the course.
>
> We don't need and don't want censorship committees. . . .
>
> But we do need stronger leadership on campus to avoid the type of overpermissive excess which gives politicians a perfect opportunity to demonstrate their own purity of behavior and thought to their constituents.[49]

Publicity about the *Equus* performance spurred the legislature to pass the screening bill and send it to the governor. Fearing the implications of the hastily-passed measure, the university community, including such groups as the Board of Regents, United Faculty of Florida (UFF), and the American Association of University Professors (AAUP), mounted campaigns calling for the governor's veto. The chancellor of the State University System, in a letter to the governor, noted that the University of West Florida had recently established an ethics committee. He suggested that the university's action, along with the letter of reprimand from the chairman of the Board of Regents, was sufficient response to the *Deep Throat* matter.[50] The chancellor also noted that passage of the bill would "stigmatize Florida's higher education system in the academic world."[51]

The faculty union was even more vehement in its denunciation of the bill. UFF president Ken Megill said a distrubing "witch hunt" atmosphere surrounded its passage.[52] Officers of the Florida State University Chapter of AAUP were likewise concerned. In a letter to the governor, they warned that the bill "would have a chilling effect upon educational innovation, professional quality, and even the direct discussion of major literary, dramatic, and artistic classics: in short, on all the basic dimensions of freedom in the classroom to discuss one's subject at the highest possible professional level."[53] The officers added that if the bill became law, they "would have no choice but to take whatever legal steps . . . necessary to oppose it."[54]

The major newspapers in Florida also opposed Fortune's bill. The *Pensacola Journal* even carried a cartoon ridiculing the legislative mentality that seemed to prevail. The cartoon showed a smiling legislator wearing a pin-striped suit and cowboy hat holding an oversized club with a nail through it. The caption read: "Relax! I'm guardin' yo' academic freedom."[55]

On June 29 Florida Governor Reubin Askew vetoed the bill calling for curriculum screening committees. The Governor stated that while showing the film was a serious mistake, it was an exception to prevailing practices.[56] Representative Fortune replied that he was shocked by the Governor's action and vowed to override the veto during the next legislative session. But as time passed and the furor over the incident diminished, the cry for screening committees subsided.

Although the Board of Regents could claim success in helping to have the screening committee bill quashed, it could not do so in defending its means of allaying public and legislative fears. As was mentioned earlier, the initial response of the Board to the *Deep Throat* incident was a letter of reprimand from its chairman. When the letter was released to the public and published, the faculty union (UFF) filed a grievance arguing that publication of a letter intended to be a part of a faculty member's personnel file was a violation of the contract between the Board and the union. Though the university, understandably not wishing to usurp the authority of the Board chairman, rejected that argument, the State University System's labor relations coordinator, Robert Carroll, thought otherwise. Ruling on a technicality, Carroll noted:

> In as much as the contents contained in the letter are evaluative in nature but were not generated or reviewed as part of the evaluation process, the letter should not be part of the grievant's evaluation file. UWF should remove the letter from the evaluation portion of the file.[57]

A memorandum of September 7 from the Dean of Arts and Sciences to the Academic Vice-President acknowledged removal of the letter.[58] No further criticism, public or private (e.g., in an annual faculty evaluation), was ever directed to me by university officials about the *Deep Throat* incident.

The Legal Proceedings

While the local community and university administrators, including those at the state level, voiced opinions on the moral and ethical aspects of allowing students to view a pornographic film, the legal right of allowing such action rested with the court—the setting for the third avenue of controversy. The videotape of *Deep Throat* had been voluntarily turned over to the State Attorney's office for review. Following his investigation, State Attorney Golden announced that he did not intend to press charges against me but that he would "seek a court order to destroy the videotaped . . . film."[59] Although he had not seen the film, he declared it was "definitely hard core pornography."[60]

The road to the courtroom was not a smooth one. The judge who had been handed the *Deep Throat* case was asked by defense attorney George Estess to step aside when it was discovered that the judge's daughter-in-law was a secretary in the State Attorney's office. A second and potentially more serious problem had to do with standing before the court. Prosecuting attorney Richard Schlering (the lawyer in the State Attorney's office who had been assigned the case) argued that the videotape carried a university identification number and therefore belonged to the university. As a consequence, the only one with proper authority to contest the film's destruction would be an official of the university.[61] Both matters were soon resolved. The initial judge recused himself, and the issue of standing was dropped when the prosecuting and defense attorneys agreed that the university would not likely be able to establish proof of ownership.

In March of 1978 a forfeiture hearing took place in the County Court. No jury was involved. The judge, Frank Bell, began the hearing by showing the videotape to those who would be called to testify as expert witnesses (members of the press were also allowed to watch the videotape). Interestingly, the State Attorney offered himself as an expert witness on community standards. The hearing lasted two days. Most of the witnesses who were called were students in the class, though several faculty testified.[62] Only one faculty member, however, testified for the State, and his point was that while he taught a media law course (at a university in another state) which included a section on pornography, he did not find it necessary to show a pornographic film.[63]

As the hearing proceeded, the prosecuting attorney focused on the point that the decision should be based solely on the content of the film, while the defense maintained that the context in which the film was shown must be taken into account. In the educational setting, defense attorney Estess argued, the film had scientific value and therefore failed the third part of the *Miller* test. That is, it failed to lack serious literary, artistic, political, or *scientific* value—a requisite to be judged obscene. At one point, the judge asked the prosecuting attorney whether he intended to call anyone who had seen the film to testify that the experience had not had educational value. The attorney replied that he did not, whereupon the defense promptly called for a directed verdict—but the motion was denied.[64]

Eleven days after the hearing Judge Bell ruled that *Deep Throat* was obscene by a reasonable doubt by the preponderance of the evidence. He declared that the film should be destroyed but noted that:

> Dr. Roberts is not on trial. This is not the State of Florida versus Dr. Roberts. It's in regard to "Deep Throat." I might also mention that academic freedom is not on trial. It could be a subissue of academic responsibility or however you want to phrase it. What is on trial is the film itself.[65]

Bell ordered a stay of his ruling so that an appeal could be made to the Florida Supreme Court.

At the appellate level, the American Association of University Professors (AAUP) filed an amicus brief which also argued that the *Miller* test had not been met. The brief pointed out that the film had been shown in a controlled setting for educational purposes and was therefore not the kind of commercial pornography generally associated with obscenity cases. It also stated that *Deep Throat* was not used to appeal to prurient interest but to educate students through critical viewing and discussion of controversial material. In such circumstances, the brief said, the film possessed political (as well as scientific) value.

It cannot be denied that the issue of obscenity regulation is a legitimate and important political question. When court decisions are continually criticized for being either too restrictive, when obscenity trials are reported in the newspapers on an almost daily basis, when some states have eliminated obscenity laws while others have strengthened them, and when there is a wide range of available political alternatives for dealing with obscenity . . . ,obscenity regulation constitutes a political issue of vital contemporary importance. Whatever may be the diverse goals of higher education, one of those goals must be to prepare students for the roles they will play as citizens and political leaders in governing our society. It is clear that a responsible citizen or legislator will have a greater appreciation of the issues involved if he or she can see the kinds of materials that are generating the current controversy.[66]

In the course of oral arguments, which took place in December of 1978, the attorney assigned to defend the State's seizure of the film (videotape) conceded that it could be used for educational purposes. Responding to questions from Justice Ben Overton, the attorney first acknowledged that examples of pornographic films could be shown to a prosecutors' association so that they would know what to prosecute. Next, the attorney agreed that a bar association could conduct a similar training program. Finally, the State's attorney conceded that with proper guidelines a college journalism class could also exhibit pornographic films. The *Pensacola Journal* remarked that the "barrage of tough questions" directed to the Assistant Attorney General was so intense that he was often left "groping for answers" and had little time to make his argument.[67]

In July of 1979 the Florida Supreme Court announced its decision.[68] It reversed the lower court order calling for destruction of the film—but on grounds which avoided the constitutional issues. Justice Joseph Hatchett, in a 6-1 majority opinion, declared that the film had been improperly seized. According to Hatchett, proper adjudication would have required the issuance of a warrant and judicial inquiry regarding probable obscenity prior to a hearing on the State's petition for confiscation and destruction of the film. But as a reply brief of the defense had pointed out, the videotape which had been voluntarily surrendered was held in a State Investigator's car for several months before being deposited with the Clerk of the Court.[69] Another six months passed before the State filed a petition for an order to find probable cause.

Hatchett also stated that the section of the obscenity statute dealing with forfeiture had been improperly applied, for it should have come into play only when a trial judge had "made a determination as to criminal conduct."[70] In other words, an individual must first be prosecuted under a criminal statute (i.e., the obscenity statute) before the disposition of the material in question can be resolved. The State Attorney had considered pressing criminal charges but declined to do so because he believed he could not obtain a conviction.[71]

Conclusions

The Florida Supreme Court's decision brought an end to the legal dispute. The State did not appeal, and the videotape was eventually returned to me.[72] Despite the fact that *Deep Throat* is still the subject of litigation in various state and federal courts, it has not been used again in the Regulation class. Reluctance to do so may underscore the damage that has been done to academic freedom, for the actions (or inactions) of the University of West Florida administration and the Board of Regents suggest that unpopular ideas or unpopular teaching methods will not be supported.

In his letter of criticism concerning the use of the film, the chairman of the Board of Regents indicated that he would continue to defend "academic freedom and constitutional individual rights of faculty."[73] Yet his words were not reassuring, for in a comparative survey of faculty of thirty-seven state universities carried out by the Educational Testing Service, the University of West Florida (the only Florida university included in the survey) ranked last in perceptions of academic freedom. When asked whether university trustees would support the principle of freedom for faculty and students to discuss any topic, only four percent of the faculty strongly agreed. Thirty-five percent disagreed with the statement, and thirty-two percent disagreed strongly. In responses to another question, seventy-two percent of the faculty either disagreed or disagreed strongly with a statement that eccentric or unpopular beliefs would not usually be frowned on by the administration.[74]

Because students and faculty are largely insulated from public and political pressure, they are perhaps freer than administrators to be idealistic in their views about academic freedom. On the other hand, those who place the parameters of academic inquiry within a context of social acceptance run the risk of transforming a cherished right into mere tinsel. The *Deep Throat* controversy pitted the university against itself and against the community and against the legislature. No person or group emerged as a winner, but a likely loser was reflected in the attitudes of West Florida faculty who may be inclined to believe that the pursuit of truth is confined to certain subject matter and certain means of exploration. More seriously, they may act on those beliefs.

15

Nazis in Skokie: Anatomy of the Heckler's Veto

FRANKLYN S. HAIMAN

Franklyn Haiman is Professor of Communication Studies at Northwestern University where he teaches a course entitled "Contemporary Problems in Freedom of Speech." Haiman is one of the founders of the Commission on Freedom of Speech of the Speech Communication Association, having served as the first chair of that Commission. He is also a member of the Board of Directors of the American Civil Liberties Union, as well as a Director of the Illinois Affiliate of the ACLU. His books in the area of free speech include Freedom of Speech: Issues and Cases *(New York: Random House, 1965);* Freedom of Speech *(Skokie, Ill.: National Textbook Company, 1976); and* Speech and Law in a Free Society *(Chicago: University of Chicago Press, 1981). Among his many articles concerning the First Amendment are: "Speech v. Privacy: Is There a Right Not to be Spoken To?" Northwestern University Law Review 67 (May-June 1972): 153–99; and "The Rhetoric of the Streets: Some Legal and Ethical Considerations," Quarterly Journal of Speech 53 (April 1967): 99–114. The following essay was presented as the keynote address at the convention of the Speech Communication Association of Pennsylvania in October 1978 and as a paper at the convention of the Speech Communication Association in November 1978. It was published in the* Free Speech Yearbook: 1978.

It was at 2:30 P.M. on Tuesday, June 20, 1978, as I sat in a federal courtroom of the Northern District of Illinois, that I watched the story of the proposed Nazi march in Skokie reach its climax. Television reporters rushed from the chambers to announce to their waiting camera crews that the last act of a drama that had attracted media attention and inflamed human passions for nearly fourteen months was over.

It ended, as it had begun, not as a case involving the Chicago suburb of Skokie, but as one having to do with freedom of assembly in a place called Marquette Park, on Chicago's southwest side. A scholarly black federal-court judge, responding to the arguments of a Jewish American Civil Liberties Union lawyer, had ordered an Irish-dominated city political machine to permit a half-Jewish Nazi to hold a rally in a park surrounded by Lithuanians. That is where self-styled Nazi leader Frank Collin had wanted to be in the first place, and that is where he could now, of his own free will, go instead of to Skokie. In the interim there had been two lawsuits that had worked their way through the Illinois court system, two other suits before federal district and appellate courts, two emergency rulings by the United States Supreme Court, torrents of radio and television coverage, and thousands of pages of print: news and feature stories, editorials, letters to editors, columns, and cartoons.

In that same period my own psyche was battered by a host of personal experiences I shall not soon forget: the sharp words exchanged with Harvey Schwartz, Skokie's attorney, on a Mutual Broadcasting System radio debate; the public disagreement in the Chicago media with my favorite U.S. Congressman, Abner J. Mikva, whose Academic Advisory Committee I chair; the survivor of Auschwitz in a local B'nai Brith audience who came out of his chair screaming "Filthy scum!" at me as he was restrained by his friends; the question-and-answer session in a Columbia Broadcasting System television studio with a live audience consisting *entirely* of holocaust survivors; Rabbi Rudolph Rosenthal suddenly sweeping his hand at my face, stopping an inch or two short of it, to make his point to a Cleveland City Club audience that some kinds of symbolic conduct (such as threatening gestures) do not merit First Amendment protection; the security guards walking me back to my car after a speech (at Northeastern Illinois University) which had stirred denunciations from members of the Spartacus League in the crowd.

But I am not here to solicit your sympathy or emotional support, for happily there has been an ample supply of that in these difficult months. For example, how can one be discouraged when he heard the ninety-four-year-old Roger Baldwin, founder of the ACLU, proclaim (last June) in his still-booming orator's voice: "My survival is a matter of luck, but the ACLU's survival is a matter of integrity"?

Having thus biased the case that I wish to present to you (as if you did not already know my First Amendment prejudices), let me proceed to the story of the Nazis in Skokie—a case study of the heckler's veto.

The Beginning of the Drama

As I have already indicated, the drama began, not in Skokie, but in Chicago's Marquette Park, a short distance from the headquarters of the so-called National Socialist Party of America (not to be confused with the National Socialist White People's Party, based in Cicero, Illinois, which claims to be the true descendant of George Lincoln Rockwell and which kicked Collin out of its party a few years earlier, presumably because of his allegedly Jewish father). And it all began, not a year and a half ago, but in 1970, when Collin first walked into our ACLU office in Chicago to complain that his First Amendment rights were being abridged by the refusal of the Chicago officials to give him a permit to speak in Marquette Park. That complaint led, through a series of legal actions, to a decision by the United States Seventh Circuit Court of Appeals in *Collin v. Chicago Park District* in 1977, finding Chicago officials in violation of the Constitution and ordering them to allow Collin to speak and hold his rallies.

Speak and rally he did, from 1972 to 1976, with only sporadic incidents of ensuing violence, for which the guilty parties—and sometimes innocent ones as well—were quickly arrested by Chicago's men in blue. But as the black ghetto spread closer and closer to the low-income white ethnic neighborhoods surrounding Marquette Park, tensions rose in the area, and the police became understandably more nervous. So, in May, 1976, Chicago Park District officials came up with a new technique for putting Collin (as well as a lot of other would-be exercisers of free speech) out of business. This was a requirement that any assembly of more than seventy-five persons (counting on-lookers, it should be noted) could not obtain a permit without posting from $100,000 to $300,000 worth of liability insurance—a kind of insurance that, even if the premiums were not prohibitive, is simply not available to high-risk groups like neo-Nazis or to their bitter foes in the Marquette Park vicinity: the Martin Luther King Jr. movement.

The Question of Liability Insurance

So Collin came back to the ACLU, we went back to the federal court, a district-court judge upheld the insurance requirement, and the Court of Appeals sent the case back to the lower court for further consideration. All this took time, of course. Meanwhile the publicity-hungry Collin sought action elsewhere. In early 1977 he wrote a letter to at least a dozen Chicago suburbs (my home town of Evanston among them) announcing his intent to grace them with his unwelcome presence. Most of them ignored his letter, but not the village of Skokie. (With a population of seventy thousand, Skokie advertises itself as the "largest village in the world.") Village officials informed Collin that their parks, too, required liability insurance.

This was a red flag to Collin, who at that point may not even have been aware of the heavily Jewish population of Skokie with its concentration of holocaust survivors and their families. But no sooner had he announced his intent to march on a public sidewalk in front of the Skokie Village Hall to protest the liability-insurance requirement of the parks, he quickly discovered, thanks to the community's reaction, what a publicity gold mine he had struck. It was at that moment, also, that the case of the Nazis in Skokie was on it's way to becoming one of the biggest media events of the 1977-78 season.

A Series of Legal Actions

Legal actions followed quickly. To condense a great deal into a few minutes let me highlight these events:

The Village of Skokie obtained a county-court injunction to prevent the Nazis' announced demonstration at the Village Hall on Sunday, May 1, 1977. So Collin decided to go there on Saturday, April 30, the day before. As an ACLU observer I was waiting on the steps of the Village Hall that afternoon—waiting along with a large and angry crowd, some equipped with boards and baseball bats. But the Nazis never arrived. I learned from a reporter with a walkie-talkie that their two vans had been stopped and turned back at the near-by expressway exit ramp.

I went immediately to a public telephone to report what had happened to David Goldberger, the ACLU attorney handling the case. He could only speculate that another injunction had been obtained, this time *ex parte*, since he had received no notice. That, in fact, is exactly what had happened. At ten o'clock that morning a county-court judge had been found at home and signed an *ex parte* injunction prohibiting the assembly on April 30 or any other time "until further order of this court."

The following week Goldberger asked the Illinois Appellate Court for an immediate review of the injunction. It declined, as did the Illinois Supreme Court. This resulted, on June 15, in an order from the United States Supreme Court (in *National Socialist Party of America v. Skokie*) directing the Illinois courts either to grant prompt review of this prior restraint on speech or to issue a stay of the injunction.

Reasonably prompt review was then granted by the Illinois Appellate Court, which narrowed the scope of the injunction to prevent only the public display of swastikas. In January, 1978, the Supreme Court of Illinois struck down the injunction in its entirety.

At the same time the Illinois high court ordered dismissal of a second lawsuit that had been wending its way through the state courts. Anti-Defamation League attorneys, dissatisfied with Skokie's legal tactics, had filed an action of their own on behalf of a group of holocaust survivors residing in the community, seeking to enjoin the Nazi march on the grounds that it would constitute a psychic assault on the plaintiffs. This unprecedented attempt to invoke a principle of tort law known as "the intentional infliction of emotional distress" as a basis for a prior restraint on a political assembly was dismissed out of hand by the State Supreme Court. The ADL's legal strategy had fared no better than that of Skokie.

New Skokie Ordinances Adopted and Opposed

Skokie officials had themselves foreseen the fate that their injunction might meet in court, so they gathered in an emergency session on Monday, May 2, 1977. They quickly adopted three new municipal ordinances, all admittedly designed to block any Nazi demonstration. The first extended the liability-insurance requirements from the parks to the streets and all other public areas. The second banned public demonstration by members of any political party wearing military-style uniforms. The third prohibited the dissemination or display anywhere in the village of Skokie of materials or symbols promoting or inciting hatred against people for reason of their race, national origin, or religion—a so-called group-libel law.

The ACLU challenged the constitutionality of these ordinances in federal court. On February 23, 1978, District Court Judge Bernard Decker found them all to be in violation of the First Amendment. However, because he felt that his opinion on the group-libel law was arguably inconsistent with a twenty-six-year-old U.S. Supreme Court precedent on that subject (*Beauhernais v. Illinois*), he granted a forty-five-day stay of his own order to give the U.S. Circuit Court of Appeals an opportunity to review his decision before a permit to march was issued.

The U.S. Seventh Circuit Court of Appeals responded swiftly. Oral argument was set for April 18 before a three-judge panel of the court. On Monday, May 22, the court handed down a ruling affirming Judge Decker's finding that the ordinances were unconstitutional. Later that week Skokie officials announced that they would seek review of this decision by the U.S. Supreme Court and would ask Justice John Paul Stevens for an emergency stay of the ruling, pending review. But meanwhile they were legally bound to issue the permit Collin had requested for a thirty-minute march in front of the Village Hall on Sunday, June 25. They did so promptly.

Headed Toward a Clash

At that point the attention of the nation's media became riveted on the Skokie story on an almost daily basis as events rushed headlong to their climax. Leaders of a federation of Jewish organizations announced plans for a massive counterdemonstration in Skokie on the date of the march. This would involve an expected fifty thousand people, including Illinois Governor James Thompson and U.S. Congressman Abner Mikva. Rabbi Meir Kahame, founder of the Jewish Defense League, promised that blood would flow in the streets. Collin, allegedly facing internal problems from members of his group who were quoted by one reporter as being "more interested in fighting the niggers than the Jews," told the press that he would call off the Skokie march if three conditions were met: First, the permit Collin now had in his possession for a June 25 march in Skokie must not be invalidated by further legal proceedings. Secondly, two new laws pending in the Illinois state legislature, designed to block the Nazi march, must fail of passage. Thirdly, Collin's right to assemble followers and to speak in Marquette Park must be fully restored.

Within three weeks Collin had everything he asked for. Perhaps this was because of the pressure generated by the bait of his calling off the march (a view I'm sure he holds); perhaps *in spite of* his threats and promises (an entirely plausible alternative explanation); or perhaps as a result of a combination of these contradictory forces (a hypothesis I believe to be closest to the truth).

Three Conditions Met

The first condition was met on June 12, when the full U.S. Supreme Court, responding to Justice Stevens's referral of the matter to the Court, refused by a 7-2 vote (Justices Harry Blackmun and William Rehnquist dissenting) to grant a stay of the Court of Appeals ruling against the Skokie ordinances. So the march could go forward even if the Supreme Court should later decide to review the case and determine for itself whether *Beauharnais v. Illinois* was still to be taken seriously.

The second condition was met the next day, when the Illinois house of representatives overwhelmingly killed the two pieces of legislation that, a month earlier, had been even more decisively rushed to passage in the state senate. One of these proposed statutes would have re-enacted the Illinois group-libel law, which had been upheld in *Beauharnais* but was later repealed by the Illinois legislature. The other, whose meaning no one, including its sponsor, could explain, would have outlawed demonstrations by groups that "arouse reasonable apprehensions that they were organized for the purpose of using or displaying physical force in promoting any political object." Under this law the use of "symbols having historic associations with political violence" or the use of "quasi-military uniforms" would be evidence of a violence-prone group.

The third and final condition was met one week later, when Federal District Court Judge George Leighton ordered the Chicago Park District to issue instantly and without the requirement of liability insurance a permit Collin had requested for a July 9 rally in Marquette Park. Actually Judge Leighton had issued an injunction nearly a year earlier against enforcement of the $300,000-liability-insurance requirement; but Park District officials, relying on the letter rather than the spirit of that order, had merely reduced the amount of insurance required to $60,000, knowing full well that no insurance of any kind was available to Collin.

After months of futile negotiations with the Park District, Attorney Goldberger had gone to Judge Leighton on May 27, 1978, asking that the Park District be held in contempt of his 1977 ruling. The June 29 hearing in Judge Leighton's courtroom was scheduled in response to that motion. Although the judge agreed with Park District officials that they were not technically in violation of the language of his order, he was sufficiently convinced of their foot dragging that he accepted a second motion by Goldberger to modify his injunction on the spot, and he ordered the issuance, *instantum,* of a Marquette Park permit for July 9.

The Outcome

What followed was anticlimax. On Thursday evening Collin predictably called off the Sunday march in Skokie, the leaders of the counter-demonstrators canceled their plans, the Governor withdrew his instructions to the National Guard, and the residents of the village of Skokie slept peacefully that weekend.

The problem posed, however, by continuing Nazi demonstrations in the city of Chicago and by racist activity elsewhere in the United States was by no means resolved by Skokie's return to suburban tranquillity. And when one examines the lines of argument against the Skokie march, repeated in legal briefs, letters to the editor, sermons from temple pulpits, and in endless face-to-face encounters, one becomes acutely aware of how fragile is our society's commitment to First Amendment values.

Arguments by Opponents of the March

The argument took many forms, but at the core of all of them was a rejection of the principle, so well expressed by Justice Louis Brandeis in *Whitney v. California* in 1927, that "if there be time to expose through discussion the falsehood and fallacies, to avert the evil by the processes of education, the remedy to be applied is more speech, not enforced silence." Rather, the opponents of the march in Skokie adopted the philosophy that certain kinds of expression, like the advocacy of genocide or the display of Nazi symbols, are so palpably evil and so devastatingly traumatic for those who see and hear such communication that the power of government is justifiably invoked to guard them from exposure to it. It may appear to demean the worthiness of their motives and to show disrespect for the depth of their feelings for me to characterize their position as a classic case of the heckler's veto, but I cannot in all honesty do otherwise. Let us look at the arguments, one by one, to see how they fit that model:

The first and commonest theme was that a Nazi march in Skokie would be like shouting "Fire" in a crowded theater—a clear and present danger outside the protections of the First Amendment. Aside from the consistent misquoting of Judge Oliver Wendell Holmes's famous admonition against *falsely* crying "Fire" in a crowded theater, the proponents of this argument failed to see the distinction between a panic-struck captive audience in an enclosed arena and a crowd warned a month in advance of what they would see if they came, of their own free will, to a public sidewalk in front of a village hall on a particular Sunday afternoon. Any clear and present danger that might occur under such circumstances would result only from violent attempts to exercise a heckler's veto against the Nazi demonstration.

But, it was then asked, is not the proposed march in Skokie a deliberate attempt to provoke such violence, an incitement to riot not protected by the First Amendment? Again the argument failed to perceive a crucial distinction. A speaker may be guilty, under the Supreme Court's ruling in *Brandenburg v. Ohio* in 1969, of direct incitement to lawless action where there is a likelihood that such action may immediately occur, but only where the speaker is advocating that action. Collin was not going to Skokie to urge his own mutilation. If violence were to have broken out there, those *in the audience* who instigated the lawlessness would have been responsible for incitement to riot, not Collin. To shift the blame for the violence in which a hostile audience engages to the target of their lawlessness, using the rationale that the target's ideas or presence are the real "cause" of all the trouble, is one of the subtlest forms of heckler's veto; for it stands logic on its head without appearing to do so.

Closely akin to the incitement-to-riot argument was the allegation, accepted by the Illinois intermediate court, that the display of Nazi symbols in Skokie would be akin to "fighting words"—another category of expression that the U.S. Supreme Court had placed outside the protections of the First Amendment. One could counter this charge, as Attorney Goldberger did, simply by noting that the fighting-words doctrine allows for punishment only after the fact, not for prior restraints, and that it does so exclusively with respect to face-to-face encounters in which one individual hurls personal insults at another individual, not in which a speaker is addressing a rally or communicating a political message to a crowd of observers.

But I would go further and suggest that the fighting-words doctrine, even thus narrowly construed, is another kind of heckler's veto—a First Amendment aberration that ought to be abandoned by the Supreme Court. The Court's own definition of fighting words is enough to discredit the doctrine among people who understand that meaning in the eye of the beholder. Said the U.S. Supreme Court in *Chaplinsky v. New Hampshire* in 1942 in explanation of the doctrine: "The English language has a number of words and expressions which by general consent are 'fighting words' when said without a disarming smile . . . such words, as ordinary men know, are likely to cause a fight." And *with* a disarming smile, I suppose, no one would be likely to fight?

Another argument against the Nazi march in Skokie, although not taken seriously by any court or lawyer, was ardently embraced by the otherwise-intelligent columnist Gary Wills, who proposed that the Nazis should be barred from the streets as an obscenity or a public nuisance. Even more than with the fighting-words doctrine, it takes a considerable stretch of the imagination to bring the display of political, even genocidal, symbols within the definition of obscenity (that which appeals to the prurient interest in sex) or of public-nuisance law (that which allows you to complain about your neighbor's stereo at three in the morning). But, assuming that that feat could be accomplished, we again would have a classic case of the heckler's veto—ideas and symbols suppressed because they are beyond the pale of acceptability to the mores of the majority.

By far the most formidable opposition to the Nazi march came from those who held that racist communication is of utterly no value in the marketplace of ideas, that it has been outlawed by the civilized democracies of Western Europe, and that we in the United States should follow suit either by adopting criminal group-libel laws or by allowing civil suits for the prevention and punishment of speech that inflicts emotional distress upon others. As well-intentioned and as authoritatively supported as this position may be, I can find nothing to distinguish it from other forms of the heckler's veto. If adopted and enforced even-handedly it would have to encompass the burning of all copies of Hitler's *Mein Kampf*, Shakespeare's *The Merchant of Venice*, *Huckleberry Finn*, and *Little Black Sambo*. The National Broadcasting Company's "Holocaust" series would have been taken off the air because of the complaints made by German-Americans in Chicago that it was stirring up hatred against them and that their children were being called "Nazis" by other children at school. Blacks would not be allowed to say that some people are "honkie bigots" and the counterdemonstrators at a Collin rally in downtown Chicago on June 24, 1978, would have been arrested and punished for shouting "Kill the Nazis" and "Death to the Nazis." In short, the measure of freedom of speech would be in the degree in which it stirred up intense feelings in one's adversaries.

Many have bemoaned—and I have been among them—the worldwide attention Frank Collin gained from that simple letter he wrote to the village of Skokie in early 1977. But, perhaps unwittingly, he and Skokie have done us all a favor. Perhaps the nation's re-examination of the meaning of the First Amendment, triggered by their actions, will leave us all with a better understanding of why it is that a society confident of its own values will defend the right of free expression even for those whose beliefs and messages it most despises.

Part Five

Ethical Perspectives

Free Speech, Persuasion, and the Democratic Process
Thomas R. Nilsen

An Ethical Basis of Communication
Karl R. Wallace

16

Free Speech, Persuasion, and the Democratic Process

THOMAS R. NILSEN

Thomas R. Nilsen is Emeritus Professor of Speech Communication at the University of Washington where he developed and continues to teach the course "The Ethics of Interpersonal and Public Communication." He is the author of Ethics of Speech Communication, 2nd ed. *(Indianapolis: Bobbs-Merrill, 1974), and a number of articles on communication freedoms and responsibilities, including: "Persuasion and Human Rights,"* Western Journal of Speech Communication *24 (1960): 201–5; "The Ethics of Persuasion and the Market Place of Ideas Concept," in Don W. Parson and Wil A. Linkugel, eds.,* The Ethics of Controversy: Politics and Protest *(Proceedings of the First Annual Symposium on Issues in Public Communication, University of Kansas, June 27–28, 1968): 7–35; and "Confidentiality and Morality,"* Western Journal of Speech Communication *43 (1979): 38–47. The following essay appeared in the* Quarterly Journal of Speech *in October, 1958.*

Since the advent of mass advertising, professional public relations, and motivation research, persuasion has been used on a scale of such magnitude with techniques of such refinement as to raise with renewed urgency the problem of its relationship to traditional democratic principles. It is the purpose of this paper to examine some of the current techniques of persuasion in the light of these principles.

1

To those of us who have lived our lives in a democratic society the democratic process may seem to be a pattern of simple and natural ways of organizing the political relationships of men. We may readily take for granted its methods, its values, its opportunities. Yet that this process is complex and difficult is attested to by the slow and laborious way societies learn to live by such means, and by the ways in which presumably democratic procedures can become inimical to the established democratic society in which they function; that is to say, by the ways in which democracy can undermine itself in the name of democracy.

How democracy began, of course, we do not know, but some speculation about its beginnings may help point up certain of its essentials. It seems reasonable to suppose that when the needs of survival and well-being stimulated the codification of reciprocal obligations among men, we had the beginnings of, or at least the basis for, democracy. We might assume that the establishment of simple codes of procedure for relationships among men fostered a primitive glimpse of human values. The elimination of totally arbitrary relationships, or arbitrary rule of men over men, may well have led to some sense of value in man as man, some inviolable essence in his nature that other men had no right to dominate.[1] This concept of value could further have influenced the procedures to make possible a greater realization of the values at first only dimly conceived. It was, no doubt, a long and painful process, with progressions and regressions. It is still going on.

To understand the implications of modern persuasive techniques we must recognize that democracy is at once a pattern of procedures and a pattern of values; the values must influence the procedures, and the procedures must continuously recreate the values, if democracy is to perpetuate itself. The values it seems to me are these: a belief in the intrinsic worth of the human personality; a belief in reason as an instrument of individual and social development; self-determination as the means to individual fulfillment; man's fulfillment of his potentialities as a positive good. The procedures are unrestricted discussion and debate, various forms of public address, parliamentary procedure, legal processes, and publicly defined rules of evidence and tests of reasoning. An educational system that will adequately equip citizens to think and to discuss is implied.

If democracy is to function, ideas need to be expressed, the ideas need to be critically examined, the best ideas need to be found, and these ideas need to be accepted by the people if they are to be effectively translated into policies. For the expression of ideas we have freedom of speech and assembly, and freedom of the press. That ideas may be examined, understood, and tested, we have discussion and debate, and tests of evidence upon which all can agree. To gain acceptance of ideas we have persuasion. Since issues are complex, interests widely disparate, and apathy only too common, persuasion plays an important part. And herein lies our problem. Persuasion can take many forms, and it can have varied effects. Since it is one of the important procedures by which democracy is carried on, we must inquire whether persuasion in any given case serves to reinforce and perpetuate the democratic process or to weaken and circumscribe it. It will be noted that our concern here is not with the end toward which people may be persuaded, but with the process of persuasion itself.

2

Persuasion, the inducement in others of belief or action, is an essential part of any society, for ultimately government, whether democratic or totalitarian, rests upon some form of support in public opinion. In a democratic society regular procedures exist to make that public opinion instrumental in affecting government. The influencing and shaping of this public opinion then becomes of extreme importance. This paper, in viewing persuasion in the democratic process, will be limited to some of the most significant persuasive techniques used by professional public relations and advertising men in political campaigns. The use of professional PR and ad men in campaigns during the past decade has intensified some of the old and introduced some new problems for democratic society.

Although our concern here is not with persuasion as used in the PR of business but persuasion as used in the political arena, some understanding of the former is necessary to an understanding of certain biases of the latter. Historically, the PR man's role has been primarily to create and foster favorable attitudes toward a business or a product. Higher sales and increased profits have been the immediate and the ultimate objective,[2] but there have been by-products of various kinds. The need for favorable public attitudes has fostered much that is good in commercial activity; it has fostered a larger social view and an increasing sense of community responsibility. It has also given rise to many skills and techniques in influencing public opinion. These techniques have grown out of the need for creating favorable public attitudes in as short a time as possible as inexpensively as practicable. All possible short cuts are taken, the most telling appeals are used, the critical faculties are by-passed as much as possible. There is in commercial selling, it would appear, a built-in bias toward simplicity and emotional appeal, and against complexity and critical appraisal. It is the past decade that has seen a dramatic introduction of these methods of merchandising on a mass scale into the area of political campaigning.

The editor of *Tide*, an ad and sales publication, remarked during the 1952 campaign that "advertising demonstrated beyond question that it can sell a good idea as successfully as it can sell a good product."[3] Among the many techniques used in the selling of ideas and candidates I shall briefly point up seven: the concentration on "issues," the emphasis on attack, the use of timing, the use of the "appeal beyond politics" and the "negative appeal," the elimination of debate, and the mass distribution of ideas. These methods, of course, frequently overlap, and are often used in combination.

The concentration on issues is sometimes explained by the PR professional as education. For instance, Leone Baxter of the Whitaker and Baxter team says:

> It's because the public relations profession, and its allied professions, know something about presenting abstract ideas, in attractive form, to masses of people who are too occupied with their daily lives to think analytically on their own account, that the average man of today is in a position to know more about the trends of human affairs than ever before in history. . . . You are helping him to understand your clients and their problems, their ideas. You are helping him to be a better citizen.[4]

But the issues on which the campaign concentrates are usually, if not always, the issues chosen by, or at least shaped by, the propaganda specialist for their impact value, and by no means necessarily because they are the real or significant issues in the campaign.

Closely related to the emphasis on "issues" is the emphasis in the campaign on attack. "To attack is to press on the public," says Mr. Whitaker, "the issues that are to one's advantage. To attack is not just to give one's side of the question but to *define* the political situation."[5] A powerful attack forces the opposition to reply and to explain, and, further, the attacked group is not able to get to the issues it considers important, or is able to get to them only after wasteful expenditure of time and resources.

In campaigns careful use is also frequently made of timing. Campaigns are given a sense of movement or build-up which has nothing in particular to do with the importance of the issues. The mass media of communication permit such a steady build-up of intensity and enable the arousing of maximum interest and excitement just before the elections. One firm reserves about 75% of its expenditures in a campaign for the final three weeks before the voters go to the polls.[6]

While the mass media do provide many opportunities for propaganda, they also impose some limitations on method. Through the mass media a great many people are reached, but they are not likely to be giving close or continuous attention to what they read or hear. As a consequence, for maximum effect issues are condensed into themes or slogans to catch the attention of the indifferent voter and to make the issues able to compete with the other mass media content such as sports, soap operas, and murder mysteries. How this indifference on the part of the people and the competition of other content are dealt with is explained by Mr. Whitaker in a statement that apparently sums up his basic philosophy:

> The average American, when you catch him after hours, as we must, doesn't want to be educated; he doesn't want to improve his mind; he doesn't want to work, consciously, at being a good citizen.
>
> But there are two ways you can interest him in a campaign, and only two that we have ever found successful.
>
> Most every American loves a *contest*. He likes a good hot battle, with no punches pulled. He likes the clash of arms. *So you can interest him if you put on a fight!*
>
> No matter what you fight for, *fight for something*, in our business, and very soon the voters will be turning out to hear you, providing you make the fight interesting.
>
> Then too, most every American likes to be entertained. He likes the movies; he likes mysteries; he likes fireworks and parades. He likes Jack Benny and Bob Hope and Joe E. Brown!
>
> So if you can't fight, PUT ON A SHOW! And if you put on a good show, Mr. and Mrs. America will turn out to see it.[7]

This philosophy leads to what is called the "appeal beyond politics." In order to compete with entertainment on the mass media, Campaigns Incorporated, the Whitaker and Baxter firm, makes politics entertainment.

Such a philosophy leads also to a primarily "negative appeal" in politics. The indifferent voter is moved by being confronted with an imminent evil, something threatening to things as they are, against which he himself must fight. Apparently it is easier to arouse people to be *against* something than to be *for* something.

Fundamental to the public relations man's approach is the elimination of debate and of competing propaganda. In 1949 the *Dallas Medical Journal* carried some advice from Whitaker and Baxter (these two people figure so largely as a source here because of their extraordinary success in this field, and the availability of their comments):

> We do not believe it is sound campaign practice to sponsor too many debates. They would make a forum for the opposition which would be difficult for them to secure otherwise, and they are too easily stacked. This is particularly true of broadcasts to the public.[8]

This is apparently standard technique in the Campaigns Incorporated firm.

> In their plan of campaign for Governor Goodwin Knight's 1954 campaign, they [Whitaker and Baxter] say, "What about debates? Our Candidate is a master of this field, so we regret to say we will schedule no debates with our opponents. We should not permit the stature of the Governor to be utilized to build audiences for his opposition."[9]

Closely related to the elimination of debate and opposing propaganda is the method of mass distribution of "ideas." This method is simply that of providing almost endless repetition of the so-called issue and virtually crowding out competing ideas. Some indication of how this method is used is provided by Whitaker's description of media used for a ballot proposition in 1948. In that year, to publicize one issue to California's 4½ million voters Whitaker's firm put out 10 million pamphlets and leaflets, 4½ million post cards, 50,000 letters, 70,000 inches of newspaper display advertising in 700 daily and weekly newspapers, theatre slides and trailers in 160 theatres playing to nearly 2 million people each week, 3,000 radio spot announcements on 109 radio stations, plus radio programs, billboards, posters, speeches, etc., reaching millions of people.[10]

3

What are the implications for the democratic process of the persuasive techniques used in this growing business of merchandizing government?

It might be argued that the philosophy and methods which have been briefly described here have long been the stock in trade of politicians in a democratic society. And this is true, with some significant differences. The politician has not previously had available to him the mass media to the degree that a well-financed public relations firm now has, nor has the politician had the professional skills and contacts necessary to use the mass media to their capacity. A modern public relations firm has the accumulated experience of many professional propagandists, the know-how to use the media. Moreover, with the engineering of a campaign concentrated in one headquarters with the bulk of the resources to work with, coordination of use of mass media is greatly increased.

A difference too can be noted in the place of the press in modern society. Political issues traditionally have been given publicity through a free press and not by professional propagandists. Now, however, as Mr. Kelley points out, "For the public relations man the press and the other media are not only distributors of information but instruments of social control, and the media have for various reasons been forced to accept this estimate of themselves."[11] He quotes a Texas editor as stating:

> The fact remains . . . that any editor worth his salt knows that he is just about as dependent upon the public relations man as they are upon him. . . . No newspaper could afford the staff it would take to turn out the vast amount of news that fills the papers every day.[12]

The scope or extent of the social control function of the press is indicated by a *Fortune* magazine statement that now "nearly half the content of the nation's better newspapers comes from publicity releases."[13] Publicity releases, we may remind ourselves, are not random revelations of information but statements carefully chosen for the effect they will have.

There is a difference too in the relationships of the present day professional persuader to the issues and to the people he persuades. The politician by himself at least had some direct contact with his constituents. He was or might become their official representative, and out of this relationship there grew at least some sense of direct responsibility. The ad man brought in to sell a candidate sees the candidate and the voters with much greater impartiality. He has a product to sell, and the voters are buyers. As one ad man put it, "I think of a man in a voting booth who hesitates between two levers as if he were pausing between competing tubes of toothpaste in a drugstore. . . . The brand that has made the highest penetration on his brain will win his choice."[14] The politician only rarely perhaps has

> approached the immaculate amorality of the political public relations man who, admitting that his candidate did not know anything about anything, said, "Let's consider this campaign clinically. After all, you don't criticize a brain surgeon's technique just because he operates on a criminal."[15]

So much for the differences between modern public relations technique and traditional political persuasion. Now what of the processes of persuasion as seen in professional public relations and their relationships to the democratic process? Certainly a basic principle in the larger democratic process is that of majority rule. This principle implies that large numbers of citizens must make definite choices, often on gravely complex issues. If freedom of choice is to have meaning there must be adequate information upon which to base the choice, and if self-determination is to have meaning there must be significant alternatives whose implications are known among which to choose. Most of the persuasive methods of professional public relations and ad men have the net effect of reducing the opportunities for free and rational choice based on adequate information. Not that it is to be expected that the whole truth is ever going to be presented. The truth is too complex, even if it were known. But much more of it can be told than is told. Perhaps the most serious violation of the basic principle comes in the implication that the truth is being told, that the issues are simple. "The theory of our constitution," said Mr. Justice Holmes, "is that truth is the only ground upon which man's wishes safely can be carried out."[16] "In the democratic thesis," says another writer, "facts provide the basis for free judgment and decision."[17]

Coupled with the lack of significant information, the oversimplification of issues, and the selection of issues for their propaganda value is the deliberate attempt to avoid competing ideas. This is done by deliberately avoiding public discussion and debate, by forcing the opposition to answer attacks, and by overpowering opposing views by sheer massiveness of material and by continuous presentation of views. Such techniques, of course, directly violate the basic principles of constructive debate so important to the democratic process. As Walter Lippmann has put it in *The Public Philosophy:*

> Freedom of speech has become a central concern of the Western society because of the discovery among the Greeks that dialectic, as demonstrated in the Socratic dialogues, is a principal method of attaining truth, and particularly a method of attaining moral and political truth. . . . The method of dialectic is to confront ideas with opposing ideas in order that the pro and con of the dispute will lead to true ideas. . . . And because the purpose of the confrontation is to discern the truth, there are rules of evidence and of parliamentary procedure, there are codes of fair dealing and fair comment, by which a loyal man will consider himself bound when he exercises the right to publish opinions.[18]

And elsewhere:

> Thus the essence of freedom of opinion is not mere toleration as such, but in the debate which toleration provides. . . . We must insist that free oratory is only the beginning of free speech; it is not the end, but a means to an end. The end is to find the truth. The practical justification of civil liberty is not that self-expression

is one of the rights of man. It is that the examination of opinions is one of the necessities of man.[19]

The need for the opposition of ideas is one of the basic tenets of the democratic faith. What makes the violation of this principle of particular significance now is that with the use of modern PR methods employing the media of the press, radio, and television, the process of debate is circumscribed, relative to the number of people involved, to a degree never before seen in our democratic society. The principle has, of course, always been violated, but the problem takes on a new dimension when millions of people can be delivered up to one speaker on one occasion. To the side with the most money to buy the most favorable time goes the opportunity for the maximum saturation with its ideas with the least possibility of competition. The saturation spot campaign is a significant example of the elimination of competing ideas, in addition to oversimplification. As explained by a PR man, its advantages are these: "(1) It gives maximum effectiveness of penetration and recall without becoming deadly to the listener and viewer. (2) It delivers this maximum just before election. (3) It occurs too late for effective . . . rebuttal."[20]

The reply might be made that this is simply another manifestation of the democratic process. Suppose the views are partisan; in the competition of the market the best views will prevail. The citizen still has a choice. If it were true that opposing sides were nearly equally represented by PR firms this might be partially true. But then we would have the interesting spectacle of a political struggle being waged not between candidates and issues but between public relations professionals, which would make success very much dependent upon financial backing and propaganda skills. It would be highly doubtful whether the significant issues in the campaign would ever be presented. As a matter of fact, however, such competition between PR firms in political campaigns is not likely to occur. As we are well aware, not one of the major public relations firms would work for the Democratic candidate in the last national election. As one executive put it: "You see how it is. If a big agency took on the Democrats' account and the Democrats won, it would simply enrage Republican clients and drive them away. On the other hand, if it took them on and the Democrats lost, it wouldn't look too good for its selling ability"[21] The public relations firms whose primary source of accounts is business, particularly "big business," are not impartial about whose side they are on in a political campaign.

But there is more than the elimination of competition in the market place that concerns us. There is also the problem of individual responsibility for what is said. In one of the Lippmann passages quoted above it is pointed out that there are rules of evidence and of parliamentary procedure, and codes of fair dealing and fair comment, by which the loyal man will consider himself bound when he exercises the right to publish opinions. There has been a strong tendency in our society to escape personal responsibility for what is said by retreat to the traditional position that it is the competition of the market place that will determine which ideas have merit. I cannot better describe the dangers of such "intellectual laissezfaire" than Alexander Meiklejohn has done. I shall quote him at length:

> There is undeniably a genuine though partial validity in the dictum that "the best test of truth is the power of the thought to get itself accepted in the competition of the market." It rightly tells us that the only truth which we self-governing men can rely on is that which we win for ourselves in the give and take of public discussion and decision. . . . But that partial insight has often been interpreted . . . to be a total characterization of the truth seeking process. And, in that form, it has become . . . a fruitful source of intellectual irresponsibility and of the errors which irresponsibility brings. We . . . have taken the "competition of the market" principle to mean that as separate thinkers, we have no obligation to test our thinking. . . . Each one of us, therefore, feels free to think as he pleases, to believe whatever will serve his own private interests. . . . Our aim is to "make a case," to win a fight, to make our plea plausible, to keep the pressure on. And the intellectual degradation which this interpretation of truth-testing has brought upon the minds of people is almost unbelievable. Under its influence, there are no standards for determining the difference between the true and the false. . . . The dependence upon intellectual laissezfaire, more than any other single factor, has destroyed the foundations of our national education, has robbed of their meaning such terms as "reasonableness" and "intelligence," and "devotion to the general welfare." It has made intellectual freedom indistinguishable from intellectual license.[22]

The persuasive techniques in question are also inconsistent with the democratic process in that they tend to eliminate checks and balances. In the area of government, no matter how able and good the man, we do not permit him arbitrarily to make laws and enforce them. We do not trust any human being with power over other human beings that is not circumscribed by careful checks and balances, except temporarily in times of emergency. The modern persuader with vast financial resources and the mass media at his disposal has in a very real sense great power. Prior to the day of publicity releases in volume, prior to press, radio, and TV chains, there were more checks and balances in the form of more independent and diversified press coverage, more direct contact with constituents, more confrontation in debate. With millions of listeners and viewers reached at once, with money to buy the time of favorite shows, with money to print fabulous amounts of literature, with a predetermined point of view on the part of major PR agencies, the checks and balances have been drastically reduced, reduced almost in proportion to the added power of the forces that need to be held in balance.

Further, the persuasive techniques we have discussed are inconsistent with the fundamental democratic view that the human being is inviolable, that he is not to be treated as a thing, as a means, but as a person, as an end. This right seems to be respected for the physical person, but the persuasive methods of the professional public relations man in political campaigns reveal a dramatic failure to respect the personality in the same way. The more the reader or listener can be made to respond in fear or anger, the more readily he responds to suggestion, the less he makes use of his critical faculties, the less he is induced to inform himself, the more successful the PR and ad men are.[23] In other words, the fewer the distinctly human qualities of reason, self-determination, individuality which men develop, the better for the political advertising profession. And the worse for democracy, which is based on the assumption that citizens can and will make informed and rational choices.

Fundamental to the whole problem of persuasion in a democratic society is the problem of ends and means. And this is of direct concern to the teacher of speech who in various forms teaches persuasion. Persuasive techniques are usually classed as means, means to some end which may be good or bad. While we may not hold that the end always justifies the means, we place the emphasis on the ends when making ethical judgments about persuasion and thus take the onus off the means. The extreme of such thinking is suggested by the familiar scalpel analogy. The scalpel is neutral; it can be used to take a life or save a life. Whether it is used for good or ill depends upon who is using it, the end he seeks. And so with persuasive techniques. This view is, of course, grievously shortsighted. The reason is simple: The scalpel does not form habits of cutting or the patient habits of behavior as a result of the operation. Persuasive methods, on the other hand, do influence behavior apart from and in addition to the particular end which they seek. When being persuaded a man is not only influenced directly or indirectly in his choice of a course of action, he is influenced in his *method of making the choice*. The problem of ethics enters when what we do affects the lives of others. How we influence others to make choices about things of importance to them is obviously affecting their lives in a significant way.

In a democratic society—I do not think it can be denied—the method of decision is vital; *how* we go about making up our minds is vital. Whether we vote for a particular candidate in a particular election may not be momentous for democracy, but how we make up our minds about candidates is indeed momentous. By constantly limiting the critical faculties in decision we are limiting the basis upon which it is possible to have a responsible citizenry, and thus we weaken the very foundations of democracy.

There is, of course, no intention here of implying that all human behavior should or can be completely "rational." Today we are aware that our behavior results from a large variety of motivations; our needs, desires, anxieties, conscious and unconscious, play an important part in what we do. We also know, however, that much careful, reflective, critical thought is needed on the part of all citizens, leaders and followers alike, if we are to deal with our myriad domestic and foreign problems within the democratic framework. Indeed, because of the large component of irrationality in all of us, all the more do we need to make a deliberate and continuous effort to increase the amount of rationally controlled behavior, based on democratic values, in all areas of common concern.

Most of the average citizen's political actions consist of making choices between alternatives presented to him. When we determine how he makes his choices, we determine to a large extent the kind of person he is and the kind of citizen he is, whether he is a person who grows in his ability to make rational choices and develops the capacities that make him truly a man, or whether he tends toward the robot whose control buttons substitute for independent choice. And we determine whether as a citizen he strengthens the democratic community or weakens it.

Freedom of speech, which includes the freedom to persuade, imposes on everyone who exercises that right an obligation to use speech so that it becomes a carrier of freedom. "Free speech is promoted by the kind of speech that makes men free."[24]

17

An Ethical Basis of Communication

KARL R. WALLACE

Professor Karl R. Wallace was chair of the Department of Speech at the University of Illinois for twenty years; in the five years preceding his death in October of 1973 he was Senior Professor of Rhetoric and Public Address at the University of Massachusetts at Amherst. In addition to his authorship of numerous books, articles, and scholarly papers in the field of rhetoric and public address, Wallace was editor of the Quarterly Journal of Speech *(1945–47) and President of the Speech Communication Association (1954). His speaking and writing activities over the years sustained a concern for high standards of ethics in public discourse. The following essay which summarizes those ethical concerns, was published in the January 1955 issue of* The Speech Teacher.

On a recent plane trip a friend of mine sat beside a citizen of Wisconsin. Inevitably the conversation came around to the junior Senator from that state. Part of the dialogue went like this:

FRIEND: What do you think of Mr. McCarthy?
CITIZEN: Well, I happen to know him personally, and I just don't like him at all. And I don't like his investigating methods, either—his badgering people and twisting their words around and acting like he owned the whole Committee.
FRIEND: It's too bad you Wisconsin people don't have a chance of turning him out of office.
CITIZEN: What'd we want to do that for? He's doing a darn good job of blasting out those Communists. There ought to be more of it.
FRIEND: If there were an election tomorrow, would you vote for McCarthy?
CITIZEN: Yes, I would.

The conversation points up the age-old problem of judging the right and wrong of human conduct. There is a similar difficulty when we come to judge the right and wrong of communication. The problem is essentially this: Does the end warrant our using any means which seem likely to achieve it? Is the public speaker or debater who believes his purpose worthy justified in using any methods and techniques which he thinks would be successful? Is the play director, convinced that his educational objectives are right, free to select any play and employ any methods of interpretation and production which seem likely to be "effective"? Is the speech correctionist, profoundly motivated to help the child with deviant speech behavior, free to adopt any techniques which seem workable?

This is an ethical problem. It is time that teachers of communication confronted it squarely. The signs of warning are about us. One of the more prominent signs is implicit in the wide-spread growth of research in communication, as may be seen in the serious study of polling techniques designed to measure the effectiveness of persuasive methods, the new interest of political scientists and bureaucrats in methods of propaganda, the progress made by linguists and psychologists in applying scientific methods to the analysis of language behavior. The facts and data thus compiled are of course valuable; nevertheless, it is somewhat disquieting to observe that such research is centered overwhelmingly on processes, operations, mechanisms, and techniques. There seems to be little, if any, prevailing interest in the *character* of the communicator or in the quality of the communicative product. Some parent groups, of course, have shown concern over the character of radio and television programs and over the comic books, but their activities have been largely sporadic and spotty. We are fascinated—often hypnotized—by what happens, how it happens, and why it happens, but we seem to be utterly unexcited by the question: *Ought* it to happen thus? What would be *better*?

There is room to mention here but one other sign of our apathy toward the ethics of communication. We can read it from our own behavior as teachers of speech. As we start out a new class in speech, or as we confront the thoughtful student who wonders if his praiseworthy purpose allows him to give his audience what it wants, we have been known to speak like this: "Remember, in this class we are studying and applying methods and techniques of speaking. Communication is a skill, a tool, and because it is a tool we are not directly concerned with who uses it and what he says. These are matters which the individual speaker must decide for himself. The main business of this course is to help you to become an effective speaker, a successful speaker. After all, the art of speaking is like the art of reasoning, or like mathematics and science, in that morality lies outside them; it is not *of* them; it is not *in* them." This kind of professional position, this disinterested attitude, this kind of easy reasoning, is leading many persons to look anew at the ethics of both the teacher and his student. Communication is in danger of being regarded as merely an art of personal success and prestige and of being forgotten as the indispensable art of social persuasion.

I

Any professional field which has reached maturity is ever alive to its ethics. Law, medicine, engineering, and journalism have their codes of ethics. The profession of teaching, too, has its code of behavior. The field of speech shows some evidence of recapturing the maturity and stability it once enjoyed, under the name of *rhetoric*, in the educational systems of centuries past. Is it not time for the teacher of the arts of speech to face up to his special commitments? We must confront questions like these: Is there an ethic of communication? Specifically, is there an ethic of *oral* communication, a morality of rhetoric? I believe that there are ethical standards which should control any situation in which speaker and writer endeavor to inform and to influence others. I shall try to indicate where we find these standards and what they are like.

In the first place, ethical standards of communication should place emphasis upon the means used to secure the end, rather than upon achieving the end itself. A political speaker may win the vote, or a competitor in a speech contest may win the prize, but it is far more important that his means and methods, the character of his skill, and, indeed, the quality of his entire product, should conform to standards formulated by competent judges and critics of speech-making. Let us discover why.

If we give much weight to the immediate success of a speech, we encourage temptation. To glorify the end is to invite the use of any means which will work. The end can be used, for example, to sanction distortion and suppression of materials and arguments. We need here only to mention that there are still popular books on speech-making which sometimes offer shocking advice. A recent manual advises the speaker that he may, if necessary, remodel a pet quotation to fill the bill, for, after all, no one will know the difference! Such advice is on a par with the shoddy ethics of the debate coach who exclaims, "If my boys misquote, it's up to their opponents to spot it." The end, moreover, can be readily called upon to justify the misleading manoeuvres, the innuendoes, and the short-cut tricks of the propagandists. The advertiser, in his zeal to sell, is constantly tempted to promise more than he can deliver. In brief, to exalt the end is often to be indifferent about means. As a result, we gradually undermine confidence in communication and, indeed, in all human relations; and with confidence gone, nothing is left but distrust and suspicion.

If we give first prize to the speaker who wins his goal, we not only unnecessarily tempt the honest and sincere man; we undermine the character of the communicator. We associate with "success" such values as popular prestige and personal ambition. We thus give a premium to the man with a compulsive drive, to him who must win at any cost; and we handicap the man who places the welfare of others above his personal gain. We give the advantage to Senator McCarthy; we hand a disadvantage to Secretary Stevens. John Morley, one of the best English critics of public address in the nineteenth century, has clearly described the risk which the popular persuader incurs when he measures his utterance by its immediate effect. To do so may undermine

> a man's moral self-possession. . . . Effect becomes the decisive consideration instead of truth; a good meeting grows into a final object in life; the end of existence is a paradise of loud and prolonged cheering; and character is gradually destroyed by the [parasite of] vanity.[1]

Finally, the worst evil which follows from an indifference to means is that we make easy the intent of the dishonest, insincere speaker. It is easy to assert high-sounding purposes; it is difficult for the listener to assess the sincerity of these assertions. In short, as Mahatma Gandhi often told us, "Evil means, even for a good end, produce evil results."

There is a better ethic than that which justifies the means by the end. It is an ethic which respects the means more than the end. It governs both the selection and the presentation of materials. Above all, the ethic measures the quality of the communicative product in terms of the communicator, rather than according to its immediate effect upon the audience. Some 2300 years ago Aristotle suggested the standard:

> [The function of speech-making] is not simply to succeed in persuading, but rather to discover the means of coming as near such success as the circumstances of each particular case allow. In this it resembles all other arts. For example, it is not the function of medicine simply to make a man quite healthy, but to put him as far as may be on the road to health; it is possible to give excellent treatment even to those who can never enjoy sound health.[2]

What does such a standard suggest? It implies, first, that a speaker does the best job he can under the circumstances; and doing his best job means that he has education, training, and competence in the art of communication. In the second place, the comparison of the speaker with the physician and with other arts implies that the standards of communication are determined by those who best know the art, that is, by the teachers and critics of communication. Finally, the passage suggests that since immediate success is not always possible, anyway, the end or purpose of a speech operates principally as a guide or direction. Purpose serves to give organization and shape to the speech, the discussion, or the play; it aids in the choice of means, but it should not dominate the moral values of either the product or the speaker.

It seems clear that the ethical standards of communication should be set by persons who know communication best, and that the standards or code they formulate will express their judgment as to what means are good, what means are bad. If the standards were clearly stated and widely understood, they could be freely used by expert and layman alike to measure the character of any case of communication.

II

Where does one look for such standards? They are derived from the function of an art. The function of any art takes its ultimate meaning from what it tries to accomplish in its social setting. What, for example, does a speaker do not only for himself, but also for society, the community?

Although there are many sides to society, its indispensable side is political. Indeed, when society behaves politically it has the technical name, *state*. And the state is simply another name for an association of men. Because it is the largest, most inclusive association we know of, its values and ends are reflected in nearly everything that its citizens do. They are reflected particularly in education and in the arts and sciences. The influence of the political society is stated in this passage from the *Ethics* of Aristotle:

> If . . . there is some end of the things we do, which we desire for its own sake . . . clearly this must be the good and the chief good. . . . If so, we must try, in outline at least, to determine what it is, and of which of the sciences or capacities it is the object. It would seem to belong to the most authoritative art and that which is most truly the master art. And politics appears to be of this nature; for it is this which ordains which of the sciences should be studied in a state, and which each class of citizens should learn and up to what point they should learn them; and we see even the

most highly esteemed of capacities to fall under this, e.g., strategy, economics, rhetoric; now, since politics uses the rest of the sciences, and since, again, it legislates as to what we are to do and what we are to abstain from, the end of this science must include those of the others, so that this end must be the good for man.[3]

The passage demands that we recognize two basic facts. First, the political society aims to help its citizens to secure whatever they consider to be the good life. Indeed, the dominant tone of a political group is set by its ethical values. Thus Communism, e.g., has one set of values, democracy a quite different set. Second, the arts and sciences serve the ideals of the political society. Indeed, they share the same ethical values and goals. The art of rhetoric—and all the arts of communication—thus embraces the ethical part of politics. This point Aristotle states flatly in his book on rhetoric, and for this reason in his system of communication he incorporates materials which he borrows directly from the fields of political science and ethical science. For example, in discussing the materials of political oratory, he talks of the good, of happiness, of virtue, and of the general welfare. He even advises the political speaker to study ways of political life in different kinds of society. In discussing the speaking of the law courts, he treats of justice and equity. Thus, the instrumental art, rhetoric, shares the controlling ideas of the master art, politics. Hence, communication inevitably must stand for and must reflect the same ethical values as the political society of which it is a part. It is clear, furthermore, that this principle is as true today as it was in Aristotle's time. Although government and politics are much more complex than they were in the days of ancient Greece, the modern political scientist acknowledges that the foundations of the state are laid in ethics.

Is it not becoming clear, therefore, that we look for the ethical basis of communication in the ideals of our own political society? That society, for all its manifest defects, is still a free and democratic society. If we can clearly state the essential values of democracy, we can then suggest an ethic of communication and the ethics of the teacher of speech.

III

A free and democratic society, first of all, is built on the notion that the individual has dignity and worth. Our society holds that government exists to uphold and preserve the worth and dignity of each and every person. A totalitarian society, on the other hand, holds that the individual lives for the state. In a democracy people are supreme and wield the ultimate power. In totalitarianism the state is almighty and is the final source of all power. The difference is crucial; it is as sharply different as black and white, as tyranny and freedom. The phrase, "dignity and worth of the individual," leads to a state of mind best described by the old-fashioned word, *respect*. Each man respects his fellow man. This fact has led some students of political science to describe a democratic society as a "commonwealth of mutual deference."

Respect for the individual leads us to a second basic belief: a profound faith in equality of opportunity. We believe that a man can best reach his greatest maturity if he has the chance. If we can say with Wordsworth that the child is father of the man, we believe that the child must have the opportunity to become the best possible father of the best possible man. We believe, furthermore, that so far as we are able, every child must be given the *same* chance. Out of such beliefs we have developed the all-important notion of *fairness*. Like the rules of any game, the laws of the political game must be as fair as we can possible make them.

We hold a third belief that has become one of the great hallmarks of a democratic society. It is the belief in freedom. Difficult as it may be to define freedom, we know well enough that each individual must be given as wide a field to roam in as he wishes. The word also means that if a person in his roaming prevents another man from ranging widely, he must so modify his behavior as to give his fellow a similar opportunity. He can do what he wants to do, so long as he does not hinder another from exercising a like range of choice and of action. So freedom always implies restraint. A person can behave as he wishes in his own home so long as he does not become a nuisance to his neighbors; he can drive his car where and how he wishes so long as he does not endanger others; he can compete as he may desire in business, in sports, in speech contests, so long as he respects the rules.

In a free and democratic society, individuals acting in concert and with deliberation make their own restraints. The restraints are called *legislation* or *laws*. They are policies or guides of conduct. Indeed, they are no different in their origin and effect from the rules of family life or the regulations of a school. Furthermore, individuals through their government set up agencies to which they delegate power for administering the laws, and they create courts charged with the responsibility of enforcing the restraints. Lincoln showed deep wisdom in saying that our political society was of us, by us, and for us. In our democratic society, moreover, we insist that the laws bear equally upon everyone.

In effect we say to our legislators and judges: "You must do your best to make laws which will be fair to everybody, and you must enforce the laws in the spirit of fairness and justice."

A free and democratic society rests upon a fourth deep and abiding belief. It is a conviction closely linked to the idea that each individual must have the opportunity of growing and developing to the limits of his ability. The conviction is that every person is capable of understanding the nature of democracy: its goals, its values, its procedures and processes. This belief assumes that persons can acquire the knowledge necessary to form opinions and decisions and to test them by means of discussion and action. As a result of this conviction, a democracy demands that knowledge be made available to all, rather than to the few; it requires that the sources and channels of communication be wide and diverse, rather than limited and one-sided. It cannot tolerate restriction and distortion. Consequently it must cherish and protect certain special freedoms: freedom of speech, freedom of press, and freedom of assembly. Without these freedoms democracy is meaningless: the life of a free society depends upon them.

Is it not evident that each person participates in a political society? that he reflects its values and uses its procedures? In his role as communicator, whether he be playwright or play producer, public reader or public speaker, he must also reveal his political character. What he says and his method of saying it reveal his choices, and the choices a man makes are always an index to his character. Theoretically, of course, a man need not speak at all; or he can choose to speak only to himself, or to refuse to discuss matters of public interest. But if he chooses to speak, he reveals his political soul.

IV

What, then, are the ethics of the teacher of speech? They are grounded in the public character of public utterance in a free society.

First, a communicator in a free society must recognize that during the moments of his utterance he is the sole source of argument and information. His hearers know this fact, and they defer to him. He in turn must defer to them. Accordingly, his speech must reveal that he knows his subject, that he understands the implications and issues relevant to the particular time and occasion, that he is aware of essential and trustworthy opinions and facts, that he is dealing with a many-sided, rather than a one-sided, state of affairs. Although the speaker might find it difficult to know when he has met such standards, he can always direct a test question to himself: Can I answer squarely, without evasion, any relevant question that a hearer might ask? If he can answer *yes* in all honesty, he has met the standard of knowledge. In the learning situation, the teacher of speech has an obligation to teach the art of inquiry and investigation, to inculcate respect for scope and depth of fact and opinion—in a word, to help build the habit of *search*. The teacher has this duty because a free society demands that communication be informative and that knowledge be shared.

How can the teacher help his students develop the habit of searching widely for both fact and opinion? There is no simple answer, of course. Many teachers, both in high school and in college, are well aware of this duty and have developed their own methods of teaching the art of inquiry. But we shall not hurt ourselves if we periodically confront these questions: Am I keeping up with information and opinion on problems that are currently discussed, so that my chances are better, rather than worse, of being a good guide and critic of what my students know or do not know? Am I making sufficient use of discussion methods, in both the classroom and private conference, to stimulate interest and inquiry? Am I habitually encouraging the classroom audience, upon hearing a student speak, to discuss the adequacy of the speaker's knowledge and the trustworthiness of his materials?

Second, the communicator who respects the democratic way of life must select and present fact and opinion *fairly*. One of his great tasks is to help preserve a kind of equality of opportunity among ideas. He must therefore be *accurate* in reporting fact and opinion; he must *respect* accuracy. Moreover, he must not intentionally warp and distort ideas. Nor must he suppress and conceal material which his audience would need in justly evaluating his argument. He must, furthermore, avoid the shortcut methods of the propagandist. He cannot make one word guilty by loosely associating it with another guilty word. He cannot indulge in the tricks of emotion, cannot juggle with reason, at the expense of sound argument. In helping himself meet the standard of justice, a communicator can always quiz himself: In the selection and presentation of my materials, am I giving my audience the *opportunity* of making fair judgments? The speaker who can answer *yes* understands what is involved in the sharing of information and opinion. He knows that he has had a special opportunity to observe, to learn, to evaluate, which most of his hearers may not have had. He knows, accordingly, that one of his jobs as a communicator is to help his hearers compensate for the lack of special opportunity. He realizes that he cannot possibly give them the same chance he has had, but he can give them the best chance that time and occasion will allow. Speaker and hearer, writer and reader, cannot have had the same experience, but they can feel that they have had. In the classroom, accordingly, the teacher of speech must inculcate what I shall call the *habit of justice*. The habit is based on respect for truth and accuracy and respect for fair dealing. Neither can be disassociated from communication in a free society. The teacher of speech must stand for truth and justice in communication because the health and welfare of a free society depend upon the integrity of the communicator.

Third, the communicator who believes in the ultimate values of democracy will invariably reveal the sources of his information and opinion. As Al Smith said, a public figure must keep the record straight. A speaker before any audience is by that fact a public person, and he is no exception to the rule. A communicator, moreover, will help his hearers to weigh any special bias, prejudice, and private motivations which are inherent in source materials. He knows that argument and fact are unacceptable if their springs are contaminated. As an investigator preparing for his speech, he has had the opportunity of discovering whether private motives, such as those of self-interest, personal prestige, and personal profit, have merely imparted a special flavor to the source or have made it dangerous to drink. Such information he should share with his hearers. And if he is not already a public character well-known to his audience, he should be willing to reveal frankly his own motivations. The critical question which he poses to himself is this: Have I concealed information about either my source materials or my own motives which, if revealed, would damage my case? The communicator who can answer *no* is in the tradition of public integrity.

In the high school and the college, the teacher of speech must devise methods and techniques which will form the *habit of preferring public to private motivations*. Public communication is responsible communication; it remembers who said what under what circumstances and for what reasons. In this respect it is utterly unlike gossip and rumor which, if not malicious, we may tolerate as idle talk for idle pleasure.

How can the teacher of speech help his young communicators toward habits of fairness, justice, and public accountability? I do not wish to preach here. Let him who is without blemish cast the first stone. Nevertheless, we shall do well occasionally to examine ourselves as objectively as we can and to conduct the inquisition mercilessly. We may ask: In all my relationships with my students, am I as fair as I can be? Do I keep clear the differences between opinion and fact, and do I distinguish between my opinion and somebody else's? When I express an opinion, do I explain its basis, or do I take a short cut and let the opinion rest on my own authority and prestige? Do I respond to questions frankly, without evasion? Am I withholding information, as "not being good for young persons," especially under the circumstances? What kind of censor am I?

Sometimes teachers effectively employ examples of what not to do. For a ready source of illustrations of unfair tactics in public address, the speeches and press releases of Senator McCarthy offer a rich hunting ground. One could start his collection of negative examples by reading Professor Barnet Baskerville's article, "Joe McCarthy: Brief-Case Demagogue," in the September number of *Today's Speech*.[4] Baskerville cites one careful study whose author checked McCarthy's initial charges of Communism in the State Department with the ascertainable facts. The investigator, Professor Hart of Duke University, examining only the charges as presented up to the fall of 1951, found that McCarthy's "assertions had been radically at variance with the facts in fifty specific instances."[5] Another examination of two 1952 campaign speeches reveals them as *"a most amazing demonstration of studied inaccuracy."*[6] McCarthy's nationally televised address which attacked Adlai Stevenson (the speech making use of documents from a Massachusetts barn) yields "no less than eighteen 'false statements or distortions' in the text which McCarthy described as having 'complete, unchallengable documentation.'"[7] Baskerville comments on the Senator's documents, often raised aloft for all to see, "The deceit lies in the significant omissions, and in unwarranted inferences drawn from impressive but often completely irrelevant documents."[8] The article could well be the beginning of a case study in personal and public integrity.

Fourth, a communicator in a democratic society will acknowledge and will respect diversity of argument and opinion. His selection of issues, his analysis of the situation, the style of his address will reflect the attitudes which signify admission, concession, and compromise. Nevertheless, his communication will not sacrifice principle to compromise, and he will prefer facing conflict to accepting appeasement. For such a communicator, the test question will ever be this: Can I freely admit the force of opposing evidence and argument and still advocate a position which represents my convictions? The great duty of the teacher of speech is to devise ways and means and to maintain a climate which will favor the *habit of respect for dissent*. Can he teach what it means to hold convictions without loss of integrity and at the same time respect the convictions of others? The teacher who can do so is not merely skillful; he is a true representative of the free society.

It is these four "moralities": the duty of search and inquiry, allegiance to accuracy, fairness, and justice in the selection and treatment of ideas and arguments, the willingness to submit private motivations to public scrutiny, and the toleration of dissent—which provide the ethic of communication in a free society.

In view of these moralities, as teachers of speech we can no longer tell even the most elementary student of our discipline that speech skills and techniques, like tools, are divorced from ethical values. We can no longer say that how he uses his art is his own private affair. But we need not be content with an ethic which is external to communication. We need not rely solely upon the familiar, classic positions: "You'd better be good, or your audience may find you out"; or "A good man skilled in speaking will in the long run be more effective than a bad man skilled in speaking." As I have tried to indicate, communication carries its ethics within itself. Public address of any kind is inseparable from the values which permeate a free and democratic community. A speaker is in a deep and true sense a representative of his constitution which defines his way of life, and therefore defines in part the social goals and methods of his rhetoric. His frame of political reference is not that of an aristocracy, an oligarchy, a monarchy, or a tyranny. In a word, there are ethical guides in the very act of communicating; and it seems to me that the guides are the same for all communicators, no matter whether they speak as politicians, statesmen, business men, or professional men.

Notes

Notes

1. From Small Acorns Mighty Oaks Grow: The Legislatures and Free Speech in Colonial Connecticut and Rhode Island

1. Leonard W. Levy, *Legacy of Suppression: Freedom of Speech and Press in Early American History* (Cambridge: Harvard University Press, 1960), p. vii.

2. Levy, p. 18.

3. Levy, p. 20.

4. Neither Levy's work nor this essay should be considered definitive histories of free expression in the colonies. Many records were not made or did not survive the ravages of time and colonial experience.

5. Horatio Rogers, *Discourse Before the Rhode Island Historical Society* (Providence: Snow and Farnhum, Printers, 1890), p. 10.

6. John Fiske, *The Beginnings of New England* (Boston: Houghton, Mifflin and Company, 1896), p. 127.

7. Charles Edward Perry, *Founders and Leaders of Connecticut, 1633–1783* (Boston: D.C. Heath and Company, 1934), p. 11.

8. Herbert L. Osgood, *The American Colonies in the Seventeenth Century* (New York: The Macmillan Company, 1904), I, p. 302.

9. Clinton Lawrence Rossiter, *Seedtime of the Republic: The Origin of American Tradition of Political Liberty*, First Edition (New York: Harcourt and Brace, 1953), p. 165.

10. J. Mark Jacobson, *The Development of American Political Thought: A Documentary History* (New York: The Century Company, 1932), p. 17.

11. Alice Mary Baldwin, *The Clergy of Connecticut in Revolutionary Days*, Tercentenary Pamphlet Series No. 56 (New Haven: Yale University Press, 1936), p. 6.

12. Zechariah Chafee, *Free Speech in the United States* (Cambridge: Harvard University Press, 1941), p. 234.

13. Irving Berdine Richman, *Rhode Island: Its Making and Its Meaning, 1636–1683* (New York: G.P. Putnam's Sons, 1902), II, p. 46.

14. David S. Lovejoy, *Rhode Island Politics and the American Revolution, 1760–1776* (Providence: Brown University Press, 1958), p. 29.

15. Dan King, *The Life and Times of Thomas Wilson Door* (Boston, 1859), p. 15.

16. Samuel Green Arnold, *History of the State of Rhode Island and Providence Plantations* (Providence: Preston and Rounds, 1899), I, p. 109.

17. John Callendar, ed., *An Historical Discourse on the Civil and Religious Affairs of the Colony of Rhode Island*, IV of *Collections of the Rhode Island Historical Society* (Boston: Thomas H. Webb and Company, 1843), p. 229.

18. Arnold, *History of the State of Rhode Island*, I, p. 205.

19. Edward Field, *State of Rhode Island and Providence Plantations at the End of the Century: A History* (Boston: The Mason Publishing Company, 1902), I, p. 233.

20. Chafee, *Free Speech in the United States*, p. 5.

21. Rossiter, *Seedtime*, p. 14.

22. Osgood, *The American Colonies*, I, p. 302.

23. Perry, *Founders*, p. 6.

24. Perry, p. 20; also, Mary Jeanne Anderson Jones, *Congregational Commonwealth: Connecticut, 1636-1662* (Middletown, Conn.: Wesleyan University Press, 1968), p. 98.

25. No quantitative comparison with Levy's work is attempted, because Levy provides no basis for it. Nevertheless, every instance of restriction dealing clearly with speech found by this author in the colonial records and secondary sources is cited herein.

26. For a discussion of a historical approach to a study of freedom of speech see John Lee Jellicorse, "Some Historical Essentials of Teaching Freedom of Speech," *Free Speech Yearbook*, III, 1972, pp. 76-84.

27. Mary Patterson Clarke, *Parliamentary Privilege in the American Colonies* (New York: Yale University Press, 1943), p. 100.

28. J. Hammond Trumbull, editor, *The Public Records of the Colony of Connecticut 1636-1776* (Hartford: Brown and Parsons, 1850-1890), I, p. 520.

29. Clarke, *Parliamentary Privilege*, p. 178.

30. John Russel Bartlett, editor, *Records of the Colony of Rhode Island and Providence Plantations in New England* (Providence: A. Crawford Greene and Brother, 1856), I, p. 213; affirmed May 19, 1657, I, p. 354.

31. Arnold, *History of the State of Rhode Island*, I, p. 257.

32. Charles P. Hoadly, editor, *Public Records of Connecticut*, VII, p. 244.

33. Bartlett, *Records of Rhode Island*, I, p. 147. A change of procedure was instituted on October 26, 1650, as revealed in Arnold, *History of the State of Rhode Island*, I, p. 232.

34. Field, *State of Rhode Island*, III, p. 39; Prescott O. Clarke, *Rhode Island and Providence Plantations* (Providence: E. A. Johnson and Co., Printers, 1885), p. 9.

35. *At the General Assembly of the Governor and Company of the English Colony of Rhode Island, and Providence Plantations, in America, June, 1776 Session Records* (Newport: Printed by Samuel Ward, 1776).

36. Bartlett, *Records of Rhode Island*, IV (Providence: Knowles, Anthony and Co., 1858), p. 580.

37. Bartlett, *Records of Rhode Island*, IV, p. 580.

38. Bartlett, *Records of Rhode Island*, V, p. 75.

39. Bartlett, *Records of Rhode Island*, V, p. 336.

40. Bartlett, *Records of Rhode Island*, V, p. 562; additional dissents may be found at pages 190, 400, 401, 438; and Bartlett, *Records of Rhode Island*, VI, pages 19, 80, 102, 133, 148, 406, 436, 464, 495.

41. Arnold, *History of the State of Rhode Island*, II, p. 263.

42. Bartlett, *Records of Rhode Island*, VI, pp. 416-427; see also p. 452 for an Assembly order to colonists to ignore the Stamp Act because it was an

outside attempt at taxation that was "unconstitutional, and hath a manifest tendency to destroy the liberties of the people of the colony." See also VII, p. 388.

43. For example, the first dissenters cited—Ellery and Bours—were returned by the Islanders to the Assembly at the next election (see *Records of Rhode Island*, V, p. 5) and given high responsibilities by the Assembly (see V, p. 79). These kinds of subsequent events appear in the records for nearly all dissenters, regardless of the chill of their criticism.

44. Bartlett, *Records of Rhode Island*, I, p. 255. Any freeman could record a protest of a decision by the Assembly or Towne Meeting for a like sum.

45. Field, *State of Rhode Island*, III, p. 97.

46. Field, *State of Rhode Island*, III, p. 97.

47. Jones, *Congregational Commonwealth*, p. 69.

48. Trumbull, *Public Records of Connecticut*, I, pp. 14–19.

49. Trumbull, *Public Records of Connecticut*, I, p. 520. Note that the Court and the Assembly were the same body, performing legislative, judicial, and executive tasks.

50. Levy, p. 63.

51. Levy, p. 63, p. 43.

52. Trumbull, *Public Records of Connecticut*, I, pp. 77–78.

53. Trumbull, *Public Records of Connecticut*, II, p. 392.

54. Trumbull, *Public Records of Connecticut*, I, p. 51. Note, first, that the precise language of Gydersly is not included in the *Records*, a deficiency repeated often; second, as is the case most of the time when a person is ordered to appear at the next session of Court, no mention of the case is made in any subsequent records.

55. Hoadly, *Public Records of Connecticut*, V, p. 492. See also the cases of Jeramy Addoms, March 5, 1644, in Trumbull, *Public Records of Connecticut*, I, p. 123; Thomas Ozmore, March 5, 1644, in I, p. 124; John Charles, February 2, 1646, in Hoadly, *Records of the Colony and Plantations of New Haven, 1638–1649* (Hartford: Case, Tiffany and Company, 1857), pp. 298–300; John Scott, March 10, 1663, in Trumbull, *Public Records of Connecticut*, I, p. 417; William Bradley, April 11, 1665, in Franklin Bowditch Dexter, editor, *New Haven Town Records, 1662–1684*, vol. II of *New Haven Colony Historical Society Ancient Town Records Series* (New Haven, 1919), p. 138; Jeremiah Ripley, May 10, 1733, in Hoadly, *Public Records of Connecticut*, VII, p. 428; John Owen, May 12, 1743, VIII, p. 519; Roger Bidwell, May 12, 1743, VIII, p. 548; also IX, p. 255, for Bidwell reversal; Daniel Scot, XI, p. 139. (Note: This is the only case in which the Grand Jury returned an indictment for spoken words. In all other cases the legislature assumed the role of accuser.)

56. Hoadly, *Public Records of Connecticut*, IX, p. 20.

57. Hoadly, IX, p. 28.

58. Hoadly, IX, p. 29.

59. Clarke, *Parliamentary Privilege*, p. 107.

60. Bartlett, *Records of Rhode Island*, II (Providence, 1857), p. 438.

61. Arnold, *History of the State of Rhode Island*, I, p. 355.

62. Arnold, I, p. 355.

63. Bartlett, *Records of Rhode Island*, II, p. 455.
64. Arnold, *History of the State of Rhode Island*, I, p. 553.
65. Arnold, II, p. 5.
66. Bartlett, *Records of Rhode Island*, VI (Providence: Knowles, Anthony and Co., 1858), pp. 276–277.
67. Act of March 1, 1662, in *Acts and Laws of His Majesty's Colony of Rhode Island and Providence Plantations in America* (Boston in New England: Printed by John Allen, for Nicholas Boone, at the Sign of the Bible in Cornhill, 1719), p. 4; see also 1663 Act in *Laws and Acts of Her Majesties Colony of Rhode Island and Providence Plantations Made from the First Settlement in 1636 to 1705* (Providence: Rider and Rider, 1896), p. 1.
68. Act of February, 1728, in *Acts and Laws of His Majesty's Colony of Rhode Island and Providence Plantations in America* (Newport: James Franklin, 1730), p. 169.
69. Field, *State of Rhode Island*, I, pp. 59–60. Gorton was charged again on October 18, 1660, for "slander of the Court," but the General Attorney of the Colony failed to appear to prosecute, so Gorton was released. See Bartlett, *Records of Rhode Island*, I, p. 76. See the cases of John Warner, April 24, 1652, in *Collections of the Rhode Island Historical Society*, II, note on p. 55; Tom Greene, June 30, 1657, in *Rhode Island Court Records*, 1647–1662 (Providence, 1922), I, p. 29; Samuell Crokke, June, 1658, I, p. 43; Edmund Calverly, October, 1664, in Bartlett, *Records of Rhode Island*, II, pp. 63–64, 98–99; William Dyre, May 3, 1665, II, pp. 107–109; William Harris, July 2, 1667, II, pp. 209, 237; William Harris, February, 1672, in Field, *State of Rhode Island*, I, p. 121; Francis Uselton, June 7, 1671, in Bartlett, *Records of Rhode Island*, II, p. 392; John Saffin, 1678, in Durfee, *Gleanings from the Judicial History of Rhode Island*, Series No. 1 of *Rhode Island Historical Tracts*, No. 18 (Providence: Sidney S. Rider, 1883), p. 128; Richard Smith, July 9, 1679, in Bartlett, *Records of Rhode Island*, III, pp. 49–50; Gabriel Bernon, 1716, IV, p. 215; John Martin, 1753, in Field, *State of Rhode Island*, III, p. 159; Samuel Thayer, November, 1756, in Bartlett, *Records of Rhode Island*, V, pp. 552–554; Samuel Thayer, January 10, 1757, VI, pp. 5, 15; John Wheaton, February 1, 1757, VI, p. 20.
70. Account of October, 1652, letter in Arnold, *History of the State of Rhode Island*, I, p. 243.
71. Bartlett, *Records of Rhode Island*, II, p. 388.
72. Levy, p. 31.
73. Levy, p. 49.
74. Levy, p. 85. It should be noted that it was not until *New York Times Co. v. Sullivan* 376 U.S. 254 (1964), that the Supreme Court, for all practical purposes, laid to rest any cause of action that a government official (or a government through an official) might have for libel.
75. Trumbull, *Public Records of Connecticut*, I, p. 14.
76. Trumbull, I, p. 77–78.
77. Trumbull, I, p. 515.
78. Trumbull, I, p. 515. See also p. 537 for a law against lying and cursing and p. 547 for the penalty.

Notes to Pages 12–13   259

79. Trumbull, II, p. 392.

80. Hoadly, *Public Records of Connecticut*, V, pp. 382–383. See also Act of May 12, 1726, VII, p. 8; Act of May 14, 1730, VII, p. 290; Act of May 9, 1734, VII, p. 499.

81. Dexter, *New Haven Town Records*, pp. 150–151. See also the case of John Jennings, 1649, in Trumbull, *Public Records of Connecticut*, I, p. 203; John Russell in Jones, *Congregational Commonwealth*, p. 119.

82. Dexter, p. 210.

83. Dexter, p. 275.

84. Dexter, p. 276. See also the cases of Dan Clarke, in Trumbull, *Public Records of Connecticut*, II, p. 416; and Mary Stephens, May 9, 1728, in Hoadly, *Public Records of Connecticut*, VII, p. 176.

85. Jones, *Congregational Commonwealth*, p. 120.

86. Jones, p. 120. See also the cases of Robert Bartlett, June 30, 1646, in Trumbull, *Public Records of Connecticut*, I, p. 142; John Bennett, 1640, I, p. 167; Danyell Turner, I, p. 194; William Wooden, December 7, 1647, in Hoadly, *Records of the Colony and Plantation of New Haven*, p. 339; John Morris, January 3, 1670, in Dexter, *New Haven Town Records*, p. 274.

87. Bartlett, *Records of Rhode Island*, I, p. 184.

88. *Laws and Acts of Her Majesties Colony of Rhode Island and Providence Plantations Made from the First Settlement in 1636 to 1705* (Providence: Sidney S. Rider and Burnett Rider, 1896), p. 11. For other laws on slander see Act of May 27, 1640, in Bartlett, *Records of Rhode Island*, I, p. 29, 159; Act of October 1652, in Arnold, *History of the State of Rhode Island*, I, p. 242; and Irving Berdine Richman, *Rhode Island: Its Making and Its Meaning 1636–1683* (New York: G. P. Putnam's Sons, 1902), II, p. 40 note; Act of May 23, 1650, in Bartlett, *Records of Rhode Island*, I, p. 228; Act of November, 1756, in Bartlett, V (Providence: Knowles, Anthony and Co., 1860), p. 556.

89. Act of 1665, in Richman, *Rhode Island: Its Making and Its Meaning*, II, p. 39. See also Acts of 1728, in *Acts and Laws of His Majesty's Colony of Rhode Island and Providence Plantations in America* (Newport: Printed by James Franklin, 1730), p. 175, 226; Act of 1748, in Bartlett, *Records of Rhode Island*, V, p. 260; this act also found in *Acts and Laws of His Majesty's Colony of Rhode Island and Providence Plantations in New England in America from Anno 1745, to Anno 1752* (Newport: printed by J. Franklin, 1752), p. 52.

90. Act of 1647, in Bartlett, *Records of Rhode Island*, I, p. 159; also, in Arnold, *History of the State of Rhode Island and Providence Plantations*, I, p. 208.

91. Act of 1663, in *Laws and Acts of Her Majesties Colony of Rhode Island and Providence Plantations Made from the First Settlement in 1636 to 1705* (Providence: Rider and Rider, 1896), p. 1; Act of 1728, in *Acts and Laws of His Majesty's Colony of Rhode Island and Providence Plantations* in America (Newport: James Franklin, 1730), p. 170.

92. Act of 1663, in *Laws and Acts of Her Majesties Colony of Rhode Island and Providence Plantations Made from the First Settlement in 1636 to 1705* (Providence: Rider and Rider, 1896), p. 14; Act of 1736, in *Laws, Made and Pass'd by the General Assembly of His Majesty's Colony of Rhode Island and Providence Plantations 1730–1736*, p. 276.

93. Act of 1663, in *Laws and Acts of Her Majesties Colony of Rhode Island and Providence Plantations Made from the First Settlement in 1636 to 1705* (Providence: Rider and Rider, 1896), p. 9.

94. Act of 1729, in *Acts and Laws of His Majesty's Colony of Rhode Island and Providence Plantations in America* (Newport: James Franklin, 1730), p. 185.

95. For the case of Smith v. Arnold see *Rhode Island Court Records, 1662–1670* (Providence, 1922), II, p. 6; for the case of George Gardener, Jr., see *Rhode Island Court Records*, II, p. 7; for Briggs v. Arnold, see *Rhode Island Court Records*, II, p. 22; for a grant of a change of venue in the case of Steven Hopkins v. Sam Ward, June 13, 1757, see Bartlett, *Records of Rhode Island*, VI, pp. 68–69; for the case of Daniel Coggeshall see Bartlett, IV, p. 21.

96. Levy, p. 140.

97. Elisha Williams, *A Seasonable Plea for the Liberty of Conscience, and the Right of private judgment in Matters of Religion, without any controul from human Authority, By a Lover of Truth and Liberty*, signed, Philalethes (Boston, 1744), p. 6, 40.

98. Levy, p. 140.

99. Trumbull, *Public Records of Connecticut*, I, p. 361.

100. Charles M. Andrews, *The Beginnings of Connecticut, 1632–1662*, Tercentenary Pamphlet Series No. 32 (New Haven: Yale University Press, 1934), p. 55.

101. Andrews, p. 55.

102. Trumbull, *Public Records of Connecticut*, I, p. 361. For the case of the Reverend Samuel Stone, acquitted on charges of violating basic law, March, 1654/1655, see Hoadly, *Records of the Particular Court in Connecticut, 1639–1663*, XXII of *Collections of the Connecticut Historical Society* (Hartford, 1928), p. 140.

103. Andrews, *The Beginnings of Connecticut*, p. 55.

104. Trumbull,. *Public Records of Connecticut*, I, p. 524.

105. Irving Brant, *The Bill of Rights: Its Origin and Meaning* (New York: The New American Library, 1965), p. 97.

106. Brant, p. 97.

107. Sir James Fitzjames Stephen, *A History of the Criminal Law of England* (New York: Burt Franklin; originally published in London, 1883), p. 303.

108. Brant, *The Bill of Rights*, p. 127.

109. Stephen, *A History of the Criminal Law*, p. 314.

110. Stephen, p. 315.

111. Brant, *The Bill of Rights*, pp. 113–115.

112. Stephen, *A History of the Criminal Law*, p. 313.

113. Levy, p. 22.

114. Levy, p. 32.

115. Levy, p. 23.

116. Levy, p. 23.

117. Osgood, *The American Colonies in the Eighteenth Century* (New York: Columbia University Press, 1924), III, p. 275.

118. Jones, *Congregational Commonwealth*, p. 134.

119. Trumbull, *Public Records of Connecticut*, I, p. 129.

120. Albert C. Bates, editor, *The Law Papers: Correspondence and Documents During Jonathan Law's Governorship of the Colony of Connecticut, 1741–1750*, vols. XI, XIII, XV of *Collections of the Connecticut Historical Society* (Hartford, 1907), II (XIII of *Collections*), p. 96.

121. Bates, editor, *The Fitch Papers: Correspondence and Documents During Thomas Fitch's Governorship of the Colony of Connecticut, 1754–1776*, vols. XV, XVIII of *Collections of the Connecticut Historical Society* (Hartford, 1918), II (XVII of *Collections*), p. 199.

122. Jones, *Congregational Commonwealth*, p. 133.

123. *Rhode Island Court Records, 1647–1662*, I, p. 29. See also Bartlett, *Records of Rhode Island*, II, p. 208, 237; Bartlett, IV, p. 22; for comparisons with other monetary figures see Bartlett, II, p. 167; for *per diem* allowances see Arnold, *History of the State of Rhode Island*, I, pp. 354–356; for pay structures, Lovejoy, *Rhode Island Politics and the American Revolution*, p. 16, for voting qualifications. Lovejoy goes on to say, "At first glance these figures seem high but money was cheap in Rhode Island owing to frequent emission of paper bills of credit."

124. See the John Warner case in Arnold, *History of the State of Rhode Island*, p. 287; also, the case of Edmund Calverly, in Bartlett, *Records of Rhode Island*, II, p. 63.

125. Levy, p. 34. Levy's work should not go unquestioned. He may have generalized hastily. For his point that "no cause was more honored by rhetorical declamation and dishonored in practice than that of freedom of expression during the revolutionary period, from the 1760's through the cessation of hostilities . . ." (p. 63) he cites one example of a Tory deprived of his right of free speech. But there are contrary examples of passion controlled. On January 12, 1776, in Cedar Point, Maryland, a seventy-year-old Tory named Mr. Lee "had called patriots 'rabble.' Fifteen hundred of them came out to give him a lesson in politics. They dragged him to a clearing and gave him a loyalty oath to sign. He refused: 'You may kill me but you shall not force me to retract one syllable. If the blind rage that contends for liberty can force me to go against my conscience, it is time to take an eternal farewell.' Lee told the vigilantes they could not force their brand of liberty on him. 'I have lived a free man and it is my resolution to die one.' No one tried to stop the old Tory as he walked away." (From the script of the C.B.S. Bicentennial Minute of January 12, 176.) Grateful acknowledgement goes to C.B.S. and Robert Markell, Executive Producer of the Bicentennial Minutes, for allowing me to use information above.

126. The art of the historian is "imaginative synthesis and re-creation from among the myriad fragments that are the residue of the past." Jerold S. Auerbach *Unequal Justice: Lawyers and Social Change in Modern America* (New York: Oxford University Press, 1976), p. 9. For essays on rhetorical history see Joe Munshaw, "The Structures of History: Dividing Phenomena for Rhetorical Understanding," *Central States Speech Journal*, 24 (1973), 29–

42; and Bruce Grombeck, "Rhetorical History and Rhetorical Criticism: A Distinction," *Speech Teacher*, 24 (1975), 309–320.

127. *Quarterly Journal of Speech*, 58 (1972), pp. 396–407.
128. Bormann, p. 398.
129. Bormann, p. 399.
130. Bormann, p. 406.
131. Thomas I. Emerson, "Toward a General Theory of the First Amendment," *Yale Law Journal*, 72 (1963), p. 893.
132. Emerson, pp. 893–895.
133. Emerson, p. 895.
134. Clinton L. Rossiter, *The First American Revolution: The American Colonies on the Eve of Independence* (New York: Harcourt, Barce and World, Inc., 1956), p. 101.
135. Rossiter, *The First American Revolution*, p. 102.
136. Rossiter, *The First American Revolution*, p. 103.
137. Irving Brant, "Seditious Libel: Myth and Reality," *New York Law Review*, 39 (1964), p. 1.
138. Leon Whipple, *The Story of Civil Liberties in the United States* (New York: Vanguard Press, American Civil Liberties Union, 1927), p. 19.
139. Rossiter, *Seedtime*, p. 164.
140. Rossiter, *Seedtime*, p. 164.
141. Rossiter, *Seedtime*, p. 168.
142. The text can be found in Trumbull, *Public Records of Connecticut*, I, pp. 20–25.
143. See Jones, *Congregational Commonwealth*, pp. xi–xii; also, Fiske, *The Beginnings of New England*, p. 127.
144. Rossiter, *Seedtime*, p. 189.
145. Rossiter, *Seedtime*, p. 189.
146. Rossiter, *Seedtime*, p. 190.
147. Rossiter, *Seedtime*, p. 191.
148. Rossiter, *Seedtime*, p. 192. See also Rossiter, *The First American Revolution*, pp. 76, 77, and 92 for the relationship of religious freedom to political freedom.
149. Stephen, *A History of Criminal Law*, II, pp. 299–300. This quotation is a summary of themes actually used in England and probably transported to the colonies.
150. Brant, *The Bill of Rights*, p. 235; also, James Madison, Report on the Virginia Resolutions, as quoted in Chafee, *Free Speech in the United States*, pp. 18–21.
151. Rossiter, *The First American Revolution*, p. 104.
152. Jones, *Congregational Commonwealth*, p. 167.
153. Jones, p. 167; Arnold, *History of Rhode Island*, 2 vols. The point of Levy's thesis is that the popularly elected representatives of the colonists suppressed free expression. Since the councils and assemblies were elected in Connecticut and Rhode Island, cases of restriction of speech by both bodies were included in this work.
154. Epaphroditus Peck, *The Loyalists of Connecticut*, Tercentenary

Pamphlet Series, No. 31 (New Haven: Yale University Press, 1934), p. 17. Only two cases were discovered where a colonist was challenged for remarks made about the king: the cases of John Scott, March 10, 1663, in Trumbull, *Public Records of Connecticut*, I, p. 417; and Matt Graves, January 3, 1750/1751, in Bates, *The Wolcott Papers: Correspondence During Roger Wolcott's Governship of the Colony of Connecticut, 1750–1754*, XVI of *Collections of the Connecticut Historical Society* (Hartford, 1916), p. 5.

155. Perry, *Founders*, p. 52.
156. Rossiter, *Seedtime*, p. 160. See Rossiter's chapter on Hooker, pp. 159–178.
157. Quoted in Perry, *Founders*, p. 53.
158. Perry, *Founders*, p. 53.
159. Fiske, *The Beginnings of New England*, p. 117.
160. Rossiter, *Seedtime*, p. 179. See Rossiter's chapter on Williams at pp. 179–204.
161. Rossiter, *Seedtime*, p. 194.
162. Fiske, *The Beginnings of New England*, p. 268.
163. Fiske, p. 185.
164. Fiske, p. 184, 186.
165. Fiske, p. 195.

2. Freedom of Expression in the Confederate States of America

1. Clement Eaton, *The Freedom-of-Thought Struggle in the Old South* (New York: Harper & Row, 1964), p. 121.
2. Clement Eaton, *A History of the Southern Confederacy* (New York: The MacMillan Company, 1954), p. 60.
3. Leonard W. Levy, *Freedom of Speech and Press in Early American History: Legacy of Suppression* (New York: Harper & Row, 1963). See also T. F. Carroll, "Freedom of Speech and of the Press in the Federalist Period: The Sedition Act," 18 *Michigan Law Review* 615 (1920).
4. Eaton, *The Freedom-of-Thought Struggle in the Old South*. For other discussions of the same period see Russel B. Nye, *Fettered Freedom: Civil Liberties and the Slavery Controversy, 1830–1860* (East Lansing: Michigan State University Press, 1963); Harold L. Nelson, ed., *Freedom of the Press From Hamilton to the Warren Court* (New York: Bobbs-Merrill, 1967), pp. 167–220; and Arnold E. K. Nash, "The Judicial Defense of Liberalism in the South Atlantic States, 1831–1861," unpublished senior honors thesis, Harvard University, 1958.
5. Harry Kalven, Jr., *The Negro and the First Amendment* (Chicago: University of Chicago Press, 1965).
6. Franklyn S. Haiman, *Freedom of Speech: Issues and Cases* (New York: Random House, 1965), p. xv; Zechariah Chafee, Jr., *Free Speech in the United States* (Cambridge: Harvard University Press, 1948), p. 437.
7. William M. Robinson, Jr., *Justice in Grey: A History of the Judicial Sys-*

tem of the Confederate States of America (Cambridge: Harvard University Press, 1941), p. 620.

8. A. L. Hull, ed., "The Making of the Confederate Constitution," *Publications of the Southern Historical Association*, 9 (1905), 274.

9. Hull, p. 275.

10. Robert Hardy Smith, *An Address to the Citizens of Alabama on the Constitution and Laws of the Confederate States of America* (Mobile: Mobile Daily Register Press, 1861), quoted in Charles Robert Lee, Jr., *The Confederate Constitutions* (Chapel Hill: University of North Carolina Press, 1963), p. 58.

11. *Journal of the Congress of the Confederate States of America, 1861–1865* (Washington, D.C.: Government Printing Office, 1904–1905), I, 19.

12. J. L. M. Curry, *Civil History of the Government of the Confederate States* (Richmond: B. F. Johnson, 1901), p. 50. See also Alexander H. Stephens, *A Constitutional History of the Late War Between the States* (Philadelphia: National Publishing Company, 1868), I, 339; Jefferson Davis, *The Rise and Fall of the Confederate Government* (Richmond: Garrett and Massie, 1938), I, 202.

13. *Journal of the Confederate Congress*, I, 39.

14. James M. Matthews, ed., *The Statutes at Large of the Provisional Government of the Confederate States of America* (Richmond: R. M. Smith, 1864), p. 3.

15. Matthews, p. 16.

16. *Journal of the Confederate Congress*, I, 872.

17. *Journal*, p. 873.

18. For an extensive and well-documented discussion of the Confederate judiciary see William M. Robinson, Jr., *Justice in Grey: A History of the Judicial System of the Confederate States of America* (Cambridge: Harvard University Press, 1941).

19. The Senate passed a bill authorizing a court composed of a chief justice and four associate justices, but the legislation was defeated in the House in the 1863 session.

20. John V. Wright, in Bradley T. Johnson, John V. Wright, J. A. Orr, and L. Q. Washington, "Why the Confederate States of America Had No Supreme Court," *Publications of the Southern History Association*, 4 (1900), 92–93. See also C. E. George, "The Supreme Court of the Confederate States of America," 6 *Virginia Law Review*, N.S., 592 (1920).

21. J. A. Orr, in Bradley T. Johnson, *et al.*, p. 98.

22. Curtis Arthur Amlund, *Federalism in the Southern Confederacy* (Washington, D.C.: Public Affairs Press, 1966), p. 83.

23. Robinson, p. 140.

24. *Burroughs v. Peyton*, 16 Va. 470.

25. *Cobb v. Stallings*, 34 Ga. 72.

26. Albert B. Moore, *Conscription and Conflict in the Confederacy* (New York: Macmillan, 1924), p. 163.

27. Sidney D. Brummer, "The Judicial Interpretation of the Confederate Constitution," *Studies in Southern History and Politics* (New York: Columbia University Press, 1914), p. 131, 8 *Lawyer and Banker* 387 (1915).

28. Moore, p. 166.

29. Joseph Gregoire deRoulhac Hamilton, "The State Courts and the Confederate Constitution," *Journal of Southern History*, 4 (1938), 425.

30. Samuel H. Hempstead, ed., *Reports of Cases Argued and Determined in the United States Superior Court for the Territory of Arkansas, from 1820 to 1836; and in the United States District Court for the District of Arkansas from 1836 to 1849; and in the United States Circuit Court from 1839 to 1856* (Boston: Little, Brown, and Co., 1856).

31. Robinson, pp. 169, 146.

32. One judge sitting in vacation held the law unconstitutional: *In re Cain*, 60 N.C. 525. Another would have done so had the issue been before the court: *Ex parte Coupland*, 26 Tex. 406.

33. E. Merton Coulter, *The Confederate States of America*, 1861–1865 (Baton Rouge: Louisiana State University Press, 1950), p. 503.

34. *Richmond Examiner*, 23 November 1864; Wilfred Buck Yearns, *The Confederate Congress* (Athens: University of Georgia Press, 1960), p. 20.

35. Coulter, p. 505; *Vicksburg Daily Whig*, February 4, 1863, cited in J. Cutler Andrews, *The South Reports the Civil War* (Princeton: Princeton University Press, 1970), p. 288.

36. Yearns, p. 20; Coulter, p. 503; Andrews, p. 531; *Richmond Examiner*, January 11, 1862.

37. *Journal of the Confederate Congress*, III, 157; Andrews, pp. 289–290. Coulter reports incorrectly that the offense was that the reporter had garbled the senator's remarks (p. 449).

38. *Journal of the Confederate Congress*, III, 100.

39. *Journal*, p. 157.

40. *Journal*, pp. 154, 156.

41. *Richmond Sentinel*, January 14, 1865; *Richmond Dispatch*, January 18, 1865; Andrews, p. 484; *Journal of the Confederate Congress*, VII, 457.

42. James M. Matthews, ed., *Public Laws of the Confederate States of America*, 1862–1864 (Richmond: R. M. Smith, 1864), pp. 174–175.

43. Charles W. Ramsdell, ed., *Laws and Joint Resolutions of the Last Session of the Confederate Congress (November 7, 1864–March 18, 1865) together with the Secret Acts of the Provisional Congresses* (Durham: Duke University Press, 1941), pp. 130–131.

44. Ramsdell, p. 11.

45. Matthews, *Public Laws of the Confederate States*, p. 129; Ramsdell, p. 21.

46. Matthews, *Public Laws of the Confederate States*, p. 78.

47. Matthews, *Statutes of the Provisional Government*, pp. 106–107.

48. Andrews, p. 375. See T. J. O'Donnell, "Military Censorship and the Freedom of the Press," 5 *Virginia Law Review* 178 (1917).

49. See, for example, Yearns, p. 153; Eaton, *A History of the Southern Confederacy*, p. 231; Robinson, pp. 398, 452; Frank L. Owsley, *States Rights in the Confederacy*, (Chicago: University of Chicago Press, 1925), p. 166.

50. *Journal of the Confederate Congress*, II, 271.

51. *Journal*, p. 272.

52. *Journal*, pp. 308, 333, 435; Robinson, p. 452.

53. Matthews, *Public Laws of the Confederate States*, pp. 1, 84, 187–189.
54. Matthews, p. 1.
55. Emory M. Thomas, *The Confederacy as a Revolutionary Experience* (Englewood Cliffs, N.J.: Prentice-Hall, 1971), p. 63.
56. John Minor Botts, *The Great Rebellion: Its Secret History, Rise, Progress, and Disastrous Failure* (New York: Harper & Bros., 1866) p. 279.
57. Matthews, *Public Laws of the Confederate States*, p. 27.
58. Matthews, p. 84.
59. *Journal of the Confederate Congress*, III, 669–671.
60. Brummer, p. 129.
61. *Public Laws of the North Carolina General Assembly (Adjourned Session, 1864)*, p. 191, cited in May Spencer Ringold, *The Role of the State Legislatures in the Confederacy* (Athens: University of Georgia Press, 1966), p. 29.
62. Ringold, p. 33.
63. Owsley, p. 191.
64. *Journal of the Confederate Congress*, VII, 81–82, 266–267.
65. Trexler, p. 177.
66. Lieut. Col. Fremantle, *Three Months in the Southern States; April–June, 1863* (New York: John Bradburn, 1864), p. 154. For examples of various press criticisms of military and civilian officials see Andrews, pp. 518–523.
67. *The War of the Rebellion: A Compilation of the Official Records of the Union and Confederate Armies* (Washington, D.C.: Government Printing Office, 1880–1901, 128 vols.), Ser. II, Vol. I, 913; hereinafter cited as *Official Records*.
68. Coulter, p. 503.
69. Coulter, pp. 457–458.
70. *Official Records*, Ser. II, Vol. I, 824–826.
71. Jefferson Davis, *A Short History of the Confederate States of America* (New York: Belford, 1890), p. 382.
72. James D. Richardson, ed., *The Messages and Papers of Jefferson Davis and the Confederacy* (New York: Chelsea House-Robert Hector, 1966, I, 184–185.
73. Eaton, *A History of the Southern Confederacy*, p. 232.
74. Coulter, p. 502.
75. Coulter, p. 501.
76. T. C. DeLeon, *Four Years in Rebel Capitals: An Inside View of Life in the Southern Confederacy* (Mobile: Gossip Printing Company, 1890), p. 289.
77. Andrews, p. 76.
78. *Richmond Enquirer*, July 1, 1861.
79. Matthews, *Statutes of the Provisional Government*, pp. 106–107. The mails, however, were open for use by reporters even when the telegraph wires were censored (Andrews, pp. 343, 439). For a description of the codes voluntarily adopted by some of the southern newspapers see Andrews, pp. 529–530.
80. *Charleston Mercury*, July 6, 1861; Andrews, p. 77.
81. *Mobile Daily Advertiser and Register*, June 19, 1863; Andrews, p. 303.

82. Andrews, p. 441; *Montgomery Daily Advertiser*, May 27, 1864.
83. Andrews, p. 369.
84. Andrews, pp. 156, 161, 515, 472–473.
85. Andrews, pp. 236–237.
86. Andrews, pp. 337, 349, 443. Reid was later arrested by the marshal of Atlanta but was released after a few days.
87. Andrews, p. 103.
88. Andrews, p. 103.
89. Andrews, p. 62.
90. *Official Records*, Ser. I, Vol. XI, Pt. iii, 636. For other such suggestions and warnings see *Official Records*, Ser. I, Vol. XXXV, Pt. i, 522; Vol. XLVI, Pt. ii, 1047; Vol. LI, Pt. ii, 626.
91. *Official Records*, Ser. I, Vol. IX, 716.
92. *Official Records*, Ser. I, Vol. XV, 771–772.
93. *Official Records*, Ser. II, Vol. II, 1556.
94. *Official Records*, Ser. II, Vol. II, 1557.
95. Andrews, p. 532; Yearns, p. 153.
96. Yearns, pp. 151–152.
97. *Official Records*, Ser. II, Vol. II, 1367–1372.
98. Robinson, pp. 199–201.
99. Coulter, pp. 386–387.
100. Eaton, *A History of the Southern Confederacy*, pp. 231–232; Coulter, p. 500.
101. Botts, pp. 279–285; *Official Records*, Ser. II, Vol. II, 1547.
102. Coulter, p. 91.
103. *Richmond Whig*, March 6, 1862; Coulter, p. 500.
104. Trexler, p. 187.
105. *Official Records*, Ser. IV, Vol. III, 203–204.
106. *Official Records*, Ser. II, Vol. I, 850.
107. Robinson, pp. 288–289.
108. *Official Records*, Ser. II, Vol. I, 845–846.
109. *Official Records*.
110. Coulter, p. 94.
111. Robinson, p. 289; *Official Records*, Ser. II, Vol. I, 834.
112. Robinson, p. 286.
113. *Official Records*, Ser. II, Vol. I, 844.
114. *Official Records*, Ser. II, Vol. I, 834.
115. *Official Records*, Ser. II, Vol. I.
116. *Official Records*, Ser. II, Vol. I, p. 907.
117. *Official Records*, Ser. II, Vol. I, p. 922.
118. *Official Records*, Ser. II, Vol. I, p. 921.
119. *Official Records*, Ser. II, Vol. I, p. 913.
120. *Official Records*, Ser. II, Vol. I, p. 917.
121. Robinson, pp. 250–251.
122. Coulter, p. 93.
123. Coulter, p. 503.

124. Andrews, p. 541.

125. Andrews, p. 541; Eaton, *The Freedom-of-Thought Struggle in the Old South*, pp. 398–399.

126. Coulter, p. 88.

127. Robert S. Tharin, *Arbitrary Arrests in the South; or Scenes from the Experience of an Alabama Unionist* (New York: John Bradburn, 1863), p. 15.

128. Coulter, p. 86; Eaton, *The Freedom-of-Thought Struggle in the Old South*, p. 392.

129. *Official Records*, Ser. II, Vol. II, 1364.

130. Coulter, p. 88.

131. *Official Records*, Ser. II, Vol. II, 1365.

132. *Acts of the Georgia General Assembly (1862; Extra Session, 1863)*, p. 137; cited in Ringold, p. 59.

133. For a more-detailed discussion of such incidents see A. W. Bishop, *Loyalty on the Frontier, or Sketches of Union Men of the Southwest* (St. Louis: R. P. Studley, 1863); Georgia Lee Tatum, *Disloyalty in the Confederacy* (Chapel Hill: University of North Carolina Press, 1934); and Ted R. Worley, "The Arkansas Peace Society of 1861: A Study in Mountain Unionism," *Journal of Southern History*, 24 (1958), 445–456.

134. *Official Records*, Ser. I, Vol XI, Pt. iii, 636.

135. Robinson, p. 628. For examples of Union suppressions of speech and press see Nelson, pp. 221–247; Dean Sprague, *Freedom Under Lincoln* (Boston: Houghton Mifflin, 1965); James Randell, *Constitutional Problems Under Lincoln* (Urbana: University of Illinois Press, 1951); and Sydney G. Fisher, "Suppression of the Writ of Habeas Corpus During the War of the Rebellion," *Political Science Quarterly*, 3 (1888), 454–488.

136. *Ex parte Merryman*, 17 Fed. Cases 9487 (1861). See also Clinton Rossiter, *The Supreme Court and the Commander in Chief* (Ithaca, N.Y.: Cornell University Press, 1951), p. 25.

137. C. Herman Pritchett, *The American Constitution* (New York: McGraw-Hill, 1968), pp. 380–381.

138. *Ex parte Vallandingham*, I Wall. 243 (1864); *Ex parte Milligan*, 4 Wall. 2 (1866).

139. Yearns, p. 154; *Journal of the Confederate Congress*, I, 393–394, 444; Robinson, pp. 199–201.

140. Andrews, p. 529; Coulter, p. 503.

141. Wickham Hoffman, *Camp, Court and Siege* (New York: Harper & Bros., 1877), pp. 77–79.

142. Coulter, p. 503.

143. Andrews, p. 469.

144. Andrews, pp. 498; 271.

145. Andrews, p. 540.

146. Fremantle, p. 220.

147. Arthur M. Schlesinger, *Prelude to Independence* (New York, 1958); cited in Levy, p. 176.

148. For a discussion of such cases, which is beyond the scope of this study, see Thomas F. Carroll, "Freedom of Speech and of the Press in War

Time: The Espionage Act," 17 *Michigan Law Review* 621 (1919); John P. Hall, "Free Speech in War Time," 21 *Columbia Law Review* 526 (1921); and Chafee, 36–305. J. J. O'Donnell, "Military Censorship and the Freedom of the Press," *Virginia Law Review* 178 (1917).

149. *Schenck v. United States*, 249 U.S. 47 (1919).

150. Coulter, p. 94; *Official Records*, Ser. II, Vol. I, 834.

151. *Official Records*, Ser. II, Vol. I, 845–846.

152. Andrews, p. 62; Robinson, pp. 201–202.

153. Sir William Blackstone, *Commentaries on the Laws of England*, IV, 151.

154. *Journal of the Confederate Congress*, VII, 457; II, 272.

155. *Journal of the Confederate Congress*, II, 435; Robinson, p. 452.

156. *Journal of the Confederate Congress*, III, 156–157.

3. The Right to Speak: The Free Speech Fights of the Industrial Workers of the World

1. "A Call to Action," *Industrial Worker*, February 16, 1910, p. 2.

2. The notion of the "exigency" in the "rhetorical situation" is developed in Lloyd Bitzer, "The Rhetorical Situation," *Philosophy and Rhetoric*, (January, 1968), 1–15.

3. William Preston, Jr., *Aliens and Dissenters: Federal Suppression of Radicals, 1903–1933* (New York: Harper Torchbooks; Harper & Row, publishers, 1963), p. 42.

4. Vincent St. John, *Industrial Unionism: The I.W.W.* (Chicago: I.W.W. Publishing Bureau, n.d.), p. 2; see also Melvyn Dubofsky, *We Shall Be All: A History of the Industrial Workers of the World* (Chicago: Quadrangle Books, 1969), pp. 105–06.

5. Dubofsky, *We Shall Be All*, p. 174.

6. Philip S. Foner, *History of the Labor Movement in the United States*, Volume IV: *The Industrial Workers of the World, 1905–1917* (New York: International Publishers, 1965), pp. 172 ff.

7. Joseph Ettor, *Industrial Unionism the Way to Freedom* (n.p.: I.W.W. Publication, n.d.), p. 18; see also, Terry W. Cole, "Labor's Radical Alternative: The Rhetoric of the Industrial Workers of the World" (unpublished Ph.D. dissertation, University of Oregon, 1974), pp. 82–88.

8. Vincent St. John, *Final Report of the United States Commission on Industrial Relations—Testimony*, Vol. II, Sen. Doc. 415, 64th Cong., 1st sess., p. 1471; see also *General Headquarters Bulletin*, IWW, 72 (November 9, 1915), p. 2 in *Government Exhibits, Transcript of Record* in the case of *U.S.A. vs. William D. Haywood, et al.*, I.W.W. Collection, Archives of Labor History and Urban Affairs, Wayne State University.

9. Foner, *Workers of the World*, p. 182.

10. Joseph R. Conlin, "The Wobblies: A Study of the Industrial Workers of the World Before World War I" (unpublished Ph.D. dissertation, University of Wisconsin, 1966), p. 45.

11. W. E. Trautmann, "The Horrors and Outrages of the Congo in Spokane," *Industrial Worker*, February 26, 1910, p. 4.

12. *Solidarity*, March 19, 1910, p. 2; cited in Dubofsky, *We Shall Be All*, pp. 183–84.

13. James F. Klumpp, "Challenge of Radical Rhetoric: Radicalization at Columbia," *Western Speech*, 37 (Summer, 1973), 146–56.

14. Klumpp, p. 148.

15. John Waite Bowers and Donovan J. Ochs, *The Rhetoric of Agitation and Control* (Reading, Mass.: Addison-Wesley Publishing Company, Inc., 1971), p. 27.

16. "The Missoula Free Speech Fight," *Industrial Worker*, October 20, 1909, p. 2.

17. Dubofsky, *We Shall Be All*, pp. 178–80; Foner, *Workers of the World*, pp. 179–81, 187.

18. Harris Weinstock, *Report of Harris Weinstock, Commissioner to Investigate the Recent Disturbances in the City of San Diego and the County of San Diego, California to His Excellency Hiram W. Johnson, Governor of California* (Sacramento: Superintendent of State Printing, 1912), 14–16.

19. Paul L. Murphy, *The Meaning of Freedom of Speech: First Amendment Freedoms From Wilson to FDR* (Westport, Connecticut: Greenwood Publishing Company, 1972), p. 21.

20. Joseph R. Conlin, *Bread and Roses Too: Studies of the Wobblies* (Greenwood, Connecticut: Greenwood Publishing Co., 1969), p. 77; Robert L. Tyler, *Rebels of the Woods: The I.W.W. in the Pacific Northwest* (Eugene, Oregon: University of Oregon Books, 1967), pp. 36–37; Foner, *Workers of the World*, p. 177.

21. Weinstock, *Report*, pp. 16–17.

22. Weinstock, p. 20.

23. Dubofsky, *We Shall Be All*, p. 173.

24. Foner, *Workers of the World*, p. 212.

25. Murphy, *The Meaning of Freedom of Speech*, p. 21.

26. General Headquarters, IWW, "Bulletin," December 10, 1915, p. 2, in *Government Exhibits, Transcript of Record* in the case of *U.S.A. vs. William D. Haywood, et al.*, I.W.W. Collection, Archives of Labor History and Urban Affairs, Wayne State University.

27. "Free Speech and Governmentalism," *Industrial Worker*, December 1, 1909, p. 4.

28. Oliver Wendell Holmes, "Dissenting Opinion," *Abrams vs. United States*, 250 US 616 (1919).

29. "Resolutions From Portland," *Industrial Worker*, December 1, 1909, p. 4.

30. Mark Stone, "An Analysis of Free Speech," *Industrial Worker*, October 20, 1917, p. 3.

31. Conlin, "The Wobblies," pp. 147–48.

4. Patriots vs. Dissenters: The Rhetoric of Intimidation in Indiana During the First World War

1. *Richmond Palladium*, April 6, 1917.

2. *Indianapolis Star*, July 7, 1917, p. 11.

3. Letter read by Inman Fowler, Indiana State Bar Association, *Proceedings of the 22nd Meeting, July 10, 1918*, pp. 17–18.

4. *Logansport Tribune*, n.d., rpt. in *Indiana Bulletin*, February 1, 1918, p. 8, (official publication of the Indiana State Council of Defense).

5. Dhe to Will Hays, January 24, 1918, Indiana State Council of Defense, Papers and Correspondence (hereafter ISCD), Series 11, Vol. 2, Archives Division, Indiana State Library.

6. Bretz to Hays, December 29, 1917, ISCD, Series 3, Vol. 5.

7. Shirk to State Council of Defense, April 17, 1918, ISCD, Series 11, Vol. 2.

8. *Indiana Bulletin*, August 24, 1917, p. 4.

9. Ripley County Council of Defense to Hays, August 4, 1917, (Typewritten), ISCD, Series 3, Vol. 15.

10. Confidential Circular, Will Hays to County Councils of Defense, June 22, 1917, ISCD, Series 2, Vol. 1.

11. *Indiana Bulletin*, November 30, 1917, p. 3.

12. *Indianapolis News*, December 6, 1917, p. 5.

13. For example, the *Lafayette Courier*, February 16, 1918, told its readers to report all cases of disloyalty to the county defense council.

14. Thomas Gregory, "Suggestions of Attorney-General Gregory to the Executive Committee in Relation to the Department of Justice," *American Bar Association Journal*, 4 (1918), 312–13.

15. The most recent and complete history of the APL is Joan Jensen, *The Price of Vigilance*, (Chicago: Rand McNally, 1968); updates Emerson Hough, *The Web*, (Chicago: Reilly and Lee, 1919), the officially authorized history of the APL.

16. Typed list, n.d., ISCD, Series 20, Part 1; Records of APL activities in Indiana are limited. In a housecleaning during 1953 the National Archives destroyed most of their APL materials, including those pertaining to Indiana, see bibliographic note in Jensen, *Price of Vigilance*.

17. Memorandum, n.d., ISCD, Series 20, Part 1.

18. One man recommended for the job, Don Hawkins, was approved by state officials, but turned down in Washington. Another, Meredith Nicholson, withstood strong pressures and refused the job for reasons of health and other obligations; Hays to Winterbotham, February 12, 1918; Winterbotham to John Wilson, March 4, 1918; Wilson to Nicholson, March 12, 1918; Nicholson to Wilson, March 13, 1918; ISCD, Series 20, Part 1.

19. Confidential, Frank Fishback, Charles Lewis, and Hugh McK. Landon to John Wilson, May 13, 1918, ISCD, Series 20, Part 1.

20. *Ibid.*

21. For example, the State Council of Defense selected the APL State Director.

22. Official report of investigation, May 14, 1918, ISCD, Series 20, Part 1.
23. *Indianapolis News*, April 5, 1918, p. 29.
24. Frank Butler to Michael Foley, July 13, 1918, ISCD, Series 3, Vol. 12.
25. Jensen, *Price of Vigilance*, p. 146.
26. Butler to Foley, July 13, 1918, ISCD, Series 3, Vol. 12.
27. *Rochester Sentinal*, Weekly Edition, May 2, 1918.
28. Indiana State Council of Defense, Proceedings of the 64th Meeting, August 20, 1918, p. 11, (Typewritten), Archives Division, Indiana State Library.
29. *Ibid.*
30. *Ibid.*, p. 20.
31. *Ibid.*, p. 22.
32. Foley to William Schrader, July 31, 1918, ISCD, Series 3, Vol. 12.
33. ISCD, Proceedings of the 64th Meeting, p. 21.
34. Hammond to Foley, August 26, 1918, ISCD, Proceedings of the 65th Meeting, August 27, 1918, p. 11.
35. *Pulaski County Democrat*, June 28, 1917, p. 4.
36. *Rochester Sentinal*, Weekly Edition, September 12, 1918, p. 1; *Rockport Journal*, October 5, 1918; *Indiana Bulletin*, February 22, 1918, p. 3.
37. *Indiana Bulletin*, February 22, 1918, p. 3.
38. Women's Section, Indiana State Council of Defense, *Manual of Registrars*, Indiana Division, Indiana State Library.
39. *Indiana Bulletin*, April 26, 1918, p. 5.
40. *Indianapolis News*, May 1, 1918, p. 5.
41. *Indianapolis News*, May 11, 1918, p. 3.
42. *Manual for Registrars.*
43. Eastinger to Foley, May 11, 1918, ISCD, Series 3, Vol. 16.
44. Foley to Eastinger, May 17, 1918, ISCD, Series 3, Vol. 16.
45. Indiana State Council of Defense, Proceedings of the 43rd Meeting, March 27, 1918, pp. 17–19.
46. Foley to Joseph Snyder, May 24, 1918, ISCD, Series 3, Vol. 5.
47. *Ibid.*
48. John Wilson to George Wagner, May 24, 1918, ISCD, Series 3, Vol. 5.
49. *Scott County Journal*, July 18, 1917; *White County Democrat*, March 1, 1918.
50. *Indiana Bulletin*, September 21, 1917, p. 7.
51. *Ibid.*
52. *Indianapolis News*, April 17, 1918, p. 12.
53. *Indiana Bulletin*, October 18, 1918, p. 2.
54. Will Wade to O. F. Rhodes, October 6, 1918, Fourth Liberty Loan-Indiana, Papers and Correspondence, Vol. 27, Part 15, (hereafter Liberty Loan), Archives Division, Indiana State Library.
55. Cards in Liberty Loan, Vol. 37, Part 15.
56. *Ibid.*
57. *Ibid.*
58. *Ibid.*

59. Telegram, Will Wade to J. J. Dunn, October 25, 1918, Liberty Loan, Vol. 37, Part 15.

60. Letters dated October 17, 1918, and October 19, 1918, Liberty Loan, Vol. 37, Part 15.

61. Card record for G. R. Chamberlain, Liberty Loan, Vol. 37, Part 15.

62. Telegram, Chamberlain to Wade, October 23, 1918, Liberty Loan, Vol. 37, Part 15.

63. Telegram, First National Bank of Peru to Wade, October 24, 1918, Liberty Loan, Vol. 37, Part 15.

64. J. Y. W. McClellan to Parker Baker, October 14, 1918, ISCD, Series 11, Vol. 2.

65. Susan Baker to State Council of Defense, October 24, 1918, ISCD, Series 11, Vol. 2.

66. *Indianapolis News*, October 24, 1917, p. 1.

67. *Indianapolis News*, October 25, 1917, p. 10.

68. *Indianapolis News*, October 25, 1917, p. 17.

69. G. M. O'Leary to Huntington Merchants, n.d., ISCD, Series 3, Vol. 8.

70. *Indiana Bulletin*, October 25, 1918, p. 2.

71. *Indiana Bulletin*, July 12, 1918, p. 2.

72. American Legion, Clay County Post No. 2, *Clay County's Answer, 1917–1919* (Chicago: Rogers Printing Co., 1919), p. 108.

73. *Indianapolis Star*, September 15, 1917, p. 6.

74. Marion County Council of Defense, Minutes, Meeting of January 20, 1918, (Typewritten), Archives Division, Indiana State Library.

75. *Ibid.*

76. *Indianapolis News*, June 28, 1917, p. 6.

77. *Indiana Bulletin*, January 18, 1918, p. 8.

78. *Indianapolis News*, July 19, 1918, p. 15.

79. *Indianapolis Star*, December 27, 1917, p. 14.

80. *Indianapolis Star*, August 31, 1917, p. 4.

81. *Ibid.*

82. *Ibid.*

83. *Indiana Bulletin*, September 21, 1917, p. 3.

84. Lt. Governor to Marion County Council of Defense, September 19, 1917; rpt. in *Indiana Bulletin*, October 5, 1917, p. 8.

85. *Indianapolis Star*, June 1, 1917, p. 1.

86. *Ibid.*

87. *Ibid.*

88. *Ibid.*

89. Michael Foley to Marshall Hacker, August 12, 1918, ISCD, Series 3, Vol. 3.

90. Ed Adams to State Defense Council, April 12, 1918, ISCD, Series 11, Vol. 4.

91. Harney to Adams, April 13, 1918, ISCD, Series 11, Vol. 4.

92. *Ibid.*

93. *Ibid.*

94. Elkhart County Council of Defense, "Secretary's Report, Meeting of July 19, 1918," in H. K. Bartholomew, *History of Elkhart County in the World War,* (Typewritten, 1925), Indiana Division, Indiana State Library.
95. *Indiana Bulletin,* April 26, 1918, p. 3.
96. *Macy Monitor,* n.d., ISCD, Series 3, Vol. 12.
97. *Peru Journal,* October 8, 1918.
98. *Macy Monitor,* n.d., ISCD, Series 3, Vol. 12.
99. *Peru Journal,* October 8, 1918.
100. *Ibid.*
101. *Indianapolis Star,* October 10, 1918.
102. "Transcript of Evidence," ISCD, Series 11, Vol. 4.
103. *Ibid.*
104. C. C. Hurst to Foley, November 2, 1918; Foley to Wolf, November 6, 1918, ISCD, Series 11, Vol. 4.
105. "Transcript of Evidence," ISCD, Series 11, Vol. 4.
106. Mrs. Helen Sumen, *Spencer County in the World's War, 1914-18,* IV, (1923), Indiana Division, Indiana State Library, p. 9.
107. Elkhart County Council of Defense, "Secretary's Report, Meeting of July 19, 1918," in Bartholomew, *History of Elkhart County.*
108. Typed report, n.d., Liberty Loan, Series 7, Part 4.
109. Earl Houck to George Harney, April 25, 1918, ISCD, Series 11, Vol. 4.
110. *Ibid.*
111. Letter signed by eight Huntington residents, n.d., ISCD, Series 3, Vol. 9.
112. *Ibid.*
113. John Cline to Treasury Department, July 9, 1918, ISCD, Series 3, Vol. 9.
114. Treasury Department to J. D. Oliver, July 15, 1918, ISCD, Series 3, Vol. 9.
115. Huntington residents to Herbert Hoover, September 23, 1918, ISCD, Series 3, Vol. 9.
116. *Indianapolis News,* April 10, 1918, p. 15.
117. *Indianapolis News,* May 6, 1918, p. 3.
118. Rockport Journal, n.d., in *Spencer County World War History,* IV, (Typewritten), Indiana Division, Indiana State Library.
119. *Indianapolis News,* June 24, 1918, p. 6.
120. Foley to Will Wade, October 7, 1918, ISCD, Series 7, Part 4.
121. *Ibid.*

5. Free Speech: The Philosophical Poles

1. E. Barker, *Plato and His Predecessors,* p. 27, quoted in Leo Strauss, *The Political Philosophy of Hobbes: Its Basis and Its Genesis,* translated by Elsa M. Sinclair (The University of Chicago Press, 1952), pp. 155-156.

2. J. Roland Pennock, "Hobbes's Confusing 'Clarity'—The Case of 'Liberty,'" *American Political Science Review*, 54 (June, 1960), 429.

3. Thomas Hobbes, *Leviathan*, (New York: E. P. Dutton & Co. Inc., 1914), p. 63.

4. *Ibid.*, p. 66.

5. Blair Campbell, "Prescription and Description in Political Thought: The Case for Hobbes," *American Political Science Review*, 65 (June, 1971), 388.

6. Hobbes, *Leviathan*, p. 89.

7. *Ibid.*, p. 113.

8. Harvey C. Mansfield, Jr., "Hobbes and the Science of Indirect Government," *American Political Science Review*, 65 (March, 1971), 108.

9. J. B. Stewart, "Hobbes Among the Critics," *Political Science Quarterly*, 73 (December, 1955), 547.

10. George Mace, "An Abuse of Words," *Western Political Quarterly*, 20 (September, 1967), 639.

11. Hobbes, *Leviathan*, pp. 110–114.

12. *Ibid.*, p. 180.

13. *Ibid.*, p. 172.

14. *Ibid.*, p. 93.

15. Laurence Berns, "Thomas Hobbes, 1588–1679," in *History of Political Philosophy*, ed. by Leo Strauss and Joseph Cropsey (Chicago: Rand McNally and Company, 1963), p. 368.

16. Hobbes, *Leviathan*, p. 116.

17. J. S. Mill, *On Liberty*, edited by R. B. McCallum (Oxford: Basil Blackwell, 1948), p. 8.

18. *Ibid.*, pp. 8–9.

19. Hobbes, *Leviathan*, p. 112.

20. Richard Lichtman, "The Surface and Substance of Mill's Defense of Freedom," *Social Research*, 30 (Winter, 1963), 470.

21. Mill, *On Liberty*, p. 28.

22. Henry M. Magid, "John Stuart Mill, 1806–1873," in *History of Political Philosophy*, ed. by Leo Strauss and Joseph Cropsey (Chicago: Rand McNally and Company, 1963), p. 693.

23. Berns, p. 368.

24. Mansfield, p. 100.

25. Mill, *On Liberty*, p. 14.

26. Magid, p. 692.

27. Willmoore Kendall, "The 'Open Society' and Its Fallacies," *American Political Science Review*, 54 (December, 1960), 978.

28. Magid, pp. 691–692.

29. John William Ward, "Mill, Marx, and Modern Individualism," *Virginia Quarterly Review*, 35 (Fall, 1959), 532.

30. Mill, *On Liberty*, p. 9.

31. *Ibid.*, pp. 24–25.

32. *Ibid.*, pp. 51–52.

33. *Ibid.*, p. 30.

34. *Ibid.*, pp. 14–15.

35. *Ibid.*, p. 40.
36. *Ibid.*, p. 53.

6. Implications of Herbert Marcuse's Theory of Freedom for Freedom of Speech

1. Herbert Marcuse, *An Essay on Liberation* (Boston: Beacon Press, 1969), 81–82. For a contrasting view see Eliseo Vivas, *Contra Marcuse* (New Rochelle, New York: Arlington House, 1971), 171–177. For a complete bibliography of Marcuse's writings see Kurt Wolff and Barrington Moore, Jr., eds., *The Critical Spirit: Essays in Honor of Herbert Marcuse* (Boston: Beacon Press, 1967), 427–433.

2. See Mortimer Adler, *The Idea of Freedom* (2 vols.; Chicago: Encyclopedia Britannica, 1958–61).

3. Thomas Hobbes, *Leviathan*, Vol. XXIII of *Great Books of the Western World*, ed. by Mortimer Adler and William Garman (54 vols.; Chicago: Encyclopedia Britannica, 1938–52), 86–113; John Locke, *An Essay Concerning Human Understanding*, Vol. XXXV of *Great Books of the Western World*, 85. See also Bertrand Russell, "Freedom in Society," in *Sceptical Essays* (London: George Allen & Unwin, 1952), 169; Harold Laski, *Liberty in the Modern State* (Harmondsworth, Middlesex: Penguin Books, 1937), 49.

4. For a discussion of Plato's theory of freedom, see Joyce Flory, "Philosophical Assumptions Underlying Plato's Theory of Freedom of Speech," in *Free Speech Yearbook, 1974* (New York: Speech Communication Association, 1974), 45–53; Plato, *The Republic*, Vol. VII of *Great Books of the Western World*, 411–412; Auguste Hegel, *The Philosophy of Right*, Vol. XLVI of *Great Books*, 16.

5. Marcuse, *An Essay on Liberation*, 82; Herbert Marcuse, "Repressive Tolerance," in *A Critique of Pure Tolerance* (Boston: Beacon Press, 1967), 102–103.

6. Marcuse, *Eros and Civilization* (Boston: Beacon Press, 1955), 35–37, 155; Alasdair MacIntyre, *Herbert Marcuse* (New York: Viking Press, 1970), 47–49, 57.

7. Marcuse, *One-Dimensional Man* (Boston: Beacon Press, 1964), 5; *Essay on Liberation*, 82; Macintyre, 77, 102–104.

8. Paul A. Robinson, *The Freudian Left* (New York: Harper and Row, 1969), 236.

9. *Eros and Civilization*, 15, 60; Robinson, 203; Macintyre, 55; Vivas, 139–161. For a more-extensive discussion of Marcuse's view of pleasure, see Herbert Marcuse, "On Hedonism," in *Negations: Essays in Critical Theory*, trans. by Jeremy Shapiro (Boston: Beacon Press, 1968).

10. *Eros and Civilization*, 46–48, 124, 155; Robinson, 202–205.
11. *Eros and Civilization*, 46.
12. Macintyre, 47–49.
13. *Eros and Civilization*, 47.
14. *Eros and Civilization*, 38–48; Robinson, 206–207.

15. *One-Dimensional Man*, 11; Macintyre, 73–74; Robinson, 204, 242.
16. *Essay on Liberation*, 85–87.
17. *One-Dimensional Man*, 49–50.
18. *One-Dimensional Man*, 11.
19. *One-Dimensional Man*, 23.
20. *Essay on Liberation*, 84.
21. *Essay on Liberation*, 85.
22. *Essay on Liberation*, 85; Robinson, 242–243; Macintyre, 21–26; Vivas, 39–40. For more specifics on Marcuse's view of revolution, see Herbert Marcuse, *Reason and Revolution* (Boston: Beacon Press, 1960).
23. *Essay on Liberation*, 86.
24. Haig A. Bosmajian, ed., *The Principles and Practice of Freedom of Speech* (Boston: Houghton Mifflin, 1971), 348.
25. Bosmajian, 355.
26. Bosmajian, 355.
27. Bosmajian, 366.
28. Bosmajian, 356.
29. Bosmajian, 366.
30. Bosmajian, 366.
31. *Essay on Liberation*, 86.
32. *Essay on Liberation*, 89.
33. *Essay on Liberation*, 90.
34. Bosmajian, 371.
35. *Essay on Liberation*, 87.
36. *Essay on Liberation*, 87.
37. For an opposing view of society see Vivas, 45–59, 211, 181–197, 244–230.
38. *Essay on Liberation*, 88.
39. Bosmajian, 360.
40. Bosmajian, 360.
41. Bosmajian, 361, 369.
42. Bosmajian, 365.
43. Bosmajian, 363.
44. *Essay on Liberation*, 90.
45. *Essay on Liberation*, 98–99.
46. Robinson, 242–243.
47. *Essay on Liberation*, 17.

7. The Supreme Court and Communication Theory: Contrasting Models of Speech Efficacy.

1. Zecharia Chafee, *Free Speech in the United States* (Cambridge, 1941), p. 23.
2. *Ibid.*, p. 48.
3. The clear and present danger test makes most obvious assumptions concerning speech efficacy. Its current viability has been called into question.

See Harry Kalven, "The New York Times Case: A Note on 'The Central Meaning of the First Amendment,'" *The Supreme Court Review*, 1964, pp. 191–221; for a rather brief contrary opinion flavored by international implications see William van Alstyne, "The First Amendment and the Suppression of Warmongering Propaganda in the United States: Comment and Footnotes," *Law and Contemporary Problems: International Control of Propaganda*, XXXI (Summer 1966), fn. 56, pp. 546–47. The concern of this essay is only with the test's propensity for forcing the Court to state causal relationships between speech and illegal acts.

4. Chafee, p. 38.
5. *Ibid.*, pp. 39–40.
6. *Ibid.*, pp. 63–64.
7. Terence H. Qualter, *Propaganda and Psychological Warfare* (New York, 1962) pp. 4–6.
8. *Ibid.*, p. 22.
9. See Chafee, pp. 38–42, and especially 53, 92–97. If falsehood was considered a defining characteristic of propaganda, then the false statement clauses of the Espionage Act may be seen as a head-on attempt to eliminate propaganda. The convictions that were obtained by proof of falsity were, finally, convictions for propagandizing. The false statement clauses of the Espionage Act amply testify to the nation's fear of propaganda as extremely dangerous.
10. Qualter, p. 22.
11. J. A. C. Brown, *Techniques of Persuasion* (London, 1963), p. 11.
12. Roger Brown, *Words and Things* (New York, 1958), p. 300.
13. *Ibid.*
14. *Ibid.*, p. 301. The statements by J. A. C. Brown and Roger Brown taken together describe the concepts of "compelling speech" and "inherent efficacy" as they are used in this essay. Judge Hand also expresses the same conceptualization: "One may not counsel or advise others to violate the law as it stands. Words are not only the keys of persuasion but *the triggers of action.* . . ." (Emphasis supplied) *Masses Publishing Company v. Patten*, 244 Fed. 535 (S.D.N.Y. 1917), 540. While no propaganda hysteria exists today under that label, people do fear "hidden persuaders," mass media, and campus and ghetto agitators. Of course, one does not fear for himself, but for a presumed irrational "mass" somewhere out there in society that gets "carried away" by the emotionalism of the agitator. The "girlish attitude" of which Empson writes is the collective attitude, not the individual attitude—unless we unconsciously fear for ourselves.
15. *Abrams v. United States*, 250 U.S. 616 (1919), 623.
16. *Milwaukee Social Democrat Publishing Company v. Burleson*, 255 U.S. 407 (1921), 415.
17. *Gitlow v. New York*, 268 U.S. 652 (1925), 662.
18. *Dennis v. United States*, 341 U.S. 494 (1951), 503.
19. *Ibid.*, 570.
20. *Schenck v. United States*, 249 U.S. 47 (1919), 52.
21. *Gitlow*, 669.
22. *Ibid.*, 673.

23. Fire, of course, is connected with the emotions, and it also has a long history of association with speech and the emotions—speakers make fiery speeches, incendiaries ignite public opinion, etc. It may be that Justice Sanford picked up Holmes' statement in *Frohwerk v. United States*, 249 U.S. 204 (1919), at 209, that if the paper in question had been circulated in the right quarters "a little breath would be enough to kindle a flame." By comparison Sanford may have felt the Gitlow literature could start a conflagration. Whether Holmes' well known example of a man shouting "Fire!" in a crowded theatre may be read symbolically as the propagandist in society is an interesting question; short of such a reading, the example shows a remarkable facility for reductionism on the part of Holmes. There are very real differences between shouting a word and making a speech, and very real differences between questions of public order and the questions confronting the Court in *Schenck*. A man might injure another's hearing by shouting in his ear, but taking such an instance as an argument for limiting communication would be wholly fanciful. Whatever the origin of the fire imagery, to which even Justice Douglas succumbs in his dissent on *Dennis*, q. v., the suspicion of emotions on the part of the Court is clearly manifested by the imagery.

24. *Gitlow*, 673. C. Herman Pritchett dismisses Holmes' statement that "every idea is an incitement" as "some fine prose," which suggests a wholly different reading of that dissent (*Civil Liberties and the Vinson Court* [Chicago, 1954], p. 26). But the contrast explicitly made in that dissent between the narrow and the broad view of incitement would seem to indicate the dissenters are illustrating the logical extension of the broad view.

25. Robert E. Cushman, "'Clear and Present Danger' in Free Speech Cases: A Study in Judicial Semantics," *Essays in Political Theory*, Milton R. Konvitz and Arthur R. Murphy, eds. (New York, 1948), p. 318.

26. *Gitlow*, 669.

27. *Whitney v. California*, 274 U.S. 357 (1927), 376–78.

28. *Dennis*, 509–10.

29. *Ibid.*, 510.

30. *Yates v. United States*, 354 U.S. 298 (1957), 324–25.

31. *Scales v. United States*, 367 U.S. 203 (1961), 228.

32. *Kingsley International Picture Corp. v. Regents of University of New York*, 360 U.S. 684 (1959), 689.

33. *Brandenberg v. Ohio*, 395 U.S. 444 (1968), 47, 49.

34. *Ibid.*, pp. 450–57.

35. *Communist Party of Indiana v. Whitcomb*, 414 U.S. 441 (1973), 448.

36. *Musser v. Utah*, 333 U.S. 95 (1948), 101.

37. *Beauharnais v. Illinois*, 343 U.S. 250 (1952), 303.

38. *Kunz v. New York*, 340 U.S. 290 (1951), 307.

39. *Ibid.*, 302.

40. *Cantwell v. Connecticut*, 310 U.S. 296 (1940), 308.

41. *Ibid.*, 309.

42. *Chaplinsky v. New Hampshire*, 315 U.S. 568 (1942), 571–72.

43. *Terminiello v. Chicago*, 337 U.S. 1 (1949), 4.

44. *Ibid.*, 3–4.

45. *Ibid.*, 26.
46. *Feiner v. New York*, 340 U.S. 315 (1951), 319–20.
47. *Ibid.*, 321.
48. I shall not examine these cases in any depth because such has already been done by Franklyn S. Haiman, "The Fighting Words Doctrine: From Chaplinsky to Brown," *Iowa Journal of Speech*, III (Fall, 1972), pp. 3–31.
49. *Cohen v. California*, 403 U.S. 15 (1971).
50. *Ibid.*, p. 20.
51. *Ibid.*,
52. *Ibid.*, pp. 23–4.
53. *Ibid.*, p. 26.
54. *Ibid.*,
55. *Gooding v. Wilson*, 405 U.S. 518 (1972).
56. *Rosenfield v. New Jersey*, 408 U.S. 913 (1972).257. *Lewis v. City of New Orleans*, 408 U.S. 913 (1972). *Lewis* was reconsidered by the Louisiana Supreme Court and returned to the Supreme Court on appeal; the Court ruled the ordinance invalid because overly broad. See 415 U.S. 130 (1973).
58. *Brown v. Oklahoma*, 408 U.S. 914 (1972).
59. See Haiman for pertinent discussion of dissents and concurrences of individual Justices, especially those of Powell, pp. 23–26.
60. *Plummer v. City of Columbus*, 414 U.S. 2 (1973).
61. *Hess v. Indiana*, 414 U.S. 105 (1973).
62. *Ibid.*, pp. 107–8.
63. Cf. Blackmun dissenting in *Gooding*, pp. 536–37.
64. Haiman, p. 16.
65. Raymond A. Bauer in *The Obstinate Audience*, Donald E. Payne, ed. (a seminar sponsored and published by the Foundation for Research on Human Behavior: Ann Arbor, 1965), p. 1.
66. *Ibid.*, p. 10.
67. *Ibid.*, p. 11.
68. So much has been published on this point that a reference is arbitrary. Of several excellent works, *The Process and Effects of Mass Communication* Wilbur Schramm, ed. (Urbana, 1957) is one of the best. See especially Schramm's article, "How Communication Works," pp. 3–36. Other references to this work will appear below.
69. Joseph T. Klapper, "The Comparative Effects of the Various Media," in Schramm, *supra.* pp. 102–103.
70. Qualter, p. 148.
71. *Ibid.*, p. 153.
72. Joseph T. Klapper, "Mass Media and Persuasion," in Schramm, *supra*, pp. 317–18.
73. George A. Miller, *Language and Communication* (New York, 1951), p. 269.
74. Roger Brown, p. 302.
75. *Ibid.*, p. 339.
76. *Ibid.*, p. 340.
77. J. A. C. Brown, p. 309.

78. *Ibid.*, pp. 310-311.
79. Bernard Berelson, "Communication and Public Opinion," in Schramm, *supra*, p. 345.
80. Daniel Katz, "The Functional Approach to the Study of Attitudes," *Reader in Public Opinion and Communication*, Bernard Berelson and Morris Janowitz, eds. (New York, 1966), pp. 51-52. (Also available in *Foundations of Communication Theory*, Kenneth K. Sereno and C. David Mortensen, eds. [New York, 1970], pp. 234-259).
81. *Ibid.*, p. 52.
82. *Ibid.*
83. *Ibid.*, pp. 52-53.
84. Paul Harris, "Black Power Advocacy: Criminal Anarchy or Free Speech," *California Law Review* 56 (May, 1968), p. 732.
85. *Ibid.*, p. 734.

8. Toward a More Realistic View of the Judicial Process in Relation to Freedom of Speech

1. Thurmond Arnold, *The Symbols of Government* (New York: Harcourt, Brace & World, Inc., 1962), p. 9.
2. *Ibid.*, p. 32.
3. *Ibid.*, pp. 52-53.
4. Jack Piano and Milton Greenberg, *The American Political Dictionary* (New York: Holt, Rinehart and Winston, Inc., 1962), p. 212.
5. *Davis v. Massachusetts*, 167 U.S. 43 (1897).
6. *Hague v. CIO*, 101 F.2d 774 (1939); *CIO v. Hague*, 25 F.Supp. 127 (1938).
7. *State v. Fowler*, 83A.2d 67 (1951).
8. *Stromberg v. California*, 283 U.S. 359 (1930).
9. *West Virginia State Board of Education v. Barnette*, 319 U.S. 624 (1943).
10. *Adderley v. Florida*, 385 U.S. 39 (1966).
11. *Edwards v. South Carolina*, 372 U.S. 220 (1963).
12. *Cox v. Louisiana*, 379 U.S. 536 (1965).
13. Oliver Wendell Holmes, *The Common Law* (Boston: Little, Brown, 1881), pp. 1-2.
14. Benjamin Cardozo, *The Nature of the Judicial Process* (New Haven: Yale University Press, 1921).
15. *Ibid.*, pp. 9-11.
16. *Ibid.*, p. 20.
17. *Ibid.*, p. 33.
18. Roscoe Pound, "Juristic Science and Law," *Harvard Law Review*, 31 (1918), 1057; "The Theory of Judicial Decisions," *Harvard Law Review*, 36 (1923), 645.
19. William O. Douglas, "Stare Decisis," *Columbia Law Review*, 49 (1949), 736.
20. *Ibid.*, p. 736.
21. Thomas Reed Powell, "Some Aspects of American Constitutional

Law," *Harvard Law Review,* 53 (1940), 532.

22. Herbert Wechsler, "The Courts and the Constitution," *Columbia Law Review,* 65 (1965), 1012.

23. Felix S. Cohen, "Field Theory and Judicial Logic," *Yale Law Journal,* 59 (1950), 265.

24. David J. Danielski, "Values as Variables in Decision-Making," *The Federal Judicial System,* ed. by Sheldon Goldman and Thomas Jahnige (New York: Holt, Rinehart and Winston, Inc., 1968), p. 244.

25. Felix Cohen, "Transcendental Nonsense and the Functional Approach," *Columbia Law Review,* 35 (1935), 833.

26. Joseph Tanenhaus, "Supreme Court Attitudes Toward Federal Administrative Agencies 1947–1956—An Application of Social Science Methods to the Study of the Judicial Process," *Vanderbilt Law Review,* 14 (1961), 473.

27. Joel V. Grossman, "Social Backgrounds and Judicial Decision-Making," *Harvard Law Review,* 79 (1966), 1551–1564.

28. *Ibid.,* p. 1553.

29. *Ibid.,* p. 1557.

30. *Ibid.,* p. 1559.

31. *Ibid.,* p. 1561.

32. Glendon Schubert, "Judicial Attitudes and Voting Behavior," *Federal Judicial System,* ed. by Goldman and Jahnige (see note 24), pp. 254–282.

33. Danielski, pp. 244–254.

34. Walter Murphy, *Elements of Judicial Strategy* (Chicago: University of Chicago Press, 1964), p. 13.

35. Walter Murphy, "Courts as Small Groups," *Harvard Law Review,* 79 (1966), 1565–1568.

36. Murphy, *Strategy.*

37. Richard J. Richardson and Kenneth Vines, "Interpersonal Relationships on Three United States Courts of Appeal," *Federal Judicial System,* pp. 145–147.

38. *Ibid.,* p. 145.

39. Theodore Becker, ed. *The Impact of Supreme Court Decisions* (New York: Oxford University Press, 1969), p. 62.

40. Jack Peltason, *Federal Courts in the Political Process* (New York: Random House, 1955), p. 14.

41. *Ibid.,* p. 14.

42. Walter Murphy, "Lower Court Checks on Supreme Court Power," *The Impact of Supreme Court Decisions,* ed. Theodore Becker (New York: Oxford University Press, 1969), p. 70.

43. *Ibid.,* p. 66.

44. Chester Newland, "Law Reviews and the Supreme Court," *The Federal Judicial System,* pp. 326–333.

45. Benjamin R. Twiss, *Lawyers and the Constitution* (New York: Russell & Russell, 1962), p. 12.

46. Melvin Wulf, "Tragedy of 'The Times,'" *Civil Liberties* (September, 1971), p. 11.

47. Arnold, p. 33.

9. The United States Supreme Court on Libel

1. *Colegrove v. Green*, 328 U.S. 549 (1946).
2. *Reynolds v. Sims*, 377 U.S. 533 (1964).
3. *Reynolds v. Sims*, p. 568. Other instances in which the Court has taken action in the absence of appropriate state or federal legislation designed to protect constitutionally guaranteed rights are: *Gideon v. Wainwright*, 372 U.S. 335 (1963) which established a defendant's right to counsel and *Escobedo v. Illinois*, 378 U.S. 478 (1963) which required police to inform a suspect of his constitutional right to remain silent before interrogating him.
4. Robert S. Hirschfield, *The Constitution and the Court* (New York: Random House, 1962), p. 151. Hirschfield concluded that the court, while not making law in the same sense as Congress and the state legislatures do, does affect public policy in these ways: (1) "positively, by extending provisions of the Constitution into areas of individual or governmental activity where they did not formerly apply, (2) negatively by 'vetoing' the policy determination of other governmental agencies, and (3) passively, by accepting the constitutional changes brought about by custom or practice." p. 188.
5. In this history of the libel decisions of the Court, I am much indebted to the excellent survey of Clifton O. Lawhorne, *The Supreme Court and Libel* (Carbondale: Southern Illinois University Press, 1981).
6. *Howell's State Trials*, 266, at 285 (U.S. 1845).
7. *Gandia v. Pettingill*, 222 U.S. 452 (1912), pp. 458–459.
8. *Gitlow v. New York*, 268 U.S. 652 (1952), p. 666, and *Near v. Minnesota ex rel. Olson*, 283 U.S. at 713.
9. *Rosenblatt v. Baer*, 383 U.S. 75 (1966), p. 85.
10. *Rosenblatt v. Baer*, p. 87, n. 13.
11. 61 L. Ed. 2nd 411, p. 421, n. 8.
12. *New York Times Co. v. Sullivan*, 376 U.S. 254 (1964).
13. *Garrison v. Louisiana*, 379 U.S. 64 (1964), p. 77.
14. *Monitor Patriot Co. v. Roy*, 401 U.S. 265 (1971).
15. *Curtis Publishing Co. v. Butts*, 388 U.S. 130 (1967). Butts was able to establish actual malice because he had written a letter to the *Post* prior to publication of the article branding the story false, but, without further investigation, the *Post* published anyway.
16. This case is included in the Butts citation, 388 U.S. 130 (1967), p. 155. Walker was unable to prove actual malice or reckless disregard of the truth by the Associated Press reporter.
17. *New York Times Co. v. Sullivan*, 376 U.S. 254 (1964), pp. 279–280.
18. *Garrison v. Louisiana*, 379 U.S. 64 (1964), p. 74.
19. *Beckley Newspapers Corp. v. Hanks*, 389 U.S. 81 (1967), p. 82.
20. *Gertz v. Robert Welch, Inc.*, 41 L.Ed. 2nd. 789 (1974), p. 802, n. 6.
21. *New York Times Co. v. Sullivan*, 376 U.S. 254 (1964) p. 266 and p. 270.
22. *New York Times Co. v. Sullivan*, p. 268.
23. *Garrison v. Louisiana*, 379 U.S. 64 (1964), p. 75.
24. *Gertz v. Robert Welch, Inc.*, 41 L.Ed. 2nd. 789 (1974) p. 805.
25. *Curtis Publishing Co. v. Butts*, 388 U.S. 130 (1967), p. 164.

26. *Gertz v. Robert Welch, Inc.*, 41 L.Ed. 2nd 789 (1974), p. 808.
27. *Rosenbloom v. Metromedia*, 403 U.S. 29 (1971), p. 44.
28. *Gertz v. Robert Welch, Inc.*, 41 L.Ed. 2nd 789 (1974) p. 812.
29. *Gertz v. Robert Welch, Inc.*, p. 811.
30. In several cases since *Gertz*, however, the Court has softened the "competent evidence" of injury requirement as, for example, in the case of *Time, Inc. v. Firestone*, 424 U.S. 448 (1976). In addition, the Court has made it more difficult for defendants to classify plaintiffs as public figures. All of this, in the view of one scholar, while indicating a somewhat greater impulse than in the past to favor plaintiffs over defendants, the Court has still left considerable "breathing space" for "even libelous falsehoods, inevitable in the open discussion necessary for democracy." (Lawhorne, p. 107).
31. *Gertz v. Welch*, 41, L.Ed. 2nd 789 (1974), pp. 805–806.
32. *New York Times Co. v. Sullivan*, 376 U.S. 254 (1964), p. 288.
33. *Beckley Newspapers Corporation v. Hanks*, 19 L.Ed. 2nd 248 (1967), p. 252.
34. *St. Amant v. Thompson*, 390 U.S. 727 (1968), p. 731.
35. *Garrison v. Louisiana*, 379 U.S. 64 (1964), p. 79.
36. *Gertz v. Welch*, 41 L.Ed. 2nd 789 (1974), p. 802, n. 6.
37. Justice Harlan's opinion in *Curtis Publishing Co. v. Butts*, 388 U.S. 130 (1967), p. 155.
38. *Garrison v. Louisiana*, 379 U.S. 64 (1964), p. 75.
39. *Farmers Educational and Cooperative Union of America, North Dakota Division v. WDAY, Inc.*, 360 U.S. 525 (1959), p. 531.
40. *Ocala Star Banner Co. v. Damron*, 401 U.S. 295 (1971).
41. *Beckley Newspapers Corporation v. Hanks*, 19 L.Ed. 2nd 248 (1967), p. 252.
42. *Curtis Publishing Co. v. Butts*, 388 U.S. 130 (1967), p. 155.
43. *Rosenbloom v. Metromedia, Inc.*, 403 U.S. 29 (1971), pp. 70, 77, 86.
44. *Rosenbloom v. Metromedia*, p. 70.
45. *Rosenbloom v. Metromedia*, p. 43.
46. *Rosenbloom v. Metromedia*, p. 84.
47. *Rosenbloom v. Metromedia*, p. 86.
48. *Rosenbloom v. Metromedia*, p. 75.
49. *Gertz v. Welch*, 41 L.Ed. 2nd 789 (1974), p. 811.
50. *Herbert v. Lando*, 60 L. Ed. 2nd (1977), p. 115.
51. *New York Times Co. v. Sullivan*, 376 U.S. 254 (1964), pp. 286, 287.
52. *Gertz v. Welch*, 41 L.Ed. 2nd 789 (1974), p. 811.
53. The recent publication by the *Washington Post* of the allegation that former President Carter had "bugged" Blair House is an instance of the sort of thing that would be discouraged.

10. Protecting Political Speech: *Brandenburg v. Ohio* Updated

(Note: the 1985 revision is documented in legal style which is unaltered below. The editors.)
1. 395 U.S. 444 (1969).
2. 395 U.S., at 447.
3. Hans A. Linde, "Clear and Present Danger Reexamined: Dissonance in the Brandenburg Concerto," *Stanford Law Review,* 22 (1970), 1163–86.
4. 274 U.S. 357 (1927).
5. 395 U.S. at 447.
6. 341 U.S. 494 (1951). This decision contains the clearest foreshadowing of the *Brandenburg* test. In upholding Dennis' Smith Act conviction, Chief Justice Vinson's majority opinion adopted the exact language of Judge Hand's lower court decision: "In each case /courts/ must ask whether the gravity of the evil discounted by its improbability justifies such invasion of free speech as is necessary to avoid the danger." 183 F. 2d 201, 212 (1950).
7. 395 U.S. at 447.
8. Staughton Lynd, "*Brandenburg v. Ohio:* A Speech Test for All Seasons?" *University of Chicago Law Review,* 43 (1975), 151–191. See also Lillian Bevier, "The First Amendment and Political Speech: An Inquiry into the Substance and Limits of Principle," *Stanford Law Review,* 30 (1978), 299–358.
9. 249 U.S. 47 (1919).
10. 249 U.S. at 52.
11. 354 U.S. 298 (1957).
12. 354 U.S. at 324–5.
13. Cases were identified using *Shepherd's Federal Citations* through March, 1985 and with a LEXIS computer search in mid-1985.
14. 414 U.S. 105 (1973).
15. 414 U.S. at 106–7.
16. 414 U.S. at 108 (emphasis added).
17. 404 U.S. 438 (1972).
18. 404 U.S. at 459–460.
19. 729 F. 2d 1270 (1984), aff'd in 4-4 vote, 53 LW 4408 (1985).
20. 729 F. 2d at 1272.
21. 729 F. 2d at 1274.
22. 729 F. 2d at 1274.
23. 460 F. 2d 746 (1972).
24. 460 F. 2d at 754.
25. 570 F. 2d 563 (1977).
26. 570 F. 2d at 571.
27. 742 F. 2d 1007 (1984).
28. Id. at 1010.
29. Id. at 1010.
30. Id. at 1015.
31. Id. at 1015–6.
32. 745 F. 2d 560 (1984).
33. Id. at 576–7.

34. Id. at 572, 577 (emphasis added).
35. 535 F. 2d 1020 (1976).
36. Id. at 1021.
37. Id. at 1020.
38. Id. at 1022.
39. Id. at 1027.
40. Id. at 1027.
41. 719 F. 2d 1258 (1984).
42. Id. at 1260.
43. Id. at 1260–61 (emphasis added).
44. 536 F. 2d 1073 (1976).
45. Id. at 1076 (emphasis in original).
46. Id. at 1078.
47. 538 F. 2d 848 (1977), A more recent case with similar facts and holding is *Gay Students Services v. Texas A&M University*, 737 F. 2d 1317 (1984), cert. denied, __U.S. ____(1985).
48. 538 F. 2d at 855.
49. 472 F. 2d 340 (1972).
50. *Younger v. Harris*, 401 U.S. 37 (1971); *Samuels v. Mackell*, 401 U.S. 66 (1971).
51. 572 F. 2d at 619.
52. Id. at 624. Also see *U.S. v. Moss*, 604 F. 2d 569 (1979).
53. 713 F. 2d 1423 (1983), cert. denied, 104 S. Ct. 2363 (1984).
54. 739 F. 2d 331 (1984).
55. Id. at 335.
56. supra n. 19.
57. Brief for Respondents at 17–18, supra n. 19.
58. 458 U.S. 886 (1982).
59. Id. at 928.
60. supra n. 27.
61. 742 F. 2d at 1015–16.
62. Id. at 1015–16.
63. But see text accompanying n. 57, supra (in which Professor Tribe implored the Court to make just such a finding).
64. Supra n. 17–18 and accompanying text.
65. 433 F. 2d 745 (1970).
66. Id. at 751.
67. 424 U.S. 828 (1976).
68. Id. at 828.
69. 413 U.S. 733 (1974).
70. Id. at 759. Also, see *Carlson v. Schlesinger*, 511 F. 2d 1327 (1975) and *Priest v. Secretary of the Navy*, 570 F. 2d 1013 (1977), in which the Court of Appeals for the District of Columbia explicitly holds that, in a military context, the *Brandenburg* test is "inapposite." 570 F. 2d at 1016.
71. 533 F. 2d 960 (1977). See also *Brown v. Johnson*, 743 F. 2d 408 (1984) (rights of gay inmates to have gay oriented church conduct services must yield to state's interest in security and discipline).

72. 497 F. 2d 981 (1974), cert. denied, 419 U.S. 880 (1974).
73. supra n. 14–16 and accompanying text.
74. 497 F. 2d at 988.
75. 408 U.S. 169 (1972).
76. Id. at 189.
77. See n. 44–46 supra and accompanying text.
78. 491 F. 2d 722 (1973).
79. Id. at 723.
80. 477 F. 2d 456 (1973).
81. 419 F. 2d 195 (1969); cert denied, 399 U.S. 906.
82. 419 F. 2d at 202.
83. 359 F. Supp. 843, aff'd on other grounds, 491 F. 2d 498 (1974), cert denied, 419 U.S. 836 (1974).
84. 359 F. Supp. at 856. See also *Gay Law Students vs. PT&T*, 156 Cal. Rprt. 14 (1979), in which "coming out" on the job as openly gay was deemed a protected political act, though not on first amendment grounds.
85. 359 F. Supp. at 855. See also *NGTF v. Board of Education*, 729 F. 2d 1270, 1278 (1984) (Barrett, dissenting): "/In a school setting/ it cannot be said that the advocacy of/ sodomy/ is mere advocacy of an abstract doctrine or belief. To hold otherwise ignores the difference between children and adults."
86. 491 F. 2d at 501.
87. Id. at 504.
88. 364 U.S. 479 (1960).
89. 364 U.S. at 485–6.
90. supra n. 27.
91. supra n. 47.
92. supra n. 41.
93. supra n. 51.
94. supra n. 27.
95. supra n. 19.
96. supra n. 71.
97. 359 F. Supp. at 846.
98. *Norton v. Discipline Committee*, supra n. 81.

11. A Rhetoric of Ritual and Desecration

1. *Dictionary of National Biography*, ed. Leslie Stephen and Sidney Lee (London, 1908), VI, 785.
2. U.S., *Congressional Record*, 90th Cong., 1st Sess., Vol. 113, Part 12, June 20, 1967, p. 16443: James H. Quillen, Representative from Tennessee, praised those early nonconformists: "In the days of the Revolution, there were colonial or regimental flags by the score, and symbols abounded from the pine trees to beavers, anchors, and rattlesnakes. The brave and daring colonists used slogans on their flags—'Liberty or Death,' 'Hope,' 'Don't Tread on Me,' and 'An Appeal to Heaven,' were just a few."

3. Alexander Sesonske, "Saying, Being and Freedom of Speech," *Philosophy & Rhetoric*, 1 (January 1968), 29.

4. Hugh Dalziel Duncan, *Symbols in Society* (New York, 1969), p. 22.

5. Aristotle, *Rhetoric*, trans. W. Rhys Roberts, 1367 b 37. The line rightly reads, "To praise a man is in one respect akin to urging a course of action."

6. Theodore Thass-Thienemann, *Symbolic Behavior* (New York, 1968), p. 22. Thienemann also states: "A symbol has a cognitive function. A sign demands a reaction in the sensory motor sphere of the physical reality; the symbol addresses man who wants to see, observe, contemplate, and asks not for the cause but for the meaning of a phenomenon. The symbol is the tool of thinking."

7. Walter Probert, "Truth and Faith in Communication and Law," *ETC.*, 25 (March 1968), 40.

8. Arnold Whittick, *Signs, Symbols and Their Meaning* (London: Leonard Hill Books, Limited, 1960), p. 4.

9. *West Virginia v. Barnette* 319 US 624 (1943).

10. Alfred Whitehead, *Symbolism, Its Meaning and Effect* (London: Cambridge University Press, 1928), p. 99.

11. Joyce Lindmark, "The Flag As A Non-Verbal Symbol," *Free Speech Yearbook: 1971* (New York: Speech Communication Association, 1971), pp. 64–65.

12. Kenneth Burke, *Counterstatement* (Los Altos, California: Hermes Publications, 1931), p. 154.

13. George N. Gordon, *The Language of Communication* (New York: Hastings House, 1969), p. 61.

14. Suzanne Langer, *Philosophy in a New Key* (Cambridge, Massachusetts: Harvard University Press, 1963), p. 292.

15. Milo M. Quaife, Melvin J. Weig and Roy E. Appleman, *The History of the United States Flag* (New York: Harper and Brothers, 1961), p. 105.

16. Quaife et al. Also see John H. Fow, *The True Story of the American Flag* (Philadelphia, 1908).

17. Walter R. Fisher, "Narration as a Human Communication Paradigm: The Case of Public Moral Argument," *Communication Monographs*, 51 (March 1984), p. 2.

18. Ibid.

19. Public Law 623, June 22, 1942. Amended Public Law 829, Chapter 806 H. J. Res 359, December 22, 1942 includes stipulations as to when display is acceptable i.e., "only from sunrise to sunset on buildings and stationary flagstaffs in the open . . . not on days when the weather is inclement . . . on all days the weather permits on or near . . . every public institution;" manner i.e., "should be hoisted briskly and lowered ceremoniously . . . when carried in a marching procession with another flag or flags, should be either on the marching right, that is the flag's own right, or if there is a line of other flags, in front of the center of that line, etc.

20. Burke, *Counterstatement*. For Burke language is symbolic action and symbolic action is real, as real as tangible objects or movement; he argues, "a word is as real in its way as a thing, otherwise there could not be the

kinds of motions and position that we call words." See Kenneth Burke, "Formalist Criticism: Its Principles and Limits," in *Language as Symbolic Action: Essays on Life, Literature and Method* (Berkeley: University of California Press, 1966), p. 480. See Franklyn S. Haiman, *Speech and Law in a Free Society* (Chicago: University of Chicago Press, 1981), pp. 25–31.

21. Stuart Chase quoted in Harold E. Briggs, *Language . . . Man . . . Society* (New York: Rinehart & Company, 1949), p. 387.

22. Langer, pp. 287–288. Americans think big. The flag which was raised over Ft. McHenry during the War of 1812 and that inspired the words of the "Star Spangled Banner" was big: 30 by 42 feet. The world's largest flag, however, in 1980 when it was first sewn, was so big that Mr. Len Silverfine, Vice President of an ad agency who thought up the idea, could not find a place strong enough to hold it. This gigantic flag measures 210 feet tall—21 stories high and 411 feet in length, almost two blocks long. See Betty Dehnam, "The World's Largest Flag, Unfolded but Never Flown," Universal Press Syndicate, 1981.

23. Lloyd F. Bitzer, "The Rhetorical Situation," *Philosophy & Rhetoric*, 1(January 1968), 5.

24. *The New York Times*, November 22, 1968, p. 52. Hoffman was convicted in a nonjury trial under a law that bans desecration of the flag. He was sentenced to 30 days in jail and a $100 fine. *Hoffman v. U.S.*, 445 F. 2d 226 (1971). His shirt within the statutory definition was ruled not actually a flag.

25. *U.S. v. O'Brien* 391 U.S. 367 (1968).

26. Thomas L. Tedford, *Freedom of Speech in the United States* (New York: Random House, 1985), p. 290.

27. Elden Rosenthal, "Symbolic Speech: A Constitutional Orphan," *Free Speech Yearbook: 1971* (New York: Speech Communication Association, 1971), pp. 69–79. Rosenthal presents four models: (1) The Preservation of Democracy (which in our opinion is a regulatory model). (2) The Safety-Valve Model which suggests that a society that can freely express itself will be less violent. (3) The Personal Freedom Model which justifies speech on individual psychological grounds and reasons that such is worthy of government protection. And (4) The Truth-Seeking Model.

28. *Ruhstrat v. People*, 185 Ill. 133, 49 L.R.A. 181, 76 AM St. Rep. 30, 57 N.E. 41 (April 17, 1900).

29. *People ex rel. McPike v. Van De Carr*, 91 App. Div. 20, 86 *New York Supplement*, 644 (February 5, 1904).

30. *Nicholas Halter, et al., plaintiffs in Err., v. State of Nebraska, Halter v. Nebraska*, 205 US 34 (1907).

31. Ibid.

32. Duncan, p. 34.

33. *Baldwin's Ohio Revised Code and Service*, 1968, 2921.05.

34. Ibid. Manufacturers rather extensively use the "flag disconnected from an advertisement." *Life*, 67 (July 18, 1969), 32, reported that Gulf Oil Company "ordered 20 million flag stickers as competition for tiger tails and giveaway games" and that the February, 1969 issue of *Reader's Digest* contained "18 million flag decals."

35. Quoted in Maymie R. Krythe. *What So Proudly We Hail* (New York, 1968), p. v.
36. *Yetta Stromberg v. People of the State of California*, 283 US 359 (1931).
37. *Baldwin's Ohio Revised Code and Service*, 1968, 2921.07.
38. Personal observation, Moratorium, Washington, D.C., November 14, 1969.
39. *Minersville School District v. Gobitis*, 310 US 586 (1940).
40. Ibid., p. 596.
41. See Leonard A. Stevens, *Salute! The Case of the Bible vs. The Flag* (New York: Coward, McCann & Geoghegan, 1973) for an account of extreme harassment of a small band of Jehovah's Witnesses by the sheriff and others in a West Virginia town in the 1940s. Nine Jehovah's Witnesses were paraded through the town linked together by rope, urged to salute the flag in front of the city hall. When the nine refused, they were called Nazis and spat upon by the crowd and the sheriff compelled them to drink large doses of castor oil. Finally, after slashing the tires of the Witnesses' cars, the mob made them drive off.
42. *West Virginia State Board of Education v. Barnette*, 319 US 624 (1943).
43. Personal interview, May 8, 1969. The university administration supported the action of the coach.
44. "An Act to Prohibit Desecration of the Flag and for Other Purposes" Public L 90-381 amends Chapter 33 of Title 18, *United States Code* by adding paragraph 700. See Title 18 Ch 33 USC p. 1141 (1964 ed., Supplement V).
45. U.S., *Congressional Record*, 90th Cong., 1st Sess., Vol. 113, Part 12, June 20, 1967, p. 16446.
46. Ibid., pp. 16444 and 16494.
47. Ibid., pp. 16454, 16447, 16448, and 16446.
48. *United States Flag Foundation v. Radich*, *Law Week*, 35 (April 25, 1967), 2613.)
49. *Radich v. New York*, 401 U.S. 531 (1971).
50. *U.S. ex. rel. Radich v. Criminal Court of New York*, 385 F. Supp. 165 (1974). This was not the first time the flag had been used in artistic form. Jasper Johns and many others have created variations on the flag.
51. U.S., *Congressional Record*, 90th Cong., 1st Sess., Vol. 113, Part 12, June 20, 1967, p. 16491.
52. Ibid.
53. Ibid., pp. 16497–16498. Edwards of California in his concluding argument against the bill said, "Our national image as a nation where free speech is protected would not be improved when it is pointed out internationally that 7 months ago, the Soviet Union amended its criminal code to include a statute much like the proposed legislation," pp. 16464–16465.
54. *Sidney Street v. State of New York*, 394 US 576 (1969).
55. In "A Study of the Czech Resistance, The Art of the Impossible," *A Center Occasional Paper*, Vol. II, No. 3, p. 47, Milton Mayer poignantly describes young Palach's funeral which took place five months after the Soviet occupation: "January is the gloomiest of months anyway, and this one

marked the first anniversary of the 'January Spring,' the renaissance of freedom crushed again in August. But on January 25, a half million people assembled on the streets of Prague for Jan Palach's funeral procession. The whole mobile population of the capital, stone silent, undemonstrative Czechs, emasculated the Empire of Schweik, in the unearthly land of Franz Kafka, where a central European did what the Buddhist monks of Vietnam had done to emasculate the Empire of the West. You can't burn a man at the stake who burns himself; he has had the last laugh, what the Germans call *Gaigenhumor*, gallows humor. But his laugh is triumphant instead of grim. He has won."

56. Harry Fleischman, "Norman Thomas: The Last Years," *Progressive*, 33 (November 1969), 36. An object lesson in general semantics demonstrates that objects when they become significant symbols cannot easily be "de-symbolized." Scott Chisholm, an instructor of English at Indiana State University, on April 14, 1967, during a unit on symbolic language in composition class, burned a small American flag in response to a challenge by a student. Mr. Chisholm was immediately suspended, and after hearings his contract for the following year was rescinded. The American Association of University Professors placed Indiana State on the list of censured institutions in the Spring of 1970. "Academic Freedom and Tenure Indiana State University," Report of Committee A, *AAUP Bulletin*, 56 (March 1970), pp. 52–61.

57. *United States v. O'Brien*, 391 US 367 (1968).

58. Vernon L. Parrington, *The Romantic Revolution in America*, Vol. II of *Main Currents in American Thought* (New York, 1927), p. 352. Quoted from the *Life of William Lloyd Garrison by His Children*, III, 412. Garrison first burned copies of the Fugitive Slave Law and the decision of Edward G. Loring in the case of Anthony Burns.

59. *Sutherland v. Illinois* and *Farrell v. Iowa* both remanded at 418 U.S. 907 (1974). Also *People v. Sutherland*, 29 Ill. App. 3d 199, 329 N.E. 2d 820 (1975) and *State v. Farrell*, 223 N.W. 2d 270 (Iowa 1974). *Farrell*, 421 US 1007 (1975) denied review. *Spence v. Washington*, 418 US 405 (1974), *Smith v. Goguen*, 415 US 566 (1974).

60. *Kime v. U.S.*, cert. denied, 51 *Law Week* 3301 (1982).

61. *Alfred Tennyson Cowgill v. California*, 396 US 371 (1970).

62. *The New York Times*, September 1, 1968, p. 31. In "Three Cheers for the Cherry, Rinso White, and (Pow!) Electric Blue!" *American Heritage*, 19 (June 1968), 33, Norman Kotker said, "Not long ago, when a very enterprising manufacturer of ladies' undergarments tried to market a girdle overprinted with stars and stripes, the Daughters of the American Revolution attacked in force until the unmentionables were withdrawn."

63. Jack Hamilton, "Raquel Welch, Mae West Talk About Men, Morals and 'Myra Breckenridge,'" *Look*, 34 (March 24, 1970), 44–45.

64. Jack Gallon in the brief of John Edward Saionz, defendent-appellant, filed in the Court of Appeals of Lucas County, Ohio, December 24, 1968, p. 13.

65. *Smith v. Goguen*, 415 US 566 (1974).

66. *Spence v. Washington*, 418 US 405 (1974).

67. *Cahn v. Long Island Vietnam Moratorium Committee*, 418 U.S. 906 (1974).

68. "Protestors Fight Flag Charges," *Civil Liberties*, May, 1970, p. 8; Victor Riesel, "Blew Nose in Flag," *Record Courier*, May 18, 1970, p. 2; "Fined Costs in Kent City Flag Case," *Record Courier*, May 14, 1970, p. 3; "Can't Have Flag on Pants," *Akron Beacon Journal-Washington Post*, May 26, 1970, p. A4; and Art Gilman, "Altering U.S. Flag for Political Causes Stirs a Legal Debate," *Wall Street Journal*, June 12, 1970, p. 1.

69. "Flags 'Flying High,'" *Akron Beacon Journal*, October 6, 1969, p. 10 and "Dixie Flag Off Sleeves," AP, *Akron Beacon Journal*, October 23, 1969, p. A15.

70. "Only U.S. Flag Will Go to Moon," UPI, *The News*, Goshen, Indiana, June 11, 1969, p. 14. The State Department's suggestion that the United Nations' flag should be flown to the moon was soundly rejected by the U.S. Congress when it was argued by Representative Burt L. Talcott of California that if the United Nations flag goes up the space agency might as well forget about extra billions it said is needed to keep ahead in the space race.

71. *Chicago Sun Times*, reprinted in *Progressive*, 28 (November 1969), 3.

12. The Worst Case of Racial Equality He Ever Saw: The Supreme Court, Motion Picture Censorship, and the Color Line

1. Lloyd Binford quoted by Theodore Kupferman and Philip O'Brien, "Motion Picture Censorship: The Memphis Blues," *Cornell Law Quarterly* 36 (Winter 1951): 278, n. 4. See also *Motion Picture Daily*, 20 January 1950, p. 1, and *Variety*, 8 February 1950, p. 19. As presented to the Memphis censors in 1950, *Imitation of Life* was a revival of a 1934 film. Starring Fredi Washington and Louise Beavers, *Imitation of Life* concerned a young woman's decision to "pass" across the color line from black to white. For a more detailed description of the film see Thomas Cripps, *Slow Fade to Black* (New York: Oxford Press, 1977), pp. 299–302.

2. The first recorded protest against a movie occurred just two weeks after Edison's first peep show parlor opened in New York. Based on moral grounds, this protest was against a film called *Dorilta in the Passion Dance*. Three years later a court ordered censorship of the film *Orange Blossoms* which featured a pantomime of a young bride preparing for her wedding night. The presiding judge in the case denounced the film as "offensive to public decency." See Richard Randall, *Censorship of the Movies* (Madison: University of Wisconsin Press, 1968), p. 11, and Robert Stanley, *The Celluloid Empire* (New York Hastings House, 1978), p. 174.

3. See Kupferman and O'Brien, p. 273.

4. *Joseph Burstyn, Inc. v. Wilson*, 343 U.S. 495 (1952). The *Burstyn* ruling revised an earlier Court decision in *Mutual Film Corp. v. Industrial Commission of Ohio*, 236 U.S. 230 (1915), which had excluded film from First Amendment protection.

5. *Burstyn V. Wilson*, 504–505.

6. Called by at least one film scholar "the most influential and controversial film in the entire history of motion pictures" *The Birth of a Nation* tells the story of the Civil War, Reconstruction, and the birth of the Ku Klux Klan from the perspective of two families. See Harry Geduld, ed., *Focus on D. W. Griffith* (Englewood Cliffs, New Jersey: Prentice-Hall), p. 8. The film was controversial because of the range and strength of the black stereotypes presented. For a full description of the black stereotypes in the film see Donald Bogle, *Toms, Coons, Mullatoes, Mammies, and Bucks* (New York: Bantam Books, 1973), pp. 1–22. Some individuals trace the passage of censorship ordinances which established treatment of race as a standard to reaction to *The Birth*. (For example, see Kupferman and O'Brien, p. 273, n. 6.)

7. Gene Monteith, "'Birth of a Nation' May Be Rescheduled," *ids* 2 February 1979, p. 8. (Note: *ids* is the modern masthead name for the student newspaper of Indiana University; the paper was formerly called the *Indiana Daily Student*, hence *ids*. The editors.)

8. Gene Monteith, "Guild Reschedules 'Birth of a Nation,'" *ids* 28 February 1979, p. 2.

9. For example, see Greg Weber, "Censor of Racist Film Not Warranted Move," *ids*, 29 January 1979, p. 4; Judy Wolf, "Guild's Gag Mocks Higher Education," *ids*, 5 February 1979; and, Thomas Bullard, "Movie Offered Historical View," *ids*, 8 February 1979, p. 4.

10. Monteith, "Guild Reschedules 'Birth of a Nation.'"

11. Gene Monteith, "'Birth' Draws Protesters to Auditorium," *ids* 20 March 1979, p. 1. Thus, rather than being suppressed the film actually was shown on campus twice: concurrently in the Auditorium and in Woodburn Hall. The Auditorium showing was sponsored by the Guild and the film was accompanied by organ music. The Woodburn Hall showing was sponsored by the Black Student unions and was not accompanied by music.

12. Aljean Harmetz, "Oscar-Winning 'Deer Hunter' Is Under Attack as 'Racist' Film," *New York Times*, 26 April 1979, Sec. C, p. 15.

13. *Ibid*. The metaphor is a game of Russian Roulette presented in the film as a form of torture used by the Vietcong against the American prisoners. The film's distributor, Universal Pictures, admits that the specific incident presented did not take place but also argues that almost all film is based on artistic metaphors.

14. *Ibid*.

15. U.S. Congress, House, Committee on Interstate and Foreign Commerce, Subcommittee on Communication and Power, *Hearings Before the Committee on Interstate and Foreign Commerce, Subcommittee on Communication and Power, 92nd Congress, 1st Session on H. Con. Resolution 9 and H. Con. Resolution 182*, Expressing the Sense of Congress Relating *to Films or Broadcasts Which Defame, Stereotype, Ridicule, Demean, or Degrade Ethnic, Racial, and Religious Groups (and all identical resolutions) April 27 and 28, 1971, 92nd Congress, 1st Session, 1971* (Washington: Government Printing Office, 1971).

16. *Ibid*.

17. *Ibid*.

18. For example see, Anne Lyon Haight and Chandler B. Grannis, *Banned Books 387 B.C. to 1978 A.D.* (New York: Bowker, 1978), especially pp. 120–122. Of particular importance to the context of this paper are two U.S. Supreme Court decisions concerning censorship of media other than film for racial reasons. One of these cases is *Anti-Defamation League of B'nai B'rith, Pacific Southwest Regional Office v. FCC*, 394 U.S. 930 (1969). In this case the Court denied *certiorari* and thus let stand the lower court decision. The case involved the League's contention that the FCC should have denied a license renewal to television station KTYM, Inglewood, Calif., because the station aired commentary offensive to persons of the Jewish faith. The League had previously protested the commentary in paid time programs by Richard Cotten to the station. In response to the League protest, the station offered the League free and equal time either to respond to Cotten's comments or time to use as the League saw fit. The League refused KTYM's offer of free time. The FCC renews the station's license without an evidentiary hearing on the content of Cotten's programs. The League argued that the FCC's action was inappropriate because "Cotten's utterances were so contrary to the public interest that a Licensee should be disqualified for renewal." (See *Anti-Defamation League v. FCC*, 403 F. 2d 169, 170). The courts rejected the League's reasoning. For the Federal Circuit Court, then Circuit Judge Warren Burger wrote that "for the FCC to promulgate rules regarding permissible and impermissible speech relating to religion would be not only an egregious interference with free speech in broadcasting, but also an unconstitutional infraction of the free exercise clause and the establishment clause of the First Amendment." (See *Anti-Defamation League v. FCC*, 403 F. 2d 169 (1968). The second case of importance to this paper is *Beauharnais v. Illinois* 343 U.S. 250 (1952). In this case the Court upheld a state conviction for distribution of leaflets which in the words of the statute, portrayed "depravity, criminality, unchastity or lack of virtue of a class of citizens, of any race, color, creed, or religion" and which exposed said persons to "contempt, derision, or obloquy" (See 343 U.S. 250, 252). Thus, in essence in *Beauharnais*, the Court upheld a group libel law.

19. Within the context of this research, the terms censor and censorship mean any attempt to examine, review, expurgate, or change all or part of a motion picture. See *Webster's New Twentieth Century Dictionary of the English Language*, Unabridged, 2nd Edition (Cleveland: World Publishing Company, 1973), p. 292. Although similar arguments could be drawn concerning censorship for ethnic and sexual group defamation, the cases which have reached the Supreme Court dealing with film all consider censorship for racial themes and therefore the research limits itself to that topic.

20. The primary film consistently engaged in censorship battles prior to the 1940's was *The Birth of a Nation*. See Kupferman and O'Brien, p. 273.

21. "More Negro Scenes Cut Out in Dixie Set New Problem for Pix Producers," *Variety*, 16 July 1944, n.p., clipping in American Civil Liberties Union (ACLU) Archives, Vol. 2548, Wisconsin State Historical Society Microfilm Room, Madison, Wisconsin. Hereafter referred to as ACLU Archives.

22. *Ibid.* The statute powering the censors action was Memphis, *Municipal Code* (1925) Sections 1131 to 1139. The code vested the local censors with "power to censor, supervise and regulate all exhibitions, plays, motion pictures, performances, pantomimes, or other presentations" and provided that the censors "have power to prohibit any exhibition which shall be of immoral, lewd, or lascivious character or which denounces, derides, or seeks to overthrow the present form of national government."

23. See Lester Velie, "Censorship in Action," *Colliers*, 6 May 1950, p. 11; "Censor Board Draw Blast of Newsmen," *Memphis Press Scimitar*, 29 October 1947; Kupferman and O'Brien, p. 273; and Ira Carmen, *Movies, Censorship, and the Law* (Ann Arbor: University of Michigan Press, 1966), pp. 206–210.

24. "More Negro Scenes Cut."

25. *Ibid.*

26. Thurgood Marshall to Roger Baldwin, 19 July 1944, ACLU Archives, Vol. 2548.

27. Roger Baldwin to Thurgood Marshall, 20 July 1944, ACLU Archives, Vol. 2548.

28. Wolff, Greenbaum, and Ernst law firm representative initials lbm to Roger Baldwin, 10 April 1945, ACLU Archives, Vol. 2637.

29. Transcript of telephone conversation between initials lbm and Harry Kosner, 10 April 1945, ACLU Archives, Vol. 2637.

30. H. L. Mitchell to Roger Baldwin, 4 August 1945, ACLU Archives, Vol. 2637.

31. Clifford Forster to H. L. Mitchell, 7 August 1945, ACLU Archives, Vol. 2637.

32. Clifford Forster to Gradwell Sears, 23 August 1945, ACLU Archives, Vol. 2637.

33. The film "relates a simple story of how a young and pretty girl is about to assume a new job as a school teacher, how the pupils expect her to be stern and are apprehensive of the new relationship, but how she generally wins the affection of the children through her athletic prowess. Among the children in the cast is a little Negro whose part in the comedy is similar to that of the little Negro 'Farina' in the former Our Gang comedies . . . in short the picture is perfectly innocuous." See *Petition for Writ of Certiorari to the Supreme Court of the State of Tennessee: United Artists and Hal Roach. Petitioners v. Board of Censors, of the City of Memphis and the Shelby County Board of Censors*, Supreme Court of the United States, October Term 1949, No. 680, p. 3.

34. Kupferman and O'Brien, p. 275.

35. *Ibid.*

36. *United Artists v. Board of Censors of City of Memphis*, 225 S.W. 2d 500, 551 (1948).

37. "Memphis Censorship Evokes Court Fight by Film Industry," *Memphis Commercial Appeal*, 20 September 1947, p. 1.

38. Harry Martin, "Movie Industry Launch Suit Against Binford Censor

Board: Bejach Issues Writ Calling Memphis Judges Into Court," *Memphis Commercial Appeal*, 8 October 1947, p. 1.

39. 225 S.W. 2d 550, 552 (1948).

40. *Ibid.*, at 550.

41. *Ibid.*

42. *Ibid.*

43. *Ibid.*

44. 236 U.S. 230.

45. Sidney Schreiber to (?) Hamilton, 17 April 1948, O'Brien Legal File, Box 40, Folder 14, Manuscript Room, Wisconsin State Historical Society, Madison, Wisconsin (Hereafter referred to as the O'Brien Legal File).

46. *Ibid.*

47. "Marie Walthen to Chester Bahn, 9 March 1949, O'Brien Legal File, Box 40, Folder 14.

48. "Memphis Censorship Needs to be Checked," *Louisville Courier-Journal*, 25 September 1947, n.p., clipping in O'Brien Legal File, Box 40, Folder 13.

49. *Petition for Writ*, p. 2.

50. *Ibid.*, pp. 14–15.

51. *United Artists Corp. v. Board of Censors of the City of Memphis*, 339 U.S. 952 (1950).

52. The film *Lost Boundries* based on a book by William L. White told the story of a black doctor and his family who passed for white in a New Hampshire community. See Samuel Bloom, "A Social Psychology Study of Motion Picture Audience Behavior: A Case Study of the Negro Image in Mass Communication," (unpublished Ph.D. dissertation University of Wisconsin, 1956), p. 14. *Atlanta Ordinance Governing the Exhibition of Motion Pictures* (1944), S. Ct. 1–12. The ordinance stated that all pictures to be exhibited in the city must first be approved by the city's duly authorized censor.

53. "Atlanta Ban on 'Lost Boundries' Goes Before Federal Court Tomorrow," *New York Times*, 5 February 1950, Section II, p. 5.

54. *RD-DR Corp. v. Smith*, 89 Fed. Supp. 596 (1950).

55. *Ibid.*

56. *Ibid.*, at 597.

57. *U.S. v. Paramount Pictures*, 334 U.S. 131 (1948). This case involved anti-trust action by the government against Paramount and other vertically integrated motion picture companies. It forced film producers to divest themselves of motion picture exhibition theatres.

58. 89 Fed. Supp. 596, 598 (1950).

59. *Ibid.*, at 598.

60. *RD-DR Corp. v. Smith*, 183 F. 2d 526 (1950).

61. *RD-DR Corp. v. Smith*, 340 U.S. 853 (1950).

62. *Ibid.*

63. *Gelling v. State* (Texas), 156 Tex. Crim 516, 247 S.W. 2d 95 (1952). *Pinky* was produced by Stanley Kramer and distributed by Twentieth Century Fox. The film told the story of a Negro woman who returned to the South after passing for white in Boston. The story line revolved around the

problems the woman had adjusting to the inferior status accorded to blacks in the South. See Edward Mapp, *Blacks in American Films Today and Yesterday.* (Metuchen, New Jersey: Scarecrow Press, 1972), p. 38.

64. Carmen, p. 54.
65. *Gelling v. State*, 247 S.W. 2d 95 (1952).
66. *Ibid.*
67. *RD-DR Corp. v. Smith*, 183 F. 2d 562 (1950).
68. 247 S.W. 2d 95, 97 (1952).
69. *Ibid.*, at 95.
70. 343 U.S. 960. In *Winters v. New York*, 333 U.S. 507, the Court struck down as unconstitutionally vague a New York statute prohibiting the dissemination of printed matter devoted to the publication of criminal stories or stories of deeds of bloodshed, lust, or crime. In part the court stated: "The line between the informing and the entertaining is too elusive for the protection of that basic right. Everyone is familiar with instances of propaganda through fiction. What is one man's amusement, teaches another's doctrine." See 333 U.S. 507, 510.
71. *Ibid.*
72. *Ibid.*
73. *Superior Films v. Department of Education of Ohio*, 159 Ohio St. 315, 112 N.E. 2d 311 (1953).
74. *Ibid.* The same or similar issue referred to by the Court was the constitutionality of the Ohio film censorship statute. Ohio Code (1943), Sect. 154-47-154-471, vested in the division of film censorship the power to allow "only such films as are in the judgment and discretion of the board of censors of a moral, educational, or amusing, and harmless character" to be shown in the state.
75. *Ibid.*, at 316. Case No. 33265. *M* was a German film based on a series of child murders which spread terror among the inhabitants of Dusseldorf in 1929. See "The Dusseldorf Murders," *New York Times Film Reviews: A One Volume Selection* (New York: Quadrangle Books, 1971), p. 133.
76. *Ibid.*
77. *Ibid.*
78. *Ibid.*, at 317. Cases No. 33282 and 33283. *Native Son* was described to the Court by Film Classics as follows: the action of the story takes place in Chicago, and part of the picture was filmed there. The role of the central character, Bigger Thomas, an embittered young Negro, is acted by Richard Wright, the author of the book. Bigger accidentally kills a white girl. After disposing of her body he attempts to extort money from her parents. After the murder is discovered, Bigger goes into hiding with his sweetheart Bessie Mears, and immediately before his capture murders Bessie in the mistaken belief that she betrayed him.
79. *Ibid.*
80. *Ibid.*
81. *Ibid.*, at 319–335.
82. *Ibid.*, at 327–328.
83. *Ibid.*, at 335.

84. *Superior Films, v. Department of Education of Ohio*, 346 U.S. 587 (1954).
85. *Commercial Pictures Corp. v. Regents of the University of the State of New York*, 305 N.Y. 366, 113, N.E. 2d 502 (1953).
86. This case involved the censorship of the movie *La Ronda* by the New York film censors on the grounds that the film was "immoral and would tend to corrupt morals."
87. 346 U.S. 587.
88. *Ibid.*
89. For example see, Murray Schumach, *The Face On The Cutting Room Floor* (New York: William Morrow and Co, 1964), p. 157, and Hope Eastman, representing the ACLU in testimony during *Hearings on H. Con. Res. 9 and H. Con. Res. 182*, pp. 37–45.
90. 343 U.S. 250.
91. 403 F. 2d 169, 174, n. 5.

13. The Birth of a Baby Photo Essay: Was it Obscenity or Censorship?

1. Sheryle Leekley and John Leekley, *Moments: The Pulitzer Prize Photographs* (New York: Crown Publishers, 1978), pp. 90–3.
2. Morris L. Ernst and Alexander Lindey, *The Censor Marches On* (New York: Doubleday, Doran, 1940), p. 53.
3. "Facts of Life," *Time*, 18 April 1938, p. 57.
4. William Manchester, *The Glory and the Dream a Narrative History of America, 1932–1972* (Boston: Little, Brown, 1973), p. 118.
5. *Ibid.*, p. 120.
6. "Facts of Life," p. 57.
7. "The Birth of a Baby," *Time*, 4 April 1938, p. 30.
8. Ernst and Lindey, *Censor*, p. 98.
9. *Ibid.*, pp. 52–3.
10. "Facts of Life," p. 58.
11. "Life Begins," *Editor and Publisher*, 9 April 1938, p. 20.
12. "Facts of Life (cont'd.)," *Time*, 25 April 1938, p. 34.
13. Ernst and Lindey, *Censor*, p. 53.
14. "Obscene Magazine Ban to be Asked," *Christian Science Monitor*, 4 April 1938, p. 9.
15. "107 Will Help Police as Censors," *Christian Science Monitor*, 5 April 1938, p. 9.
16. "Censorship Plan Brings Results," *Christian Science Monitor*, 7 April 1938, p. 9. There was no specific reference to the name of the magazine, although later articles did point out that the periodical under question was the April 11 issue of *Life*. It should be noted that the magazine censorship board submitted the issue to Timilty for his ruling. This leads to the question of whether there was some dispute among the newsdealers as to the "obscenity" of the photo essay, thus requiring them to submit the issue to Timilty for a final ruling, according to the plan agreed to several days before.

17. "Picture Magazines With Pages Deleted Sold by Newsstands," *Christian Science Monitor*, 9 April 1938, p. 9.

18. "Pittsfield, Mass," *Memphis Commercial Appeal*, 7 April 1938, p. 1.

19. "Life Ban Spreads to Pennsylvania," *New York Times*, 10 April 1938, p. 21.

20. Paul Blanshard, *The Right to Read: The Battle Against Censorship* (Boston: The Beacon Press, 1955), p. 156.

21. "Boston Bans Another," *New York Times*, 11 April 1938, p. 6.

22. "Ten Cities Ban Life's Birth Issue," *New York Times*, 8 April 1938, p. 6.

23. "Wide Ban on 'Life' for Birth Pictures," *New York Times*, 9 April 1938, p. 15.

24. "Hue and Cry Goes Up In Conservative Boston," *Memphis Commercial Appeal*, 8 April 1938, p. 2.

25. "Timilty to Ask Magazine's Ban," *Christian Science Monitor*, 9 April 1938, p. 11.

26. *Ibid.*, p. 9.

27. "St. Louis Police Take 'Life' Off Newsstands," *St. Louis Post-Dispatch*, 9 April 1938. For a similar account of these events, see "Seize Magazine Declared Lewd," *St. Louis Globe-Democrat*, 9 April 1938, p. 1. In this particular article, it was mentioned that Rogan was to appear before Judge Simpson's Court of Criminal Correction on April 14. However, no mention of this appearance, nor any mention of a dismissal of charges was contained in either of the St. Louis newspapers for several days surrounding this date. Also, a search for a reported case dealing with Rogan produced nothing. One can speculate that the charges were eventually dropped, and thus nothing was noted either officially or in the area newspapers.

28. "Furor Over a Magazine's Pictures," *St. Louis Post-Dispatch*, 9 April 1938, p. 4.

29. "Civil Liberties Committee Objects to 'Life,'" *St. Louis Post-Dispatch*, 11 April 1938, p. 4.

30. "Life Ban Spreads to Pennsylvania," p. 21.

31. "Committee Protests Magazine Seizure," *St. Louis Globe-Democrat*, 12 April 1938, p. 8.

32. "All But 50 Copies of Seized Magazine Returned to Agent," *St. Louis Post-Dispatch*, 12 April 1938, p. 3.

33. "City Officials Ban Magazine's Camera Study of Childbirth," *Memphis Commercial Appeal*, 8 April 1938, p. 1.

34. *Ibid.*

35. "Furor Condones, Condemns City's Ban on Life Magazine," *Memphis Commercial Appeal*, 9 April 1938, p. 1.

36. *Ibid.*, p. 3.

37. *Ibid.*, p. 1.

38. "Ban Magazine With Pictures of Childbirth," *Chicago Daily Tribune*, 9 April 1938, p. 16.

39. "Allman Lifts Temporary Ban on Sale of Magazine," *Chicago Daily Tribune*, 10 April 1938, p. 18.

40. "Expert Publicity," *New Orleans Times-Picayune*, 9 April 1938, p. 8.

The only mention of the ban in New Orleans encountered in this study came from news sources outside of the city. See, e.g., *Memphis Commercial Appeal*, 8 April 1938, p. 1; and *Time*, 18 April 1938, p. 58.

41. "Life Ban Spreads to Pennsylvania," p. 21.
42. "Facts of Life," p. 57.
43. "Furor Condones, Condemns City's Ban on Life Magazine," p. 1.
44. "Wide Ban on 'Life' for Birth Pictures," *New York Times*, 9 April 1938, p. 15.
45. *Ibid.*
46. "Publisher of 'Life' Arrested in Test," *New York Times*, 13 April 1938, p. 46.
47. "Foley Condemns 'Sneering at God,'" *New York Times*, 25 April 1938, p. 9.
48. "Wide Ban on 'Life' for Birth Pictures," p. 15.
49. "Life Ban Spreads to Pennsylvania," p. 21.
50. *Ibid.*
51. "Publisher of Life Pushes Court Test," *New York Times*, 12 April 1938, p. 6.
52. "Publisher of 'Life' Arrested in Test," p. 46.
53. "Larsen Wins Point in Indecency Trial," *New York Times*, 20 April 1938, p. 46.
54. 5 N.Y.S.2d 55, 57 (N.Y. Sp. Sess. 1938).
55. "Court Clears 'Life' on Baby Pictures," *New York Times*, 27 April 1938, p. 3.
56. 5 N.Y.S.2d at 56.
57. *People v. Finkelstein*, 114 N.Y.S.2d 810, 813 (N.Y. Magis. Ct., 1952); *People v. Finkelstein*, 156 N.Y.S.2d 104, 109 (N.Y. Magis. Ct. 1955).
58. *People v. Mishkin*, 207 N.Y.S.2d 390, 394 (N.Y. Sp. Sess. 1960).
59. *Bantam Books v. Melko*, 96 A.2d 47, 59 (N.J. Super. Ct. Ch. Div. 1953).
60. *State v. Scope*, 86 A.2d 154, 157 (Del. Super. Ct. 1952).
61. *Capitol Enterprises, Inc. v. City of Chicago*, 260 F.2d 670, 675 (7th Cir. 1958).
62. "A Lively Issue," *Editor & Publisher*, 16 April 1938, p. 20.
63. Blanshard, *The Right to Read*, p. 156.
64. Olga G. Hoyt and Edwin P. Hoyt, *Censorship in America* (New York: The Seabury Press, 1970), p. 42.
65. Morris L. Ernst and Alan U. Schwartz, *Censorship: The Search for the Obscene* (New York: The Macmillan Co., 1964), pp. 114–5.
66. "Mrs. Roosevelt Approves 'Birth of a Baby' Pictures," *St. Louis Post-Dispatch*, 18 April 1938, p. 9.

14. *Deep Throat* in Deep Trouble on a College Campus: An Academic Freedom Case Study

1. *Roth v. United States*, 354 U.S. 476 (1957)
2. For an interesting discussion of the "average person," see George N.

Gordon, *Erotic Communication* (New York: Hastings House, 1980), pp. 148–150. For a legal update see *Pinkus v. United States*, 436 U.S. 293 (1978).

3. See Justice Harlan's opinion in *Manual Enterprises, Inc. v. Day*, 370 U.S. 478 (1962) and Justice Brennan's opinion in *Jacobellis v. Ohio*, 378 U.S. 184 (1964).

4. *Paris Adult Theatre v. Slaton*, 413 U.S. 49 (1973), p. 103.

5. *Miller v. California*, 413 U.S. 15 (1973).

6. *Ibid.*, p. 43.

7. *Jenkins v. Georgia*, 418 U.S. 153 (1974), p. 161.

8. *Jacobellis v. Ohio*.

9. In some cases, students submitted a concurring opinion, agreeing with the majority or minority decision but for a different reason.

10. In the court case that later transpired, a transcript of an audiotaped lecture in which voluntary viewing was emphasized was submitted as evidence. Also, students who testified in court stated that viewing was voluntary.

11. Dot Brown, "'Decency' Group to Decide Community Standards," *Pensacola Journal*, 22 April 1977, pp. 1B & 3B.

12. The student was employed by the local commercial television station (WEAR) and was at work when he was contacted and asked to come to the State Attorney's office immediately. The urgency of the request upset the student who called me and an attorney in trying to determine why he had been contacted and what his course of action should be. In the meantime, the State Attorney and his assistant went to the station and personally served a subpoena and questioned the student. Later, it was discovered that the student's name was furnished by the daughter-in-law of the State Attorney's assistant. She was a member of the Regulation class but had not viewed the entire film, nor had a friend of hers who was in the class. The State Attorney wished to question someone who had seen the film in its entirety, and the student at the television station was the only class member whose name she and her friend could recall.

13. The question of whether the complaint originated inside or outside the State Attorney's office was never satisfactorily resolved. In the hearing at the County Court, the prosecuting attorney told the judge that Felicia Smith (the daughter of state legislator Ed Fortune, and daughter-in-law of the State Attorney's assistant, Wayne Smith) was the one who complained. But in a personal conversation with me, Ms. Smith said she never complained but simply mentioned the class assignment to her husband, and later to her father-in-law.

14. *Pensacola Journal*, 13 May 1977, pp. 1A & 3A.

15. *Pensacola Journal*, 20 May 1977, pp. 1A & 10A.

16. A typical letter to the editor exclaimed: "What amazes me is the cry which goes up from some in the university community about academic freedom. Just how far do these people think freedom ought to go in the name of education?" *Pensacola Journal*, 16 June 1977, p. 20A.

17. The newspaper later decided that showing the film was not proper. Referring to the incident, an editorial noted: "It was, in our opinion, an error of

judgment. But it touched off such a furor and caused so much negative public reaction that we doubt its like will occur again anywhere around the state—and if it does there are already plenty of university regulations to handle the situation." *Pensacola Journal*, 19 August 1977, p. 16A.

18. *Pensacola Journal*, 14 May 1977, p. 8A.
19. WCOA editorial, 19 May 1977.
20. WEAR editorial, 18 May 1977.
21. The station manager, sensitive to the personal attack rule of the Fairness Doctrine, offered to let me or someone else in the class respond to his editorial.
22. WEAR editorial, 25 May 1977.
23. WEAR editorial, 27 May 1977.
24. *Pensacola News-Journal*, 29 May 1977, p. 3E.
25. *Santa Rosa Free Press*, 30 May 1977.
26. *Pensacola News-Journal*, 29 May 1977, p. 3E.
27. *Pensacola News-Journal*, 29 May 1977, p. 6B.
28. WSRE Newscast, 22 March 1978.
29. *Pensacola Journal*, 23 May 1977, p. 4A.
30. Ed Stanford, past president of the Christian Business Men's Committee and the one responsible for the ad being placed, expressed his views further in a Tampa newspaper article. Philip Morgan, "'Deep Throat' Fuss Festers," *Tampa Tribune and Tampa Times*, 12 June 1977, pp. 1-A & 28-A.
31. John Wingard, personal letter, 20 May 1977.
32. Anonymous letter, received 27 March 1978.
33. W. B. Oakes, personal letter, 1 June 1977.
34. Chrys S. Holley, letter to President Robinson, 23 May 1977.
35. *Ibid.*
36. Student Council Memorandum, 12 May 1977.
37. Mary Barrineau, "UWF President Calms Faculty Freedom Fears," *Pensacola Journal*, 19 May 1977, pp. 1B & 3B.
38. *Ibid.*
39. Marshall M. Criser, personal letter, 24 May 1977.
40. E. W. Hopkins, Jr., personal letter, 27 May 1977.
41. Mary Barrineau, "'Deep Throat' Showing 'Bad Judgment,'" *Pensacola News*, 26 May 1977, p. 1A.
42. United Faculty of Florida press release, 26 May 1977. Most of the material in the press release was published in an article the following day. Mary Barrineau, "Regent Criticizes 'Deep Throat' Showing," *Pensacola Journal*, 27 May 1977, pp. 1A & 14A.
43. Letter to Marshall M. Criser, 4 June 1977.
44. Mary Barrineau, "Showing of Porn Film Morally Wrong—Fortune," *Pensacola Journal*, 17 May 1977, p. 1A.
45. SB 1230, Florida Legislature, 1977 (The bill would create s. 240.146, Florida Statutes).
46. "House Votes to Allow Censorship on Campuses," *Pensacola Journal*, 24 May 1977, p. 1A.

47. Mary Barrineau, "Mock Sex Act Spurs Campus Censorship Bill," *Pensacola Journal*, 1 June 1977, p. 1B.

48. Mary Barrineau, "Student Denies Sex in Scene from 'Equus,'" *Pensacola News-Journal*, 5 June 1977, pp. 1B 7 4B.

49. *Pensacola Journal*, 1 June, 1977, p. 8A.

50. John Hanchette, "Censorship Opposition Mounting," *Pensacola Journal*, 25 June 1977, p. 1B.

51. *Ibid.*

52. Mary Barrineau, "United Faculty Calls for Veto," *Pensacola News*, 3 June 1977, pp. 1A & 2A.

53. Letter to Governor Reubin Askew, 28 June 1977.

54. *Ibid.*

55. *Pensacola Journal*, 7 June 1977, p. 10A.

56. *St. Petersburg Times*, 30 June 1977, pp. 1B & 2B.

57. Chet Kaufman, "Roberts Wins Grievance on Letter," *Pensacola Journal*, 2 September 1977, pp. 1B & 4B.

58. Memorandum to Arthur H. Doerr from Lucius F. Ellsworth, 7 September 1977.

59. Mary Barrineau, "No Charges Pressed in Film Controversy," *Pensacola News*, 17 May 1977, pp. 1A & 2A.

60. Mary Barrineau, "Golden: Film Clip 'Hard-Core' Porn," *Pensacola Journal*, 14 May 1977, pp. 1A & 4A.

61. University officials had indicated through their attorney that they would not pursue the matter. Likewise, a request from the chairman of the University of West Florida Faculty Council to the chairman of the Board of Regents for legal assistance in my behalf went unheeded.

62. Dennis Kaufman, "Deep Throat Obscenity Rule Expected Today," *Pensacola Journal*, 21 March 1978, pp. 1 & 2.

63. *Ibid.*

64. *Ibid.*

65. Monde Murphy, "Bell Rules 'Deep Throat' Obscene," *Pensacola News*, 31 March 1978, p. 1A.

66. Brief Amicus Curiae of the American Association of University Professors, filed in *Roberts v. Florida*, Case No. 54, 135, pp. 16 & 17.

67. Bill Kaczor, "State Concedes 'Deep Throat' Could be Used Educationally," *Pensacola Journal*, 23 December 1978, pp. 1C & 2C.

68. *Roberts v. Florida*, 373 So 2d 672 Fla. (1979).

69. Appellant's Reply Brief, filed in *Roberts v. Florida*, Case No. 54, 135, pp. 5 & 6.

70. *Roberts v. Florida*, p. 675.

71. Hanover, "Deep Throat Obscenity Rule Expected Today," p. 2.

72. Although the litigation had been emotionally taxing, it did not produce a serious financial strain. My attorneys, George Estess and Fletcher Baldwin (the latter a constitutional law scholar who helped argue the case before the Florida Supreme Court), did not charge for their services. Money raised from legal defense funds (one initiated by University of West Florida faculty;

another supported by the Speech Communication Association) and a donation of $500 from the *Playboy* Foundation were used to pay for various expenses (mainly travel) which we incurred.

73. Criser, personal letter.

74. Mary Barrineau, "Schools Survey Ranks UWF Last in 2 Areas," *Pensacola Journal*, Gulf Coast Section, 25 July 1978, p. 1.

16. Free Speech, Persuasion, and the Democratic Process

1. See Walter Lippmann, *The Good Society* (Boston, 1937), pp. 374–376.

2. The success of PR and advertising in business is attested to by the enormous increase in money invested in it in recent years. See Vance Packard, "The Growing Power of the Ad Man," *The Atlantic Monthly*, CC (September 1957).

3. William L. Miller, "Can Government be Merchandized?" *Reporter*, IX (October 27, 1953), 11.

4. *Ibid.*, p. 13.

5. Stanley Kelley, Jr., *Professional Public Relations and Political Power* (Baltimore, 1956), p. 48. I wish to acknowledge a special indebtedness to Mr. Kelley. His timely book came to my attention while I was gathering material for this paper. In his book much of my work was done for me, and I have used his material liberally.

6. *Ibid.*, pp. 51–52.

7. *Ibid.*, p. 50.

8. *Ibid.*, p. 74.

9. *Ibid.*

10. *Ibid.*, p. 54.

11. *Ibid.*, p. 204.

12. *Ibid.*

13. *Ibid.*, p. 205.

14. Robert Bendiner, "How Presidents are Made," *Reporter*, XIV (February 9, 1956), 18.

15. Miller, p. 12.

16. Walter Lippman, *Liberty and the News* (New York, 1920), p. 13.

17. Ralph Block, "Propaganda and the Free Society," *The Public Opinion Quarterly*, XII (Winter 1948–49), 678.

18. (Boston, 1955), pp. 124–130.

19. Walter Lippmann, "The Indispensable Opposition," *The Atlantic Monthly*, CLXIV (August 1939), 189.

20. Kelley, p. 189.

21. William H. Hale, "The Politicians Try Victory Through Air Power," *Reporter*, XV (September 6, 1956), 20.

22. Alexander Meiklejohn, *Free Speech and Its Relation to Self-Government* (New York, 1948), pp. 86–87.

23. For a discussion of modern advertising technique and "motivation re-

search" see Vance Packard, *The Hidden Persuaders* (New York, 1957), and his article referred to above.

The recent development in persuasion known as the "invisible sell" suggests the frightening lengths to which those who sell are willing to go in influencing behavior.

24. Max Ascoli, *The Power of Freedom* (New York, 1949), p. 67.

17. An Ethical Basis of Communication

1. *The Life of Richard Cobden*, 2 vols. (London, 1908), I, 223.
2. *Rhetoric*, 1355 b 9–14. Trans. W. Rhys Roberts, in *The Works of Aristotle Translated into English under the Editorship of W. D. Ross*, XI (Oxford, 1924).
3. *Nicomachean Ethics*, 1094 a 17-1094 b 7. Trans. W. D. Ross, in *The Works of Aristotle Translated into English under the Editorship of W. D. Ross*, IX (Oxford, 1925).
4. II (September, 1954), 8–15.
5. *Ibid.*, II, 5.
6. *Ibid.*
7. *Ibid.*, II, 13.
8. *Ibid.*

Annotated Bibliographies

The following bibliographies pertain to journals in speech communication published through 1984. Essays published in this anthology are excluded.

Essays on Freedom of Speech from the National and Regional Speech Communication Journals

JOHN J. MAKAY

Arnold J. William E. "A Field Study of Attitudes Toward Freedom of Expression and the Flag." *Free Speech Yearbook* (1973): 21–37.
    This essay builds on the findings of Barbour and Goldberg with regard to American attitudes and free speech issues. Specifically it focuses on attitudes toward freedom of speech and the flag to determine attitudes and replicate previous research about First Amendment statements. The results support the claims made previously by Barbour and Goldberg.

Bailey, Dennis. "Free Speech, The Massachusetts Bay Colony, and its Problems With Covenant and Rhetorical Deviance." *Free Speech Yearbook* (1984): 80–91.
    This essay is concerned with the history of free speech in America; it reviews two events from the early seventeenth century history of the Massachusetts Bay Colony and describes the concept of covenental theology as a rationale for the controlled theocratic society that characterized the Colony. Bailey describes the rhetorical genres used by ministers involved in free speech controversy.

Barbour, Alton, and Alvin Goldberg. "Survey Research in Free Speech Attitudes." *Free Speech Yearbook* (1971): 28–35.
    This essay summarizes the findings of investigators who studied free speech attitudes held by Americans and compares past findings with recent surveys. The authors suggest that Americans are poorly informed about their constitutional rights of free speech and that a large number of Americans, young and old, are willing to restrict the free speech of others. They maintain that the evidence about free speech attitudes is not encouraging.

Barbour, Alton. "Some Psychological Dimensions of Free Speech Attitudes." *Free Speech Yearbook* (1978): 68–71.
    This article reports on efforts made at the University of Denver to gain empirical data about persons who would allow freedom of expression and others who would restrain it.

Bellows, Jeff. "On Citizenship and Technocracy. *Free Speech Yearbook* (1974): 64–73.

The purpose of this essay is to critically examine three basic constructs for democracy: an informed public, alternatives for direction in life, and the means of human expression. The author explains the nature and role of myth in American religious and political belief with regard to democracy and examines the fundamental constructs which have implications for freedom of speech.

Boase, Paul H. "Samuel M. (Golden Rule) Jones: Unorthodox Champion of Free Speech." *Free Speech Yearbook* (1980): 32–39.

This essay focuses on the rhetoric of Samuel M. Jones, the Golden Rule Mayor of Toledo, Ohio, from 1897 until his untimely death in 1904. Jones' social philosophy and the political and economic reforms he promoted were based on the same fundamental premises that support First Amendment rights. Boase profiles Jones as an important free speech advocate who had a highly positive impact on the community he served.

Bosmajian, Haig. "Fire, Snakes, and Poisons: Metaphors and Analogues in Some Free Speech Cases." *Free Speech Yearbook* (1981): 16–22.

This essay examines several landmark U.S. Supreme Court opinions on freedom of speech. The author analyzes the use of metaphors and analogues in defining the character of a variety of anti-World War I, anti-conscription, and anti-capitalistic speeches, writings and groups. He calls attention to the role, power, and distortion of the use of metaphors and analogues as central to Supreme Court arguments in First Amendment decisions.

Bosmajian, Haig. "Speech 'And the First Amendment.'" *Today's Speech* 18 (Fall, 1980): 3–11.

This essay, making initial reference to Milton's *Areopagitica*, examines the U.S. Supreme Court's rulings on symbolic behavior as speech protected by the First Amendment. Distinctions between various kinds of symbolic speech are suggested as the author argues that both jurist and layman must examine and re-examine the definitions and grounds upon which freedoms of speech, assembly and petition are grounded.

Cahill, Corrine M., and William A. Haskins. "The First Amendment Issue of Obscenity: A Phenomenological Analysis." *Free Speech Yearbook* (1984): 30–41.

The essay contends that the U.S. Supreme Court's interpretation of obscenity is unclear, and the author's advance the argument that one approach for clarifying the court's position is through a phenomenological method. After reviewing phenomenology from a methodological perspective, the author analyzes obscenity as an individual value and with regard to the relationship between social and individual value.

Center, Don. "The Baskette Collection: A Research Report." *Free Speech Yearbook* (1976): 78–82.

This report identifies and describes materials for historical research on freedom of speech. The author describes the Baskette Collection as the largest free speech collection in the nation, and he provides a concise background on the activities of Ewing Baskette, who was assistant cataloguer at the Illinois State Library until his death in 1959. Items in the collection are listed.

Chandler, Daniel Ross. "A Comparison of John Milton's *Areopagitica* with Thomas Erskine's Addresses on Free Speech." *Free Speech Yearbook* (1978): 98–112.
 The author concentrates on Milton's pamphlet and twelve speeches from Erskine. He claims the rhetorical situations encountered by Milton and Erskine governed the invention of the rhetoric and contends that while both men championed free speech, both acknowledged limitations imposed on it.

Chandler, Daniel Ross. "International Exchange of Scientific Information During Crisis: A Case Study in the Right to Communicate." *Free Speech Yearbook* (1980): 58–66.
 This essay focuses on the tension between the United States and Communist nations as it existed in the international exchange of scientific information after the Soviet invasion of Afghanistan and the internal exile of Andrei Sakharov. The author recalls tense exchanges between prominent international technical organizations and officials in the Carter Administration over restrictions of communicative freedom among scientists.

Cline, Timothy R., and Rebecca Cline. "Gaining Access to the Media: Some Issues and Cases." *Free Speech Yearbook* (1975): 35–56.
 The authors consider the tension between speakers having the right to speak freely and the constraints of access to the mass media. Cases for and against media access are reviewed, and authors examine access to the media from the perspective of the listener, the speaker and the media.

Cline, Rebecca, and Timothy R. Cline. "The Opinions of William O. Douglas: Defining and Defending Freedom of Speech." *Free Speech Yearbook* (1981): 78–98.
 This essay explicates U.S. Supreme Court Justice William O. Douglas' interpretation of the First Amendment and identifies the philosophy which guided him. The authors analyze his written opinions concerning the term "speech," permissible limits of free speech, and presuppositions constituting his philosophy and their impact on his First Amendment decisions.

Crocker, Lionel. "Training to Exercise Freedom of Speech." *Western Speech Journal* 7 (March, 1943): 1–5.
 This essay reviews the history and status of public speaking in American colleges and universities and their value for exercising the right to free speech. The author grounds his assessment in traditional as well as modern rhetorical theory and practice.

Day, Louis A. "The High School Press and the First Amendment." *Free Speech Yearbook* (1978): 92–97.
 This essay focuses on the high school newspaper and freedom of expres-

sion. Day contends that the First Amendment pronouncements of press freedom are made binding on the States through the Fourteenth Amendment and that school officials must uphold these freedoms. She focuses on the scope of the First Amendment's protection for high school papers and First Amendment restrictions.

Denman, William N. "'Them Dirty, Filthy Books:' The Textbook War in West Virginia." *Free Speech Yearbook* (1976): 37–45.
The 1974 textbook controversy in Kanawha County, West Virginia, is recounted in this essay. The author examines the issues and events that involved a free speech controversy, one which captured national attention through the mass media. Denman describes the attitudes of parents protesting the books as well as the supporters of the material.

Eich, Ritch K., and Charles M. Feldman. "Suppression of Expression: Rights in Jeopardy." *Central States Speech Journal* 27 (Fall, 1976): 225–29.
The focus of this essay is on free expression in the academic setting. After summarizing the traditional view of free speech in academia, the authors point to contemporary challenges entailing suppression of ideas. The essay presents a three point plan of action to assure and encourage free and full speech in colleges and universities.

Enholm, Donald K., and J. Justin Gustaines. "Plato and the Totalitarian State." *Free Speech Yearbook* (1984): 58–65.
This essay examines the concept of communication in Plato's *Republic* and advances the argument that Plato's view of communication in his ideal society conforms closely to that of modern totalitarianism. The authors maintain that the *Republic* and Plato's view of communication are characterized by a central direction and control of the entire communicative process to provide power for the ruler, to arrest change and to serve the good of the nation.

Erickson, Keith V., and Carroll R. Haggard. "Freedom of Expression and the Law Enforcement Officer." *Communication Quarterly* (Fall, 1977): 21–27.
This essay examines the legal status and arguments supporting and rejecting free expression in regard to police officers. The study focuses on the First Amendment rights of police and discusses police expression rights, the views of the courts on free expression by public employees, and points to a paradox—police protect our freedoms but forego their own.

Ewbank, H. L. "Freedom to Teach, to Learn, and to Speak: Rhetorical Considerations." *Free Speech Yearbook* (1974): 29–34.
The purpose of this essay is to consider important free speech conditions which provide a satisfying learning environment that is encouraged and protected by the First Amendment. Ewbank reminds us that as a whole, the discipline of rhetoric, the First Amendment and the bases of academic freedom determine the opportunity for free expression in the American educational experience.

Flory, Joyce. "Philosophical Assumptions Underlying Plato's Theory of Freedom of Speech: A Comparison With the Theory of Democratic Individualism." *Free Speech Yearbook* (1974): 45–53.

This essay examines the individual from Ralph B. Perry's view and contrasts this view with Platonic theory with particular regard to free expression. The author provides an illuminating analysis of Plato's theory of freedom of speech as it shows what separates Platonic theory from a democratic individualistic theory and the good of the individual.

Foley, Joseph M. "The Information Society: A New Threat to Freedom of Speech." *Free Speech Yearbook* (1984): 51–57.

Foley's essay presents a careful consideration of the proposition that the cost of information in society has serious implications for free speech. The author contends that in the information society information becomes the basis for economic activity and that professionals in the field of speech communication must play a vigorous role in monitoring the impact of the information society on freedom of speech.

Francesconi, Robert. "Freedom of Expression and Rhetorical Art: The Problems of Avant-Garde Jazz." *Free Speech Yearbook* (1979): 38–46.

This essay is underscored by the theme of the power of forces in the entertainment industry to control artistic expression. Francesconi sketches the rhetorical nature of avant-garde jazz and examines charges of racism linked with the suppression of musical expression. He argues that the contemporary avant-garde forms of jazz in the Civil Rights Movement were suppressed by discrimination.

Freeman, Douglas N. "Free Speech and Foreign Policy Decision-Making." *Free Speech Yearbook* (1976): 7–16.

The purpose of this essay is to analyze contemporary foreign policy deliberations and advance the argument that the decision-making process has been handicapped by barriers to free speech. The obstacles to free speech are examined in terms of acquiesence and token dissent by policy-makers.

Freeman, Douglas N. "Freedom of Speech Within the Nixon Administration." *Communication Quarterly* (Winter, 1976): 3–10.

This essay examines the freedom government officials in the administration of President Richard Nixon had to evaluate public policies and programs. The author surveys the role of free speech in intragovernmental decision making and Nixon's style of leadership, and he argues that freedom of expression was significantly controlled during the formulation of both domestic and foreign policy.

Gill, Ann M. "X-Rated Political Broadcasting: A Test of the First Amendment." *Free Speech Yearbook* (1984): 123–34.

This essay argues that Congress or the Supreme Court should act in the areas of political, indecent or profane speech in a way that clarifies rather than confuses First Amendment doctrine. The study examines current law, a case involving Larry Flynt, publisher of *Hustler* Magazine, and suggests changes to modify the law while keeping First Amendment freedom intact.

Goding, William E. "Antagonism and a Free Society." *Free Speech Yearbook* (1974): 13–20.
> This essay responds to the question: "What is apt to occur when hostility is present together with either pro or con free speech attitudes?" Goding used established attitude scales to distinguish free speech attitudes and high and low hostility levels. Open-ended interviews were completed, and a number of important findings are reported.

Gorden, William I. and Robert Kelley. "A Look at the Fire Symbol Before and After May 4, 1970." *Free Speech Yearbook* (1974): 18–28.
> Fire has been explicity associated with free speech in America, the authors indicate, since 1919 when Justice Holms reasoned, "The most stringent protection to free speech would not protect a man falsely shouting fire in a theatre and causing a panic." This essay focuses on the relationship of fire and the rhetorical threat of fire to the events surrounding May 4, 1970.

Gorden, William I., A. Bennet Whaley, and Marie A. Whaley. "Conceptualization of a Measure of Patriotism." *Free Speech Yearbook* (1983): 83–88.
> This paper presents the development of an instrument to assess patriotism in the United States. The instrument examines items generated around categories about use of the flag, freedom of speech, patriotic ritual and patriotic belief. The study tested a three-fold definition of patriotism focusing on attitudes, constitutional ideals, rituals and the national symbol.

Goss, Patricia. "The First Amendment's Weakest Link: Government Regulation of Controversial Advertising." *Free Speech Yearbook* (1975): 21–34.
> This essay examines the legal basis for distinguishing commercial expression from that directed at public decision making. Government efforts at regulating commercials is discussed, and the author presents possible solutions to the inadequacy of legal safeguards. She points out that the U.S. Supreme Court has regarded communication designed solely for profit as not being constitutionally protected.

Haiman, Franklyn S. "Freedom of Speech As An Academic Discipline." *Free Speech Yearbook* (1976): 1–6.
> Haiman provides information about the beginnings of what has become the Commission on Freedom of Speech in the Speech Communication Association. Furthermore, the author examines the following types of research in the area of freedom of speech: historical-critical research, case or field studies, experimental studies, effects studies, attitudes research and critical analyses.

Haiman, Franklyn S. "Justice Brennan and the First Amendment, 1956–1984." *Free Speech Yearbook* (1983): 33–42.
> Haiman indicates that civil libertarians usually identify former U.S. Supreme Court Justices Hugo Black and William O. Douglas as the judicial patron saints of the First Amendment. The author further argues that Justice William Brennan Jr., appointed by President Eisenhower, has contributed more to shaping and fortifying First Amendment law than Justices Black and Douglas combined.

Haiman, Franklyn S. "Nonverbal Communication and the First Amendment: The Rhetoric of the Streets Revisited." *The Quarterly Journal of Speech* 68 (November, 1982): 371–83.
> This essay examines the developments that have occurred since the author's seminal essay, "The Rhetoric of the Streets," (listed below), and assesses their impact on freedom of speech as well as communication theory. The author discusses key issues and cases where nonverbal expression such as flag desecration, sexual explicitness and economic boycotts are central to First Amendment discussions by the U.S. Supreme Court.

Haiman, Franklyn S. "The Rhetoric of the Streets: Some Legal and Ethical Considerations." *The Quarterly Journal of Speech* 53 (April, 1967): 99–114.
> In the midst of public demonstrations against America's involvement in the Vietnam War and within a period of national racial strife, the author critically examines the existing protest rhetoric by exploring key lines of criticism directed at the "street rhetoric." The legal and ethical challenges to new rhetoric raises, he reveals, new questions about First Amendment protection and other ethical matters.

Haiman, Franklyn S. "Speech Communication: A Radical Doctrine?" *Central States Speech Journal* 34 (Summer, 1983): 83–87.
> This is a published account of Haiman's keynote address at the 1983 Central States Speech Association Convention. He contends that speech communication as studied and taught is a doctrine that is radical and subversive and paradoxically, also a deeply conservative ideology. Support for his points comes from a thirty-five year career devoted to free speech concerns.

Haiman, Franklyn S. "Why Teach Freedom of Speech?" *Free Speech Yearbook* (1970): 1–4.
> This essay advances major points about how the profession of speech communication rests on the assumption that freedom of speech, as a political principle, is sufficiently understood and accepted in society to give substance and meaning to the activities of the profession. The oral communicator, the author maintains, needs to know the rights and responsibilities of free speech.

Haney, Roger D. "Obscenity and Pornography: Legal Arguments and Empirical Evidence." *Free Speech Yearbook* (1976): 46–59.
> In 1976 President Lyndon B. Johnson created a Commission on Obscenity and Pornography under a congressional mandate to examine existing obscenity laws. This essay reviews significant research on pornography in terms of key Supreme Court cases on obscenity in an effort to evaluate the recommendations of the Commission.

Haun, Martha Womack. "Immanuel Velikovsky: A Case Study in the Suppression of Scientific Ideas." *Free Speech Yearbook* (1979): 27–37.
> This essay argues that the scientific establishment functions as an institutional inhibitor of free expression of scientific ideas and has consciously

suppressed the paradigm of Immanuel Velikovsky. Velikovsky, trained as a physician and psychoanalyst, declared that ancient literature contained descriptions of global catastrophies, and this became the core of his paradigm.

Haun, Martha Womack. "Spinoza on Freedom of Thought and Speech." *Free Speech Yearbook* (1977): 47–53.

Benedict De Spinoza (1632–1677), author of *Tractatus Theologico Politicus*, stirred unrest among his readers. This essay examines the general philosophy of Spinoza with special emphasis on ideas related to individual freedom of expression and the relationship of that freedom to sovereignty of the state.

Hendrix, Jerry. "The Speech Communication Classroom and the First Amendment: Two Views." *Free Speech Yearbook* (1972): 85–91.

In this essay the author points to two fundamental obligations of communication educators: to maintain an open, objective forum for free expression of all points of view in speech classes and to evaluate students' speeches according to principles of communication without the use of any bias from the teacher's political orientation.

Herbeck, Dale. "The Regulation of Pornography in the New Media." *Free Speech Yearbook* (1984): 92–108.

This essay addresses the debate about regulating sexually explicit material in the news media, which includes video cassettes, videodiscs, cable and direct broadcast satellites. The author explores the extent of pornographic material in the new media, reviews existing forms of regulations, and argues that sexual material in the new media should be treated as it is in print media.

Hilper, Fred P. "The Influence of a Course in Ethics and Free Speech in Changing Student Attitudes." *Free Speech Yearbook* (1972): 66–75.

This essay stems from research on attitudes toward free speech, especially with regard to restricting rights guaranteed by the Constitution. Using a sample of undergraduate and graduate students, the author tests hypotheses with regard to students' approval of free speech and students changing their attitudes in favor of free speech after completing a course in ethics and freedom of speech.

Howell, William S. "Introduction: Freedom of Speech and Change in American Education." *Free Speech Yearbook* (1971): v–ix.

The essay points to the *Free Speech Yearbook* as an effective effort by the Speech Communication Association to counter forces that inhibit freedom of speech. Howell reviews recent trends and pressures involving free speech issues in education, and this is followed by Richard Gregg's detailed syllabus and bibliography for the study of issues in freedom of speech.

Hudson, David D. "The Effects of Censorship on the Valuation of Sexually Explicit Messages." *Free Speech Yearbook* (1980): 51–57.

The author argues that communication research has generally dealt with studying the effects that exposure to certain messages might have on individuals and often raises the question: "Does access to certain types of information have adverse effects on the audiences' behavior?" He examines an alternative question: "What might be the attitudinal effects of restricting the availability of a message an individual wishes to obtain."

Hunsinger, David. "Freedom and Responsibility in First Amendment Theory: Defamation Law and Media Credibility." *The Quarterly Journal of Speech* 65 (February, 1979): 25–35.
This essay deals with the conceptual relationship between freedom, responsibility and First Amendment theory. The author explores the conflict between charges of defamation and media reporting, power and credibility of mass media in terms of public trust or distrust, and reassessing defamation in First Amendment theory. He then argues for a private remedy against media abuses.

Jamison, David L. "Parliamentary Confidentiality and Free Speech: A Legal View." *Free Speech Yearbook* (1977): 35–45.
In this essay the author considers the privileges of confidentiality in a legislature and highlights the unique aspects of the right to free speech for members of a parliamentary body. He examines pertinent cases and questions about disclosing controlled information and the ultimate arbiter for determining the public's right to know.

Jellicorse, John Lee. "Some Historical Essentials of Teaching Freedom of Speech." *Free Speech Yearbook* (1972): 76–84.
This essay provides strong guidelines for teachers of freedom of speech. The author emphasizes the following major objectives: to understand and teach a philosophy of freedom of speech, to understand and teach laws about freedom of speech (what they are and what they could be), and to understand and teach the historical forces that condition freedom of speech.

Jensen, Richard J. "Denial of Freedom of Speech in Jock Yablonski's Campaign for the United Mine Workers Presidency." *Free Speech Yearbook* (1980): 21–31.
This essay turns to the UMWA as an organization in which significant reform is difficult to achieve. The author contends that the difficulty in bringing about change lies in the fact that the leader has absolute control over the organization. The essay details reasons why Jock Yablonski decided to challenge Tony Boyle and the restrictions on the challenger's freedom of speech in his efforts to gain the leadership.

Jensen, Richard J. "Freedom of Expression: The Mormons for ERA." *Free Speech Yearbook* (1982): 1–14.
A striking and highly publicized challenge to a religious issue of the ERA was mounted by Sonja Johnson through "Mormons for ERA." The author focuses on the rhetoric of this organization because of its use of public com-

munication to attack church leadership and maintains its members spoke for other women advocates who challenged the positions of their churches against women's rights.

Johannesen, Richard L. "The Crisis in Public Confidence in Public Communication." *Free Speech Yearbook* (1971): 43–49.
   This essay points to the need for a dialogic attitude to prevail in public communication transactions, for mutual confidence and trust are vital for complete communication. The author points to a mounting crisis in public confidence with regard to truthfulness in public communication, and he draws illustrations from statements made by a variety of public communicators.

Johnson, Mark. "The FCC: The Urge to Censor." *Free Speech Yearbook* (1978): 73–81.
   This essay explores the Federal Communication Commission, censorship in broadcasting and free speech issues. The special relationship between broadcasters and the First Amendment is explained by highlighting the attempts of the FCC to enforce section 1464, Title 18, of the U.S. Code as incorporated in the FCC Act of 1934. Specific cases are used to illustrate FCC efforts at censorship.

Kahn, Frank J. "From 'Fairness' to 'Access' and Back Again: Some Dimensions of Free Expression in Broadcasting." *Free Speech Yearbook* (1974): 1–10.
   The purpose of this essay is to consider the FCC's "Fairness Doctrine" against a backdrop of two decisions made by the U.S. Supreme Court: The *Red Lion* decision (1969), and *CBS v. DNC* (1973). With an eye toward First Amendment principles, the author reviews the rationale of the "Fairness Doctrine" and the U.S. Supreme Court's actions in both cases.

Kane, Peter E. "Public Figure Libel After *Sullivan: Goldwater v. Ginzberg*." *Free Speech Yearbook* (1983): 43–50.
   In the case of *The New York Times v. Sullivan* The U.S. Supreme Court stated that public figures with access to the media must prove more than factual error in order to successfully sue for libel. The first major case involving a public person was the suit of Senator Barry Goldwater against Ralph Ginzburg and *Fact* magazine. The author examines the basis of the Goldwater suit, the evidence and arguments used and the appeals court responses.

Kane, Peter E. "William H. Rehnquist: Ideologist on the Bench." *Free Speech Yearbook* (1975): 10–20.
   This essay evaluates Justice Rehnquist's position regarding freedom of speech issues and speculates about his future decision making with regard to freedom of expression. The analysis examines Justice Rehnquist's opinions on free speech matters, and his judicial behavior is reviewed to examine how his attitude may be evidenced in Court decisions.

Keyser, Lester V. "The Watergate Scandal and the Mass Media: The Early Phases." *Free Speech Yearbook* (1974): 54–63.

This essay examines the free speech implications in the troubled relations between President Richard Nixon and mass media professionals in regard to the Watergate scandal. The author contends that the press chronicled the phases of the Watergate drama in a highly professional manner and maintains the early phases constituted the most challenging period in the history of American journalism.

Kneupper, Charles W. "No On Proposition 6: The San Francisco Campaign." *Free Speech Yearbook* (1981): 36–41.

This essay is important not only to readers with free speech concerns but to those concerned with communication and the status of gays. Proposition 6 appeared on the November 1978 California ballot, and aimed at teachers, it was to require active discrimination against gays. The author analyzed campaign rhetoric, press coverage, political outcome and implications.

Le Duc, Don R. "'Free Speech' Decisions and the Legal Process: The Judicial Opinion in Context." *The Quarterly Journal of Speech* 62 (October, 1976): 279-87.

This essay analyzes the legal process in terms of communication by way of major free speech cases. The author summarizes the legal process and turns specifically to three famous cases: the *Schenck* Case (clear and present danger), *Memoirs of a Woman of Pleasure* (without redeeming social value), and the *Red Lion* case (the public's right to know). The author offers a legal analysis of the cases and an analysis of law as a communication process.

Leeper, Roy V. "Rawls's *A Theory of Justice* and Freedom of Expression." *Free Speech Yearbook* (1976): 83–96.

The author points to a lack of justification universally accepted as a philosophical underpinning for the First Amendment freedom of expression. After citing scholars who have contributed to philosophical bases for free expression, the author focuses on John Rawls' *A Theory of Justice* (1971) by analyzing Rawls' treatment of liberty and how his system could have modified several major free speech cases.

Lindmark, Joyce. "The Flag as a Nonverbal Symbol." *Free Speech Yearbook* (1971): 64–68.

Lindmark focuses on the contradiction between the traditional patriotic meaning for the U.S. flag and evidence that the flag has been disregarded in some parts of the collective mind of America. Flag desecration was witnessed during the Vietnam era and raised public concern over apparent disrespect of, and danger for, America. The author discusses both flag supporters and detractors.

Linsley, William. "The Supreme Court and the First Amendment." *Free Speech Yearbook*.

In every volume from 1972–84, the author reviews actions by the U.S. Supreme Court on cases involving the First Amendment and free speech issues.

Litterst, Judith H. "Civil Disobedience and the First Amendment Toward a Balance." *Free Speech Yearbook* (1973): 1–12.
> This essay identifies four key questions concerned with civil disobedience, and after examining definitions of civil disobedience, Litterst discusses objections raised against the use of civil disobedience. Finally, the author presents justification for its limited use as a legitimate political protest protected by the First Amendment.

Lower, Frank J. "Julian Bond: A Case Study of a Legislator's Freedom of Speech." *Free Speech Yearbook* (1974): 35–44.
> This essay focuses on Julian Bond, perhaps one of the most significant contemporary black spokespersons. Specifically the author deals with the infringement on Bond's freedom of speech, his being denied a seat in the Georgia Legislature, the U.S. Supreme Court decision in *Bond v. Floyd* (1966) and the status of Bond's First Amendment rights.

Makau, Josina M. "Judicial Invention in First Amendment Governmental Regulation Cases." *Free Speech Yearbook* (1983): 1–19.
> Looking at judicial invention in First Amendment cases, the author shows that appropriate responsiveness to the rhetorical constraints imposed on judicial invention in First Amendment cases is vital to free speech. She also shows that the constraints are applicable to all judicial invention and specifically to judicial invention in First Amendment governmental cases and that in some First Amendment cases it falls short of rhetorical demands.

Makau, Josina M., and J.P. Williams. "Perspectives on Pornography and Free Speech." *Free Speech Yearbook* (1984): 109–22.
> This essay reviews the complex area of First Amendment law as it relates to the debate over the censorship of pornography; the liberal versus conservative dichotomy; differences between erotica and pornography (and its implications) and the claim that increased levels of violence in obscene materials create dangers to human rights. The authors call for continued research on free speech and pornography.

Markham, David. "Federal Censorship of National Open Forum Radio." *Free Speech Yearbook* (1971): 36–49.
> Markham discusses the principle of free speech as it applies to the mass media. The author reports a conflict of attitudes concerning broadcasting between important legislative and federal administrative figures. He turns to "open forum radio" supported by donations from listeners and efforts of a U.S. Senate subcommittee to censor a Pacifica Foundation station for presenting an obscene poem on the air.

Martin, Robert F. "Freedom of Expression in Southern Asia I: Political Realities and Cultural Expectations: Freedom of Speech in Thailand. *Free Speech Yearbook* (1981): 1–8. (For essay II, see Merriam).
> This essay provides a historical perspective on the development of freedom of expression in Thailand. The author contends Americans and Thais share

a common constitutional provision for freedom of speech, but government restrictions in Thailand have been considerable. The struggle of reformists to ensure freedom of speech in a country with a history of sovereignty and a rule of absolute power is clearly outlined.

McCarthy, Michael J., and Peter E. Kane. "Freedom of Expression in Shopping Centers." *Communication Quarterly* 22 (Summer, 1974): 45–48.
The purpose of this essay is to review the legal history of the general controversy over the use of privately owned shopping centers for First Amendment purposes. The study summarizes the pertinent court decisions and points to a reversal of a liberal trend, in which, the author claims, legally established and settled First Amendment rights were abrogated.

McGaffey, Ruth. "Anti-Pornography Campaigns: A Case Study." *Free Speech Yearbook* (1982): 27–39.
Since the U.S. Supreme Court in 1973 gave individual communities freedom to use local standards in regulating the sale of sexually explicit materials, the author notes there has been a shift in the strategy of anti-pornography groups to crusade for local anti-porn ordinances. Focusing on free speech conflict and persuasive communication, this essay examines an anti-pornography campaign in LaCrosse, Wisconsin.

McGaffey, Ruth. "Free Speech in Marquette Park: A Realistic Look at the Marketplace of Ideas." *Free Speech Yearbook* (1978): 1–16.
The issue of whether or not a speaker must be allowed to speak, even if police or military forces must be called upon for protection, is central in this essay. The author analyzes a rhetorical situation in Milwaukee which focused on the appearance of Nazi spokesman Frank Collins of the National Socialist Party of America.

McGaffey, Ruth, "Group Libel Revisited." *The Quarterly Journal of Speech* 65 (April, 1979): 157–70.
This study, grounded in events spawned by Nazi groups in Milwaukee, Wisconsin, poses a question of national scope: "Is group libel legislation a viable answer to the activities of hate groups?" The author explores the history of group libel laws and their constitutional validity, and analyzes arguments for and against such legislation.

McGaffey, Ruth. "Judicial Decision-Making: A Study in Dissonance." *Free Speech Yearbook* (1979): 16–26.
With the First Amendment in mind, this essay provides a historical analysis of decision making and shows that with an application of dissonance theory to the process of judicial decision making, additional insight can be gained. The author examines factors in individual, judicial decision making and persuasion in the judicial process. Consistency theory is applied to explain judicial behavior.

McGaffey, Ruth. "Local Option on the First Amendment." *Free Speech Yearbook* (1974): 11–17.
The purpose of this essay is to examine the idea of local option versus na-

tional standards with regard to obscenity. The author attempts to determine the meaning of "community standards" and the effects such standards may have on freedom of speech.

Medhurst, Martin J. "The First Amendment v. Human Rights: A Case Study in Community Sentiment and Argument from Definition." *Western Journal of Speech Communication* 46 (Winter, 1982): 1–19.
This essay, a case study, analyzes the rhetorical strategy and arguments of a counter campaign against gay rights and how the rhetoric of conservation reaction was successful in defeating gay-rights proposals. The essay is also offered as a corrective to pronouncements about the generic characteristics of conservative resistance rhetoric.

Meeske, Milan D. "Editorial Advertising: A New Form of Free Speech." *Free Speech Yearbook* (1973): 51–65.
This essay examines the paid political advertisement. The author considers cases to show how the courts have responded to the question: "Is advertising protected by the First Amendment?" He reviews restrictions on an individual's ability to speak directly to an audience because of the U.S. Supreme Court's decision to recognize the right of a broadcaster to determine who can speak through advertising.

Meeske, Mike. "Minority Ownership of Broadcast Stations: The Diversification Policy." *Free Speech Yearbook* (1977): 81–86.
Discrimination in the broadcasting industry frames the concern of this essay, particularly with regard to the issue of the licensing of a broadcast station to a minority group which aims to use the outlet to espouse its views. The author traces the development of the minority issue and considers the future implications of the rulings in two major decisions: *TV9, Inc. v. FCC* and *Garrett v. FCC*.

Merriam, Allen H. "Freedom of Expression in Southern Asia, II: The Contribution of Jayaprakash Narayan in Preserving Free Expression in India." *Free Speech Yearbook* (1981): 9–15.
This essay interprets the influence of Jayaprakash Narayan on the struggle for free expression in modern India. The author provides historical background for Narayan's political activity, a discussion of his political movement in the mid 1970s and his imprisonment by Indira Gandhi for his public plea for civil disobedience. He analyzes statements by Narayan and explains the moral imperatives of both Gandhi and Narayan.

Minnick, Wayne C. "Teaching Free and Responsible Speech: A Philosophical View." *Free Speech Yearbook* (1972): 1–19.
This essay examines the philosophical implications of the proposition that communication educators have a right and an obligation to inculcate favorable attitudes toward freedom of speech. The author rejects a Skinnerian view of training students about free speech to serve predetermined goals and offers an argument to promote self-actualization through free expression, a view guided by the work of Abraham Maslow and Carl Rogers.

Muchnik, Melvyn M. "Responsibility and Survival: Free Expression and Political Broadcasting on Public Radio and Television Stations." *Free Speech Yearbook* (1973): 38–50.
> This essay describes the purpose of public broadcasting with regard to political coverage, the history and regulations which support and impinge on this purpose and the "assault on public broadcasting" resulting from its efforts to report on controversy in political campaigns. The author focuses on a state's attempt to ban programs of a political nature and problems of funding public broadcasting.

Murray, Michael D. "J. B. Stoner and Free Speech: How Free is 'Free?'" *Western Journal of Speech Communication* 38 (Winter, 1974): 18–24.
> In 1972 J. B. Stoner, aspiring to the U.S. Senate as a representative of Georgia, broadcast a series of paid racist advertisements over radio and television stations in Georgia and Tennessee. This essay examines public response to Stoner's remarks and the FCC decision concerning those statements. The author indicates that the First Amendment makes no distinction between various communication media.

Murray, Michael D. "To Hire a Hall: An Argument in Indianapolis." *Central States Speech Journal* 26 (Spring, 1975): 12–20.
> This essay focuses on the free speech controversy over the cancellation of an initial meeting of professionals to form a state chapter of the ACLU. The meeting was to be held in the East Room of the Indiana War Memorial in 1953. The study responds to key questions about the documentary telecast, "An Argument in Indianapolis," on Edward R. Murrow's television news program, "See It Now."

Orr, Jack C. "Truth, Knowledge, and a Democratic Respect for Diversity." *Free Speech Yearbook* (1980): 16–20.
> This essay attempts to uncover an epistemological base which best describes a democratic respect for diversity and free speech on a universal scale. The author draws on current trends in communication theory and aims to serve both analytic and practical purposes. Four major propositions about respect for diversity, truth and free expression are presented.

Osborn, Wilbur J., and William I. Gorden. "A Freedom of Speech Survey of Student Opinion in a Basic Speech Course." *Free Speech Yearbook* (1970): 52–62.
> Osborn and Gorden examine one of four major objectives of a basic course: to develop an understanding of the nature and role of speech communication in a free society. The authors present the results of a survey of 741 students about freedom of speech. The results of the research help support the free speech objective for the basic course in speech communication.

Parker, Richard A. "Between Rhetoric and Disloyalty: Free Speech Standards for the Sunshine Soldier." *Free Speech Yearbook* (1975): 1–9.
> This essay focuses on the military court's view of a proper standard for governing political expression, a perspective which encompasses a wide

spectrum of issues. The author's perspective turns to the men conscripted or compelled to enlist in military service during the Vietnam War years and turns to the case of Roger Priest, a Navy seaman who publicized his opposition to America's war policy.

Parkerson, James W., and Waldo Braden, George Brian, Donald Graham, Monroe Lippman, and Ray Murphy. "What Can Be Done By Teachers of Speech to Preserve Freedom of Speech: A Symposium." *Southern Speech Journal* 19 (March, 1951): 333–340.
    This symposium includes brief and substantive statements by each member in response to key questions pertaining to threats against freedom of speech. The symposium raises the primary question: "What can teachers of speech do to preserve freedom of speech?" Each participant responds to this question.

Patterson, J. W. "ACLU Limitation on Free Speech: The Case of Elizabeth Flynn." *Free Speech Yearbook* (1972): 31–39.
    The author argues that the American Civil Liberties Union denied Elizabeth Gurley Flynn many of the same procedural and substantive safeguards it supports for those it defends in court. Flynn, an ACLU charter member, was ousted from the Board of Directors in 1940 because of her membership in the American Communist Party and because of her criticism of the ACLU Board.

Phifer, Greg. "Westmoreland in Tallahassee." *Free Speech Yearbook* (1978): 162–66.
    On February 16, 1978, U.S. Army General William Westmoreland was hooted from the platform on the campus of Florida State University where he was about to speak on ratification of U.S. Panama Canal Treaties. His decision not to speak was the result of angry protests over his role in the Vietnam War. The author analyzes the free speech issues in discussing reactions from the campus, the ROTC Commanding Officer and the official university action.

Phifer, Greg. "H-Bomb 'Secrets' and the *Progressive*." *Free Speech Yearbook* (1980): 99–114.
    This essay is concerned with the issue of whether "prior restraint" is justified in the case of *Progressive* magazine's 1979 publication of Howard Morland's article "The H-Bomb Secret: How We Got It—Why We're Telling It." The author examines federal laws about secret restricted data, the basic issues in a case between the *Progressive* and the government, First Amendment implications and the eventual publication of the article.

Phillips, Gerald M. "Freedom of Speech and Minority Rule in the Talmud." *The Quarterly Journal of Speech* 47 (February, 1961): 36–40.
    In this essay the author gives attention to two specific rhetorical matters in the Talmud: freedom of speech and majority rule. He notes that in Talmudic history the processes of discussion and debate in search of *halachah* are evident along with a doctrine of free speech and disputation. The essay

underscores the right of a person to speak and act freely as long as God's existence was not denied or the rights of others jeopardized.

Pierce, W. Barnett. "On Fooling the People, Whether Some, Most or All of the Time: An Examination of the People's Right to Know." *Free Speech Yearbook* (1970): 69–81.
This essay presents reasons for and against government control of information. The author acknowledges free speech guarantees framed by the writers of the First Amendment and points out that the counterpart of freedom of speech is the people's right of access to information. The author examines government control of information, cases against and for government control, and also provides analysis.

Pollitt, Daniel. "Haircuts and School Expulsions." *Free Speech Yearbook* (1970): 82–94.
The length of male hair styles was highly controversial in schools around the nation. School officials and other concerned citizens sought to expel male students from school when they violated the implied or explicit dress code. This essay points out how the courts ruled in favor of student expressions with dress and hair styles and presents the free speech implications surrounding this issue.

Ragsdale, J. Donald. "*Last Tango in Paris, Et. Al. v. The Supreme Court:* The Current State of Obscenity Law." *The Quarterly Journal of Speech* 61 (October, 1975): 279–89.
This essay analyzes the state of obscenity law as shaped by the U.S. Supreme Court's decision and dissents on June 21, 1973, and June 24, 1974, and by litigation which principally involved the controversial film, *Last Tango in Paris*, starring Marlon Brando. The author discusses obscenity, freedom of speech, the development of an obscenity criteria and the application of the obscenity criteria in litigation.

Rice, George P. Jr. "Freedom of Speech and the 'New-Left.'" *Central States Speech Journal* 21 (Fall, 1970): 139–45.
This essay analyzes the relation of free legal speech to the "New Left" from six points of view: ancestral opinions have contemporary influence; major constitutional provisions which protect free speech; the major causes of disorders existing at the time the essay was written; a definition of the "New Left," the weapons used by its adherents; and the counterblows of society.

Rice, George P. "The Meets and Bounds of Speech and Law." *Central States Speech Journal* 13 (Autumn, 1961): 8–10.
This essay examines the basic relation of speech and law with regard to freedom of speech and assembly and the right to remain silent. By "meets and bounds," the author means "the points where various practical aspects of public address, including copyright, slander, constitutional limitations, and tort liability come into direct contact with civil and criminal rules of law with consequences to the speakers, the audiences, and the public."

Rice, George P. Jr. "The Right To Be Silent." *The Quarterly Journal of Speech* 47 (December, 1961): 349–54.
> Rice contends that the status of the legal right to be silent may occasionally be equal in importance to the right to free legal speech. The position taken in the essay is that free speech is one side of a fundamental human right, and the right to silence is the other side. The author is concerned with the fact that minimal litigation has not clarified the right to silence as much as speech and assembly.

Rice, George P. Jr. "What Do Students Care About Freedom of Speech?" *Communication Quarterly* 3 (November, 1955): 19–21.
> This research report provides evidence about what some college students think of certain aspects of freedom of speech in America. The researcher obtained data from 1000 students in two states: Indiana and New York. He makes several insightful claims based upon his findings and urges communication educators to stress free speech and assembly in their classes.

Rodgers, Raymond S. "Absolutism and Natural Law Argument: William O. Douglas on Freedom of Expression." *Southern Speech Communication Journal* 48 (Fall, 1982): 22–37.
> This essay focuses on the term "absolutism" in the context of the First Amendment interpretations by U.S. Supreme Court Justice William O. Douglas. The study reveals that Douglas' positions did not advocate absolute freedom to communicate and also suggests that jurisprudence should not be a means of labeling a justice, but a schema for classifying arguments.

Rodgers, Raymond S. "Movement on the Periphery: Foreign Travel as a First Amendment Right." *Free Speech Yearbook* (1982): 50–69.
> This study examines the history of U.S. Supreme Court litigation concerning the right to foreign travel. The author explains the qualified nature of the right in terms of First Amendment cases preceding a dubious ruling in *Haig v. Agee*, where the Court ruled that the Secretary of State may revoke the passport of a person whose activities abroad "are causing or are likely to cause serious damage to the national security or foreign policy of the United States."

Rodgers, Raymond S. "The Jurisprudence of Censorship: Philosophic Bases of Anti-Pornography Arguments. *Free Speech Yearbook* (1978): 82–91.
> This essay examines principles that have warranted laws to enforce institutionalized censorship: the harm principle, the principle of legal paternalism, the principle of legal moralism and the offense principle. The author indicates each has been used to justify the legal censorship of pornography and determine to what extent they rely on the tenets or natural-law theory in either its Thomistic or modern formulations.

Rodgers, Raymond S. "The Rhetoric of Legal Realism: William O. Douglas on the First Amendment." *Free Speech Yearbook* (1981): 23–35.
> Rodgers reports a study which led to the conclusion that the First Amend-

ment opinions of Justice Douglas provide evidence for the possible existence of a rhetorical genre grounded in the jurisprudence of "legal realism." The author reviews the philosophy of legal realism and defines it as rhetorical genre. He examines actual opinions using the definition as a theoretical guide.

Roncelli, Janet M. "Book Censorship: A Strategy of Order for the Fireman in *Fahrenheit 451* and Moral Majority, Inc." *Free Speech Yearbook* (1983): 20–32.
 This essay provides a comparative analysis of the firemen in *Fahrenheit 451* and the Moral Majority. The analysis is limited to the strategy of book censorship as a method for maintaining and achieving order in society. The author uses a dramatistic method to analyze the strategy of book censorship and suggests implications for free speech.

Rosenthal, Elden. "Symbolic Speech: A Constitutional Orphan." *Free Speech Yearbook* (1971): 69–79.
 The author contends that constitutional protection is not guaranteed for nonverbal communicative conduct (symbolic speech). He cites convictions over flag desecration and printed objectionable words as examples of the inconsistent decisions in terms of symbolic expression and the First Amendment. Rosenthal maintains that conduct that is primarily communicative should receive an equal degree of First Amendment protection.

Rossiter, Charles M. Jr., and Ruth McGaffey. "Freedom of Speech and the 'New Left': A Response." *Central States Speech Journal* 22 (Spring, 1971): 5–10.
 This is a study designed to determine whether teaching techniques which demand varying amounts of involvement in class activities by students would result in different amounts of attitude change about free speech issues. The researcher hypothesized that lessons which demand involvement would result in a greater attitude change than would lessons taught in the lecture/discussion fashion. The results of the research support the hypothesis.

Rossiter, Charles M. Jr., and Ruth McGaffey. "Freedom of Speech and the 'New Left': A Response." *Central States Speech Journal* 22 (Spring, 1971): 5–10.
 This essay takes exception to an analysis of freedom of speech and the 'New Left' which appeared in volume 21 of the *Central States Speech Journal*. The authors present alternative views of the problem treated by George P. Rice. They contend that Rice did not accomplish what he set out to do, and they detail their objections.

Ryan, Halford P. "Free Speech in Ancient Athens." *Free Speech Yearbook* (1972): 20–30.
 Freedom of speech in Classical Greece was constantly changing. The purpose of this essay is to determine how free speech evolved as Greek history progressed in Athenian times. The essay refers first to Homer's *Iliad* and, by reviewing the democratic evolution of the Athenian constitution

under Solon, Cleisthenes, and Pericles, shows to what extent people in Athens increasingly enjoyed free speech.

Sanders, Wayne C. "Common Law Tort and Contract Erosion of the At Will Rule: New Paths Toward Freedom of Speech in the Private Sector." *Free Speech Yearbook* (1984): 1–12.
   This essay addresses both the general topic of freedom of speech in the contemporary organizational setting and the erosion of the "at will rule" by means of tort of wrongful discharge actions or breach of contract actions. The author shows that an increasing minority of states are using this means to protect employees from employer retaliation against free speech.

Sanders, Wayne C. "The First Amendment and the Government Workplace: Has the Constitution Fallen Down on the Job?" *Western Journal of Speech Communication* 47 (Summer, 1983): 253–76.
   This essay examines the changes in First Amendment protection afforded public employee speech after the landmark 1968 U.S. Supreme Court decision in *Pickering v. Board of Education* and the assumptions about organizational communication which underlie the charges. The author finds that free speech in public organizations is unnecessarily more limited than free speech in society at large.

Samosky, Jack A., and John M. Suter. "The Mimic-War at Miami: A Case Study of 19th Century Speaker Bans." *Free Speech Yearbook* (1982): 70–77.
   This study examines a case on the issue of whether speakers are to be banned from campus appearances. The authors first examine the history of the issue with regard to various literary societies and then focus specifically on the Miami societies in Ohio. They examine the struggle with an administrative ruling that the names of proposed speakers be submitted to the university faculty for approval.

Scanlon, Ross. "Freedom, Knowledge, and Public Address." *The Quarterly Journal of Speech* 35 (October, 1949): 310–15.
   Scanlon argues for freedom of speech as a primary concern for teachers of speech communication. Written in the wake of the threat of Nazi tyranny and in the face of Communist restrictions on freedom in Communist ruled nations, the author examines the close link in American democracy between freedom of speech and freedom of thought as essential to conditions for human progress and public satisfaction.

Schliessman, Mike. "Free Speech and the Rights of Congress: Robert M. LaFollette and the Argument From Principle." *Free Speech Yearbook* (1978): 38–44.
   Schliessman claims that the worst infringement by the federal government on personal freedom came in the period of the U.S. involvement in World War I. He contends that in waging war under Presidential powers, Woodrow Wilson attempted to curtail dissenting speech while Wisconsin's Senator Robert M. LaFollette spoke fervently in opposition in his address on "Free Speech and the Right of Congress to Declare the Objects of War."

Schuetz, Janice. "Alexander Solzhenitsyn's Approach to the Philosophy and Functions of Free Expression." *Free Speech Yearbook* (1981): 69–77.
   This essay examines Solzhenitsyn's approach to free expression by reviewing the history of free expression in the Soviet Union and presenting Solzhenitsyn's position as it is expressed in his major works. The author analyzes the dissident's letter to the Soviet Congress, *Cancer Ward*, the Nobel Prize Speech, a collection of essays from *Samizdat* and his Harvard commencement address.

Schuetz, Janice E. "Human Rights in El Salvador: A Case Study of the Advocacy of Archbishop Oscar Romero." *Free Speech Yearbook* (1982): 40–41.
   Archbishop Romero, a well known advocate of human rights, was assassinated while saying a funeral mass in 1980. This study focuses on free expression in El Salvador, the national security system and evangelism in response to the curtailment of civil liberties. The author provides an examination of the themes of free expression in four sermons of Archbishop Romero.

Sharp, Harry. "Freedom of Speech and the Federal Election Campaign Act: The Problems of Reform Legislation." *Free Speech Yearbook* (1984): 135–55.
   This essay advances the argument that the Federal Election Campaign Act is reform legislation that is well intended but which does more harm than good. The study examines the Act as passed and amended in response to judicial review, as well as the First Amendment issues of public disclosure, campaign contributions and expenditures, independent expenditures and FECA administration.

Shmuker, Anita. "Long-Hairs, Hard Hats, Hard Heads, and Fuzzy Thinking." *Free Speech Yearbook* (1970): 63–68.
   Shmuker states that verbal discourse in public rhetoric is being attended to less seriously than nonverbal display. The author contends that communication educators need to help promote a social environment characterized by free speech. She warns that "when symbolic speech seems to supplant verbal discourse out of a loss of faith in the power of words to heal and to persuade, our society is in danger."

Silvers, Dean. "Access Rights to the Mass Media: The Hidden Channels." *Free Speech Yearbook* (1980): 40–50.
   While the author contends that the free speech clause of the First Amendment has been recently strengthened, the individual's right to free expression, he suggests, has been weakened. The essay takes a step toward creating a strengthened right to free speech through an individual's right of access to the media at the state and local levels.

Slaughter, H.K. "How Free Is Labor's Speech?" *Today's Speech* 7 (February, 1959): 8–10.
   The author takes the reader inside a steel mill to illustrate the point that the grievance committeeman in industry is a key factor in the degree of free speech a worker can have. The essay underscores the importance of

freedom of expression within the industrial environment and how an organizational leader can provide a key constraint to freedom of speech.

Smith, Stephen A. "The Uncivil Servants: Public Employees and Political Expression." *Free Speech Yearbook* (1983): 51–61.
 This essay reviews the governmental philosophy embodied in the Hatch Act, as amended by Congress and interpreted by the U.S. Civil Service Commission and the U.S. Supreme Court. The author examines the internal consistency of the philosophy as it is applied to different classes of executive branch employees and offers suggestions to promote free expression and maintain safeguards.

Suffet, Stephen L. "The Resistance and the Court: the Punitive Draft Cases." *Free Speech Yearbook* (1971): 50–63.
 This essay focuses on the problem during the Vietnam War era of "noncooperators (distinct from "conscientious objectors). Men registered for the military draft who ended compliance by destroying their draft cards and refusing to obey the Selective Service. The author suggests that noncooperation, supported by ACLU arguments for free speech, was not fully successful. He examines pertinent court cases.

Tedford, Thomas L. "Unprovable Assumptions? The Reasons and Empirical Evidence of Twelve Who Favor Censorship." *Free Speech Yearbook* (1978): 156–60.
 This study was prompted by statements in favor of censorship made by a spokesman for Citizens for Decency Under Law and U.S. Supreme Court Justice Warren Burger. The author chose the work of twelve contemporary advocates of censorship to determine reasons for censorship, empirical evidence to support the reasons, definitions of "obscenity" and "pornography" and views on whether or not government censorship should be continued.

Towers, Wayne M. "Empirical Research and Some Major Supreme Court Decisions on Free Press/Fair Trial Conflicts." *Free Speech Yearbook* (1978): 60–67.
 The focus of this study is the free press/fair trial controversy, where a free press overlaps with difficulties of judicial decision making. The analysis is centered around four major U.S. Supreme Court decisions which preceded the case of *Nebraska Press Association et. al. v. Stuart*.

Towne, Ralph L., and Frederick J. Specken. "Robert Green Ingersoll: A Case Study of Free Speech." *Today's Speech* 10 (November, 1962): 10–12.
 This essay calls to attention the nineteenth century rhetoric of Robert G. Ingersoll as a key to understanding the meaning of basic freedoms, particularly freedom of speech. Ingersoll, known as "The Great Agnostic," was an extremely popular lecturer, and the authors point out how his speaking is a pertinent guide for communication in contemporary times.

Tucker Amelia Gay. "*Arnett v. Kennedy:* Restrictions on Public Employee's Freedom to Criticize." *Free Speech Yearbook* (1976): 31–36.

This essay analyzes the U.S. Supreme Court decision on *Arnett v. Kennedy*, which involved a public employee's right to criticize his or her employer, a decision released April 16, 1974. The decision did not favor Kennedy's position over statements made as a public employee, and the author speculates on this decision in relation to the conservative nature of President Nixon's appointees—Justices Burger, Rehnquist, Blackmun, and Powell.

Ulrich, Walter. "The Creation of a Legacy: Brandeis' Concurring Opinion in *Whitney v. California*." *Southern Speech Communication Journal* 50 (Winter, 1985): 143–55.

This essay examines the strategy used by U.S. Supreme Court Justice Louis Brandeis in his concurring opinion in *Whitney*. The author points to the neglect by rhetorical critics to study legal decisions and analyzes the Brandeis opinion. The author, with a special eye to freedom of speech, considers the clear and present danger concept, the case, and discusses Brandeis' rhetorical strategy.

Veenstra, Charles. "The House Un-American Activities Committee's Restriction of Free Speech." *Communication Quarterly* 22 (Winter, 1974): 15–22.

This essay discusses several ways in which free speech was restricted by the Un-American Activities Committee of the U.S. House of Representatives. The failure of the courts to protect these rights relative to the procedures of this Committee is also described. The author shows how the individual's First Amendment rights were not adequately protected when they appeared before HUAC.

Wiethoff, William E. "Milton's Viable Attack on Prior Restraint in the *Areopagitica*." *Free Speech Yearbook* (1984): 42–50.

This essay examines the viability of an attack on censorship by John Milton in relationship to contemporary concerns. The author shows Milton's *Areopagitica* as a summary of arguments against prior restraint and its pertinence for First Amendment cases. He suggests the *Areopagitica* awaits translation into contemporary language and legal tests.

Windt, Theodore O. "Freedom of Speech, Commitments, and Teaching Public Speaking." *Free Speech Yearbook* (1972): 88–91.

This essay is a response to arguments by Jerry Hendrix about the students' right to speak. The author bases his arguments on two premises: the traditional image of a professor of speech communication as an objective evaluator is neither desirable nor real; and, a professor has the right and responsibility to limit the range of topics for student speeches.

Yoder, Jess. "Contributions of Sixteenth-Century Anabaptist Heretics to First Amendment Freedoms." *Free Speech Yearbook* (1977): 25–34.

This study focuses on the impact of the Anabaptists who demanded religious freedom in the sixteenth century. The author points to the unique relationship of freedom of expression with freedom of religion under the First Amendment and shows the influence of the Anabaptists on freedom of speech in Europe. He maintains their views on freedom of speech and religion are written into the First Amendment.

Essays on Communication Ethics from the National and Regional Speech Communication Journals

DAVID L. JAMISON

Aly, Bower. "Speech in the Service of Tyranny and Freedom." *The Speech Teacher* 3 (March, 1954): 81–88.
  Reprints Professor Aly's opening address to the 1953 S.C.A. annual meeting. Speaking at the height of McCarthyist-fed fear, Aly forthrightly criticizes pending Justice Department efforts to limit the protections of the First Amendment. He challenges speech teachers to defend freedom by being alert to the techniques of tyranny.

Andersen, Kenneth E. "Communication Ethics: The Non-Participant's Role." *The Southern Speech Communication Journal* 49 (Spring, 1984): 219–28.
  Traditional perspectives put responsibility for ethical quality in communication on the sender. Andersen argues that receivers who may act on the message have equal ethical responsibility. Further, since communication affects all, even those not directly involved in the communication act have significant ethical responsibility.

Bormann, Ernest G. "Ethics of Ghostwritten Speeches." *Quarterly Journal of Speech* 47 (October, 1961): 262–67.
  Because the ghostwriting of speeches involves deception, it raises ethical problems. Bormann argues that we must impose on our public figures and political leaders the same ethical standards we impose on our students and ourselves: to assure that the ideas and the "self" which speakers present to audiences are truly their own.

Brigance, William N. "Demagogues, 'Good' People, and Teachers of Speech." *The Speech Teacher* 1 (September, 1952): 157–62.
  This essay maintains that ethical speech training is essential in a free society and aims at protecting the welfare of that society by imparting significant information to listeners able to think for themselves. The responsible speaker utters the truth, is intellectually honest, doesn't mislead, and lifts the tone of public discussion.

Brown, Frank E. "To What Extent Candor." *Quarterly Journal of Public Speaking* 1 (April, 1915): 93–95.
  This article is a reply to a call for complete candor in discourse by Profes-

sor Charles Henry Woolbert. Brown argues in reply that candor is not always easy to define, and further, that if a rule of candor were to be rigorously applied, much that is useful in speech would disappear.

Brummett, Barry. "A Defense of Ethical Relativism as Rhetorically Grounded." *The Western Journal of Speech Communication* 45 (Fall, 1981): 286–98.
   Brummett argues that ethical values arise from, and are legitimated by, cultures. Social groups and communities generate values, and rhetoric is the process within culture which does the generating. Values are grounded in argument: we have values not merely because we live in a culture, but because we are persuaded in a culture.

Buchanan, Paul S. "Logic or Bunkum in Persuasion." *Quarterly Journal of Speech Education* 11 (April, 1925): 157–62.
   Buchanan maintains that it is both unethical and ineffective to appeal strictly to emotion, an audience's line of least resistance. Teachers must instruct students not to become "masters of a knack of words," but forcefully to put the truth before an audience and be able to gain their decision by force of reason.

Burgess, Parke G. "The Rhetoric of Moral Conflict: Two Critical Dimensions." *Quarterly Journal of Speech* 56 (April, 1970): 120–30.
   In eras of rapid cultural change, revolution is fundamentally moral. Rhetoricians need a cultural perspective that takes account of a speaker's resorting to moral motives. For this reason, critics must explicitly link strategic with moral dimensions in discourse to reveal the nature, choice and effects of rhetorical strategies.

Capel, Robert B. "Speech in the Atomic Age," *The Southern Speech Journal* 12 (September, 1946): 1–4.
   Capel reminds speech teachers that they fail in their responsibility if they concentrate too much on speech technique and not enough on the aim of "developing character in our students."

Chesebro, James W. "A Construct for Assessing Ethics in Communication." *Central States Speech Journal* 20 (Summer, 1969): 104–14.
   Kenneth Burke's dramatism provides the critic with a complete model for assessing a speaker's ethical behavior. The pentad is used in this article as a classificatory construct for communication behaviors. Chesebro then points out how Burke's ratios serve as a tool for assessing situational factors in developing a process-based understanding of rhetoric and ethics.

Courtney, L. W. "Speech in Community Life." *The Southern Speech Journal* 15 (March, 1950): 219–21.
   Since democracy depends on individual worth, and because people are influenced by speech, the worth of speech requires consideration. Efforts at discourse must reflect a sense of fairness, honesty and truth. Promoting effective speech may help direct human behavior into desirable channels and make "language criminality" more easily recognizable.

Crable, Richard E. "Ethical Codes, Accountability, and Argumentation." *Quarterly Journal of Speech* 64 (February, 1978): 23–32.
  Crable connects political accountability with general ethics. Accountability for any action results from ethical codes which govern our view of the "rightness" of action. Our emphasis in communication studies should not be on developing ethical codes, but on how such codes can be used argumentatively in the context of ethical change.

Cripe, Nicholas M. "Debating Both Sides in Tournaments is Ethical." *The Speech Teacher* 6 (September, 1957): 209–212.
  In a reply to Richard Murphy's article (*q.v.*), Cripe argues that Murphy has applied the wrong standards of ethics, since tournament debate is a different form of public address than other debate. If a debater presents the best possible arguments for the side represented, that is ethical debating.

Cushman, Donald P., and Gerard A. Hauser. "Weaver's Rhetorical Theory: Axiology and the Adjustment of Belief, Invention, and Judgment." *Quarterly Journal of Speech* 59 (October, 1973): 319–29.
  Richard Weaver's rhetorical theory, which separates the dialectical and rhetorical processes of invention and judgment, allows rhetors to transcend cultural pluralism in constructing their appeals. Ethical values are significant in this process, since there is always a better and a worse choice. Those who can discriminate, choose the better.

Day, Dennis G. "The Ethics of Democratic Debate." *Central States Speech Journal* 17 (February, 1966): 5–14.
  The relationship between democracy and debate establishes an ethic for debate. Since the highest obligation of debate is the fullest exposition of arguments, educational practices should encourage this ability, much as switch-sides debating does. This ethic of debate may become a starting point for a statement of the ethics of public address.

Diggs, B. J. "Persuasion and Ethics." *Quarterly Journal of Speech* 50 (December, 1964): 359–73.
  Diggs argues that ethical persuasion is a sharing of reason that contributes to universal knowledge and well-being. Persuaders must acknowledge that the persuasive act is part of society's logical and moral training. Persuaders not only must have the right to persuade, but further, are obliged to do so in a morally correct way.

Dobkin, Milton. "The Forensic Director and Citizenship." *Western Speech* 22 (Fall, 1958): 203–6.
  Introducing a symposium on the educational value of forensic activity, the author argues that it is unwise and dangerous to ignore a forensic director's informal, non-academic role in citizenship training. Students observe what the coach says is right, and teaching by example is often the most effective way.

Duffy, Bernard K., and Susan Duffy. "Fundamentalism, Liberal Education, and Freedom of Speech: An Issue for the Public Speaking Instructor." *Communication Education* 33 (October, 1984): 309–16.

    The authors address the problem of how to deal with doctrinaire religious fundamentalists in public speaking courses. After outlining some of the problems such students create, the authors suggest that teachers identify proselytization and distinguish it from persuasion, ban proselytization, tell students why, and continue to evaluate all speeches by consistent criteria.

Erlich, Howard. "'. . . And By Opposing, End Them.' The Genre of Moral Justification for Legal Transgressions." *Today's Speech* 23 (Winter, 1975): 13–16.

    The author identifies and comments on the rhetorical strategy of invoking moral law (a "higher law" than that broken) when speakers attempt to justify illegal acts done to advance major causes. He uses Thoreau's defense of John Brown and Stringfellow's defense of the Berrigan brothers to illustrate how speakers attempt to identify an accused with a class of morally superior beings.

Eubanks, Ralph T., and Virgil L. Baker. "Toward an Axiology of Rhetoric." *Quarterly Journal of Speech* 48 (April, 1962): 157–68.

    Aimed at teachers, this article argues for an educational emphasis on an axiological rhetoric, a "rhetoric of commitment." By boldly becoming axiological, concerned, that is, with the study and transmission of human values, rhetoric can enhance moral culture and deepen the relationship of discourse to ethics and justice.

Ewbank, Henry L. Jr. "On the Ethics of Teaching Speech Content." *Central States Speech Journal* 8 (Fall, 1956): 23–25.

    Student plagiarism, lack of information and fabrication of evidence show that not enough attention is being paid to the teaching of content. The ethics of teaching require that teachers treat content as vital. We must stress analysis of topics, hold speakers responsible for their own ideas and be as widely informed as possible.

Ferre, John P. "Contemporary Approaches to Journalistic Ethics." *Communication Quarterly* 28 (Spring, 1980): 44–48.

    Journalists need an ethic which can guide them in reporting news. Current approaches are deficient: issue-based theories only describe ethical problems, while theoretical approaches disregard the importance of justification. We need a rationally justifiable theory which defines the good and helps resolve moral issues.

Fisher, Walter R. "Toward a Logic of Good Reasons," *Quarterly Journal of Speech* 64 (December, 1978): 376–84.

    Claiming that humans are as much valuing as reasoning beings, Fisher seeks to enhance development of a logic of good reasons. He explores values in rhetoric, defines good reasons, posits a five-part reconceptualization of a logic of good reasons and suggests ways of implementing this analysis in rhetorical reasoning.

Flynn, Lawrence J. "The Aristotelian Basis for the Ethics of Speaking." *The Speech Teacher* 6 (September, 1957): 179–87.
> In asking whether ends justify means in persuasion, we can find a useful guide in Aristotle's determinants of a moral act: object of the act, intent of the agent, circumstances. Thus, in considering the ethics of discourse, we should examine what the speaker does, why he does it, and under what accompanying circumstances.

Freeman, Patricia Lynn. "An Ethical Evaluation of the Persuasive Strategies of Glenn W. Turner and Turner Enterprises." *The Southern Speech Communication Journal* 38 (Summer, 1973): 347–61.
> Following Nilsen's view that analysis of communication ethics must include assessment both of the course of action urged and the means of persuasion used, Freeman concludes that Turner was unethical because the action urged (personal financial aggrandizement) and his means (propaganda techniques like bandwagon and plain folks) are unethical.

Gulley, Herbert E. "The New Amorality in American Communication." *Today's Speech* 18 (Winter, 1970): 3–8.
> The author uses examples from advertising and politics to support the thesis that American discourse shows a drift toward irresponsibility in public utterance. Because audience ignorance, apathy and "moral confusion" are partly to blame, better courses in speech communication can help address the problem.

Haiman, Franklyn S. "Democratic Ethics and the Hidden Persuaders." *Quarterly Journal of Speech* 44 (December, 1958): 385–92.
> Subliminal advertising techniques are but technological advances on aims as old as the sophists: speakers seeking uncritical acceptance of their views. These techniques violate democratic ideals by taking advantage of man's exploitability. In response, critics must measure the ethics of speakers by their behavior (not motive), and audiences must learn to protect themselves from manipulation.

Haiman, Franklyn S. "A Re-Examination of the Ethics of Persuasion," *Central States Speech Journal* 3 (March, 1952): 4–9.
> Philosophically, persuasion is an autocratic act, hard to square with democratic ideals. When we use the powerful weapons we call persuasive devices, we undertake an awesome responsibility: deciding what ends justify such means, and yet leaving both the bodies and minds of our listeners free to choose.

Haiman, Franklyn S. "The Rhetoric of the Streets: Some Legal and Ethical Considerations." *Quarterly Journal of Speech* 52 (April, 1967): 99–114.
> Haiman analyzes three criticisms of the tactics of the "new rhetoric" of the 1960's: that tactics lead to anarchy; depart from legal limits of time, place, and manner; and contradict ethical ideals of "rational discourse." He concludes that such tactics may ethically be justified when gross power imbalances render ordinary norms of democracy inapplicable.

Hample, Dale. "Purposes and Effects of Lying." *The Southern Speech Communication Journal* 46 (Fall, 1980): 33–47.
> Three studies are used to answer an ethical problem: why do people lie? Results suggest that lies are intentional, for personal benefit, and usually a means of social or economic defense in a disadvantaged situation. Lies create uneasiness in liars, even when the results are satisfactory.

Hansen, John D. "Speech in a Nation at War." *Quarterly Journal of Speech* 28 (October, 1942): 271–74.
> Hansen argues that the speech profession in wartime has an ethical obligation to promote free discussion of ideas. This would include presenting information not readily available to the general public, keeping debate over critical issues alive and combating misinformation and propaganda.

Hilpert, Fred P. Jr. "The Influence of a Course in Ethics and Free Speech in Changing Student Attitudes." *Free Speech Yearbook* (1972): 66–75.
> This article reports the results of a 1971 study of university students who completed a course in freedom of speech. Results showed a significant increase in attitudes approving of free speech when students completing the course were compared with control groups.

Hunsaker, David M. "Freedom and Responsibility In First Amendment Theory: Defamation Law and Media Credibility." *Quarterly Journal of Speech* 65 (February, 1979): 25–35.
> Extended media protection from libel suits (after *New York Times v. Sullivan*), especially in light of increased media power, raises ethical problems. How can the press be kept responsible? Hunsaker argues that maintaining the private remedy for defamation is a needed check on media abuse and that limits on the remedy are a First Amendment issue.

Jensen, J. Vernon. "An Analysis of Recent Literature on Teaching Ethics in Public Address." *The Speech Teacher* 8 (September, 1959): 219–28.
> Jensen's review of the literature suggests that writers on ethics stress obligations toward truth, political society, liberal arts, the speech profession and students. Key questions writers have asked include: what is the source of ethical standards, how can practices be made consistent with standards, and what are the ends and means of persuasion?

Johannesen, Richard L. "Richard M. Weaver on Standards for Ethical Rhetoric." *Central States Speech Journal* 29 (Summer, 1978): 127–37.
> Understanding Weaver's theory of rhetoric requires understanding his Platonism, political conservatism and belief that rhetoric is axiological. With this basis, Johannesen derives from Weaver's *The Ethics of Rhetoric* five standards or guidelines for ethical behavior.

Johnson, Robert C. "Teaching Speech Ethics in the Beginning Speech Course." *The Speech Teacher* 19 (January, 1970): 58–61.
> The article reports the results of a survey of California speech instructors. The major finding was that a vast majority of respondents believed that

discussing ethics was part of their responsibility, but that less than a third devoted class time to it as a special topic.

Johnstone, Christopher Lyle. "Ethics, Wisdom, and the Mission of Contemporary Rhetoric: The Realization of Human Being." *Central States Speech Journal* 32 (Fall, 1981): 177–88.

Understanding rhetoric-as-epistemic poses an ethical problem: knowing what are rhetoric's ends. Since rhetorical activity generates opportunities for humane knowing, it allows us to embrace humanness. We must commit to a humanistic ethical system based on nurturing and treasuring values that bring quality to our lives.

Kantner, Claude E. "Social Responsibility in Speech Education." *The Southern Speech Journal* 14 (September, 1948): 67–73.

During the time of great growth in speech education, educators were strangely silent about ethical problems in speaking. Teachers must make an active effort to encourage the development of ethical standards, to stress the speaker's obligation to use language to foster human cooperation.

Klopf, Donald W., and James C. McCroskey. "Debating Both Sides Ethical? Controversy Pau!" *Central States Speech Journal* 15 (February, 1964): 36–39.

The controversy over whether debating both sides is ethical should end. The overwhelming majority of the forensics community believes that academic debate is a game with special rules. It is not real life, so its ethics are relativist. In its context, therefore, switch-sides debating is ethical.

Kruger, Arthur N. "The Ethics of Persuasion: A Re-Examination." *The Speech Teacher* 16 (November, 1967): 295–305.

Kruger argues that persuasion theorists have been interested only in results, not in how they are achieved. Since rational belief is the goal of persuasion, it is unethical for the advocate to try to induce belief by an appeal to emotion. Likewise, teaching students to exploit an audience's weaknesses is pedagogically indefensible.

Leroy, David J., and F. Leslie Smith. "Perceived Ethicality of Some TV News Production Techniques by a Sample of Florida Legislators." *Speech Monographs* 40 (November, 1973): 326–29.

Politicians are persistent news critics, claiming at times that questionable or unethical techniques are used to distort the news. Journalists, however, may perceive these same techniques as standard, noncontroversial editing practices. This experimental study did conclude that some common production behaviors were considered by a sample of legislators to be unethical.

McGuire, Michael. "The Ethics of Rhetoric: The Morality of Knowledge." *The Southern Speech Communication Journal* 45 (Winter, 1980): 133–48.

An ethic of rhetoric must take into account rhetoric as a way of knowing and also rhetoric's conditionality. This article uses Nietzsche as a guide toward an aesthetic, message-centered rhetoric. The author posits an ethic of rhetoric which understands that judgments in rhetorical criticism are judgments about the morality of knowledge.

McLeod, Alan Lindsey. "The Ethics of Radio Announcing: A Dilemma." *Today's Speech* 5 (April, 1957): 30–31.
Radio announcers are perceived by the public as advocates for the products, causes and persons for whom they speak. This can lead to an ethical problem when an announcer is called upon to speak for causes/persons/products in which they do not believe. The solution must lie in better guidance from station management.

Minnick, Wayne C. "A New Look at the Ethics of Persuasion." *The Southern Speech Communication Journal* 45 (Summer, 1980): 352–62.
Revising an earlier position, Minnick asserts that the best way to judge the quality of a persuasive message is to assess the short and long-term consequences it will have. This evaluation must include not only consequences which reflect the persuader's conscious choices, but unintended consequences produced by the materials and strategies employed.

Murphy, Richard. "The Ethics of Debating Both Sides." *The Speech Teacher* 6 (January, 1957): 1–9.
Murphy examines and rejects nine arguments advanced on behalf of debating both sides, concluding that if the practice is defensible it is so only in terms of pedagogy, not ethics, and only if debate is a closed-club activity. If debate is to be training for the public platform, then a public utterance should be a public commitment.

Nilsen, Thomas R. "Criticism and Social Consequences." *Quarterly Journal of Speech* 42 (April, 1956): 173–78.
Nilsen maintains that since speeches are aimed at influencing human behavior, they inevitably have an ethical component. Critics assessing speech effect must, therefore, include ethical judgment. This can be done by relating speeches to their social consequences by evaluating how the speech reflected the values a society seeks to realize.

Nilsen, Thomas R. "Persuasion and Human Rights." *Western Speech* 24 (Fall, 1960): 201–05.
Nilsen proposes recognition of a "right to information" as a human right. Such recognition would oblige persuaders to present information enabling listeners to exercise rights of choice. The ethics of persuasion would mean that speakers need as strong a commitment to a listener's right to know as to a counter-persuader's right to reply.

Oliver, Robert T. "Ethics and Efficiency in Persuasion." *The Southern Speech Journal* 26 (Fall, 1960): 10–15.
This essay maintains that speakers do not have to choose between truth and persuasive devices that "work." While unethical persuasion may sometimes work in the short term, truth can be efficient as well. The teacher's challenge is to teach persuaders to advance their goals ethically.

Pellegrini, Angelo M. "Public Speaking and Social Obligations." *Quarterly Journal of Speech* 20 (June, 1934): 345–51.
> To avoid charges of teaching sophistry, speech teachers must inculcate four ethical principles: public speaking's value is intellectual, not economic; speeches must exhibit intellectual honesty and an appeal to reason; content must not be trivial; and "demagoguery must be actively hated."

Ray, John W. "The Moral Rhetoric of Franz Theremin." *The Southern Speech Communication Journal* 40 (Fall, 1974): 33–49.
> Theremin, a nineteenth-century German theologian, developed a theory of rhetoric. Theremin's treatise, *Eloquence a Virtue*, is an important contribution to making moral issues an essential part of rational discourse.

Rieke, Richard D., and David H. Smith. "The Dilemma of Ethics and Advocacy in the Use of Evidence." *Western Speech* 32 (Fall, 1968): 223–33.
> Survey results show that college debaters have an ethical commitment, but also that the system rewards certain behaviors of marginal ethicality. The writers propose, therefore, a plan for improving debaters' ethics: increasing the rewards for effective/ethical use of evidence, increasing as well a judge's scrutiny of evidence.

Rogers, Jimmie N., and Theodore Clevenger, Jr. "'The Selling of the Pentagon': Was CBS the Fulbright Propoganda Machine?" *Quarterly Journal of Speech* 57 (October, 1971): 266–73.
> The authors suggest that CBS-TV failed in its obligation to the public when it did not credit Senator Fulbright as the source of the message in its heralded investigative report, "The Selling of the Pentagon."

Rogge, Edward. "Evaluating the Ethics of a Speaker in a Democracy." *Quarterly Journal of Speech* 45 (December, 1959): 419–25.
> Rogge exhorts speech critics to be concerned with ethics, to look beyond effect to examine the "rightness" or "goodness" of speeches. Standards for judging "rightness" are established by a society and vary with the speaking situation. How a speech conforms to society's "mores of persuasion" is a key element in understanding discourse.

Scanlan, Ross. "Freedom, Knowledge, and Public Speaking." *Quarterly Journal of Speech* 35 (October, 1949): 310–15.
> Scanlan states that in a slave state speakers are trained in thoughts, in a free state, in thinking. Freedom of speech becomes not so much an end in itself as a means to freedom of thought. And freedom of thought is an essential condition for human progress.

Schrier, William. "The Ethics of Persuasion: A Defense of Rhetoric." *Quarterly Journal of Speech* 16 (November, 1930): 476–86.
> Speech is not inherently sophistic. While there *is* false persuasion and unscrupulous speaking, speech should be taught as an ethical subject. Using appeals to emotion and factors of attention need not be unethical if speakers are sincere and honest in purpose. "Persuasion ethics is general ethics," says Schrier.

Smith, Donald H. "Social Protest . . . and the Oratory of Human Rights." *Today's Speech* 15 (September, 1967): 2–8.
> Smith points out that some of our most revered historical figures were not consistent advocates of human rights. Teachers of speech have an ethical and pedagogical obligation to tell students the truth about our democracy and its heroes.

Smith, Joseph F. "The Moral and Ethical Responsibility of College Theatres." *Western Speech* 17 (May, 1953): 181–85.
> To be true to the spirit of the liberal arts, theatre directors must acknowledge an ethical responsibility: to drama itself, to cast and crew, to the public. Smith supports the view that a director must be both an educator and an artist.

Speech Association of America. "The Ethics of Free Speech." *Quarterly Journal of Speech* 39 (February, 1953): 94.
> Here is published the *Statement of Principles and Code of Ethics of Freedom of Speech*, adopted unanimously by the Speech Association of America on Dec. 31, 1952. The Statement, a ringing endorsement of free speech and a strong condemnation of efforts to suppress it, came at the height of the McCarthy era.

Sproule, J. Michael. "Using Public Rhetoric to Assess Private Philosophy: Richard M. Weaver and Beyond." *The Southern Speech Communication Journal* 44 (Spring, 1979): 289–308.
> Believing that Weaver's key contribution is his claim that an advocate's definitional arguments reveal vital information about his philosophy, Sproule argues that in order to make judgments about the moral worth of a rhetor's philosophy, a critic must scrutinize both the validity and motivation for a rhetor's use of definitional terms.

Strine, Mary Susan. "Ethics and Action in Conrad's *Heart of Darkness*." *Western Speech* 36 (Spring, 1972): 103–8.
> Conrad's great novel presents the dilemma of imperialism in its social-moral complexity. Viewed as a rhetorical act, *Heart of Darkness* is a social indictment, dramatizing the lack of a realistic, morally defensible course of action for ethical citizens in the age of imperialism.

Thonssen, Lester. "The Social Values of Discussion and Debate." *Quarterly Journal of Speech* 25 (February, 1939): 113–17.
> This essay shows that discussion and debate are effective instruments for developing intellectual integrity. Teachers must guide students in learning debate principles, must not "glorify technique," and must make debate an "instrument of straight thinking." When properly instructed, students learn ethical values (open-mindedness, fairness), and become better societal problem-solvers.

Tussman, Joseph. "Controversy and Academic Freedom." *Western Speech* 19 (October, 1955): 251–56.

In debates over academic ethics, some have argued that controversial teachers have no place in the university. But being true to the principles of academe (truth-seeking and moral action) requires an exchange of views. For moral, political, and intellectual health, partisan debate must be part of academic life.

Utterback, William E. "The Appeal to Force in Public Discussion." *Quarterly Journal of Speech* 26 (February, 1940): 1–6.
Concerned by the death of democratic processes in Mussolini's Italy and Hitler's Germany, Utterback calls for reestablishment of traditional principles of public debate. These ethical principles reject the appeal to force and pressure politics and rely instead on allegiance to truth and the use of reason in solving human problems.

Wallace, Karl R. "The Substance of Rhetoric: Good Reasons." *Quarterly Journal of Speech* 49 (October, 1963): 239–49.
Rhetoric must reassert concern with the subject matter of discourse, assertions about human behavior and conduct. These assertions, based in ethical judgments, are for Wallace the essence of rhetoric. Wallace borrows the term "good reasons" from ethics to describe and help us understand these assertions.

Watkins, Lloyd I. "Ethical Problems in Debating—A Symposium," *The Speech Teacher* 8 (March, 1959): 150–56.
Four scholars present personal views on the ethics of contest speaking. They stress maintaining the educational focus of these activities and keeping the coach-as-teacher primarily responsible for the ethics of the activity.

Wieman, Henry Nelson and Otis M. Walter. "Toward an Analysis of Ethics for Rhetoric." *Quarterly Journal of Speech* 43 (October, 1957): 266–70.
The authors take the position that while rhetoric may be amoral, people should not be. Humans possess unique capacities for symbol use and for appreciative understanding. An ethics of rhetoric based on these characteristics suggests the need for speakers to create conditions favorable to mutual understanding. The art of persuasion is, therefore, indispensible to moral law.

Wiley, Earl W. "The Rhetoric of the American Democracy." *Quarterly Journal of Speech* 29 (April, 1943): 157–63.
The role of the democratic orator, Wiley says, is to rise above faction and partisanship to find the democratic criteria for truth. Truth balances between individual prejudice, which the speaker is free to express, and group ideals, which he/she is equally free to espouse.

Thomas L. Tedford is Professor of Communication and Theatre at the University of North Carolina at Greensboro. He is a member of the Commission on Freedom of Speech of the Speech Communication Association, having served as the Commission's chair and as editor of its newsletter and yearbook. He is a member of the Board of Directors of the North Carolina Civil Liberties Union. His articles concerning the First Amendment have appeared in the *Speech Teacher*, the *Free Speech Yearbook*, the *English Journal* and the American Library Association's *Newsletter on Intellectual Freedom*. Tedford is also the author of *Freedom of Speech in the United States* published in 1985 simultaneously by Random House and Southern Illinois University Press. The book received SCA's H. A. Wilchens Memorial Award for scholarship in speech and law for 1985.

John J. Makay is Associate Professor of Communication at the Ohio State University where he teaches such courses as "Presentational Communication," "The Rhetoric of Social Movements" and "The Rhetoric of American Issues." He is a member of the Commission on Freedom of Speech of the SCA, having served as vice-chairperson and convention program planner of the Commission from 1982 to 1985; he was elected Chair of the Commission in 1985. A member of the ACLU, Makay is also the author of numerous books, articles, and convention papers, with an emphasis on the areas of rhetoric and public address.

David L. Jamison is Professor of Communication and Department Head at the University of Akron. He is a member of the Commission on Freedom of Speech of the SCA, having served as editor of the Commission's newsletter from 1981 through 1984. His essay "Parliamentary Confidentiality and Free Speech: A Legal View," published in the 1977 *Free Speech Yearbook*, won SCA's H. A. Wichelns Memorial Award in recognition of its excellence in free speech scholarship. Other articles by Jamison concerning speech and law have appeared in *The Ohio Speech Journal* and the *A.C.A. Bulletin*. In addition to his career in teaching, Jamison is an attorney active in several professional organizations including the American Bar Association and the Ohio State Bar Association.

KF
4772
.A75
P47
1987

Perspectives on
freedom of speech